...ssors of the first Marquess of Anglesey

...ston
...)

Thomas, 3rd Baron Paget = Nazaret Newton
(1543/4 –1589)   (d.1583)
           1565

...e Knollys

...Frances Rich (d.1672)

...O'Rorke

...Whitcombe (d.1740/1)

Josias de Robillard = Maria de la Rochfoucault
Chevalier, Seigneur   g/dau of Charles, Duc
de Champagné   de la Rochfoucault (d.1730)
(d.1689)

Josias de Champagné = Lady Jane Forbes
(1673–1737)   (dau. of 2nd Earl
          1705   of Granard) (d.1760)

Lieut-Colonel Isaac Hamon = ?

Arthur Champagné Dean of Clanmacnoise (1714–1800) = Marianne Hamon (d.1784)
...mpagné (1746–1817)

ONE-LEG

ONE-LEG

The Life and Letters of

HENRY WILLIAM PAGET

First Marquess of Anglesey
K.G.

1768-1854

by

THE MARQUESS OF ANGLESEY
F.S.A.

LEO COOPER
London

First published in Great Britain in 1961 by
Jonathan Cape

This edition republished in 1996
by
LEO COOPER
190 Shaftesbury Avenue London WC2H 8JL
an imprint of
Pen & Sword Books Ltd
47 Church Street,
Barnsley, South Yorkshire S70 2AS

© The Marquess of Anglesey, 1961, 1996

A CIP record for this book is available from the British Library.

ISBN: 0 85052 518 7

The right of The Marquess of Anglesey to be identified as
author of this Work has been asserted by him in accordance with
the Copyright, Designs and Patent Act, 1988

Printed in Great Britain by Redwood Books

TO
THE MEMORY OF
M.A.
WHO FIRST
ROUSED IN ME
AN INTEREST
IN MY
GREAT-GREAT-GRANDFATHER

SUMMARY OF THE CHIEF EVENTS

IN THE FIRST MARQUESS OF ANGLESEY'S LIFE

	aet.	
Master Bayly		
Birth	0	1768
Mr Paget		
Westminster School	8	1777
Lord Paget		
Oxford	16	1784
'Grand Tour'	18	1786
M.P., Caernarvon	22	1790
Raising of 80th Regiment	24	1793
Netherlands campaign	25	1794
First marriage	26	1795
M.P., Milborne Port	27	1796
Lieutenant-colonel, 7th Light Dragoons	28	1797
Helder campaign	31	1799
Colonel, 7th Light Dragoons	33	1801
Major-general	33	1802
Lieutenant-general	40	1808
Corunna campaign	40	1808
Elopement	41	1809
Walcheren campaign	41	1809
Divorce	42	1810
Second marriage	42	1810
Death of his father	44	1812
Earl of Uxbridge		
Waterloo campaign	47	1815
Created Marquess	47	1815
Marquess of Anglesey		
Knight of the Garter	50	1818
General	51	1819
Master-General of the Ordnance (1)	58	1827
Lord Lieutenant of Ireland (1)	59	1828
Recall from Dublin	60	1829
Lord Lieutenant of Ireland (2)	61	1830
Visit to Russia	71	1839
Colonel, Royal Horse Guards	74	1842
Master-General of the Ordnance (2)	78	1846
Field Marshal	78	1846
Death of Lady Anglesey	85	1853
Death	85	1854

CONTENTS

MAPS

ILLUSTRATIONS

'The Ordnance going off and relieving Guard'. The Marquess of
Anglesey succeeded the Duke of Wellington as Master-General of
the Ordnance in 1827

> Etching by George Cruikshank (1792-1878) of a cartoon by W. H.
> Merle. May 11th, 1827
>
> Anglesey is shown bestride the cylinder of 'the Regent's bomb', holding
> a rein attached to the jaws of the bronze monster. On the bomb sits
> Wellington, holding his Field Marshal's baton, and saying, 'I've done
> the state some Service — but no more of that.' A winged figure of
> Fame flies after the Duke holding out a laurel wreath. Anglesey's left
> leg (he in fact lost his right one) terminates in a cork transfixed by a
> giant corkscrew. Behind is the Horse Guards.
>
> 'The Regent's bomb', a giant mortar (or bomb), was uncovered on
> August 12th, 1816, the Regent's birthday, on Horse Guards Parade. It
> was a gift from the Spanish Regency in memory of Wellington's victory
> at Salamanca, after which battle it had been abandoned by Soult, who had
> used it to bombard Cadiz from the unprecedented distance of three and
> a half miles. A stand for it in the form of a monster intended for Geryon
> (the mythical Spanish monster-king), on account of his connection with
> Gades (Cadiz), was designed by Lord Mulgrave (Wellington's pre-
> decessor as Master-General of the Ordnance) and cast at Woolwich
> Arsenal, Geryon symbolizing Napoleon overcome by Hercules (Well-
> ington). See George (Mrs M. D.), *Catalogue of Political and Personal
> Satires ...in the British Museum,* IX, 1949, 696
>
> In the possession of the British Museum   170

The Marquess of Anglesey as Lord High Steward at the Coronation of
George IV, aged 53

> Anon., 1821
> In the possession of the Trustees of the Goodwood Collection   192

'The Man Wot Could Not Drive As He Liked'. The Marquess of
Anglesey was recalled from the Lord Lieutenancy of Ireland for his
advocacy of Catholic emancipation in the winter of 1828-9. He
defended his conduct in the House of Lords in May 1829

> Engraving (coloured impression) by 'A Sharpshooter', May 12th, 1829
> Anglesey is shown wearing a coachman's coat almost identical with that
> worn by Wellington in a number of caricatures made during his
> Premiership which show him as a coachman. In this case, however,
> the coat is left open to disclose a fashionable collar and stock, the
> 'Paget Blue Coat' and white trousers. Anglesey's whip is broken and
> in his hand he carries his letter to Dr Curtis
> In the possession of the British Museum   193

The Marquess of Anglesey with his dog 'Nep' shooting blackcock from
horseback on Cannock Chase, aged 61 (see p.296)

> Richard Barrett Davis (1782-1854), 1829-30
> In the possession of the author   224

The Duke of Wellington and the Marquess of Anglesey.

> Caricature sketch by George Cruikshank (1792-1878), no date, possibly
> about 1829
>
> In the possession of the British Museum 225

'An in and an Out'. The Marquess of Anglesey became Lord Lieutenant
of Ireland for the second time upon the fall of the Duke of Wellington
in November 1830

> Lithograph by Robert Seymour (1800?-36), from *The Looking Glass,*
> December 1st, 1830
>
> Anglesey ('an In'), who carries his right boot over his shoulder, and
> whose right trouser leg flaps loose, sarcastically asks Wellington ('an
> Out') whether he has 'any commands for Ireland', and receives the
> laconic reply: 'No.' 240

'The Retort Courtious. (Anecdote in the Chelmsford Chronicle)'.

> Lithograph by Robert Seymour (1800?-36) from *McLean's Monthly
> Sheet of Caricatures*, Feb. 1st, 1831
>
> O'Connell in levée dress says: 'Whatever I may say of your government
> I beg your Lordship will not think there is anything personal.' Anglesey
> replies: 'Very good Mr O'Connell & give me leave to say that if you proceed
> as you have done you'll be hang'd but don't think *this* any-
> thing personal.' 244

'The Tinker'. Early in 1831 the Marquess of Anglesey issued a number of
Proclamations designed to curb Daniel O'Connell's agitation for
Repeal of the Union; these did not have the desired effect

> Lithograph by Robert Seymour (1800?-36) from *McLean's Monthly
> Sheet of Caricatures,* Feb. 1st, 1831
>
> Anglesey, wearing an old-fashioned artificial leg, holds a large pot, two
> of the holes in which he has mended with 'Proclamations' (*sic*); the
> pot, however, has sprung a third leak, and liquid is pouring from it.
> The handle of the pot terminates in the bewigged head of O'Connell.
> Anglesey addresses Lord Grey, the Prime Minister: 'Here Goody Grey
> I can do no good with your Irish stew pot as fast as I mend one hole
> another breaks out.' 249

' "Good morning to you Daniel" – "Will I nat get lave to spake"?' In
January 1831 Anglesey arrested O'Connell, who was given
bail in the sum of £2,000 (see p. 248)

> Anon., engraving (coloured impression), Jan. 23rd, 1831
>
> Anglesey holds the key to the padlock which silences O'Connell, and
> upon which is written 'Recognisance My Self £1,000 2 Sureties 500
> each', in reference to the conditions of bail
>
> In the possession of the British Museum 256

The Marquess of Anglesey, aged 83
   Wax relief by Richard Cockle Lucas 81800-83), 1851
   Presented by Anglesey to his son Lord Clarence Paget, in February 1852
   In the possession of the National Museum of Wales   369

ACKNOWLEDGMENTS

Among the many individuals who have supplied me with material and advice, often at considerable inconvenience to themselves and always with benefit to this book, I should like especially to thank the following: Mr Ronald Armstrong, Mr C. T. Atkinson (whose vetting of the chapter on the Waterloo campaign proved invaluable), Mr R. L. Atkinson, Mr Denys Baker (who drew the numerous excellent maps), Sir Gavin de Beer, F.R.S., Mr K. Darwin, Mr C. E. P. Davies (for assistance in the legal aspects of Chapter VI), Mr J. Conway Davies, Dr Richard Drögereit, Mr M. H. Evelegh (Secretary of the Royal Yacht Squadron), the late Maj.-Gen. G. Farmar, C.B., C.M.G., Mr Noel Fosbery, Mr Roger Fulford (whose encouragement and active help over a long period have placed me permanently in his debt), Miss M. Gollancz, Brig. P. H. Graves-Morris, D.S.O., M.C., Mr E. Heatley, Brig. O. F. G. Hogg, C.B.E. (for placing at my disposal his unrivalled knowledge of the Ordnance Office), Mr H. Montgomery Hyde, the late Earl of Ilchester (for the immense pains which he always took whenever, which was often, I asked his advice), Mr E. Gwynne Jones (Librarian of the University College of North Wales, for much assistance in arranging papers and answering innumerable questions), Maj. W. Le Hardy, M.C., the late Evelyn, Lady Le Marchant, Mr R. B. McDowell (for giving freely of his unrivalled knowledge of nineteenth-century Ireland), Sir Owen Morshead, K.C.B., K.C.V.O., D.S.O., and Mr R. C. Mackworth Young, of the Royal Library, Windsor (for their patience and efficiency in the face of numerous importunate inquiries), Mr T. H. McGuffie (for his limitless aid on points of military history), Miss Carola Oman, Mr Clarence A. E. Paget, the late G. R. Y. Radcliffe, D.C.L., Professor Glyn Roberts, Lieut.-Col. G. A. Shepperd, Dr K. Spalding (for lengthy translations from the German), Mr F. B. Stitt, Brig. A. R. J. Villiers, Mr S. G. P. Ward (for allowing me to pick his brains on the details of the Corunna campaign), the Duke of Wellington, K.G., and Mr A. S. White.

Of the numerous institutions which have placed their services at my disposal, I should like above all to single out for gratitude the London Library.

To Lady Phyllis Benton, the owner of Sir Arthur Paget's papers (without which Chapter VI could not have been written), and to the late Lady Paget, G.B.E., who went to great pains on my behalf to catalogue and transcribe large numbers of them, my profound thanks are due.

No author could feel more grateful than I do for his publishers' forbearance, care and wise advice. Finally, my debt to Mrs Gordon

Acknowledgments

Waterfield and to Mr Thomas L. Ingram is great, the one for much typing and retyping, the other for undertaking a vast amount of research of which I should have been quite incapable. At all stages of the work their advice and criticism have been exceeded in value only by the patience which my wife has shown over many years.

A.

Plas Newydd,
   February 1961

ONE-LEG

NOTES AND SOURCES

The *alphabetical* references in the text of this book relate to
the substantive notes (pp. 343-87). The *numerical* references
relate solely to sources and dates (pp. 393-413).

PART I

————————— * —————————

CHAPTER ONE

*Deliberate maturelye in all things. Execute quyckelye the Determynations.
Do justice without respecte.... Be affable to the good and sterne to the evill....
Thus God will prosper youe, the King favour youe and all men love youe.*
William, 1st Baron Paget to the Earl of Hertford (temp. *Henry VIII*)¹

FIELD MARSHAL HENRY WILLIAM PAGET, first Marquess of
Anglesey, K.G. — referred to by his descendants as 'One-Leg' or
'the Waterloo Marquess' — was known for the first of his eighty-five
years as plain Master Bayly. On April 11th, 1767, his father, Mr Henry
Bayly, son and heir of Sir Nicholas Bayly, an obscure baronet of Scottish,
Welsh, Irish and English extraction,ᵃ took as his wife Miss Jane Champagné, who was descended from two families of French Huguenot
refugees and an Irish earl.ᵇ At the time of their marriage,² Jane was twenty-
two and Henry twenty-five. One of their daughters writing twenty-one
years later described the circumstances of what was clearly a love-match.
'When Papa married Mama,' she wrote, 'he was only a Lieutenant in the
Army.... Tho' loved to a degree by his mother, not a favorite with his
father, who was violent against his marriage, he *did* marry.... Mama too
was as *determined* as possible, for the whole family were teasing her to
marry another person.'³

Henry Bayly, who was far from being wealthy, had every reason to
hope that before long he would become so, and within twenty years of his
marriage his most sanguine expectations had been realized. In middle age
he found himself one of the richest peers in the country, possessed of
immense territorial and parliamentary interests. To understand the
circumstances of this remarkable transformation it is necessary to go back
to the year 1549, when William Paget, one of Henry VIII's 'New Men',
was created Baron Paget de Beaudesert.ᶜ To make sure of his succession
(though he had four sons) the first baron contrived that his peerage
should be transmittable through the female line in the event of the male
line dying out.ᵈ This in fact happened two and a half years after the
Baylys were married, for on November 17th, 1769, the eighth Baron

19

Paget died unmarried and intestate.ᵉ This insignificant bachelor had a
distant cousin, Miss Caroline Paget, who by her marriage to Sir Nicholas
Bayly became Henry Bayly's mother. Though Caroline Bayly had died in
the year before her son's marriage, she was the link through which the
barony passed to him. (See Chronological Table I.)

Thus three years after their wedding, by a tortuous line of descent,
Mr and Mrs Henry Bayly found themselves Lord and Lady Paget. Nor
was the barony an empty title, for the material rewards of a career such as
the first Lord Paget's were great. Not only had he acquired the lucrative
spoils of the dissolved abbey of Burton-upon-Trent, but, at the hands of
his royal master, he had received substantial grants of land and money
elsewhere. Henry Bayly, when he became ninth baron, succeeded to a
splendid heritage. Not least of the good things which fell to him was the
mansion of Beaudesert, built on the edge of Cannock Chase. Queen
Victoria, talking to Lord Melbourne of the origins of the great names of
her day, thought Paget sounded Norman, but her Prime Minister had
another view about the family name. 'Their ancestor,' he said, 'asked to
have a *patch* of land, which was this great Beaudesert, and it was given to
him, but they said to him, "You must call yourself Patchet." '⁴

*   *   *

Eleven years after his first accession of rank and wealth, the new baron
found himself master of a second fortune. In 1752 a wealthy West Country
landowner by the name of Peter Walterᶠ made a will which provided that
in the event of his own line failing, all his possessions should pass to the
heir of Sir Nicholas Bayly. Why he should have done so remains a
mystery to this day.⁵ Nevertheless, when his only surviving brother died
without male issue in 1780, the strange terms of Peter Walter's will were
put into effect, and Henry Paget came into extensive lands in Dorset and
Somerset.ᵍ Two years later, on the death of his father, Sir Nicholas
Bayly, he succeeded, at the age of thirty-eight, to the comparatively
modest estates in Ireland and North Wales which went with the baronetcy.
The total territory which now was his was of the order of a hundred
thousand acres. Of these an important part was at this time yielding income out of all proportion to its agricultural value, for coal, lead and
copper lay not far beneath its surface, and the end of the eighteenth
century was not the time for neglecting such precious commodities.

In 1784 the earldom of Uxbridge, which had been created for the seventh Lord Paget[h] and had died out with the eighth, was revived for the ninth, and Henry Bayly's metamorphosis was complete.

*   *   *

Of Master Bayly's mother, Jane Champagné, at the time of her marriage little is known. From later evidence it becomes clear that her husband made an excellent choice. The letters which she wrote to her family, preserved over many years, as well as numerous household accounts, always kept in her own neat, unhurried hand, show that she was gentle and pious, and full of intelligent common sense. In her offspring she inspired genuine affection and respect: the encouragement and tactful advice which she poured out for their benefit prove her to have been an admirable and influential mother. Nearly thirty years after her death, her eldest son, then aged seventy-seven, recalled that his 'excellent mother, wonderfully nervous as she was, was a Pattern' when her sons were away at the war; for the more they were exposed, 'the more I really believe she was gratified, and all this for the true love of us.'[6] In appearance she was birdlike: attractive rather than beautiful, with a slight, well-proportioned figure and easy, dignified carriage, her face marred by a too lengthy and pointed nose, which she was wont to describe as 'Gothic'. Her mouth was small and delicate, and the very large and intelligent eyes which dominated her face were topped by well-defined eyebrows. These were even more prominent in her husband, whose portraits show him to have justified Peter Pindar's couplet,

> And he who lours as if he meant to bite
> Is Earl of Uxbridge with his face of night.[7]

His 'louring' looks and swarthy hue belied his character. All the vast opportunities which came his way failed to fire him with personal ambition. His outstanding characteristics (if so positive a term can be applied to so negative a man) were his lack of personal aspirations and his love of ease, though on occasion he could sacrifice both for the advancement of his sons' careers. He had, besides, a reputation for whimsy[8] and a dry sense of humour, both of which, no less than his disinclination for business and letter-writing, sorely tried his family and friends. There is a story handed down in the family which well illustrates his brand of humour. On one occasion, it is said, a son of the house took leave of his father at

Beaudesert and rode off to London. After some hours of fast riding he was overtaken by a groom, who asked him to return home at once upon urgent business. Galloping back as fast as he could, he entered his father's room — to be met with: 'Oh, my boy, you forgot to close my door.'

Lord Uxbridge's loyalty to his sovereign was unswerving. George III never had a more constant and unquestioning parliamentary supporter, for Uxbridge saw to it that the House of Commons seats of which he disposed were filled by relations and friends in steady support of the Tories. His personal friendship with the King, and Lady Uxbridge's with Queen Charlotte, were close: the stationing of Uxbridge's regiment of militia at Windsor over many years brought them into frequent contact. A further tie was a mutual love of music. This, in Uxbridge's case, led him on occasions to patronize promising young musicians, and to set them up in their careers. Among those he befriended was the composer and organist George Baker, who in his seventeenth year left his parents in Exeter to try to make a musical living in London. So as to attract attention, it is said, and being short of money with which to buy instruments, he collected a quantity of horseshoes of varying sizes and strung them across the street. One day Lord Uxbridge, who happened to be passing, heard him playing upon them and was so entranced by the boy's ingenuity and skill that he there and then took him into his household and arranged for his musical training.[91]

ii

Being convinced how great your desire is that I should read this term, and conscious that I should in some measure make up for your goodness to me, I conclude with assuring you that I will exert myself.
Henry William, Lord Paget, to his father, from Oxford[10]

Henry William Bayly was born on May 17th, 1768, in the parish of St George the Martyr, London. Besides the fact that his name changed from Bayly to Paget before he was two years old, little is recorded of his early childhood. It seems that much of his time was spent between London and Kingston-on-Thames, at both of which places his parents kept establishments, his mother being five times confined in one or the other between 1769 and 1775.

At eight and a half he was admitted to Westminster School as a town-boy, and there he stayed, moving up from form to form in the conventional manner for seven years[j] until his matriculation at Christ Church,

Oxford, in 1784. This was the year of his father's elevation to the earldom: from then onwards he was known by the courtesy title of Lord Paget.

Early in life, while still at school, he settled upon a career for himself. Many years later he declared that he

'had ever a passion for the Navy at Westminster; every shilling I had went in boat hire, and old Roberts[k] trusted me so, that he kept a suit of sails of larger dimensions for me and for George Hobart, who had much the same taste. I tried hard to go to sea. Curzon, then a Midshipman, the present Admiral, was some years older than me. He was often at my father's. He drew ships and talked of his career till I was mad to follow him. But it would not do.'[11]

Lord Uxbridge felt that the Navy was an unsuitable profession for his son and heir, and Paget was considerably galled to see his younger brother William, when only fourteen, leave Westminster before him, to become a midshipman.[1]

At Christ Church, Paget spent less than two years. Only two letters from that period survive. In one of them, condoling with his father on some interruption 'of that domestic quiet which appears to you so sweet', he observes, 'My taste, I fancy, is either not yet properly settled, or else it is corrupted, as I generally find that a family living in retirement is melancholy; indeed most retirements, *Oxford excepted*.' Soon after leaving the University, without taking a degree (though, as was the custom of the day for noblemen's sons, he was 'created' Master of Arts), he wrote, in answer to a paternal lecture:

'It is very true that I am not a good scholar, that I have no great knowledge in the classics, and that my time at Oxford has been less employed, and less profitably than a person very anxious about me might have wished, yet I cannot reproach myself with that absolute ignorance, that averseness to knowledge that you express, and I must say that my desire has been and is very great to be well acquainted with the history of all, and particularly my own country, and that besides the pleasure which I have in acquiring that knowledge, I am still more inclined to it from the anxiety and kindness to me on your part, and the real necessity I am under of knowing its laws, etc.

'I am afraid your wishes are carried rather beyond that of my knowledge, and that you wish me to prove it by becoming a public man; I cannot say that that is, at present, my desire (rather otherwise), and that, from a motive less culpable (if at all so) than that of indolence.'[12]

CHAPTER TWO

We stopped at Lausanne, and supped at the *table d'hôte*; where my school-fellow, Lord Paget, now the Marquess of Anglesea, sat opposite me. He seemed to wish to enter into conversation with me, and I am sure, I was more than equally anxious to chat over with him 'auld lang syne'; but *Westminster pride* allowing neither of us to make the first overture, we parted, as we met, in dignified silence.

Frederic Reynolds, the dramatist, in his autobiography[1]

IN the 1780s the education of an earl's eldest son was incomplete without a 'Grand Tour'. Shortly after leaving Oxford, therefore, Paget was packed off to the Continent with a servant, a courier, a travelling carriage and M. St Germain, his tutor. For over two years he remained abroad, doing the round of the Courts of Europe, seeing the sights and completing his studies. The letters which he wrote to his mother and father throw light on his character and interests at this early stage in his life.[2]

The first winter was to be spent in Lausanne, but at Strasbourg, on the way, there was an unforeseen delay. M. St Germain wrote to Lord Uxbridge to give the reason:

'You will undoubtedly be much astonished, My Lord, to receive still another letter from Strasbourg and to learn that we have stayed several weeks in a town where we intended only to stop a few days. I must tell you the reason. Lord Paget was so unfortunate, before leaving London, as to visit some female who had been recommended to him as a safe person, & this creature assured him most vigorously that the enjoyment of her person would never have any burning [*cuisantes*] consequences. He was so weak as to believe her but it was not long before he felt that he had been the victim of his imprudent credulity. He only told me about it a few days before our arrival in Strasbourg. This town contains a large garrison, and venereal disease is therefore common enough. I came then to the conclusion that there must be doctors there to whom it was well

known. No sooner was I out of the carriage than I ran to a banker of
my acquaintance to beg him to give me the name of the doctor who
had the greatest reputation for dealing with this kind of disease. He
mentioned a Dr Lachans and praised him as one of the most honest
& understanding men in France. I went to his house at once and
brought him to Lord Paget after making him swear to give me his
frank opinion of Lord P's condition and tell me if I could without
danger take him to Lausanne where I should do well to put him in
the hands of the famous Tissot. The doctor's reply, after examining
Lord Paget, was that up till now he saw no symptom that might
cause alarm, but he could not answer for certain, until, after several
days of giving medicines, no dangerous symptom appeared. This
reply decided me to stay on here & to entrust Lord Paget to his
care. I have every reason to be satisfied. His remedies have had an
entire success & every day he gets better & better and I have just
this moment heard that in two days everything will be over. The
doctor assures me on his honour that your son will then be radically
cured & that five days later he can leave Strasbourg with complete
peace of mind. I could not vex you in speaking of Lord Paget's
disease before being able to console you with the news of his certain
cure. But give no sign, My Lord, of knowing anything of what I have
had the honour to report to you here for I have an idea that your son
will confide in you in a day or two.[a] One is never really made wise
but by one's own experience. I hope with my whole soul that what
Lord Paget has now experienced will teach him for all time a good
lesson & show him once & for all the nature of a whore! In God's
name refrain from worry & count above all on my zeal & on my
every care.'[s]

This was a bad start, especially as from the first Paget found the constant
company of his worthy tutor rather irksome.[b]

At the end of January 1787 M. St Germain sent a further report to
Lord Uxbridge from Lausanne:

'Everyone here is most pleased with [Lord Paget's] good humour &
his good manners. He spends some time every day in reading; he is
attentive to his tutor's lessons. He comes with me regularly to the
little gatherings in this small town. He seems not unpleased with
the supper parties given for us two or three times a week. And when
there is no supper party, we come quietly back to our lodging

towards half-past nine & we talk till midnight. Fortunately there are no English here to disturb our rule of life.'

But luckily for Paget, not long after he had completed a spring tour of Provence, the calm dreariness of the Lausanne routine was broken. At Westminster, his two particular friends had been the Marquess of Worcester, two years his senior, and his younger brother, Lord Charles Somerset. These young gentlemen had embarked on their Tour some time after Paget, and he made strenuous efforts to persuade his father to allow him to get away from Lausanne so as to meet them. At the end of 1786 he had written: 'I have received letters constantly from Worcester and Somerset, who are now probably in Paris. I am sorry to say that nothing is more improbable than our meeting, according to the present plans of each party, as they are fixed at Dijon for some time; and that place, I fear, is not once mentioned in the whole course of my route.'

M. St Germain, aware of his charge's restlessness — and of the reasons — wrote that as Paget had made sufficient progress in French to be able to get on well in the course of his travels, he had proposed to him

'that we should start for the South of France at the beginning of March, as agreed between us in London. He asked me for time to consider the matter, he who until now had always shown a great wish to travel to Marseilles to await & join his brother [William] & Capt. Finch. I did not understand the reason for this change of fancy, but understood shortly afterwards when Lord Paget suggested a departure for Germany at the end of March in order to be at the reviews in Berlin at the end of May, a moment when his dear friend Somerset should also be there. This latter circumstance alone prevents me from falling in with his plan. I told him that I could not, without your consent, change anything in the plans arranged with you, My Lord, before our departure. Lord Paget answered that this was quite reasonable and that he would at once write to Lady Uxbridge on the matter.... He is patiently awaiting her answer and your commands.

'As a matter of fact it is of no importance whether Lord Paget starts by the French provinces or the German. The journey through this latter country is even more essential to a young man of good breeding. Its large & small Courts can furnish more amusement & more instruction. But in order that these Courts may instruct and amuse, one must stop for a certain time. It is above all important that a young Englishman should not be there with one of his old schoolfellows with whom he will not fail to laugh at everything he sees, and conclude that everything that is not like London is a "*damned boar*". He must *travel* in Germany and not rush through it post haste. But the children of the Duke of Beaufort must rush all the time, because they should leave Rheims in the month of April and be back in England before the end of the year after visiting both France and Germany and having stayed in Paris for some weeks.

'Besides, you know, My Lord, the reasons why I fear the company for Lord Paget of Lord Charles Somerset, however charming the latter may be. He has certain tastes in common with your son which might turn out fatal to the destiny of them both. That for horse-racing for example. I have the impression that it is losing its hold over Lord Paget & it no longer, at least, forms the constant subject of his conversations with me. But this half-extinguished fire might well be re-lighted by the conversations of our dear Somerset. He has also another inclination, My Lord — you will understand me. One can control it well enough when one is alone but gives oneself up to it when one meets again the friend with whom one formerly enjoyed great adventures.

'I am touched by the tender friendship which unites these two lords and it ... is delicate & difficult to prevent them from meeting again. Weigh the arguments for and against, My Lord, and then take whatever decision seems to you appropriate.'⁴

Lord Uxbridge replied that there was to be no change of plan, and Paget, writing on February 25th, 1787, for the moment gave up the struggle:

'Although I like M. St Germain much, and am with him on the best footing, yet it would have not a little contributed to my happiness to meet (now and then, at least, in travelling), friends, instead of being almost constantly alone with one whose misfortunes and extreme calamities in life must, necessarily, render him melancholy and triste. I could not help saying this to justify a little my request, but however unhappy the refusal may have made me, I shall here totally drop the subject.'

Nearly a year later he wrote to his mother from Vienna that he had the best opinion of his tutor, 'but you surely don't imagine that I can prefer him as a companion? He is now laid up with gout.'

M. St Germain, in a letter to Paget's uncle, the Rev. George Champagné, showed much concern at the perpetual correspondence with Lord Charles.

'It is very difficult,' he writes, 'impossible, even — to stop this correspondence based on a similarity of age, birth, tastes & that pleasantest of ties, perhaps, & the most lasting, a childhood friendship.... I continue to be most satisfied with your nephew's conduct, and entirely so with his sentiments. He is frank, truthful, noble & generous. He loves Lord & Lady Uxbridge tenderly, and the fear of displeasing them, of hurting them, is a motive which I urge almost always with success to reclaim him from some little lapse or to keep him back from it. Yet all my efforts until now have been insufficient to awake in him any curiosity, any desire to educate himself to a reasonable extent. It is very rare that he stops even for a moment to examine any object, & this indifference breeds, inevitably, whims, sarcasm, boredom — a boredom that drives us often enough from some town before we have had time to explore it.

'Lord Paget puts also too much faith in his first impressions (this self-sufficiency, anyway, is natural at his age). If the first set of people among whom we chance to alight in any place is not agreeable, then Lord Paget concludes, irrevocably, that there is no other set there, & refuses to make the smallest effort. That means that we spend alone together almost every evening after the theatre. It is in this way that we spend them at Marseilles & we are here already for twelve days. We were introduced to the Governor, the Duc de Gilles, the most charming man in the world, but he is very deaf & his house is not, perhaps, very amusing — So our young man having made the discovery will in no case return there. Several other houses in Marseilles have been condemned & treated by him in the same fashion.'⁵

In August when he was at Lausanne Paget was at last joined by Worcester and Somerset — with unfortunate results, for he became involved in an escapade in their company which much upset his parents. On the 8th he told his father the story:

'My dear Father

'Lest report should have fallen into either extremity about our late singular adventures, I will briefly recount them to you, that you may contradict all false reports (if any there are) about our imprisonment; the cause &c &c.

'We had had races in the morning & on our return dined together, & leaving table in rather *more than ordinary* spirits, we walked about the town [of] Geneva some time; at last it occurred to one of those who lived in the country, that he, by applying to the first magistrate, might be able to procure the keys of the town (I must here say, tho' it's almost too ridiculous to mention, that we voted *taking Geneva,* but on the Centinels being very civil and good-natured it ended in our giving them money instead of attacking them). On asking then for the keys, the Syndic [chief magistrate] remonstrated with us on the impropriety of our demand & assured us of the impossibility of a compliance with our request. — We then (as report goes for I confess I don't recollect) abused him excessively & made a great noise so as very much to disturb his wife who was then ill — of which being informed, we all retired & were walking down the street, when a strong guard came to seize us, — (here they accuse [us] of having attacked them & of having knocked down several of them, not a word of which I believe to be true, for this simple reason that an armed centinel would never receive an insult, much less a blow, from unarmed persons — & we received no hurt from them;) they at length took us to the guard room, where having been some time & having made some disturbance at being detained as we thought unjustly, we were conducted to prison — examined at different times, kept as strict as any criminals, & at the end of six days released at the request of the Duke of Gloucester, who espoused our cause with great warmth. Nor did the Duke lay himself under any obligations to them in obtaining our liberty; he on the contrary, demanded that we might be put into his hands as brother to the King of England. So much for a very absurd frolick, but which is allowed by all, to have been treated with much too great severity.ᶜ I am aware of the uneasiness it may have occasioned you & my mother at the first relation of it. 'Tis this idea that has hurt me & made me feel much on the occasion. For the rest, I look upon it as a ridiculous rather than serious affair. We were at the Duke's last Saturday to thank him, &c, he rather laughed &

treated it as a trifling affair; he behaved most handsomely thro' the whole. Worcester, Somerset and I go there again next Saturday in our way to the Glaciers & the rest of Switzerland. I beg my duty to my Mother and love to my brothers and sisters and am my dear Father

'Your dutiful affece Son
'PAGET'ᵈ

When his mother and father refused to take the matter as lightly as he did, he wrote to 'offer comfort' to Lady Uxbridge:

'tho' how to begin I know not, being ignorant ... from what part of my conduct you have taken such alarm. If it is the riot and imprisonment, I have nothing more to say.... If it is from the set of men with whom you saw I was, ... I can, I believe, comfort you by assuring you that mere accident allotted me (out of a party of 20) the gentlemen you allude to as companions in this unlucky adventure.... I cannot express the extreme pain and grief that I feel on this occasion, but it is all occasioned by the affection & regard I have for you & my father, and not from the cause or consequence of our riot.

'I feel that I have been guilty of an extreme folly, & have been punished like a malefactor.'

To his father he readily owned it 'to have been a mad absurd business, yet you will forgive me if I cannot see it in the very atrocious point of view you represent it in.' 'With respect to gaming,' he adds, 'I feel safe in assuring you that you will never have cause of complaint on that subject — but [as] to horseracing — I feel such an inclination as makes me afraid to pledge my word to you upon it, tho' at the same time I feel that I owe much to your opinion and wishes, to which I could much more easily make a sacrifice than to any pecuniary considerations.'

Meanwhile Lord Uxbridge had written his thanks to the Duke of Gloucester. The Duke's reply is worth quoting.

'*Chateau de Coppet*
Septbr. 8th 1787.

'My Lord,
'I received the other day your letter of the 23d. of August. I return you my thanks for the manner you have Expressed yourself to Me, for the part I took in a late affair about My Lord Paget at Geneva. I

did only what I thought my Duty as an English Prince; I am exceedingly glad to have been of use to Lord Paget, and hope you will have certainly no more reason to be under any fear for any Youthful scrapes for the future. He spoke to me so feelingly and properly about it. The conduct of the Magistrates to me personally was very flattering and I told them I should represent it to the King as a mark of their Duty, and Attachment to him. I remain My Lord,

'Your's

'WILLIAM HENRY'⁶

*   *   *

As a result of many months at Lausanne and two tours in France, Paget was now more or less master of French ('I have so far gained ground in French that I know how ill I speak it; which, I think, is being very much improved') and was even embarking on a study of Italian ('It is said to be so easy a language that it may be learnt in three months'). Thus equipped, he set out for a year's sojourn in Vienna. 'Here I am,' he wrote at the end of November 1787, 'already launched into the *grande monde,* and acquainted with every lady without knowing a single name or even feature, for, so quickly was I conveyed through the circles, that not one visage has made the least impression upon me. I was presented, last Sunday, to the Emperor and the Archduke and Archduchess. I have been twice at Prince Kaunitz's and I dine there to-day.'

Paget's letters from Vienna show him to be increasingly aware of the charms of the opposite sex. He spent much time in the house of the Comte de Thun. 'Himself I have never seen,' he writes, 'but Madame de Thun receives people every night: no supper, no tea drinking, no cards, no formal circles; but a house open from the end of the Opera to one or two o'clock in the morning, where liberty and ease are uninterrupted.... She has three daughters who are handsomer and more agreeable than any three sisters in the world, I am persuaded.' Six weeks later he assures his father that he is 'not *in love* with any of them'.

Except for the de Thun salon, Paget soon tired of the social life of Vienna. As to the appearance of the city, it had 'the best possible. In my idea, it has much more the look of a considerable capital than either London or Paris; the entrance is very striking, as the road through the suburbs is extremely wide and most regularly built, and of an immense extent. There is a great space between the entrance of the town itself and the suburbs, in order (in case of an attack) to be able to defend it.'

He was already much engrossed in military matters. The first and most detailed things he has to say about each new place nearly always refer to the fortifications or lack of them and to the composition and strength of the garrison. Of Lille he writes: 'This is one of the handsomest and dearest towns I ever saw, immensely fortified and well garrisoned, there being now here four regiments of infantry and two of horse.' Of Nancy: 'This is really the first town I have been at since I landed that is not fortified; what a wonderful number of troops, too, they have in them all. At Metz there are four regiments of infantry, one of Artillery, and two of cavalry, one of which consists of 1400 men; the artillery hit a small mark at an immense distance 24 times in 25; the bets were that they would hit it but 20 times.' The day after his arrival at Strasbourg he marvels that the Rhine 'five hundred miles from its mouth' should be 'nearly as broad as the Thames at Westminster. The bridge is made of wood and may be moved in an instant on a sudden alarm.' He then describes the garrison in detail: 'I have seen them manoeuvre all together. The Germans are the finest men I ever saw, all of an immense size and stout.'

Paget's interest in military affairs had nothing to do with the official opening of his career as a soldier. To his mother he wrote from Lausanne on June 6th, 1787:

'I must beg my father to procure me a commission in the Stafford [Militia]; for I feel much the want of an uniform & shall still more in Germany, as on all occasions where a frock is too negligée or a dress Coat too troublesome, an uniform comes in between & is perfectly proper. I am only sorry that I have not a better title to an uniform than as a *Militiaman*. Pray send me Buttons; I would not have a coat as I am somewhat changed in shape since I left England. I don't much taste the idea of a *Militiaman*.'

Lord Uxbridge replied that he would obtain for his son a commission in the Anglesey Militia. Paget thanked him, adding: 'I shall make up the Anglesea uniform *en attendant*. War I think seems less thought of than it was at least by the English; the newspapers say tho' that the King of Prussia is marching an army of 60,000 men into Holland.'

In Vienna the preparations afoot for war against the Turks were of particular interest to Paget. In January 1788 he wrote that the Emperor intended to join his army almost immediately

Jane Champagné, Lady Paget, mother of 'One-Leg' aged about 36

Henry Bayly, Lord Paget, father of 'One-Leg' aged 38

Jane Champagné, Dowager Countess of Uxbridge in old age. From a drawing by her daughter-in-law, Lady Harriet Paget, said to be 'a wonderful likeness'

'but he has put it off, & it is even reported that a reconciliation is on foot. It appears to me very unlikely, as his preparations have been so rapid & determined, that he will certainly give up his pursuits with great reluctance. He has now an army of 162,000 men, — the completest & best established troops that perhaps ever marched — & with the 15 Battalions which are ordered to join them, he will have 180,000 men, close to Turkish frontiers. His regiments are of 1200 men, he has most of them 100 men overcomplete & some have even 300 above the complement.

'I should like very much to see a campaign here, as in England there seems to be no chance of a war — but the Emperor don't much like Volunteers.'

War was actually declared on February 9th, 'which however did not in the least damp the brilliancy & gaiety of the assembly that evening.'

'I received a famous letter from my Brother William the other day, he was then about to leave Smyrna for Leghorn, where he begged I would meet them, coolly assuring me that from Vienna to that place it was nothing of a journey & he adds "Besides that, it will be the finest thing in the world for you, for about that time the Turks & Russians commence Hostilities & I make no doubt but we shall see a good many actions & in short have a great deal of fun; you will never have such opportunity again for I think you are *the sort* to like that kind of fun.... " I confess that in the summer I should like to join them.'

Paget followed the progress of the war minutely, but 'all bad news is carefully smothered here & the good published with extreme pomp, consequently it is difficult to know what is really going forward; as yet nothing of consequence has been done.' In spite of the censorship, and the fact that letters were liable to be opened, he managed at the end of May to get the following through:

'The Emperor is cutting the very worst figure possible, he is almost at the foot of Belgrade with a most immense army, most perfectly supplied, and he does not stir a step — nobody can account satisfactorily for this delay — People choose to say that he is waiting in order to *defeat* the great Turkish army which approaches, and that then Belgrade will fall without a blow.... If I could possibly get permission to approach the army, it would perfectly make up for the loss of the Berlin reviews — But I have very little hopes — Volunteers [the Emperor] protests against, & Visitors he receives most unkindly.'

Then, just before he was due to return home, Paget had a sad story to tell: '*My* Emperor is at a very low ebb. My letter would not pass were I to tell you the truth and my opinion. The Turks are the finest boldest fellows in the world — They give every day the most wonderful proofs of an universal intrepidity.'

'October 3d 1788.... Everything is in confusion here. The Emperor retreats and the Turks advance as speedily....

'Never was such management, such injustice, such want of resolution as in a certain person; never such discouragement & such discontent as in troops. They will, however, soon be quit of these troublesome enemies, as in about 6 weeks all the Asiatick troops retire into their own country to spend the winter. Vienna is a desert, and half the people one sees are in mourning.'

At this time Paget made two excursions from Vienna, one into Hungary and the other to witness the autumn manœuvres of the Prussian Army at Neisse and Breslau. In Hungary he visited

'one of the most magnificent chateaus possible, belonging to the Prince D'Esterhazy.... He has an immense establishment and tho' economising to a great degree, spends about £50,000 a year. Those strangers who choose to be presented to him he lodges & receives

with every mark of attention & hospitality. Those who go in-
cognito are furnished with carriages to see the Parks, Gardens &c.
He has an Italian Opera & German Play who perform alternatively.
The Theatre which is the most elegant and handsomest I ever saw
he built himself. Tho' the Opera is not of the first rate, yet they are
very tolerable — and the excellence of the Orchestra, of whom
Haydn, the illustrious Haydn is at the head, makes great amends for
the moderate Vocal Performers. He has a great collection of curio-
sities of all countries — and a tolerable Gallery of Pictures. I am no
connoisseur but I found some strikingly good. All this I admire, but
I cannot forgive the superfluous magnificence of having a body of
Guards, in the midst of his own most peaceable harmless tenants. The
Chateau is of an immense extent, he has capital rooms for 50 masters
with their servants — I could not help remarking the overflow of
Clocks and immense great Glasses — of the former there are above
400, many of which are richly set in diamonds. Notwithstanding all
this Plasnewydd or Beau Desert are a Paradise to it, according to my
taste.'

The Silesian Reviews he describes in detail and with enthusiasm, adding
that he was

'greatly flattered with the unbounded civility and attentions that I
met with. Fêtes, suppers & a ball were given to his Majesty [Frederick
William II, nephew and successor to Frederick the Great, who died in
1786], which were most numerously attended. Every body then
moved to the camp — And in the evenings — *open tent* was kept by
the Princess de Hohenloe. An aide de camp provided quarters for
the English — They were comfortable as much as a clean barn &
plenty of straw could make them. We always dined with the Field
Officers.'

*   *   *

Paget's passion for everything connected with the sea and boats,
already developed at Westminster, and to remain with him throughout
life, intrudes into nearly every letter. He had not been long at Lausanne
before he was complaining 'that there is not one pleasure boat on the
finest piece of water imaginable'. 'How I should enjoy myself here if I had
but the little skiff that I used to sail in when in Angelsea; but alas! that is a

pleasure they have not an idea of here. The chief amusement is card playing.' He was for ever pressing for news of his father's Anglesey yacht. 'I am very anxious to hear about the *Mona*, I hope that she did not lose her golden "druid and harp" during the Equinox; I rather suspect she has; I advised them to *take a spare one*.'

Horses were an equal passion — one he shared with many of his contemporaries. He was always anxious for news of horses and their riders, and for details of the hunting and racing events at home. To shooting he was not yet as attached as he later became: perhaps because he was not accomplished enough. At Treisdorf on his way to Vienna he went out shooting several times, '& had I not been the worst shot in the world,' he reported, 'should have made great havock.... Lenox and myself after firing till our guns were hot, brought home one miserable hare, and that too with the assistance of a dog.' He was better as an athlete than as a shot, for when in Geneva he boasted that he had beaten 'the most famous runner in England, a *Mr Charles Parkhurst*. He gave 3 yards in 100, but started so much before me, that all people from our running say that I am as fast & good as him.'

ii

... that chearfullness the Pagets are so famous for.
                     Queen Charlotte[7]

The delights of Europe were not such as to prevent Paget from being happy at the prospect of returning home. From Vienna in February 1788 he wrote: 'Pray write me word when you expect me in England — I have not the least curiosity to see either Italy or Paris but wish very much to see you all.' His wish was granted at the end of the year.

Paget emerges from his Grand Tour a normal, high-spirited, non-intellectual Englishman, convinced of the superiority of his race and class, without affectations, and tolerant of foreigners (though by them, he reported, 'Englishmen are thought to be all mad to a certain degree'). While he hankers after the sports and occupations of home, his approach to the wonders of the Continent, whether the splendours of the Alps ('Mont Blanc has been lately conquered for the first time'), the magnificence of the Courts, or the precision of the Prussian cavalry, is always straightforward and level-headed. He had acquired fluency in French, a smattering of German and Italian, and had made acquaintance with those in authority in Europe. Many years later he wrote: 'The first taste I took for the Army was attending the Silesian Review in 1788. I was particularly attentive to the cavalry. They then rode beautifully and manoeuvred with great celerity and precision. When I came home, I looked in vain for anything like it. I thought of trying my hand in that profession, but other occupation diverted me from it.'

General Donkin, a family friend, gives a charming picture of the family, a year after Paget's return, when for the first time Lord and Lady Uxbridge and their twelve children were all under the same roof for Christmas:

> With theme that's noble, beautiful & great
>   At Beau Desert this eve I fain would treat;
> And will attempt this Christmas eighty-nine
>   To sing the virtues of the Uxbridge Line;
> The finest offspring that I ever saw,
>   In mind and person all without a flaw!

> My Lord & Lady, a most gracious pair,
>   Father & Mother of twelve children rare!
> The Sons are seven of heroick line,
>   The Daughters five: skilled as the Muses nine
> In acts harmonious & in works divine.
>   Lord Paget eldest of this noble race
> Form'd for the Council; soon will take his place
>   In Senate, and debate with manly grace.
> William a seaman bold, a British tar,
>   Neptune's chief favorite thunderbolt of war!
> Arthur the learned, fit for Church or law
>   Either to preach or plead or case to draw.
> Perhaps no parents on the British Isle
>   Can shew or boast of such a glorious file.
> Edward, with solemn mind and serious face,
>   Methinks in pulpit would become His Grace.
> See Charles his brother in bold feats of sport!
>   Brownlow the youngest of this hopeful race
> By none excelled but with the whole keeps pace;
>   Whose mind enlarges as his days increase;
> An earthly cherub! Nature's Masterpiece!

The matchless daughters let me now define,
   The first of these is Lady Caroline;
Then Ladies Jane, Louisa, Charlotte mild,
   And Lady Mary a most beauteous child!
These five as graceful as the seven are brave!
   What high delight must their fond parents have
To view twelve offspring lovely to behold;
   Pleasure heartfelt beyond what can be told![8]

*   *   *

At the earliest moment after his return from the Continent, Paget was introduced into Parliament. In the election of 1790, which returned Pitt to power with an increased majority, he was elected unopposed for the Borough of Caernarvon, where Lord Uxbridge's influence was unchallenged. Whether he even put in an appearance in the town is not clear, but there was, of course, no need for him to do so in any case. In 1796 he gave up Caernarvon and sat, instead, for the 'rotten borough' of Milborne Port, on his father's Dorsetshire estate. There he remained until 1804, when, because he '*decidedly* and *conscientiously* differed'[9] from his father on some political topic (probably connected with the return of Pitt to power in the place of Addington, or with the resumption of war with France), he gave up the seat.[e] He resumed it for the short Parliament of 1806-7, when Portland succeeded Grenville as prime minister, and remained in it until his father's death in 1812. It does not appear that he ever made a speech in the Commons in all the years of his membership of it, though his letters to his parents and brothers show that he had decided views on some of the great questions of the day.

iii

The town talk of a marriage between the Duchess of Rutland and Lord Paget.

                             Horace Walpole to Miss Berry (1791)[10]

For a rich young nobleman, the years immediately preceding the start of the French Revolutionary war were the perfect background for a life of pleasure. Paget did not neglect them. On the shores of the Menai

Strait there was built for him his own yacht, and much of the high summer was spent in gratifying his ruling passion. The winters found him increasingly attached to the hunting-field. On Christmas Eve, 1790, a young friend dined 'at a *grand couvert* at Uxbridge House, where', he reported to Arthur Paget, 'Master and Mistress, Brothers and Sisters were all perfect in my eyes. I must not leave out', he went on, 'that we had the best dinner in the World. Paget set off at 9 o'c. to go and hunt the Lord knows where.... I think he seems to flirt with the beautiful Duchess of Rutland.' At a country house party ten days later the same correspondent reported that 'the Dss of R. cut no small figure as you may suppose. She and Paget were hard at it the whole time *ding dong*, but *où nous en sommes* I cannot make out ... each one somehow or other seemed afraid of being jilted by the other; this I say is foolish, for both being of the same mind, a proper understanding ought to ensue.' Nearly a year later, the affair was still in progress: 'The Duchess and the Lord of P.', it was reported, 'go on still but they contrive to make each other wretched instead of happy.'[11]

Mary Isabella, Duchess of Rutland, was the youngest daughter of the 4th Duke of Beaufort, and the aunt, therefore, of Paget's friends the Marquess of Worcester and Lord Charles Somerset. Her husband, the 4th Duke of Rutland, had died aged thirty-four in 1787, leaving five children, the eldest of whom, by the time Paget fell in love with her mother, was fourteen years of age. In short, Paget, aged twenty-two, was in love with a widow of thirty-four. All agree that she was exceptionally beautiful and a woman of immense fascination. Paget was by no means the only young man who wished to marry her.

In 1791 there came out a scandalous newspaper called *Bon Ton*. One of the first stories it carried in its brief career gives a pretty picture of a prank in which Paget was a leading figure. Under the heading 'Amorous Conflagration — A Farce in Two Acts', there is given a Dramatis Personae, which includes, besides others, 'Duchess of R——d' and 'Lord P—g—t'. The scene is a hunting-box belonging to Mr Meynell, and it is supposed that the young Duke of Bedford and Paget, the one enamoured of the Marchioness of Salisbury and the other of the Duchess, 'to avoid suspicion of *design*', contrived 'to obtain a Fox-hunt with the famous hounds of Mr M—yn—l', and to secure invitations for the objects of their affections as well. The select party was to include for propriety's sake, besides their host, the good-natured and unsuspecting Earl and Countess of Essex. After the day's sport, all returned to the hunting-box where they were regaled with hospitality, 'and Mr M—yn—l, to complete his kindness, appeared solicitous that the two ladies and their two Adonises, should repose there that night'; this, Lady Essex in her innocence seconded on account of the weather. At length, when all were in bed, 'the two expecting lovers, according to appointment, met in the parlour ... [where] they had prepared a small quantity of gun-powder, and other combustibles.' To this they set fire,

> 'without any design but that of frightening the guests into a state of confusion favourable to their design upon the ladies; but, unfortunately, the quantity was more than sufficient and they were obliged to vociferate the danger, lest the house should be actually consumed before the inhabitants could effect an escape. Lord P——t, running up stairs, met the terrified Duchess in a state of *unadorned* loveliness, and securing her in his arms, carried her through the smoke to ... a snug corner of an adjacent hayloft, where he immediately took care to prevent the possibility of her taking cold, by surrounding her with *his own clothes.'*

Young Bedford meanwhile had done the same for his Marchioness in an adjacent oat-barn, while Mr Meynell 'who having taken a cup too freely, happened to be the last alarmed', jumped from a window, breaking his fall upon a dunghill. 'As the stable was the most natural place for Mr M. to repair to', there he went and to 'his no small astonishment, *soho*'d the Duchess and her gallant protector in a situation both laughable and loving.' The fire was put out by the servants, but not before the wearing apparel in the house had been destroyed, obliging 'our heroes and heroines to remain *in statu quo*, until they could be accommodated by the neighbouring gentry.'[12]

Horace Walpole says that Lord Uxbridge forbade Paget to marry the Duchess, which is likely enough. Nevertheless, his name was still connected with hers as late as October 1794.[13] She in fact never married a second time, and died in 1831 at the age of seventy-seven.

CHAPTER THREE

Lord Paget remains at Guernsey with his Regiment, and is much commended as an officer, having made it one of the finest Regiments in the Service.
Lord G. Leveson-Gower, February 22nd, 1794[1]

SEVEN months after the opening of the war with revolutionary France, Paget learned at Beaudesert that an expedition was to go to the Continent and that regiments were to be raised.

'The moment I heard it,' he wrote many years later, 'I jumped upon my horse and galloped to Ivy Bridge, from whence I rode post all night without stopping to Hertford Bridge. Then I dined and went by chaise into London. I instantly wrote to Mr Pitt [the Prime Minister] to beg to see him. He appointed the next day. I told him my anxiety to raise a Regiment of Cavalry. He received me most kindly, but told me Cavalry was not then wanted; that I might raise a Battn. of Infantry and have the rank of Lieut.-Colonel. I instantly closed with him [and] got my father's leave, who generously contributed everything that was necessary to effect the object.... Contrary to the practice of the day, my father was put to great expence in raising the Regiment. Many Commissions were given away, which in other hands would have been sold.'[2]

On September 12th, 1793, Paget obtained the 'Letter of Service' which gave him command of the battalion which he was to raise. It was to be known as the 'Staffordshire Volunteers', or 80th Regiment of Foot. His 'Conditions for young Gentlemen, above sixteen years age, getting Ensigncies' in the regiment included the furnishing of fifteen men, none of whom was to be

'under five feet six inches high, or upwards thirty years old, with a good countenance, straight, and wellmade. Each man to be carefully examined by a surgeon before he is attested.... Each recruit to furnish himself with four good shirts, two pair of shoes, a set of

41

brushes and blackball, one black stock and clasp, two pair of stockings, and one haversack, combs and powder bag.'

One of the regimental officers, writing home at this time, describes the uniform which Paget devised for the officers:

'The facing is yellow, the epaulette gold and gold laced hat and white feather with a very handsome sword. This is the afternoon dress, in the morning we wear a Jacket, blue pantaloons to the ancles, with a border of about three inches of yellow leather and the same all up the fork, and a bearskin helmet hat and white feather and half boots under the pantaloons. The effect is quite what you would expect from Lord Paget's taste. It looks particularly well on Horse Back.'

The initial establishment of the regiment was seven hundred rank and file, later expanded to a thousand; the majority of these were volunteers from his father's Staffordshire Militia.

Less than three months after its embodiment, the 80th was sent to Guernsey, where Paget set about moulding his recruits into a fighting regiment. By the end of April 1794 he had five hundred men under arms. On the occasion of a review by the Governor of the island, their colonel was able to report to Lord Uxbridge that they were tolerably steady. He had no reason, he wrote, to be dissatisfied 'considering the time, our situation in the Island and the badness of the weather (I wish every one who is to see us was aware of half these uncommon difficulties).' As the summer wore on, he became increasingly impatient to quit Guernsey, a place 'barren of all amusement'. The senior officers, nevertheless, managed to be quite gay. On hearing that Sir John Warren had captured three French frigates in the Channel, they sat down to a dinner given by Major Harness. Nine of them got through 'three dozen of Claret besides Port and Madeira. Lord Paget', wrote Harness, 'was put into my bed.'

* * *

In mid-June Lord Moira left England with ten thousand men to reinforce the small British force already in the Netherlands, but Paget and the 80th were not of the number. In February he had asked Lord Moira to take the regiment with him when he went, but Lord Uxbridge at that time had thrown every obstacle in the way.[5] In May, however, Uxbridge heard from Moira that it was positively arranged that the 80th should join him immediately, though in the result this did not happen.[6] To Beaudesert Paget addressed a stream of angry letters.

'The 80th Regt.', one of them read, 'has been long under orders for Embarkation and still longer under promise, that whenever Lord Moira moved, it should. With their usual regard to Faith, Ministers and their Servants have overlooked us and we are in *statu quo*. I should think little of it, were it not that the 88th Regt. who out of 800 men can actually bring but 300 upon a Parade ... are just gone up the Scheldt. However I am at His Majesty's Disposal for the war, and I shall not say any more about it.... I have now 4 Companies under tents that were condemned last war. To see a Regiment dropping off thro' neglect is really heartbreaking. In the heat of a Campaign these things are unavoidable, but in cool blood every one must suffer who knows of it.'

So as to learn what life in the ranks was really like, Paget and another officer lived for a week entirely on soldier's fare. Not many officers in the eighteenth century would have undergone a similar experience. One of his majors, indeed, declined to share in the experiment, fearing 'the effects of so slender a diet and water at this season of the year [April] in a spot that's remarkably aguish'.[7]

At the end of May the regiment held a field day which caused its colonel to be delighted with their performance. 'My lads,' he said when it was over, 'I shall give you your colours on Monday, and I hope you will all come to dine with me. I will try to get you a good dinner, and bring your wives and children with you.' For the meal he ordered a pound of roast beef, a pound of plum pudding, a pound of bread, a pound of potatoes and a quart of ale each, for a thousand people.[8] After the consecration of the colours, Paget made 'a most beautiful and manly speech, saying that the King had done him the honour to present him with these colours; that he felt the honour and the duty of so sacred a gift; that in executing this trust he knew he had but to present them to his Regiment, who would support them with their lives in defence of so gracious a sovereign and in guarding the honour, the laws, the religion and the prosperity of their country. "From you they never will receive a stain and as long as I command you I shall feel confident and happy." ' 'Lord

Paget's speech,' wrote one of his officers, 'from his rank, his person, his situation with us and from the affectionate and graceful manner of his utterance could not fail of powerful impression. The Governor shed tears.'[9]

*   *   *

Paget's anxiety to arrive at the seat of action was intensified by the galling fact that his brother Edward, though eight years his junior, had been in the theatre of war nine months, and in April, though only eighteen, had gained command of the 28th Regiment, the famous 'Slashers', whom he was to lead for many years to come. Of Lord Uxbridge Edward now asked, 'Where is Paget? Have I the least chance of seeing him and his Regt. brigaded with the 27th & 28th? Can you conceive — *27th, 80th, 28th* — such a Brigade & Paget commanding it too, which he would do were he here. I fear the Castle is built too high & must fall.'

The 80th had not long to wait, for by September 1st it was embarked, and on the following day it sailed. A week later Paget found himself no further off than Deal. 'Thank God', he wrote, 'we are at last quit of Guernsey, the most odious place I ever set foot into & I trust that the Duke of York [commander-in-chief on the Continent] will soon send for us from Flushing. I find that we are to be under Lord Mulgrave. I believe he is a good fellow & barring his brother's jealousy at my commanding him, I dare say we shall do very well.'

Ten days later he wrote from 'H.M.S. *Hind*, Lat. 56, St Abb's Head bearing N.W.' to inform his father that 'the 80th had laid a week in the Downs waiting for a fair Wind when we heard of a strong Squadron of French Frigates being off the North Sand Head. You know my passion for the sea & my curiosity to be witness to a sea fight, and will easily imagine that I could not let this opportunity slip.' There followed a description of his cruise with the Navy, which proved fruitless as far as the French frigates were concerned, but which lasted far longer than he had expected. 'I confess I did not think that our Cruize could last above 2 or 3 days, or I don't think that I should have come.... The 80th cannot move till we return, or I should be a little uneasy at quitting them, & as I heard when we were off Flushing that 2 Regts. had reembarked I suspect that our destination may be changed.' A little uneasiness would have been justified in the circumstances, for he failed to return to Deal (having 'scudded under a Close Reefed Maintop Sail & Fore Sail the whole way' from the Naze of Norway) until 28th September, nearly a fortnight after he had set out. Next day he wrote to his father:

'I must begin this letter by owning that I am the greatest *Etourdi* that ever lived yet that I am always lucky enough to get well out of every Scrape. Think of my having fallen into a cruise for a fortnight when I expected to have assisted in the Taking of 5 French Frigates in a few hours. Think of my Regt. having in the meantime sailed for Flushing & think of my feelings when I returned into the Downs.'

Many years later, he wrote:

'To my dismay I found that my Regt had sailed 3 days before. I instantly ran to the Admiral (Peyton) a very crusty old fellow to ask for a conveyance to Flushing.... I found him most kind. He asked after the Squadron of which he had not heard a word, for we had run from all the small craft, and had nothing to detach as we had gone along. I gave him an account of our proceedings and he instantly placed at my disposal what he called his favourite little *Fanny*,—a nice fast lugger of about 60 tons. I was soon at Flushing, where I learnt that the Regt. had been embarked in *Scuyts* [schuyts: Dutch canal vessels] and had sailed for Bommel. I soon got a vessel and followed and had the good fortune to get there just as the first company was disembarking. My joy was excessive; I believe it was not less thro' the whole Regt.'

The 80th arrived in Holland at a time when the initiative gained earlier in the campaign by the Allies, notably at Wattignies by the Austrians and at Beaumont by the Duke of York, had long been lost to the enemy, ably and energetically led by Pichegru. The Austrians were on the point of retiring behind the Rhine, leaving the British no alternative but to give up the line of the Meuse for that of the Waal, whence they had started a year and a half before.

The 80th was at once posted to the right centre of the line about fifty miles from the coast, having 'the honor of being the advanced Post of this part of the Duke of York's Army'. The state to which the regiment was reduced by mid-October angered its colonel. Three hundred and thirty-five men were sick, a hundred were employed in marching prisoners to the coast, and 200 were detached for work with another Regiment.

''Tis the most cruel case that ever was,' he wrote, 'we had not 30 sick

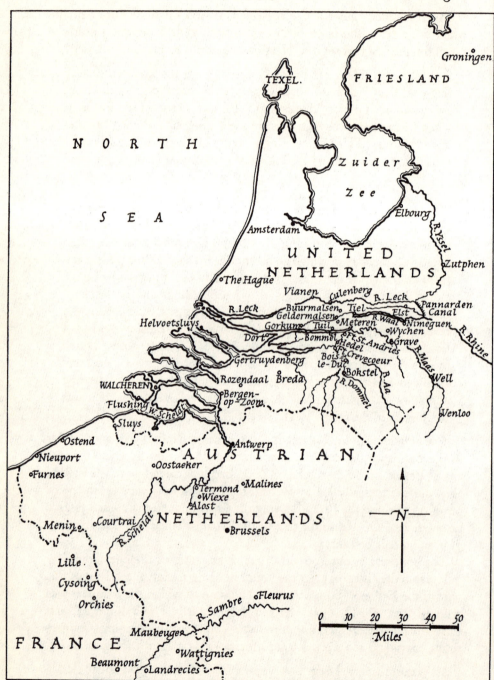

MAP I: THE NETHERLANDS CAMPAIGN OF 1794-5

when we left Guernsey & they put us into Transports that had been in the West Indies & a species of Yellow Fever broke out among them. Is not this heart-breaking!

'I am just relieved from infinite anxiety by the arrival of General Abercrombie [Sir Ralph Abercromby, commanding under the Duke of York] as I have been commanding in this town [Bommel] since my arrival, and on a proper arrangement in this little place much depends, in order to cover the Retreat (shd it be necessary).'

This, the first of the campaigns of the Revolutionary War, was one of the last to be fought in a truly civilized manner, as witness Paget's description of front-line warfare in the 1790s.

'Nothing', he wrote, 'can be more moderate & *Gentlemanlike* than the present Mode of carrying on the war between us & the French. Our Sentries & theirs never fire on each other & all Officers are allowed to ride about peacably, tho' within half Gun Shot of their Piquets. I yesterday rode to a Village opposite Crevecoeur & had some conversation with a Carmagnole Captain who had come over the river upon some business; & a Hessian Officer dined the other day with Pichegru near Bois-le-Duc & was most elegantly entertained, but it is with the British that they are particularly polite. Other Nations are not so safe with them, for, after conversing some time the other day with some Officers of ours, two Dutchmen came & they immediately fired at them.'

Paget found himself '*on excellent terms* with Head Quarters, & particularly the Duke of York, who on Edward's and my expressing a wish to be Brigaded together, immediately made a fresh arrangement'.

At this stage, it looked as if the campaign was over, for the Austrians, believed to have come to a secret understanding with the French, failed to fulfil promises of support for a November offensive, and the French party in Holland gained ground daily. The British Army retired to the north bank of the Waal, and hoped to stay there for the winter. Half the British troops were sick. What hospitals there were were short cuts to the grave, and the onset of winter accelerated the decimation of an underpaid and ill-clad army. Paget could not conceive how his thousand men had dwindled so fast. He attributed all their misfortunes to the West Indian transports. 'Those', he wrote on December 17th, 'who were not violently infected were in some degree tainted & we cannot get our heads up. All

my best men are dead, & strange to say, the little ugly fellows, who were
scarcely considered as belonging to the Regt. at Guernsey are the only
ones that hold out.... I own to you that they disgust me at present. I
long to bring them into action that I may expend them & get a fresh set.'

Had the Army been quietly settled in winter quarters, Paget thought of
applying for leave of absence at about this time,

> 'and should have had infinite pleasure in surprizing you all at
> Uxbridge House, but for the present it is quite out of the question,
> as not a day passes, but some Orders are given out respecting the
> intention of the Enemy to attempt to cross the Waal, and reports
> are eternally coming from one quarter and another that the very
> hour of the attack is determined on. Now, though I firmly believe
> that they have no such rash intention, yet such a thing might
> happen & as I think that we shall cut them up completely, I rather
> wish to be of the fête. If we make any retrograde movement, I
> promise to join you immediately.'

The officer commanding the 33rd Regiment, not far away, was in the
same frame of mind. 'I intend to go to England in a few days,' wrote
Lieutenant-Colonel Arthur Wesley (not yet Wellesley, let alone Wellington), 'that is to say, if the French remain quiet.'[10] But the French, unlike
the Allies, had no intention of remaining quiet. In the last days of the year
Pichegru crossed the hard-frozen Waal and was not checked until some
miles to the north of it. Here the local commander discovered that the
French were but two thousand strong. Acting on this information, the
Hanoverian general, Walmoden, who had assumed command of the army
on the Duke of York's return to England, attacked on December 30th
with five regiments, including the 80th. A sharp fight took place, and the
enemy was driven back across the river with heavy loss. British casualties
did not exceed fifty. In old age Paget recalled his baptism of fire:

> 'My *Coup d'Essai* in Command occurred about this time. It was
> determined to drive the French back over the Waal.... A corps was
> put in motion under the general direction of Sir D. Dundas; Lord
> Cathcart was by a circuitous road to turn the enemy's left — another
> Brigade was to come along the Dyke upon their right flank —
> General Gordon in whose Brigade was the 80th, was to attack Tuyl,
> being the centre of the position. Sir David and General Gordon were
> both present, but the ground was enclosed & covered with snow.

Gordon was gouty and could not walk. Sir D. was unable to get over the fences and their horses could not leap — they were therefore thrown out. I had a capital little horse that could leap anything, and easily kept with the advance. The result was the French were instantly dislodged — 6 guns were taken and they retired across the River, which however was frozen over and in so rough a state that the sharp shooters found much cover behind the broken ice. Our skirmishers could not dislodge them. I looked around for the Generals — missed them, found myself in command. Tired of this skirmish and supposing that we were to push across, I had ordered the advance, when Sir David appeared. I told him what had happened and what was ordered. He immediately exclaimed "God's so!" (always his ejaculation!) "don't move a step, defend yourselves here, but do not stir an inch." I believe I would have been in a monstrous scrap in a few minutes if the General had not so happily arrived. The French were in force in Bommel and had a strong artillery and Lord Cathcart's corps had not yet arrived, but I foolishly didn't know when to stop.'

Major Harness declared that Paget's 'determined coolness in this little affair, charging at the head of the Regiment, charmed every soldier in it.'[11] To his father at the time, he modestly wrote: 'the 80th were fortunate enough to be engaged & did very handsomely.'

By January 15th, 1795, Walmoden decided that the French pressure was so great that he must give up even the Leck, the last river defence line for thirty or forty miles. There now began one of the worst retreats known to history. The extreme cold, coupled with a lack of the most elementary supplies of food and clothing, combined to destroy the last vestiges of discipline. In a period of four days, more than six thousand men were frozen and starved to death. The survivors reached the west bank of the Yssel on January 19th. On the 21st Paget was writing from

'Elbourg on the Zuyder See.... Surely Messieurs les François ought to be satisfied with what they have for the winter. Alas! It is too humiliating to depend everything wholly on the Movements of the Enemy. What would not 50,000 British do! Pray send them to us. We are now, tho' still the advanced corps of the Army, at such a distance from the *Foe*, that you will not feel nervous about us, but there have been times lately when we had a pretty fair chance of being cut off. By all hands, the hardships that Dundas's Corps of the Army has undergone for some weeks, it is allowed, were never surpassed

& the extraordinary thing is that there are any Soldiers still fit for duty, as not a man of them has had his Accoutrements off since we marched from Teil & we in general laid out the whole time in the fields. Our last march from Culenberg to this place [a distance of more than forty miles] has been perhaps the most rapid thing that ever was, but it saved us.'

At this time Paget was delighted by a visit from his brother Arthur, who three years before, at the age of twenty, had entered the diplomatic service. He had been sent earlier in 1794 to Berlin as envoy-extraordinary to King Frederick William with the object of persuading him to reconsider the Prussian abandonment of the defence of Holland. He got no satisfactory assurances, and made his way back to England via Brunswick and Holland.

'Notwithstanding your hint that he might drop in upon us,' wrote Paget to his father, 'I did not think it likely that even he would volunteer coming among us at this time, for we are a set of miserable dogs; however, as I am a pretty good *Caterer*, he gets on tolerably well. It is an age since I last saw him, & most delighted we were to meet.... He talks of staying with us a few days & if in that time our Corps makes any movement to the Rear, or that there is a determined prospect of being quiet for some time, I will then accompany him to England for a few weeks.'

*   *   *

While Walmoden was writing in exaggerated vein to the Duke of York: 'Your army is destroyed, the officers, their carriages, and a large train are safe, but the men are destroyed', Paget was expressing the

'fear that it has been a most anxious time to most people in England; since our communication with it has been interrupted by the late intense frost ... the latest accounts that you must have had, were not such as to tranquillise you upon the fate of the Army in general and particularly on that of our Corps. It has indeed, since that time gone thro' many hardships & performed a march that has surprised the Old Stagers. The 6th Brigade (which, by the by, I have the honor to command) & a Brigade of Heavy Cavalry, the whole under Ld Cathcart, were sent towards Groningen to cover the retreat of considerable depots of the Emigrés. We took up a position near that town for 4 days, when having effected our purpose, we crossed the Ems the day before yesterday. Such figures were perhaps never seen. This Brigade has long deemed useless Shirts or Stockings, but we are now pretty nearly without Coats, waistcoats, Breeches or shoes....

'It is ridiculous to relate that Ld Cathcart's Corps was completely lost sight of by the rest of the Army & that we met a few days ago Officers who were sent from Headquarters to cautiously explore & feel for us, the most dismal accounts having been propagated, such as our having been surrounded & cut up to a man by the Dutch, ditto by the French, and so on. The fact is that barring excessive fatigue & constant night marches we have lived like Princes. In all the Villages & farm houses where we cantooned, Officers and men had always excellent dinners provided for them by the owners gratis. Their civility to the body has been unbounded, but *en revanche*, they have murdered most of our Stragglers.'

As Cathcart was quite out of touch with headquarters, orders which should have reached him, in fact miscarried. When after he had crossed the Ems these instructions eventually caught up with him, he realized that he had been intended to remain to the west of the river. Accordingly he recrossed it and took up positions dominated by a strong fort. Of this he gained possession by sending Paget forward with some cavalry and the light infantry companies. While the horsemen beset the place to prevent messengers from summoning assistance, and Paget parleyed with the garrison, who were attempting to lift the drawbridge, some of the light companies slipped past and secured both drawbridge and gate.[11] Paget, however, does not himself mention this neat little exploit.

'Poor Arthur', he wrote at this time, 'was completely nicked by his kind visit to us.... Had it been possible I assure you that I should have accompanied him to England, but ... we have been most constantly employed on very important Service, besides I have not been long enough in my new Command to be able to quit it yet. You know every child is fond of a new Play thing.'

He was able to report that his maternal uncles Forbes and Joseph Champagné, both senior regimental officers and old soldiers from the American War ('they were greatly useful in forming the Regiment and in instructing me, for I had everything to learn!') were in high force, and that he and

Edward ('he is an excellent fellow') had grown so fat as to be unrecognizable.

By the end of April the last remnants of the army, Paget and the 80th included, had been embarked at Bremen in transports sent out from England.

Arthur Wellesley in after years pointed out the most important gain of the campaign when he declared 'I learnt what one ought not to do, and that is always something.'[13]

ii

> There was a time, I confess, when I did not look upon the Cavalry of our Service as a good school for soldiers, but your Lordship has in great measure changed my sentiments on that head.
>
> *Marquess Cornwallis to Lord Paget,* 1804[14]

Paget was now confronted by a problem common to a number of his fellow officers at the time. He had found himself in command of a brigade after little more than a year's service as a soldier, and yet he had no formally established rank whatever. To General Abercromby and others he had put his case on a number of occasions: though everyone agreed that he had a perfect right to regular rank in the Army, nothing had been done about it. What he particularly wished was to avoid subjecting his father to the very expensive process of purchasing rank for him.

'I should be glad to know', he had written from Holland, 'which is the most serviceable to a Country at War — An Officer who raises a Regiment, disciplines & brings it into the field, or one who without joining any Regiment at all, by dint of purchasing Rank after Rank, at last commands an old Regiment. Yet such is the case of Ld. Craven who now commands the Buffs, having been for a few weeks a Captain in my Regt.'

He asked his father to carry the point with the King direct, who 'would certainly do it at once, & then I need not be obliged to a set of bargainers. … Of course, I must retain my rank from 12th of September, 1793. This will probably give me the rank of Colonel if the War lasts, & at all events I shall serve with more pleasure, when I know that I am upon the footing with those about me.' Lord Amherst, the veteran Commander-in-Chief, whom Uxbridge approached on the subject, suggested that the only way to achieve permanent rank was for Paget to begin at the foot of the ladder.

To this process he was agreeable so long as no expense was entailed. 'I have no objection', he wrote on January 21st, 1795, 'to going thro' the Ceremony of Ensigning &c &c &c, but I would not accept of Rank one day younger than my present Commission. I am now one of the oldest Lt. Col's of this Army, which is not to be given up.' Once this process had been completed, he felt that it would be 'the easiest thing in the world to get a Lt. Colcy. of Light Dragoons which is the height of my ambition, but it must be in some Regiment on the Continent, as I am very anxious to see one dashing Campaign in that line.' All was arranged satisfactorily, for between March 11th and June 15th, 1795, he rapidly (on paper only) ran through all the ranks from lieutenant to lieutenant-colonel,[a] becoming a fully established colonel-in-the-army on May 3rd, 1796. On April 6th, 1797, he obtained 'the height of his ambition', for on that date he assumed command of the 7th (Queen's Own) Light Dragoons (later to become Hussars), a position which he held for forty-five years.[b]

His desire to see more service on the Continent was not to be gratified for over two years; but employment at home had its compensations. During the three months after his return from Germany, he had become engaged to and had married Lady Caroline Elizabeth Villiers, a younger daughter of the 4th Earl of Jersey. 'Car' Villiers, whose mother was for many years the favourite of the Prince of Wales, was twenty-one at the time of her marriage, and a girl of a simple, dreamlike beauty. As to her character, there is too little evidence for an opinion to be given, but for over nine years, according to her own version,[15] she lived very happily with Paget. In that period she gave him three sons and five daughters.

On June 8th, 1795, Lord Jersey received Paget's 'regular proposal' for his daughter's hand, which he accepted without hesitation, 'trusting with confidence that in every respect her happiness will be obtained'.[16] The wedding took place on July 25th, by special licence of the Archbishop of Canterbury, in her father's house in Grosvenor Square. The honeymoon seems to have lasted for a fortnight only,[c] probably because Paget had to go off to see to the reconstitution of the 80th.

*   *   *

When, two years later, he took over the 7th Light Dragoons, he found that many improvements were necessary to bring the regiment up to the high standards upon which he insisted. In this task he was exceptionally fortunate to have as his second-in-command John Le Marchant (whose distinguished cavalry career was terminated by a musket-ball in 1812). To him he left the task of thoroughly reforming the regimental discipline, which of late had been grossly neglected. Le Marchant, indefatigable and relentless, incurred considerable odium among the troopers, who on one occasion greeted with inordinate cheers Paget's appearance on the parade ground after a long period of absence. 'His Lordship', says the editor of Le Marchant's memoirs, 'immediately checked his horse, and addressing the men in terms of dignified rebuke, expressed his entire approbation of Lieutenant-Colonel Le Marchant's conduct whilst in command, and observed that they were proving the necessity of the strictest discipline, by an act of insubordination, which he considered as a personal insult to himself.'[17]

Le Marchant, though he admired Paget, did not at first get on with him. 'Lord Paget's is such an overgrown fortune', he wrote to his wife in August 1797, 'that it will be unpleasant to live in the same place with a person whose military rank is only my equal; but by the profusion observed by him in every instance in his mode of life, I shall always be considered in a very secondary point of view, money being the great engine of popularity.'[18] Eleven months later, when the regiment was to leave Canterbury for Guildford, Le Marchant had settled down with his commanding officer; complaining that though the regiment was much improved generally the officers were 'a bad set', he goes on to tell his wife that he is 'very well with them all, but it is by being intimate with none but Colonel Barne and Lord Paget. We three agree very well together, and in time hope to weed the Regiment of the black sheep.'[19] This they achieved by inducing a number of officers to leave the regiment either by purchase or exchange. Among the new blood brought in was Paget's brother Berkeley, who at the age of eighteen was given a cornetcy.

*　　*　　*

On June 6th, 1796, Paget became a father for the first time. On that day Car presented him with a daughter, who was christened Caroline after her mother. Thirteen months later his son and heir was born, and to him was given the name Henry, after his father. There followed, in 1798, a second daughter, named Jane after old Lady Uxbridge, her paternal grandmother. The arrival of this third baby was succeeded by a comparatively long period of nearly two years during which Car had a respite from the business of bringing little Pagets into the world.

CHAPTER FOUR

The noble Duke of York
He had ten thousand men;
He marched them up to the top of the hill,
And marched them down again.
Anonymous jingle

SINCE the British army had been driven from the Netherlands in 1795, the war with France had been waged, on the part of England, almost exclusively at sea. By the summer of 1799 the Government had decided that the time had come to set foot once more upon the Continent. Ministers therefore set in motion a well publicized enterprise known euphemistically as the 'Secret Expedition'. On August 27th Sir Ralph Abercromby, England's most experienced general, loudly protesting at the lack of preparation, was landed with the first wave of the invasion, upon the northernmost tip of Holland. Within two days the whole of the Dutch fleet at the Helder had passed into the hands of Britain without the firing of a single shot. Abercromby, for lack of transport and in face of unexpected native hostility, was unable to take advantage of this initial (and only enduring) success of the campaign. A week after landing he had advanced only a short distance. There, on the Zype canal, he awaited the arrival of the Duke of York (who was once again to be supreme commander) and the main expeditionary force, including 18,000 Russians subsidized by Britain.

Among the British troops were the 7th Light Dragoons with Paget at their head. In July the regiment had been quartered at Old Bracknell, near Windsor. While there, the King had inspected it and been much pleased with its appearance and field movements. In August the regiment had moved to Hornchurch in preparation for embarkation, and had duly arrived off the Helder on September 12th.

More than three weeks after the first landing, the Duke declared himself ready to advance. This lengthy breathing-space enabled General Brune, the energetic French commander, to assemble a formidable force in strong

55

defensive positions. His line ran from Bergen in the west, to Oudkarspel, about five and a half miles to the north-east, with its right flank more or less uncovered. With the object of turning it and then menacing the enemy's rear, Abercromby set off to capture Hoorn on the Zuider Zee

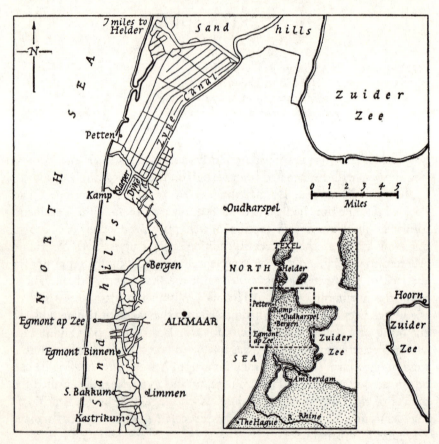

MAP 2

THE HELDER CAMPAIGN OF 1799

with 10,000 men. This operation, in which he failed due to the exhaustion of his troops, was intended to support the Duke of York's frontal attack upon the main enemy positions which was launched at dawn on September 19th. This proved a fiasco. The Russians had been assigned the place of honour on the right of the line, and together with a British brigade and the 7th Light Dragoons, they had orders to eject the French from their positions in the sand-hills which surround the village of Bergen. To the left of this column were two others: all three were to attack at dawn, but a body of Russian infantry on the extreme right decided for no clear reason to advance along the sea-shore at about two o'clock in the morning, a good two hours early. They were led appropriately enough by a general named Schutorff. When the Russian commander-in-chief, General Hermann, learnt what had happened, he decided to support his insubordinate subordinate. He therefore ordered his troops on Schutorff's immediate left to advance along the Slaeper dyke. To Paget he gave orders for two squadrons of the 7th to support the impatient Russian general, and two to escort a troop of British horse artillery. All this was set in motion while it was still completely dark. When the Russians first came across the enemy outposts they lost all discipline, and yelling at the tops of their blood-curdling voices, fired off every weapon they could lay hands on. The only casualties were sustained among themselves. Some of them penetrated as far as Bergen, but there they were cut down by enemy chasseurs, and the Russian retreat which followed quickly developed into a rout.

The other two columns had set off at the appointed time as soon as it was light. When the Duke learnt of the defeat of the Russians on the right, he began the process, which continued for most of the day, of throwing in more and more British troops in an attempt to steady the Russians. When that failed he drew liberally from the other two columns in an effort to hold the French counter-attacks. By nightfall, after sustaining over four thousand casualties, the great Anglo-Russian Army found itself back where it had started. Paget had been engaged for most of the day, but his first essay in command of cavalry in action had resulted in no casualties to his regiment.[1]

There was nothing for it but to attempt another frontal attack, and after delays due to the weather, the Duke on October 2nd launched his army in four columns against an enemy who had not failed to strengthen his positions. The right-hand column under Abercromby was ordered to march against Egmont-op-Zee and to turn the enemy's left flank. It consisted of three infantry brigades (one of them commanded by General John Moore), and part of the reserve: in all, about eight thousand bayonets. It was accompanied by Paget in command of one troop of horse artillery and nine squadrons of cavalry, numbering at least seven hundred and twenty sabres. When, nine days earlier, the initial plans for the attack had been made, it had been intended that Abercromby's column should be accompanied solely by the 7th Light Dragoons, but in the interval, two squadrons of the 11th (and possibly another of the 15th) had been added to Paget's command. It was wise thus to place the majority of the cavalry in the right-hand column, as only on the beach was there any possibility of manœuvre for horsemen.

At six in the morning, one squadron of the 7th and the two guns of the horse artillery troop led Abercromby's column out of Petten. As they debouched into the sand-hills near Kamp, small groups of the enemy retired before them. While Paget led the cavalry along the beach — the right-hand horsemen actually riding through the surf — the brunt of the fighting was taking place on his left among the dazzling white of the sand-hills. Here the infantry's progress was painfully slow: the enemy was numerous and took full advantage of the peculiar difficulties presented to the attackers by the sea of sand which stretched inland in great waves, preventing men on one side of a crest from seeing their comrades on the other. As the day, which had opened fine and warm, wore on, casualties mounted (Moore was badly wounded) and the men became increasingly exhausted. Towards evening the weary infantry were furiously attacked about two miles from Egmont, and only after a desperate struggle was the enemy driven back. At this point Abercromby wisely decided that his troops were too jaded to attack the enemy in the strong position to which they had been driven among the sand-hills before Egmont, and it seemed that the action was over. As protection, he ordered Paget to thrust forward the troop of horse artillery. Its escort of dragoons had just dismounted to rest behind some dunes out of view of the enemy when, before the astonished gunners knew what was happening, they found themselves surrounded by French hussars, attempting the capture of their guns. General Vandamme, who had just arrived on the scene, thought the guns unprotected and an easy prey. But it so happened that about twelve officers and N.C.O.s had remained in their saddles, among them Paget. Losing not a moment, this group charged straight at the French hussars and engaged them furiously, giving the rest of the escort time to mount and join them. The enemy horsemen were then chased nearly to Egmont itself, not a single man of the squadron employed reaching his lines.

The losses of the 7th on this day were two men and four horses killed and eleven men and twenty-five horses wounded. At one moment during the battle a report that Paget had been taken prisoner caused a detachment of the 7th to rush forward rather impetuously to recapture their colonel; the report proved false, 'and although', wrote Cannon in his records of the regiment, 'His Lordship felt it necessary to restrain this excess of ardour, he could not withhold an expression of his feeling of the good intentions of his brave corps.'[2]

Egmont-op-Zee was claimed as a victory, though it had proved a costly one, and the French withdrew at leisure from the village the following morning. In his dispatch four days later, the Duke paid special tribute to Paget, 'who commanded the Cavalry upon the Beach, and whose exertions are deserving of every praise'.[3]

*   *   *

Encouraged by the events of October 2nd, the Duke determined to continue the attack. He therefore ordered an advance on the 6th, so as to make contact with the enemy in his new position before launching a full-scale offensive the next morning. But it so happened that Brune had chosen the same day for a partial counter-attack, so that as soon as the British columns had occupied the lightly held villages immediately in their front, they found themselves engaged in a general action, for which they were not prepared. General Essen, who had taken over command of the Russians after Hermann's capture at the battle of Bergen, had wandered on south of the rest of the Allies, reaching the village of Kastrikum, where he found the opposition unexpectedly vigorous. More and more British and Russian troops were rushed forward to his aid, and casualties mounted. A stubborn battle followed, the French eventually driving the Russians back along the two roads to South Bakkum and Limmen, and capturing their guns. Essen's position was perilous, for immediately in his rear was a stream with a broken bridge over it, and the French cavalry who followed up the bayonet attacks of the infantry were on the point of driving the hapless Russians to the bank of the stream, when they were saved at the last moment. A small party of dragoons of the 7th and 11th had been skilfully hidden by Paget behind some sand dunes on the road to the north of Kastrikum which runs through South Bakkum. As the enemy cavalry charged past Paget's ambush, he suddenly crashed into their left flank.[a] The extraordinary suddenness of this surprise attack by a small body of determined men had the effect of completely demoralizing the French cavalry, who quickly communicated their panic to the infantry behind them. In a matter of seconds the whole attacking force, cavalry and infantry, perhaps three thousand men, was in disordered retreat. They raced back to Kastrikum as fast as they could go. Seldom had an ambush proved more entirely successful.[b] By his brilliant charge, Paget had given the Russians time to recover their guns, repair the bridge, and cross the stream. As night fell and the fighting ceased, they were able to return to Bakkum and Limmen in perfect safety.

That same night, though the Allies had gained ground and taken many prisoners, the lieutenant-generals represented to the Duke that he should retire. Difficulties of transport and supply and the lateness of the year, combined with increasingly unfriendly relations between the Russians and the British, decided the Duke to accept their advice. He retired once more to the old line of the Zype. Negotiations were opened on October 14th, and a convention signed four days later, thus bringing the campaign to an end. The troops were re-embarked, and after delays due to bad weather, they sailed for England. The 7th were split into small parties on board fourteen different ships. Paget, who with fourteen men was carried in the *Mistley* transport, was lucky to escape the fate of some of his officers and men, for the muster-roll of the regiment shows them as 'taken by the French on passage to England'.[4]

By the first days of November most of the regiment had landed at Ramsgate and was moving to quarters near Canterbury.[e]

ii

Paget, Lady Paget, and little Car were in town lately ... and his kindness and affection to myself ... commanded my warmest gratitude.

Charles Paget to Arthur Paget, 1805[5]

There was little scope for the use of cavalry in the small number of foreign expeditions which left the shores of England between 1799 and 1808. For much of that period the British Isles were threatened with imminent invasion, and the need for troops to counter it kept the majority of the army at home. These were the factors which condemned Paget to eight years without a sight of the enemy. In April 1802 he was promoted to the rank of major-general and given the command of a cavalry brigade, with his headquarters at Ipswich. In the same year he was returned unopposed for the second time as Member of Parliament for Milborne Port, and spent, in consequence, a part of each year in London attending in an inconspicuous way to his Parliamentary duties. The rest of his days were spent either at Beaudesert and Plas Newydd, or at Wretham, an estate near Ipswich, famed for its partridge shooting, and for which he gave five hundred guineas a year. There he lived in state with some thirty servants.

Joseph Farington, the artist, heard that for the year 1804 Paget's bill for coals and small beer alone came to £500. 'He pays his bills', he added, 'with great regularity.'[6]

A glimpse of what he was like at this period is provided by his sister Louisa Erskine, who, writing to her husband in 1801, says:

> 'Car [Lady Paget] and I laughed heartily at what you told me of Paget. We agree in thinking that *his indifference* and cold manner upon all occasions must not a little astonish *you* who are so very much the reverse of what I am sorry to say he rather piques himself upon. How strange that anybody should affect what is so very un-amiable. I am convinced that Paget *au fond* has great feeling but he study's so to appear devoid of it that I fear it will end in his being so.'[7]

This looks very much like the frustration of an insufficiently employed man-of-action. Four years later Louisa paints a more attractive picture: talking of her young daughter, she tells her brother Arthur 'that Paget doats upon her; I never saw him take so much notice of any child but his own, in short you know he professes hating all Children but his own, except our little Loui.'[8]

In 1803 when the invasion scare was looming large, he refused to put off a shooting-party with his brother Arthur. 'By the arrangements that I shall make', he wrote from Norwich, 'I can be at Ipswich in 6 hours after the intelligence of the first movement of the foe is known. There are certain little previous ceremonies attending an attack of the nature of that expected, which pretty much preclude the possibility of surprise, *ergo* I shall have no scruples in shooting & dining with you *each day*, even tho' I should think it necessary to spend the nights here under arms.'[9] Two years later, when the scare was at its height, Louisa reported from Beaudesert that orders had been issued for officers not to be absent from their posts even for a night. 'In spite of which,' she wrote, 'Paget (who is excessively *lungeous* at the Monster [Napoleon] for always beginning his threats in the shooting season) proposes (if he can possibly get leave) coming down here for a little black game shooting.'[10]

In August 1803 Sir Sidney Smith, the victor of Acre, arrived off Suffolk aboard the *Antelope*. Young Major Hussey Vivian of the 7th describes how a party which included Paget was very nearly drowned on its way to the ship. 'The wind was hard and we struck on the bar of the Alde river, and if all the sailors and Lord P. and myself had not jumped out up to our middles in water to lighten the barge, she must have gone to pieces; for the sea was making a fair breach over her, and the ladies were just as wet as if they had been drawn through a pond. When we got into deep water the boat was full half-way up the leg. So much for water parties!'[11]

*   *   *

At about this time in his career, Paget was gaining for himself the reputation of a dandy which was to remain with him for life. In the 7th Hussars he set an immensely high sartorial standard: one extremely wealthy young officer, Ball Hughes, known later in society as 'The Golden Ball', gained fame as the great imitator of his colonel, 'whom he took', wrote Captain Gronow, 'as a model for his coats, hats and boots; indeed everything that his noble commander said or did was law to him.'[d] Lord Melbourne, talking to Queen Victoria in 1838, said that George IV, though he liked Paget, was jealous of his figure, 'and used to say to the Tailor, "Why don't you make my coats fit like Paget's?", which made us laugh,' wrote the Queen in her Journal, 'as the King might well think his own figure wasn't quite as slim as Lord Anglesey's.' Wellington's friend, Alava, the Spanish general, 'was highly amused once at Brussels [in 1815] at hearing a discussion between Lord Anglesey and [Hussey] Vivian about their dress', wrote a fellow officer. 'Vivian came to consult his master about what dress he should wear at a levée, and they were talking about it just like ladies. "Oh, we must put on our yellow boots and pelisses." Old Alava came away laughing, "Well, I never should have supposed that those two fellows had anything in their heads." '[12]

*   *   *

On August 29th, 1800, Car gave birth to her fourth child, a daughter, who was baptized Georgiana. There followed the fifth, sixth, seventh and eighth additions to the family, who arrived at almost exactly annual intervals, Augusta on January 26th, 1802, William on March 1st, 1803, Agnes on February 11th, 1804, and Arthur on January 31st, 1805. Arthur, who became a favourite of his father's, died from a hunting accident in Yorkshire, a month before his twentieth birthday.

CHAPTER FIVE

As you are sending 5000 cavalry, I suppose we shall have my friend Paget again; I shall like this, as he certainly understands our arm.
Charles Stewart from Spain to his brother, Lord Castlereagh, Secretary of State for War, October 8th, 1808[1]

THWARTED by the English Navy from his designs upon England herself, Napoleon, after Trafalgar, turned his energies towards the conquest of India and Britain's rich possessions in the East. For this to succeed it was vital that Gibraltar and Cadiz should be securely in his hands, and that, as a first step, Portugal should be bludgeoned into adherence, as her unfortunate Regent put it, 'to the cause of the Continent'. In the late summer of 1807 this process was complete, and one of England's last allies had been prised from her. At the end of October, by the secret Treaty of Fontainebleau, Napoleon had partitioned Portugal between Spain and France. To Lisbon he had at once sent off an army under General Junot, who arrived there at the end of November. A clause of the treaty provided that, should the English land in the Peninsula, the French were to occupy the north-eastern provinces of Spain in support of Junot. Napoleon invoked this clause long before any such landing had been contemplated in London, and in February 1808 he employed the most shameless treachery to gain without bloodshed the four fortresses which were the bastions of Spain. In the process, he first secured the abdication of King Carlos, and then kidnapped Ferdinand, his more popular heir.

As the French army, a hundred thousand strong, swept through Spain, the Spaniards at first welcomed it as their liberator from a corrupt tyranny, but as soon as they learnt how Ferdinand had been tricked, their innate loathing of the foreigner caused them to effect an extraordinary volte-face. By the end of May 1808 the rebellion against the French had spread throughout the country. The Portuguese were quick to follow suit, and by the end of June the forces at Junot's disposal occupied no more than two frontier fortresses and the immediate neighbourhood of Lisbon.

63

Spain, at this time, as a satellite of France, had been at war with England for four years; now her situation was speedily reversed. Even before the establishment of formal peace between Spain and England, appeals for help had reached London from certain of the provincial Juntas, and it was fortunate for both countries that for once there was a

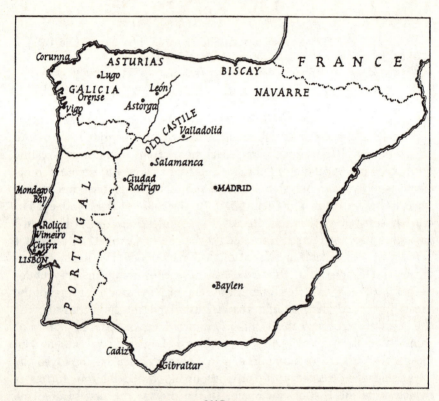

MAP 3

SPAIN AND PORTUGAL IN 1808

sizeable English army at hand to take advantage of the situation. At Madeira, 3,000 men were kicking their heels. In transports off Gibraltar were a further 4,000 under Major-General Spencer. In Ireland, 9,500 were preparing under Sir Arthur Wellesley for a madcap expedition to revolutionize Venezuela, and Sir John Moore was about to return from an ill-contrived Swedish project, with a force of 10,000. Encouraged by reports of the effectiveness of the Spanish resistance, the Government, with

Lord Paget as Lieutenant-Colonel of the 7th Light Dragoons (Hussars),
aged 30

'Car', Lady Paget aged 26, first wife of 'One-Leg' with their eldest
daughter, Caroline, aged 4

commendable speed, decided to send out Wellesley's force to aid the peoples who so daringly opposed the master of Europe.

Wellesley's orders were to create the maximum diversion possible for Spain in Portugal, and to see what he could do to expel Junot. Sailing ahead of his troops to get as much information as possible about the progress of the Spanish rising[a] and the size of the French forces, he directed his army to land at Mondego Bay at the mouth of the Douro. There it was joined by Spencer's 4,000, and on August 9th began its march on Lisbon. On the 16th, Wellesley encountered part of Junot's army sent from the capital to meet him, and soundly beat it at Roliça the following day. A further two brigades then joined him from England, bringing the strength of his army to about 18,000 men.

Meanwhile Moore had arrived off the coast of Galicia, with Major-General Edward Paget on his staff, and Lieutenant-General Lord Paget among his divisional commanders.

It was a blow for Paget to learn that the Horse Guards in its wisdom had designated him for command of nothing more than an infantry division. On the day of the battle of Roliça, he was writing to his brother Arthur, from Vigo Bay, where he had arrived in a man-of-war from England:

'When I saw you, I had every prospect, as I thought, of a brilliant situation. I had seen the distribution by which it appeared that I was to command a most eligible Corps. It was composed of what Cavalry there was in the Expedition — some light Artillery, I believe, & Infantry, chiefly Light. All this is changed; I find myself destined to lead a division of Infantry — Pleasant! The fact is that by Moore's having two Generals above him, he is as a *douceur* complimented with the Reserve (with all the good things). This is natural enough — It is quite right, & God knows I am most fully aware that he is much more competent to such a charge than I am, but you will admit, that having had this corps in expectation myself, I may without being accused of being unreasonable, feel a little uncomfortable. And the fact is that I really do feel so completely. In short — Will they or will they not send out a good corps of Cavalry — If they do, they shall see if I like the Service — If they do not, I already foresee that I shall be *no where*, & that I had much better be any where else. I don't know that I should make a good *Chef de Cavalerie* — but I am sure, I shall make a very bad *Officier de Ligne*, for I

c

detest the idea, & whatever one does not like, one does ill.... I am all for Cavalry Cavalry Cavalry — This won't do for me I see — I am *nowhere*.'²

As it happened, Paget was to be employed neither with infantry nor cavalry for some time to come; instead he was to return to England in bitter disappointment before his chance came. For a tricky situation concerning the chief command of the expedition had been developing for some time, and it now came to a head.

Wellesley was low in the list of lieutenant-generals in the army. There were many senior to him whose experience extended well beyond his; notable among these was Moore. The Horse Guards looked askance at Ministers' appointment of so junior an officer as Wellesley to command so important a force, but since he was himself a Minister, being Chief Secretary for Ireland, he was far more acceptable to the Cabinet than was Moore. Further, though the Horse Guards, strongly supported by the King, believed, with justice, that Moore was the foremost soldier in the army, and the obvious choice for the command, he was no friend to Ministers, whose erratic conduct of military operations he at times quite openly deplored. If Sir Arthur Wellesley was not to retain the command-in-chief, Ministers were determined that Sir John Moore should not have it. They dug out, therefore, two ancient and extremely senior generals, and sent them off to Portugal, Sir Hew Dalrymple as commander-in-chief, and Sir Harry Burrard as second-in-command. 'The Gentlemen', as Wellesley ever afterwards remembered them, were entirely unsuited to the command of a large expeditionary force.

Sir Harry arrived first, and though he did not take over command till Wellesley had won the battle of Vimeiro on August 21st, he refused to allow the success to be followed up. Scarcely had he deprived the army (and himself) of the fruits of victory, when Sir Hew appeared upon the scene. To the chagrin of Sir Arthur, Dalrymple was even more cautious, and all hopes of an early entry into Lisbon evaporated. Junot, however, as a direct result of Vimeiro, sent a flag of truce, and Sir Hew proceeded to negotiate an armistice with him, Sir Harry and Sir Arthur both being present. This was succeeded by the Convention of Cintra — by which the French were to be evacuated from Portugal and taken in British transports to France with all their arms and possessions, including, in the event, their booty. From now on, said Canning, he would spell 'humiliation' with a 'Hew'.

While the Convention was being negotiated in Lisbon, the senior officers had an opportunity of meeting the French commander. Major Colborne relates that 'when Lord Paget was presented to Junot he was in a general officer's uniform, at that time a very unbecoming dress, and Junot, going up to Graham, said, "J'ai toujours supposé que Lord Paget était le plus beau garçon d'Angleterre, mais je ne le crois pas du tout." However, when next day he came to dine in his splendid Hussar uniform, Junot changed his mind. "Ah, il faut avouer à present qu'il est très-beau." '³

'The Portuguese campaign', wrote Paget to his father, two days before the signing of the Convention, 'is, I suspect, at an end, and I have had no share whatever in it. In two actions which Wellesley had before Moore's corps landed, the French were well beaten, and are now negotiating. They appear to have managed very ill indeed, and I almost think that they had the original intention to give themselves up to us from a fear of falling into the hands of the natives. ...

'Wellesley's corps has certainly been superior to the French in both actions, but more particularly so in the first. Full opportunity, however, was given to prove the perfect courage and steadiness of the soldiers, and the quickness and ability of the chief. He is, I really believe, an excellent officer. Every officer speaks well of him. He is very quick, and full of resources. He has lodged me for two days, and I had during that time an opportunity of observing that he possesses much method and arrangement. He is, besides, the luckiest dog upon earth, for it is by a sort of miracle, or rather by two or three combined, to detain Moore's corps, that he has been enabled to do this by himself. I feel it to be a real misfortune to me, as a soldier, that I am above him on the list, for I think there is a good chance of its cutting me off from all service. We who came out with the latter division of the army are in the most awkward predicament imaginable. I must say that it is borne with the most perfect good humour, but it cannot go on. We all *really and sincerely* rejoice that Wellesley and his division have done the thing without us, because it reflects the greatest credit upon them, and that the same thing divided amongst the two corps together would have been of little service to any, as we should so greatly have outnumbered the enemy. Still, however, we are as I say, most awkwardly situated. Wellesley's corps still continues collected and under his orders, and in Moore's (of much less strength) there are four Lieut.-Generals[b] almost without commands. I was yesterday put in order to command the cavalry, which, if assembled, would only consist of eight squadrons, with a Brigadier-General under me, but which, in fact, is only four weak squadrons of the German Legion. I really feel that if our Commander-in-Chief had even the inclination he can do no more for me, because all the other Lieut.-Generals are older and more experienced officers than myself, and as even by this unsatisfactory arrangement I am put in the way of Charles Stewart, for whom the command of this little brigade was certainly intended, and which is just suited to his rank, I feel a delicacy in interfering at all, and have therefore made up my mind for the present to retire.'

Charles Stewart wrote at this time to his brother, Lord Castlereagh, the Secretary of State for War, 'Paget ... has open'd his mind to me, and [expressed] his disinclination to interfere with myself in the handsomest manner.... He feels he cannot command here what his rank and situation entitles him to, and in depriving me of what is suited to me would be like the dog in the manger.'[4]

Paget decided before retiring to see the army into Lisbon, and if there should be occasion to fight, give all assistance he could. His decision to apply for leave of absence was taken in good humour and after discussing the matter with Moore.

'I only think,' he wrote, 'as indeed most do, that Ministers were unwise in not giving Wellesley openly the chief command at once, without sending out to be mere spectators a parcel of older officers, or that if they thought him too young for so large a command, they should have at once made an equal distribution of the forces — and perhaps the former would have been the wiser arrangement.... One of the disadvantages of my situation is this, that I can *literally get nothing*, which never happened to me in any other service. If I apply for anything in Moore's corps I am told, "I understand your Lordship's division is in Sir A. Wellesley's army"; and if I apply to those in the latter they tell me, "Your Lordship had better apply to Sir John Moore's army, as you belong to that."... It is, I do believe, unavoidable, and therefore I take it all in good part, for there cannot, I am sure, be a greater nuisance in an army than a useless, unattached General Officer and his suite. But if ever I do find myself at the head of thirty or forty squadrons, I will make up for it and live like a prince.'

The crux of the matter was Wellesley's lack of seniority. The problem that was to deprive Paget of any part in Wellesley's great Peninsular campaigns which followed Corunna was already a real one. 'If Wellesley should have the Command-in-Chief', he wrote, 'I could not of course serve, and', he continues, with excellent judgment, 'I must, in candour, say that I do think he is very capable of it.'[5]

In common with most of his contemporary officers, Paget had a very real respect for Moore, and it would clearly have been to his interest that Sir John should have the command-in-chief, which was undoubtedly his right; yet Paget's two days as Wellesley's lodger had shown him the peculiar qualities of the victor of Vimeiro, and he had been honest enough to acknowledge them.

So ended the first phase of the Peninsular War. Public opinion demanded a court of inquiry to investigate the Convention of Cintra, but received no satisfaction from its findings, and Paget, like Dalrymple and Wellesley, sailed homewards; they to give evidence before the court, and he to bide his time in a short-lived state of frustration.

He can hardly have guessed as he sailed northwards that at last his great chance was almost at hand. His brother Edward, who had remained in Portugal, reported to Lady Uxbridge on October 10th the arrival of 'a letter from Sir J. Moore to announce his appointment *to command*. Huzza! No more conventions!' And on the following day: 'From suspense and uncertainty all is suddenly converted into confidence, from the appointment of Sir John Moore to the command.... I think we now bid fair for a most important, and, I hope, brilliant campaign or two. Nothing, I trust, will prevent Paget's taking the command of the cavalry. I know his name is down for that command, and I also know that it will be a subject of serious disappointment to Sir J. Moore if he does not take it.'[6]

Paget was offered it and took it. On what he made of it, at least as much as on his Waterloo record, any assessment of his worth as a cavalry leader must depend.

ii

Never was any one so well equipped for a campaign as I am. My horses are capital and in perfect order. My baggage is upon the best possible footing, and can keep pace with the Hussars. My staff is very good. I have the best cook and the best set of servants that ever were collected, and I have a little corps of cavalry that cannot be surpassed.

Paget to his father, December 4th, 1808[7]

The fiasco which had resulted from the Government's efforts to exclude him from the earlier command, the consequent unpopularity of Ministers, and the influence of the King, were the factors which combined to secure for Moore now, when it seemed that his career was over, the command of the largest army the country had sent abroad since the days of Marlborough.

The news of Vimeiro coming soon after the Spanish victory at Baylen in July, had decided the Cabinet to prepare a large force under Sir David Baird. This was ready to sail from Falmouth three weeks before Moore was given supreme command. Baird was ordered to land at Corunna with his 19,000 men, while Moore was given the option of either taking his 20,000 by sea from Lisbon to Corunna or marching there by land. He decided to go by land. At the end of October all his troops were on their way to the frontier. His orders, necessarily vague, were to join his own army to Baird's and move forward to support the Spanish armies facing the French on the river Ebro. In pouring rain and over mountainous terrain, Moore's army struggled to the frontier, and it was the second week in November before they were over it. Meanwhile, on October 13th, Baird had arrived off Corunna, with Paget commanding his cavalry.

Both Moore and Baird now began to experience the difficulties which co-operation with the Spaniards presented. The body with which they had to deal was the newly created Supreme Junta at Madrid, consisting of thirty-four members each exercising equal powers. There was neither a commander-in-chief nor a general staff. Baird was forbidden to disembark at Corunna until permission had been granted by the Supreme Junta, and in consequence did not complete the landing of his first 12,000 until November 4th, and, granted no aid by the suspicious people of Galicia, made very slow progress along the mountain road to Astorga.

Napoleon, all this time, had been reinforcing with great speed, and by November 12th had completely destroyed the Spanish armies of Estremadura and Galicia, which were to have formed up on Moore's left, and

whose commanders' petty jealousies had made it easy for him to defeat
them in detail. As a result, Valladolid, which Moore had designated as his
rendezvous with Baird, was in French hands, and the Grand Army of
perhaps 200,000 men was in a position to make highly problematical the

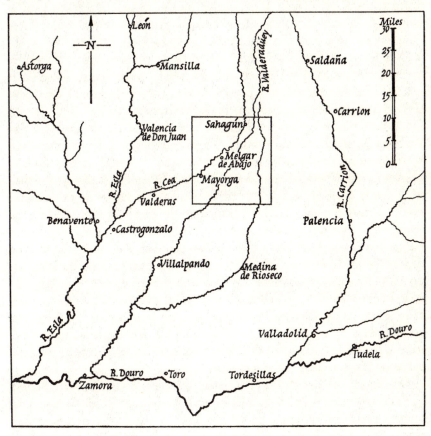

MAP 4

PART OF OLD CASTILE IN 1808

junction of the two English armies. The inefficiency of the Spanish
commanders, and the delays forced on Baird by the obstruction of their
countrymen, had placed Moore in a terrible position. As there was now
only General Castaños's army left intact, the whole basis of the campaign
— that there were Spanish armies to be aided — was on the point of
vanishing.

Baird had been expected with his whole force at Astorga by the middle of November, but by then he had not covered half the 170 miles which lay between Corunna and that place, and Paget's cavalry was still disembarking on the 15th. Edward Paget, in command of Moore's advance guard, wrote to his mother from Ciudad Rodrigo on the 13th that he had heard from Moore (who had reached Salamanca) of Paget's arrival at Corunna. 'We are now three of us here, and the Devil is in it if out of that number you are not fortunate enough to save the expense of wash-leather gloves before Christmas, especially as I command the advance corps, Paget the cavalry — which are always almost at the advanced posts — and Berkeley a squadron or two of Hussars, which Paget will, of course, send as forward as he can, for the honour of the family.'[8]

On the 17th the cavalry left Corunna for Astorga. On the previous day Berkeley Paget wrote to his father, 'Paget marches with my division, and we mean to take our guns. He has plenty to do, indeed, I do not think he has time to write to England. We have 160 or 170 miles to Astorga, which will occupy us thirteen days, including two halting days. I do not imagine he will remain long with my division, as he will probably soon be tired of going only three or four leagues a day. He will, I think, make the best of his way to Astorga, and wait there till we come up.'[9] Hussey Vivian, who now had direct command of the 7th, wrote while on the march, 'I had the good fortune to be quartered in the same house with Lord Paget, & consequently fared very well as to eating: but our lodging was ... miserable; ten of us in one little room, and an ante-chamber full of lice, fleas, and all sorts of vermin.... At Bahamonde [?], having heard that there were woodcocks in a wood facing the house, Lord Paget went out, and succeeded in bringing home a couple.'[10]

On his arrival at Lugo, Paget received an express from Baird stating that he had received very bad news, that he found himself in the most critical situation, and that he wished very much to have his cavalry commander with him. 'I, of course, set out instantly on post horses,' wrote Paget, 'and contrived to ride seventy-four miles in the first nine and a half hours, which being upon tired bidets and over mountains was no bad work.' He reached Astorga on the next day, and found nothing but long faces. 'Blake's[c] army [the Army of Galicia] had been beaten and totally dispersed. The Estramadurians had shared the like fate.... Sir J. Moore had expressed his determination to fall back the moment the enemy advanced from Valladolid, and he recommended Sir David Baird to look to his own safety.' When Paget arrived, he found that Baird had already started to withdraw. 'I flatter myself', he wrote, 'that I very considerably contributed to retard, at least, this operation.... In fact the retrograde movement was stopped, but they [Baird's army] soon took alarm again, retired, then advanced, and are now finally gone off.'[11]

In a letter to Arthur he sums up the predicament in which England's only army found itself. Of the remnants of the Spanish armies he says:

'None of these are equipped, many half naked, & they cannot be considered in a state to keep the field. I know of no reinforcements any where — The game therefore is considered as completely up. Our Government must have been most grossly deceived in regard to the situation of the Spanish Armies, the Resources of the Country & the Dispositions of the People. We do not discover any *enthusiasm* any where. The country appears to be in a state of complete Apathy. ... I have no doubts whatever that a junction of Moore's & of Baird's Corps is impossible. We cannot venture into the plain, till the arrival of the Cavalry, which will not be all come up till the 3d of Decr. Supposing the French did not till then advance in force between, it would still be a very hazardous operation, as they are immensely superior in that Arm — but this will not be the case.... Even if we were to form the junction, we have now no ulterior object. There is no Spanish Army & altho' 30,000 Men, which we should be, might probably beat the first Corps that tried with us, still that could do no good, & there is *no salvation* for the *Spanish Nation*, take my word for it.'[12]

The retreat of Baird's force now started in earnest. Paget stayed with the infantry rearguard at Astorga to await the arrival of the cavalry which was to cover the infantry's front, and 'all I pray for is that the Enemy will allow our Infantry to remain sufficiently long in their Position to enable the Hussars to give them one brush.' More gloomily, and with a prophetic flash, he declares that if very closely and heavily pressed, they may be obliged, if it comes to re-embarkation, 'to destroy most of the Horses & save the Men. How most sincerely do I rejoice that the Duke of York did not come here. An Angel could do us no good, & Mr Cobbett, & our Governors the Editors, would without hesitation have attributed all the disasters of the Spaniards to him.' Of the cavalry still struggling on to Astorga, he reported that they

'are very ill put up, & tho' marching thro' a country with some resources, suffering from want of faith in Spanish Contractors &

want of skill & Method in our Commissaries. Still we have managed *much* better than our neighbours. The Horses suffer a great deal in their feet, & I have been obliged to make the men lead them a great part of the way. Oh! we could have done well, I am sure we could, if we had had the opportunity. I am in despair. The fates are against us. The French have been too quick. Neither Moore nor Baird can help themselves. All we can do is to give the Foe a good Black Eye if he is impertinent in our Retreat. *Tout ceci me dégoute du Gouvernement & du Service. Il n'y a pas d'honneur à gagner. On peut bien le perdre.*'

Baird sent Paget off on November 25th to try to find out from the two Spanish commanders, Romana and Blake, what forces they had left, what their intentions were, and to gain more certain intelligence of the enemy.[12] He saw Romana at Leon, and found his army utterly feeble, consisting of not more than 5,000 men, mostly the débris of Blake's army, and these ill-equipped in every respect.

Appalled at the thought of a retreat and re-embarkation — 'what an ignominious thing is it to go off and embark' — Paget

'sent in a proposal to endeavour to march to the right by Orense, and so into Portugal, with the most effective part of the cavalry, and I have even determined to take with me four guns, although it is stated to be impossible, but we have so often been taught by the French that nothing is impossible that I have resolved to try it. The roads will be desperate, and there are several rivers to pass, but as I shall be without infantry, and as the enemy might push a small corps of Light Infantry across Portugal (and a very small corps would be a very desperate annoyance to us), and might even stop our march without a few shrapnell-shells to assist us, I shall force through all the difficulties that may occur for the artillery, and by hook or by crook get them on.'[14]

Nothing, however, came of this audacious plan.

Moore was now faced with two alternatives. Either he must play for safety and withdraw his own force to Portugal and that of Baird to its transports, or, in spite of the tremendous odds against him (and by now he knew pretty well the size of Napoleon's army), still make an attempt

to assemble both. While there were any organized Spaniards in the field
— General Castaños was still intact in the north-east — he felt that it was
his duty, in spite of the risk to his army, not to abandon them completely.
But he had scarcely sent off a letter to Baird to stop his retreat when he
heard that Castaños had been trounced at the battle of Tudela. All, it
seemed, was over. Moore sent orders for Baird to re-embark at Corunna
and for his own troops to return to Lisbon.

Paget, still at Astorga on December 4th, wrote to his father that Baird
had received Moore's dispatch that morning, approving the former's
arrangements to retire,

'but desiring that if he has still a regiment of cavalry forward, he
will send it to him. I have caught at this, have written to Sir D.
Baird, and by every argument that has occurred to me have shown
the propriety of my advancing with three regiments and six pieces
of Horse Artillery, and begged and entreated, and begged again, that
he will allow me to make this movement with 1200 or 1500 of the
Hussars.ᵈ If he does not consent, or if he prevents *me personally*
from going, I solemnly declare that I never will serve again. It will be
the finest operation in the world. A rapid march over an immense
plain — a perfect sea which has been overrun by the enemy's cavalry
— with a compact body of British cavalry and artillery, ready and
willing to fall upon almost anything in *its own way* that presents itself.
Here I am in a state of the most complete trepidation until I get his
answer. He is at Villa Franca. I have sent two orderly officers to him,
and everything is quite ready for a start. If it don't take place *I cut.*
It will be the only pleasant thing that can happen to us, if Sir J.
Moore retires, for, as for assisting in the defence of Portugal, I
confess I have no taste for it, and if the French fairly possess themselves of Spain, believe me, Portugal has no chance whatever. It will
fall *to a certainty*.... Bonaparte is too much for all Europe. He *will*
place his brother on the throne of Spain, and he will plant his
imperial eagles at Lisbon.'¹⁵

Paget got his way, and marched on the 5th with about 1,200 cavalry and
six pieces of horse artillery. Between the 8th and 10th he reached Zamora
and Toro and extended his troops north of the Douro between these two
places, and as far east as Tordesillas.

Eight days earlier, Moore had received the astonishing intelligence that Napoleon, instead of turning westwards to fight the British, had proceeded to march upon Madrid. It is almost certain that the Emperor still believed the *whole* British force to be retreating towards Lisbon; but whatever reasons lay behind the decision to reoccupy the capital, with the French advance guard before Madrid, Moore was given the one thing he most desperately needed, a breathing-space in which to effect his own retirement into Portugal, and Baird's return to his transports. He could now gain both these objects without being attacked with overwhelming force. But on the very day that Paget with the best part of Baird's cavalry was leaving Astorga to join him, Moore heard that the populace of Madrid had once again risen, as they had on May 2nd: this time to deny Napoleon entry to their capital. The British commander now took a decisive step. An urgent appeal for help reached him from Madrid, but since his force was clearly too small and too distant to commit to the relief of the capital, he determined instead to harass the French communications in the north, thereby drawing off at least part of the pressure on Madrid. He considered the obvious risks worth taking, in preference to an ignominious withdrawal from Spain without effecting anything. Napoleon had left only 20,000 men under Soult in the whole of the north-west, and Moore felt that, faced with such comparatively small opposition, he could join up with Baird and have a very good try at defeating the 'Duke of Damnation' (as Soult, Duke of Dalmatia, was nicknamed by the British troops), before Napoleon could come to his aid.

In halting the retreat, Moore warned his commanders to be prepared to resume it at a moment's notice, for as he noted in his diary on December 9th, 'the courage of the populace of Madrid may fail.' It quickly did; the capital capitulated on the 3rd, and Moore heard the news on the 9th.

It was now certain that the retreat was inevitable, but at about this time, reconnaissance had revealed that the French did not know that Moore was anything like so far north as the edge of the Castilian plain. It was this information, confirmed by the enemy's evacuation of Valladolid, which induced Moore to make his second great decision. He would now see what damage he could do before he was forced to make a run for it. That he was justified in his decision, captured documents which came to hand three days after he had begun the advance amply proved. Soult, these disclosed, with two divisions totalling only 18,000, had orders to clear the country between Galicia and the Douro, where some ineffective Spanish resistance was all that was expected. It appeared that he was already moving across the Carrion River towards the west. With the greatest speed Moore's army converged on Baird's, and by December 20th they had met; the infantry at Mayorga, the cavalry at Melgar de Abajo. Great speed was necessary to effect the junction, for if Soult was to be defeated it must be soon, as he could not now remain much longer in ignorance of the whereabouts of the English. Further, Junot's corps, so recently evacuated from Portugal, was known to be marching to join him.

The moment his army was concentrated, Moore redistributed it into four divisions and two light brigades. Paget's command consisted of his brother Edward's reserve division, and of course the cavalry, which consisted of five regiments, divided into two brigades.[e] His two brigadiers were John Slade, who was nearly useless,[f] and Castlereagh's brother, Charles Stewart, who possessed ability and enterprise.[g]

As soon as Soult had learned that Baird's troops were moving in his direction, he had concentrated his two divisions at Carrion and Saldaña with Debelle's and Franceschi's cavalry brigades in covering positions at Mayorga and Sahagún. His intention was to wait for reinforcements from Junot, and when they came, to attack either Romana, with whose cavalry Debelle had been in touch as far north-west as Mansilla, or Baird at Astorga. He was still unaware that Moore had moved northwards to join Baird, and the credit for this ignorance on Soult's part goes largely to Paget, for had he not, earlier in the month, persuaded Baird to allow him to join Moore, with a considerable force instead of with the one regiment of cavalry which was all that had been asked for, there would have been virtually no troops available to screen the northward march of Moore's army. As it was, in spite of active reconnaissance by Franceschi, Paget was able, with complete effectiveness, to mask the junction at Mayorga, and to lead Soult to believe that it would still take place at Valladolid. Debelle, at Sahagún, seems to have been so occupied with Romana's reconnoitring parties in the Mansilla area that he was still ignorant, on the evening of the 20th, that Paget was at Melgar de Abajo, only twelve miles down the river Cea from Sahagún.[h]

iii

The cavalry have been performing really prodigies of valour, and Paget always at the head, and in the thick of everything that has been going on. He is, in this respect, quite a boy, and a cornet instead of a lieut.-general of cavalry, but in every other he is the right hand of the army. We all row him for exposing himself in the manner he has been doing, and I hope he will recollect that he is the Lieut.-General in future.

Edward Paget to his father, December 28th, 1808[16]

On December 17th, patrols from the 15th Hussars established that about seven hundred French cavalry were moving northwards out of Medina de Rioseco; on the 19th, at about eight o'clock in the evening, the 10th and 15th Hussars together with four horse-artillery guns arrived at Mayorga in a severe snow-storm. They had been marching since six in the morning from Villalpando, some twenty to thirty miles to the south-west. The enemy, it was learned, had left Mayorga on the Sahagún road some hours before the British cavalry entered it. During the night, the 10th, the 15th and the four guns pushed on to Melgar de Abajo. The following evening Paget called together his commanding officers and their adjutants and gave them orders for a night attack on Sahagún, where it was now known that Debelle's cavalry brigade was stationed.

The night of December 20th was bitterly cold. The snow, which lay in drifts as much as four feet deep, was frozen hard, and there were inter-mittent showers of sleet. The surface of the tracks had become sheeted with ice, and the men were obliged to dismount and lead their horses. Several small rivers were frozen so hard that even the guns could be taken across them in safety.

Paget's orders[1] for the march entailed leaving Melgar de Abajo at one in the morning and arriving before Sahagún at six thirty. His object was to effect a complete surprise; his fear, that Debelle might escape before he could be brought to action. He therefore planned a pincer movement: Slade was to lead the 10th and the four guns along the west bank of the Cea, to 'make a show and if possible push into the town',[17] while Paget[1] was to take the 15th along the east bank of the river, so that he could cut off the enemy's retreat once Slade had driven them from the town.

The first part of the plan worked smoothly enough, and some miles north of Melgar, Paget and Slade parted company. But about four and a half hours after starting, the leading division of the advanced guard of the 15th fell in with a French forward picket, charged it and took five

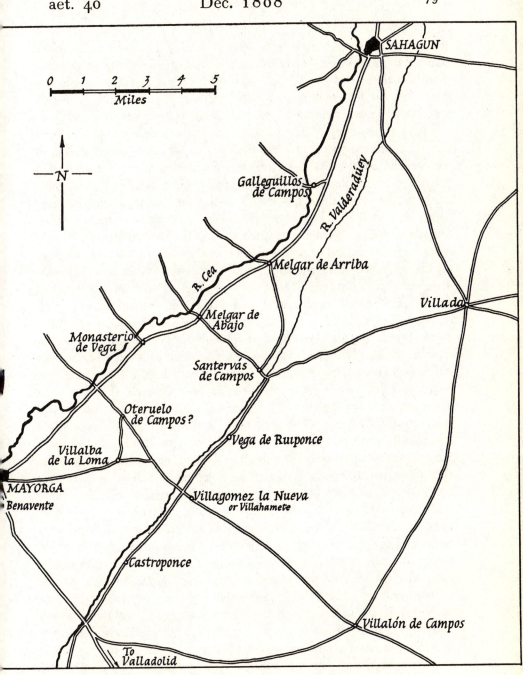

MAP 5: THE ENVIRONS OF MAYORGA AND SAHAGÚN, 1808

prisoners. Unfortunately, due to the darkness of the night, a small number of the French horsemen escaped to give the alarm to Debelle's main body in the town. It says much for the alertness of the French that when the alarm was given, the men were sleeping in the stables beside their horses, which were ready saddled and bridled; consequently it took them only a very short time to assemble at the eastern gate of Sahagún.

Paget, meanwhile, aware that the alarm must have been given, drove on with increased speed, and was just in time, as day began to break, to see Debelle starting to move off on the Carrion road. 'I marched in column parallel,'[k] he wrote next day, 'but a good deal behind them, gaining however upon them. At length seeing they must be caught, they halted and formed.' This they did behind a rugged ravine or ditch. Debelle possibly expected this ditch to stop or disarray Paget's charge, otherwise it is unlikely that the French cavalry would have remained at the halt to receive it; on the other hand, we know from accounts given by prisoners that in the grey light of dawn the French believed that they had encountered Spanish cavalry, and doubtless the ditch would have proved more of an obstacle to them than to the elite of the British horse.[1] However that may be, the 15th found no difficulty in charging across it.

When he saw the enemy halt and form, Paget, as he told his brother Arthur, 'pursued a little further to secure them, halted, wheeled into Line & charged, just as you have often seen us do at Ipswich'. The two regiments engaged on the enemy side were the 8th Dragoons and the 1st Provisional Chasseurs à Cheval, and as the 15th gave three cheers followed by shouts of 'Emsdorf and Victory',[m] the chasseurs fired upon them from the saddle with their carbines. But nothing could now stop the 15th's devastating charge delivered at the gallop, and the chasseurs were instantly broken. The 8th Dragoons, in line immediately behind, were completely disordered by the chasseurs falling back upon them, and in their turn broken. A few moments of utter confusion followed, with friend and foe intermingled, Debelle himself being thrown and trampled upon. 'In many places', reported Captain Gordon, 'the bodies of the fallen formed a complete mound of men and horses.'[18] Many of the Frenchmen continued fighting desperately even as they lay under their horses, while about two hundred of them managed to struggle free and make good their escape in every direction. There followed numerous little charges against small groups of the enemy as they retreated, but, as Paget put it, 'the pursuit was sadly disorderly.[n] I gave the Regiment a good scolding for it after the affair was over, & the answer they gave me was three cheers, & a request that I would accept as a token of their regard the two best Officers' Horses° that were taken. You would be pleased', he told Arthur Paget, 'if you were to hear all they say about me. I cannot write it.... I rode Harlequin, — he carried me admirably over the roughest & most difficult ground that can be imagined.'[19]

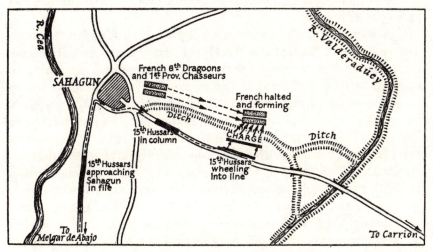

MAP 6

THE COMBAT OF SAHAGÚN, DECEMBER 21ST, 1808

Thus ended the combat of Sahagún, described by Oman as 'perhaps the most brilliant exploit of the British cavalry during the whole six years of the war', and by Fortescue as 'a brilliant little affair, and very creditable to Paget'. As a result of it Debelle's brigade was virtually wrecked, and all its baggage and a large amount of plate and money taken; several Frenchmen were killed, nineteen wounded; two lieutenant-colonels, one captain, ten lieutenants and about one hundred and fifty men taken prisoner, as well as many horses and mules. Of the 15th only two men were killed, and the colonel, adjutant and quartermaster and about twenty men[p] wounded. In all, the action had lasted for less than an hour.[q] Moore's comment was typical of him: 'It was a handsome thing, and well done.'

*   *   *

As the victorious cavalry took possession of the quarters so recently occupied by the enemy, Moore's infantry followed in their wake, and by nightfall had joined them at Sahagún. Preparations were immediately made for the main attack upon Soult. After resting his troops for two days, Moore's right-hand column was on the point of setting off early on the morning of the 23rd, when the news which he had long expected and feared reached his headquarters. Napoleon was, at long last, marching to destroy the impudent general who ought, by now, to have been well on his way to Lisbon.

The orders for the attack were immediately cancelled, and in the course of Christmas Eve Moore began his epic retreat. The troops were deeply disappointed; their immense exertions on the advance were not to be rewarded, as they had hoped, with a pitched battle; instead there was to be what seemed an inglorious withdrawal with nothing accomplished. Paget was prominent among the generals who tried to dissuade Moore from so dispiriting a course,[20] but neither he nor they could know that their commander had already saved Spain. By his audacity he had drawn the Emperor's vast army to attack him, thereby giving the Spaniards in the south the breathing-space they needed in which to reorganize their government and armies for the struggle ahead. By deciding to retreat when he did, Moore almost certainly saved his army from complete defeat. It now remained for him to extricate it as speedily as possible. To achieve this, everything must be done to steal two marches on the enemy.

iv

Lord Paget will remain with the cavalry to give us notice of the approach of the enemy; hitherto the infantry have not come up; but they are near, and the cavalry surround us in great number: they are checked by our cavalry, which have obtained by their spirit and enterprize, an ascendancy over that of the French which nothing but great superiority of numbers on their part will get the better of.

Moore to Castlereagh, December 28th, 1808[21]

As the infantry divisions of the army began their retreat from Sahagún in two columns, one to cross the Esla at Valencia de Don Juan, and the other at Castrogonzalo, the cavalry made demonstrations against Carrion and Saldaña. It was of the first importance that Soult should be kept in ignorance of the retreat, and consequently Paget directed the cavalry to be as active and pushing as possible. For two days Franceschi's outposts were harassed and driven in to such effect that Soult was convinced that a major assault was about to be launched against his position. As a result, Napoleon was led to suppose that the whole of the British army was still in Soult's immediate front. Acting on this belief, he planned to encircle it. This he would certainly have done had Moore in fact been in the position which the activity of the British horse had so successfully indicated. As it was, when, on the 27th, Soult closed in from the north-east, Ney from the south-east and Napoleon from the south, they found the trap empty. The bold handling of his cavalry had given Moore that lead which was essential to the success of the retreat. Though this had started on the 24th, it was not guessed at by the enemy until the evening of the 27th.

On Christmas Eve the two columns of the main army crossed the Esla without molestation, while the cavalry, on Christmas night, withdrew south-westwards towards Valderas.[r]

A partial thaw now set in. Incessant rain by day was succeeded by hard frost at night, and as the men lay down exhausted, their wet clothes froze them to the ground. All this was bearable for the cavalry, who were constantly engaged with the enemy and at every encounter conscious of their superiority over them; but for the infantry and artillery who had been marching backwards and forwards without a sight of the French for many weeks, it seemed that this new retreat following so swiftly on their recent advance would deprive them of their last chance of being tested in battle. As they trudged sullenly on, with the thick clay-mud up to their knees, discipline began to break and the numbers of stragglers increased alarmingly. The cavalry, in these circumstances, had to exert every nerve to keep the enemy advance guard at bay for as long and as effectively as possible. To achieve this they had to contend against thirteen enemy regiments with only five of their own on a front of thirty miles. For four days (from December 26th to 29th) nearly every troop was constantly in action from dawn to dusk. Never had cavalry been more severely tried, nor, indeed, more skilfully handled. 'By this time', wrote the historian of the British Army, 'the contempt of the British for the French horse was such that they cheerfully engaged greatly superior numbers.'[22] Napoleon himself, when the fighting was over, though he underestimated the strength of the infantry, put the British cavalry at between four and five thousand sabres, whereas in fact at this time there were less than two thousand five hundred.

*   *   *

On Christmas Day the baggage of the cavalry had been sent ahead to Mayorga. Next morning the baggage was captured by a small number of French cavalry, and as the main English body came up to the town they found it occupied by the enemy: but after a little skirmishing the enemy was driven out, and the baggage and a few prisoners which had been taken with it recovered.

'I took 2 Squadrons of the 10th', wrote Paget in his most staccato style, '& found 2 Squadrons [of the 15th Chasseurs of Ney's Corps] without, & a small party in the town; I advanced with one Squadron,⁸ ordering the others to support; they fired as we came thro' the gateway, & retired to some high ground. We attacked them again, they again fired, by which they killed two & wounded one Horse. They stood firm, we broke them, killed several, wounded 20, & took Prisoners, 1 Officer, 100 Menᵗ and 50 Horses.... *We* are in the greatest favor. The Army is retreating & it is high time it should, for there are no Spaniards & lots of French. We are all well but a good deal harassed.'[23]

This remarkably successful little encounter illustrates well the audacity of Paget's cavalry-handling at this time. He thought nothing of launching one squadron uphill through deep slushy snow against two drawn up in a position of their own choosing.

*   *   *

On the 27th, the 18th Hussars were attacked no less than six times, and on each occasion they turned and charged with equal success enabling their retreat to continue unmolested until the next attack. In one of these charges, a single troop routed a French squadron, killing twelve men and capturing twenty.

The wear and tear on the horses was appalling, and at the end of each day many of them had to be shot, for Paget had ordered that as soon as a horse was unable to keep up, it was to be destroyed. To a cavalryman this was a fearful act, and many a tear was shed as trusting friends were destroyed. On the other hand, the losses of men in all five regiments were negligible. In perfect order they fell back. During the evening of the 27th the greater part of them crossed the Esla and made for Benavente. Meanwhile, protected by Craufurd's light infantry brigade, a party of engineers prepared the massive bridge at Castrogonzalo for destruction. Except for an occasional skirmish between the hussars of the King's German Legion and the 15th Chasseurs, the work of demolition went on unhindered. During the 28th, the mass of the Imperial cavalry arrived before the bridge, and for most of the day the French sought in vain to find a ford suitable for a crossing. Towards the evening General Lefebvre-Desnoëttes, who commanded the elite of Napoleon's cavalry, tried to force the bridge with dismounted men, but without success. The last of the German hussars then crossed it, and in the early hours of the 29th it was blown up.

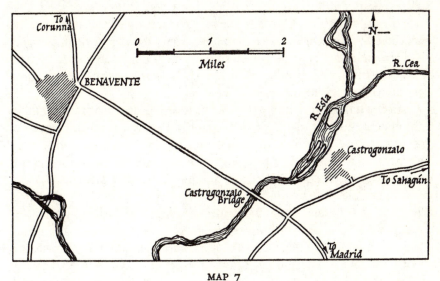

MAP 7

THE ACTION AT BENAVENTE, DECEMBER 29TH, 1808

At every likely crossing of the river (which was swollen by heavy rains into a torrent) Paget posted pickets to watch for attempts to ford it. The main body of Moore's army had by now reached Astorga, and only the rearguard and the cavalry were left at Benavente. That his splendid cavalry should be held up on the Esla infuriated the Emperor, and he ordered them to cross it instantly. Lefebvre-Desnoëttes at last found a passable ford, which enabled him to get across with over five hundred men. 'About nine o'clock', wrote Paget in his official statement of the action, 'I received a report that the enemy's cavalry was in the act of crossing the river at the ford near the bridge. I immediately sent down the picquets of the night under Lieutenant-Colonel Otway, of the 18th, having left orders that the cavalry should repair to their alarm posts.'[24]

But the outlying pickets could not assemble in time, and the leading *chasseurs* of the Imperial Guard succeeded in pushing Otway back to within a short distance of Benavente. He soon rallied, but as more of the enemy came ashore, he was again being forced back, when a timely reinforcement of the German hussars enabled him to check his attackers until further help could arrive.

At this point up galloped Paget, 'twirling his moustachios',[u] as an onlooker put it, and said, 'You see, there are not many of them. I wish to draw them on till the 10th are ready, but I don't know what they may have on the other side. Our lads, the picquets, are up to a charge.'[25] With him came Stewart who at once took over from Otway and again charged the French, but without decisive results. While the confused mass of men and horses struggled together, further French horsemen came up, pushing Stewart right back to the walls of Benavente.

Paget, who had instantly galloped off to bring up the 10th from their cantonments around the town, arrived with them at the crucial moment: just as Lefebvre was about to launch another attack with superior forces against Stewart. Instead of bringing them out into the open to support their hard-pressed comrades, Paget skilfully concealed them from view so as to be able to attack the left flank of the enemy's charge; at the same time he directed Stewart to retire before the onrush, in order to gain more favourable ground on which to receive it. As the French general came on at speed to within a hundred yards of Stewart's line, he was horrified to see the 10th with the forbidding figure of Paget himself at its head, bearing down upon him from the left, the 18th in support. His nerve broke, and just as Paget was on the point of crashing into him, he wheeled about and made a dash for the river. Accompanied by delighted shouts of 'Vivan los Ingleses' from the watching populace and by the cheers of the infantry spectators in the town, a tremendous race now developed over the three or four miles which divided Benavente from the river. For a time the mass of the enemy preserved some sort of order, though the laggards were mercilessly cut down, or forced to give themselves up. Yet as they reached the river bank, the same men who the year before had routed 30,000 Russians in Poland gave way to terror. Some plunged, one on top of the other, into the swollen river: others, whose mounts refused the water or were wounded, became prisoners. One of these was Lefebvre-Desnoëttes himself, who quite properly was among the last to reach the river bank. As the French swam across the river, the British cavalry fired at them with their carbines. Before long some of the enemy were able to form up on the opposite bank and return the fire, but three guns of the horse artillery, which at this moment arrived on the scene, dispersed them with a few rounds of grape-shot. The French cavalry did not again attempt to cross the river that day, and Moore gained further vital hours for his retreat to the sea.[v]

* * *

As the army left the plains and entered the mountains of Galicia, Edward Paget's famous reserve division replaced his brother's cavalry, and bore the brunt of the rearguard action for the rest of the retreat.

The men of Edward Paget's own regiment were 'highly diverted' one morning, at the height of their gruelling march, when some cavalry came up to them reporting the approach of the enemy in force. They were forming outside the village in which they had stayed the night when up came a dragoon, who was hailed by an officer lying in one of the carts much fatigued and probably ill, with a faint 'Dragoon, what news?'

'News, sir!' he was answered. 'The only news I have for you is that unless you step out like soldiers and don't wait to pick your steps like bucks in Bond Street of a Sunday, with shoes and silk stockings, damn it! you'll be all taken prisoners.'

'Pray, who the devil are you?'

'I am Lord Paget,' came the reply. 'And pray, sir, who are you?'

'I am Captain Donavan of the 28th Regiment, my lord.'

'Come out of that cart directly. March with your men, sir, and keep up spirits by showing them a good example.'[26]

Not long afterwards Paget and Stewart were both put out of action by one of the diseases which became prevalent among the troops. They were lucky, where officers and men were daily falling by the wayside from exhaustion and exposure from which many failed to recover, to escape with nothing worse than ophthalmia.[w] Paget, who for some days was practically blinded by it, was given leave to make his way to Corunna ahead of the army. One who saw him pass said that he looked 'very interesting; he had a white handkerchief bound over his eyes', while the officer who led his horse, clothed in a blanket in which he had cut a hole for his head, looked just like a Pyrenean shepherd.[27] Throughout his career Paget suffered on occasion from the disease. A quarter of a century later he was writing from Naples 'in a dark room almost blind with ophthalmia',[28] and it is very likely that the agonies of tic douloureux (facial neuralgia) from which he was to suffer for the last thirty-five years of his life were a direct result of this first attack upon his eyes.

Paget had not been long in Corunna before he was informed of Brigadier Slade's arrival in the town. Apparently he too had obtained leave to proceed ahead of the army, on the plea of indisposition. He had established himself in comfortable quarters, taken a dose of calomel and retired to bed, when Paget sent him a peremptory order to return to his brigade without a moment's delay; 'and forced him to set out at night, in a soaking rain regardless of his pathetic remonstrances and intestinal commotions!'[29]

On January 11th, 1809, the main army at last came in sight of the sea. Within the next few days the fleet of transports which was to carry the wretched army home arrived from Vigo. The cavalry were the first to embark, but as there was no room for all the horses in the ships, large numbers of them had to be destroyed on the beach, to prevent their falling into the hands of the enemy, thereby fulfilling Paget's gloomy prophecy of six weeks before.

He was not a witness of the battle of Corunna on the 16th, for he was already at sea in H.M.S. *Cossack* when he heard the heavy firing from the heights behind the town. The news of its success was brought out to him by boat: at the same time he learned that his gallant chief had fallen 'like Nelson in the hour of victory'.

CHAPTER SIX[1]

In 1809 there was an event which caused great scandal at the time, and affecting as it did the relations between the greatest military commander and the greatest cavalry leader of the day, had its effect upon history.

A. F. Fremantle, England in the Nineteenth Century[2]

P AGET, who landed in England on January 20th, 1809, came home to face a personal problem which had remained unresolved for at least a year. The cause of the trouble was simple enough. During the early months of 1808 the usual series of musical parties had been held at Uxbridge House, and among those who often attended them were the three step-sisters of Earl Cadogan, members of a family which had been close friends of the Pagets for many years. With the second of these young married ladies, Paget, who attended his father's parties whenever he could, fell desperately in love. Nor, though she too was married and had children, did Lady Charlotte Wellesley spurn his advances.

Opportunities for the indulgence of their passion constantly presented themselves. During the spring of 1808 Lady Charlotte (known universally as 'Char') was recommended a course of riding for her health, and it so happened that her husband, Henry Wellesley[a] (who was Sir Arthur Wellesley's youngest brother), was able neither to provide her with a suitable horse nor (since a Secretary to the Treasury must put in a few hours' work each day) to accompany her on her rides. Paget, on the other hand, could and did provide both steed and escort.

'At length,' stated Sir Arthur Wellesley in a memorandum written later on his brother's behalf, 'Lady Charlotte being considerably advanced in her pregnancy[b] the riding parties ceased; & about this time Mr Wellesley had perceived the extraordinary attention paid to Lady Charlotte by Lord Paget, & had in consequence remonstrated with her upon the subject. Towards the close of the Session of Parliament of 1808 [in July] Mr Wellesley removed to Putney Heath [from Berkeley Square] & from that time till the return of Lady Charlotte to London in the Month of February 1809, Mr Wellesley had every reason to believe that no meeting took place between Lady Charlotte & Lord Paget.'

In fact, as she later admitted, she was not only in the habit of meeting him frequently (particularly between Paget's arrival in England after the Convention of Cintra and his return to Spain in early November) but also maintained a constant correspondence with him.

As early as January 1808 Charles Paget had found his sister-in-law, 'poor dear excellent Car [Lady Paget], with as much or more reason to complain than ever'. He told his brother Arthur that Paget's conduct towards her and her consequent misery at that time had induced her 'as near as possible to take that most decisive step which you so wisely made her promise never to take without a previous communication with yourself. *This* you fortunately told me, which enabled me to remind her of her promise, & for God's sake for the present to postpone undertaking anything of the kind.' Charles besought her if she should be driven to so extreme a course, '*not* to fly for protection to any of her own family, but to ours.... Of course,' he went on, 'whoever received the poor dear soul would incur the direful wrath of Paget, but in such a cause, much as I esteem being on the best possible footing with him, I should glory in sacrificing it if it depended on doing what would be but justice to so amiable & wretched a creature as she is. I am persuaded that there is one, but one single thread that binds her, & that is the misery she would incur at separating from her children.' In this unhappy state Car continued throughout the year. While Paget was fighting in Spain that winter, she wrote to thank Arthur Paget for offering to mediate between her husband and herself. 'It is *now useless*,' she asserted. 'I feel however as anxious about him as if he loved me, and as you may suppose am in a constant fright.' In another letter to Arthur written on January 18th, 1809, she declared herself very happy that her husband had

'distinguished himself as he wished to do & that he is safe and well, but if I was to tell you that I feel on this occasion as I sh'd have done *even* this time last year I should *deceive* you — it is not possible, I can't look forward to any happiness with him again, every letter that I receive convinces me of the truth of what I say. You remark his letter was like a newspaper, they are *all* too much so, to please me

— the *only* difference in any that I have had — is *dear Car* at the beginning & end. Now as I am *quite* sure that *very* different letters are sent by the same Post it makes me *now* feel as I ought to have done long ago.'

Char, the recipient of these 'very different' letters, now recovered from the birth of her baby, removed to a house in Curzon Street from Putney Heath in the second week of February. She told her husband that since so many unpleasant things had been said of her and Paget last year she was resolved 'not to go out this year'. Wellesley then asked her what her feelings were for Paget, and his for her. 'I regard him', she replied, 'as a common acquaintance & I believe he liked my society last year but I have no reason to believe that he thinks of me in any way that can be objectionable.' Wellesley then told her not to deprive herself of any London amusements which might give her pleasure, to continue to treat Paget as a common acquaintance, but to avoid particularly the riding-parties. He added that his confidence in her was unbounded.

But Paget's triumphant return from Spain proved too strong a temptation: the lovers almost at once took up where they had left off five months before. The riding-parties indeed were not resumed: tête-à-tête walks in Green Park took their place. On three or four occasions young Tom Miller, the Wellesleys' footman, whose job it was to follow his mistress at a respectful distance while she took the air, was, to his infinite surprise, told to leave her and not to return for an hour or two, a thing which he had 'never known her to do before'. Paget would then take over the escort till he observed the return of the bewildered footman.

By March 3rd matters had come to a head. On that date Paget told Charles 'that his only hope in an *éclat* not taking place rested on no less than the death of Henry Wellesley', who had retired to bed with a serious liver complaint. From this letter it is clear that Paget and Char had already made up their minds to elope. Paget had gone so far as to speak to Car most distinctly upon the subject of *her* future. He seemed, as Charles told Arthur,

'to feel no doubt not only of a present attachment between her and Lorne [the Duke of Argyll, who was still known familiarly by the courtesy title of Marquess of Lorne which he had held until his succession to the Dukedom in 1806] but of a future either legal or illegal connection. The first he supposes in the event of his deserting Car and her gaining a Divorce and her subsequently becoming

Duchess of Argyll, or secondly in his going on with the intercourse which now subsists between himself and Lady Charlotte Wellesley (without a blow up^d) which would, as he says, justify her in the illegal process. This is the way, my dear fellow, he talks, and it is quite marvellous that on subjects so enormously dreadful he should be able to be so cool and deliberate. To Car I spoke this morning. I told her that which Paget had, it appeared, already mentioned to her. She took all I said in good part and solemnly vowed there was nothing to create the slightest fear in our minds as to any understanding between herself and Lorne. She owned the greatest friendship and regard for him (two dangerous feelings to cherish) but no more — and that it was cruel in the greatest degree that being entirely deserted by her husband she might not receive common civilities from a friend without being liable to such insinuations.'

Charles explained to her that he did not mean to question her conduct but only to put her on her guard upon 'a subject that had not only been mentioned by Paget but had already begun to gain some observation in the world'.[e] These two letters provide conclusive evidence that Car's name was already linked with the Duke of Argyll's even before Paget ran away with Charlotte, and are of importance when considering Paget's behaviour, since Car, as will be seen, married the Duke immediately after her divorce the following year.

In passing, it is worth noting that Argyll and Paget, who were almost exact contemporaries, had been close friends ever since they shared a house in Vienna when both were engaged upon their Grand Tours in 1787. At that time Paget described Argyll as 'the best creature in the world'.[s]

ii

Oh! That that nefarious damned Hellhound should have so entrapped that before noble fine creature.

Charles Paget to Arthur Paget, March 9th, 1800

Divest yourself of prejudice and enquire about her, and you will find that she is one of the most amiable and agreeable women in Society — devoid of all affectation, uncommonly modest, perfectly virtuous, exemplary in her conduct towards her family, truly but not ostentatiously religious, uncommonly beloved by all who know her well. Of high rank and married into a family of high rank. An attachment is unfortunately formed between us. It is fought against for a long time. Alas, not long enough — passion gets the better of reason and finally we are driven to the necessity of the present step.

Paget to Charles Paget, n.d. [*March-April*], 1809

During the first days of his illness, Henry Wellesley noticed that although his wife was 'not deficient in attention to him, there was not that appearance of affectionate kindness which he had observed upon former similar occasions'. This made him so uneasy that on the night of Sunday, March 5th, he got up from his sick-bed and went to his wife's room while she was dressing for dinner. He found the door locked, and while waiting for her to open it, heard the rustling of papers. This suspicious noise and the state of confusion in which he found her when she opened the door 'induced him to tell her that he was convinced she was carrying on an improper correspondence with Lord Paget', a charge which she then tried to evade. Later that evening he pursued his accusations and made use of strong language, which gave Charlotte the opportunity of leaving the room on the grounds that her husband was too angry to be reasoned with; but not before he had shouted in his fury that she or he must quit the house the following day 'for that he knew everything'. This declaration gave Charlotte just that small justification for which she had been waiting. At about noon next day she went as if to take her daily stroll in the Park, but almost at once dismissed the footman (an order to which he was becoming quite accustomed) and hailed a hackney-coach. But before she had done either, Charles Arbuthnot, a close friend of her husband's, passed her in Half Moon Street. When he crossed the street to greet her, she forestalled him by saying, 'Pray don't speak to me', and when he persevered, hurried on her way. Arbuthnot, much alarmed by such strange behaviour, went straight to Curzon Street, where he found Wellesley highly agitated, saying that he had sent after Charlotte to

Green Park, and that after the row which they had had the previous evening he feared that she had destroyed herself. Arbuthnot then set out on a search which yielded no results whatever. During the evening he received a letter in which Charlotte confessed to having left her husband.

Wellesley and Arbuthnot, in conclave that night, made it their first object to find out where she had gone to. They were aided by the fact that some new clothes directed to Charlotte were delivered at the house earlier in the evening. These she had ordered four days before from Mrs Ware's linen shop, saying that she wanted some 'linen for day as well as night for a friend in the country', and giving 'particular orders that the articles were to be *kept by Mrs Ware till they were called for*'. These instructions had been misunderstood, so that when at nine o'clock a servant (probably one of Paget's) called at the shop for the clothing, he discovered that it had already been delivered at Wellesley's house. Mrs Ware immediately sent an assistant there to retrieve it, which gave Wellesley the looked-for chance of communicating with his wife. This he did by following the shop assistant back to Mrs Ware's. Of that lady he then inquired who had ordered the things and what they were. He was no sooner answered than another person, sent by Charlotte to collect the parcels, entered the shop. To this messenger Wellesley entrusted a letter for his wife, in which he offered to take her back.

That same evening Arthur Paget received the following note:

'My dear Arthur,

'At the very instant that your letter arrived, I received a message from a person in a Hackney Coach in Park Lane to come immediately.

'An *Eclat* took place last night and Lady Charlotte Wellesley, dreading a further discussion this morning, that event which we have long dreaded, has actually taken place. I pity you all. Pity us in return — we are in want of it.

'Adieu —

'PAGET'

On receiving the summons to come to her immediately, Paget, after changing into his shabbiest clothes so as to avoid recognition, joined Charlotte in the hackney-coach and ordered the coachman to drive to an address in Mount Street. Arrived there, he rushed upstairs to the first-floor apartments of his old friend and aide-de-camp, Baron Tuyll,[1] who was sitting, all unsuspecting, at his midday meal. In the greatest haste, and

to the astonishment of the Baron, Paget announced that there was a lady
in the coach, and begged that she might use his lodgings for a few hours.
Taken thus by storm, Tuyll had no alternative but to accede to his
general's request. Charlotte was then brought in, while Tuyll went out,
tactfully avoiding an encounter with her. When later in the day he
returned, Paget disclosed to him her identity and asked whether they
might have the use of the lodgings for some days to come. To this Tuyll
agreed, taking himself off to a near-by hotel. So as to deceive his landlord,
he told him that the strangers were friends of his from the country, under
pecuniary embarrassments, and this seemed to satisfy him.

At seven in the morning of the next day Char replied to Wellesley's
offer of the previous evening, by the following letter to Arbuthnot:

'It would be the Height of Ingratitude,' she wrote, 'were I not to try
to convey my thanks to Henry for his most kind and generous offer
of taking home a Wretch who has so injured him. I dare not write to
himself but I implore it of you to say everything which Gratitude
and Feeling can suggest to express my Sense of the Kindness of his
Conduct. His note was forwarded to me this Morning — but
degraded and unprincipled as I must appear in the eyes of everybody,
believe me I am not lost to all Sense of Honor which would forbid
my returning to a husband I have quitted, to children I have abandoned. Indeed, indeed, my Dear Mr Arbuthnot, if you knew all you
would pity more than blame me. Could you tell all the resistance
that has been made to this most criminal most atrocious attachment,
could you know what are my Sufferings at this Moment you would
feel for me. Henry has not deserved this of me. We have had some
differences and he may perhaps have sometimes been a *little* too hard
to me, but I can with truth assert & I wish you to publish it to the
World that in essentials and indeed in trifling subjects, he has ever
been *kind to me to the greatest Degree*. Nor has the Person (who
may be supposed to have attempted to lower him in my estimation in
order to gain my affections) ever spoken of him to me but in the
Highest Terms of Respect. About my dear dear children I must say
one word. Do you think I dare hope ever by any remote or indirect
means to hear sometimes of them? You know how much I love
them, you are aware of their merits and what I must feel at having
quitted them but I have the satisfaction, the inexpressible comfort
of knowing they will be taken care of by their Father though their

Mother has abandoned them. My dear little Henry and Charlotte, God bless you.'

To this in the afternoon, she added a postscript:

'Since writing the enclosed I am come to Town — if it is not repugnant to your feelings I think I should like to have one interview with you but not if you object to it in any way. The bearer can bring you to me instantly if you will see me, but if not ask no questions.'

The bearer was none other than Baron Tuyll, who had with him Admiral Bentinck, a friend of both Paget's and Charlotte's. Arbuthnot did not hesitate. He at once accompanied these gentlemen back to Mount Street, where he had an interview with Charlotte alone, during which she 'declared distinctly that she could never think of returning home after the Iniquitous Act she had been guilty of with Lord Paget'. He then saw Paget and Charlotte together and remained with them some time.

Wellesley now made one final effort, and himself wrote to Char on March 8th, saying that 'for the sake of her welfare, and that of her children, he would consent to receive her again, provided she would return and break off all correspondence or connection with the person she was then with; but that she must return instantly, for the next day would be too late.' This letter he charged Arbuthnot to deliver to Charlotte in person, but she would not see him, writing him instead a further note in the same sense as her earlier one.

Tuyll found himself during this eventful week the bearer of a number of letters between the occupants of his rooms and their families. Some of these have survived, most of them not: an important one which no longer exists was Paget's confession of guilt addressed to his father, in which he is reputed to have told him of his vain desire when in Spain to escape from his guilty passion by death in the field.

Two days after the elopement Lord Uxbridge addressed a pathetic appeal to Char, of which a copy is extant:

'Dear Madam,

    'Let me on my knees implore you to listen to the prayer of an aged & perhaps dying Father, and to restore my Son to his distracted Family, which for ever will render me your Grateful & Faithful Servant,

                                                'UXBRIDGE'

'Uxbridge House, March 8th, 1809.'

Lord Paget as Colonel of the 7th Light Dragoons (Hussars) aged 39-40

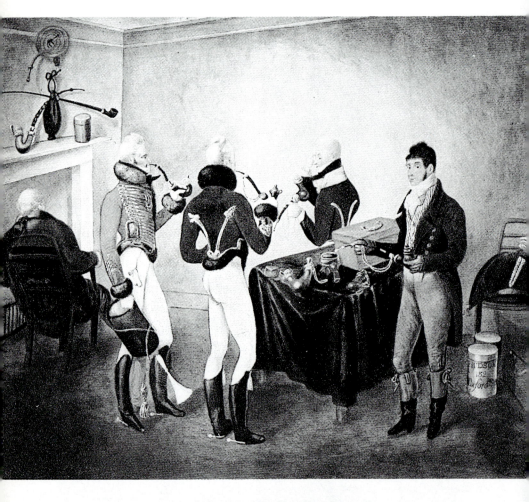

A Scene at Ipswich Barracks

Lord Paget (second from left) with his father (first left), his brother Berkeley (fourth from left), and the Duke of Cumberland, trying out a variety of pipes bought from his Oxford Street shop to the Cavalry Barracks at Ipswich by the tobacconist, Joseph Hudson

The original was lately in the possession of the late Sir Chartres Biron, a descendant of Joseph Hudson, who for many years used it as an advertisement for a special type of pipe tobacco, known as 'the Paget tobacco'. This could still be obtained under that name as late as 1900

On a number of occasions during these hectic days Paget's relations came to plead with him to return to his wife and to abandon Char. On March 9th Charles wrote to Arthur, who was not at the time in London: 'Not a bit better My dearest fellow are things in this Town. I have been with Paget till this instant (just six) & he only repeated the same set of conversations we have before had with him. In short all is over, & I apprehend they will leave town as soon as they have determined *where* to go to.' Lord Graves, Paget's brother-in-law, wrote next day: 'As for poor Paget I am afraid his case is desperate — he is still in Town with that *maudite sorcière*. Baron Tuyll gave some hope this morning so that we began to think better, but I have heard nothing more, which confirms my fears. The people in the streets talk of it — even the mob — & I am afraid every one sees Paget's conduct in the most unfavourable light.'

Old Lord Uxbridge in the meantime had become so enraged at what he considered the folly of his son and heir that he threatened to cut him off without a farthing, and it was only with the greatest difficulty that he could be prevented from forcing his way into the lovers' presence.

Naturally enough, the effect of her husband's desertion left poor Car in a state of great misery. Lady Uxbridge and her sons and daughters did all they could to comfort her. Four days after the elopement Charles went round to see her at Paget's house in Brook Street. He was told that Mr Singleton, a legal friend of Paget's, was with her in the drawing-room.

'This however', wrote Charles, 'did not prevent my desiring to see her and she immediately came out of the room to me and we entered into her little bedroom where she then shewed me a scrap of paper in Paget's hand in these words, or to this effect "Admit the bearer Singleton and you'll not repent it". It then appeared that *he* had been (instead of one of us) deputed by Paget to go to her to offer on Paget's part a meeting with her that evening in Grosvenor Square. Car was violently indignant at this and at the secrecy which he, Singleton, wished her to observe as to the transaction. The first she positively declined. The second she said she should not observe as *we* were much fitter to be trusted with secrets between Paget and herself than he was. Thus I believe she dismissed this wretch who I hear left the house in a rage. Car then wrote a most perfect letter to Paget amongst other things saying that tho' the sight of him for the last time would kill her, still that she could not forego the gratification of once more beholding him. She pressed his giving her the meeting in

D

his own house, to which she promised, if he desired it, that no other
creature than herself should be privy, but that as to meeting him in
the street, it was impossible, as her weak state of body and wretched
state of mind would not enable her to undertake it. This letter I took
to Paget. I marked him well whilst he read it. It evidently affected
him much. I observed this and tried to work more upon him by introducing how interesting I had just seen poor little Car [his eldest
daughter, Caroline, aged thirteen] looking and how unhappy all his
dear children appeared and how lonely and dismal his house looked
without him. This is the string which touches him to the quick....
It is evident from his own words that neither passion or affection
retain him in his present chains, for he positively told me that
excessive guilt and shame precluded his emancipation more than anything else. I then with as much force as my abilities enabled me to
express myself said that surely guilt and shame would increase upon
him in proportion as he continued in it and that he might at that
moment return to his family and live with us all at least, if he could
not bear to see the world. I also said that it was *quite* impossible
that he could be long connected with Lady Charlotte Wellesley and
I asked him *how long* he thought he could answer for himself. He
answered, *forever*, for tho' he might *loathe* her person — still upon
principle he must ever be her protector. As I found him in the kindest
possible tone, I ventured to say that his acting on principle would not
long survive his fancy for her person and that it must ultimately end
by his return to his own family, which he tried to convince me was
impossible, for his shame would ever render it out of the question
shewing his face again even amongst us.

'Before I left him I pressed his going to see Car in Brook Street
but he stopped me short by saying that he could not collect firmness
sufficient even in the dark to enter his own doors and that if, by any
possible accident any one of his children, should appear, the inevitable consequence would be that his tortured mind would be so
distracted between them and the object (pointing to the next room)
that he should return to his lodgings and put an end to that existence
which, as he said, would to God had been put an end to on one of
the many occasions I could [*sic*] when in Spain. I then said "Paget if
you can't go to the house, and as she positively is unable to undertake
meeting you as you have proposed in the circle of Grosvenor
Square, I shall propose your giving her the meeting in a Hackney

coach," to which he assented and I was appointed to arrange this
with her accordingly at half past ten. Poor Car and I walked out of
her house to the bottom of Upper Brook Street where I had a
Hackney waiting. I had scarcely opened the door of it and handed
her in when Paget came up, touched me on the shoulder and said,
"Ah, is that you Jack?", whereupon he jumped into the coach and
after drawing up the windows on both sides they continued together
forty minutes during which time I continued within hail. At about
the expiration of that period I saw the door of the coach thrown
open. Out Paget jumped and *ran off*. I immediately went up to the
carriage and finding poor Car overwhelmed with violent grief and
bathed in tears I got into the coach till they had sufficiently subsided
to allow her to walk home — where poor thing I conveyed her, and
after seeing her somewhat composed I left her. My God, how
dreadful, and all this unbounded misery and disgrace and for the
most wicked and profligate whore and liar that ever hell itself could
or ever will produce.'

The newspapers meanwhile had loaded their pages with fact and
rumour: indeed the celebrated scandal of the Duke of York and Mrs
Clarke for a while took second place in the popular press. It was confidently stated that Henry Wellesley and Paget had fought a duel and that
Paget 'had atoned, with his life, the injury offered to a husband's honour'.
Another paper asserted with equal untruth that Sir Arthur Wellesley had
pursued the fugitives, overtaken them on the Oxford Road, and inflicted
a dangerous abdominal wound upon the ravisher of his ailing brother's wife.
   On March 11th Paget and Char escaped from Mount Street before the
public curiosity had discovered their hiding-place, and so great was the
secrecy that to this day it is impossible to discover where they went.[g]
   At this point Char's family decided to take strong measures. Baron
Tuyll was given a letter for her signed jointly by her brothers, requiring
that she should at once give Paget up, and in the event of her refusing
to do so, threatening that one of them should call him out. Tuyll undertook to deliver the letter, so long as he was not followed, since he had
promised on his honour not to divulge Paget's whereabouts. According
to Lord Enniskillen (Paget's brother-in-law), Charlotte's brothers were
'most violent. They *will* have her or the most fatal consequences may be
the result. The elder brother offers her his entire protection. I trust the
fear of losing her last resources and the dread of Paget's life (as the

lewdness is now pretty well over it is supposed) may work upon her —
It is our last shift & if this does not do, Paget must be lost for ever.'

On the night of March 14th, a week and a day after the elopement, the
Duke of Sussex sent for Paget's brother-in-law, Lord Graves (who
years later became Comptroller of the Duke's Household), to say that
Char's brother, Henry Cadogan, had 'just arriv'd, attended by a friend,
Exprès to call out Paget. His [the Duke's] surgeon had just told the
Duke so, for the second had been at the Surgeon's to put him in requisi-
tion saying — "you will be ready to attend me at any time in the course
of the day — or when I send for you." ' Charles thought that 'fellows that
mean really to fight do not take these sort of precautions *days* before the
conflict', and added that he himself ought to be the last to interfere on
such an occasion, as he thought that if the threatened duel took place, 'it
might by some miracle dissolve the cursed connection as it now exists'.
However, 'that d——d meddling Duke threatened to give the information at Bow Street for the apprehension of the Parties'. Graves besought
His Royal Highness to do no such thing, as he thought an interference in
a matter so delicate to both parties highly improper and indecorous.
Next day nothing further transpired, Graves telling Arthur that 'both
Mr H. Wellesley and Cadogan vote that stinking Pole Cat not worth the
shedding blood. Damn her! How Paget's stomach will heave in the course
of six months, when she seizes him in her hot libidinous arms.'

Cadogan now made a most liberal and handsome offer: if Char would
give up Paget he would 'sell out of the Army in order entirely to devote
himself to her protection. She however is inexorable', wrote Charles, '&
will not even consent to seeing her Brother. Paget at the same time says
that he will not attend to any Challenges from anybody, but that if
Henry Wellesley or the Cadogans feel themselves aggrieved they may
come to his lodgings & shoot him.'

Car, so that she might get away from it all, removed early in the week
to a cottage outside London belonging to Lord Kinnaird. There she
stayed some days while Stoke, a house of Lord Sefton's which he had
kindly offered as a refuge, was made ready for her and the children. She
was very wretched, of course, but at least she did not lack sympathizers.

On Thursday, March 16th, two interviews took place. Cadogan saw
his sister for three hours, and Dr Dodeswell, a friend of Paget's, had a
long talk with his client. The result, as triumphantly announced by
Charles, was 'that *the* wretched subject [took] a favourable turn, inasmuch
as that the parties have agreed to a *month's separation* from each other *to*

reflect & if possible to vanquish their passions for each other.' 'Now', wrote Enniskillen, 'every Engine should be at work to put a final stop to it, for how long this separation will be I know not. I wish I could get some huge Paddy to satisfy her lust and outdo Paget.' On the night of the 11th the lovers parted. Char for the time being stayed under Dr Dodeswell's roof. 'As for Ld. P.', wrote Tuyll, 'I cannot say where he is, but am inclined to think that he went into Norfolk with Singleton.' Charles saw Paget on Monday night 'for a full hour and so far from his expressing anything like a probability of ultimate good coming from this measure [the separation], he repeatedly asserted the impossibility of it, and (to use his own words) it would be as much out of the question for them to control or vanquish their passions & affections for each other as it would be for him to attempt at the head of the 7th to overpower the united forces of Buonaparte; that one of two things *therefore* must take place after the month's separation, both or either of which they were prepared to adopt, the one being allowed to retire together & seclude themselves for ever from the sight of man; the only other alternative: *self-destruction*.' On Tuesday night Charles delivered to Paget a note from Car which gave an account of the children. 'His agitation & affliction were excessive on reading it, insomuch that he literally burst out into tears & threw himself upon me for support, exclaiming that his heart was broken — & he wondered how his intellect had been retained so long.'

The experiment of temporary separation lasted a very short time. On March 23rd Charles reported that Char had sent Paget a summons which he felt called upon to attend to with alacrity. 'They are now actually together again, but their plans are not settled whether to continue in or leave town. If they do the latter we have still to see what the Cadogans are made of.' Henry Cadogan proved what he was made of by writing Paget the following letter:

'*Cook's Hotel, Dover Street,*
March 28, 1809

'My Lord,
    'I hereby request you to name a time and place where I may meet you, to obtain satisfaction for the injury done myself and my whole family by your conduct to my sister.

    'I have to add that the time must be as early as possible, and the place not in the immediate neighbourhood of London, as it is by concealment alone that I am able to evade the Police.

'H. CADOGAN'

Paget's reply, dated two days later, acknowledged receipt of the letter, and added,

'I have nothing to say in justification of my conduct towards your sister, but that it has been produced by an attachment perfectly unconquerable. She has lost the world upon my account, and the only atonement I can make is to devote myself, not to her happiness (which with her feeling mind is, under the circumstances, impossible) but to endeavour, by every means in my power to alleviate her suffering. I feel, therefore, that my life is hers, not my own. It distresses me beyond description to refuse you that satisfaction which I am most ready to admit you have the right to demand: but upon the most mature reflection, I have determined upon the propriety of this line of conduct.

'My cause is bad indeed: but my motive for acting thus is good: nor was I without hopes that you would have made allowances for this my very particular situation, and thereby have largely added to the extreme kindness you have already shewn to your sister upon this afflicting occasion. I have the honour to be Sir

'Your obedient servant

'PAGET'

'P.S. On referring to the date of your letter it becomes necessary to assure you that I have only this moment received it.'

Cadogan communicated his own letter and Paget's answer to his intended second, requesting that gentleman, a Mr Sloane, 'in order that what has passed may not be misrepresented' to show the correspondence to any of his friends that might wish to read it. 'It is not unknown to you', he continued, 'that I have by concealment alone been able for some time to evade the Police, who having anticipated the step I was likely to take, are continuing in pursuit of me. Under these circumstances it would ill become me to apply to the conduct of Lord Paget the expressions that my feelings at this moment dictate: and I shall therefore leave it to you and others to determine whether the line he has thought proper to adopt on this occasion is or is not the most honourable.'[h]

The exact movements of Char and Paget at this stage are obscure. It seems that they retired for a time into Devonshire, where eventually Paget received a further challenge from Cadogan. They were back in Mount Street by May 6th, for on that day Henry Wellesley's legal representatives called there so as 'to see them together'. This was a necessary part of the evidence in the action for 'criminal conversation' which Wellesley had instituted against Paget, as a preliminary to divorce proceedings. This action came before a jury in the Sheriff's Court on May 12th, and Paget suffered judgment by default, thereby acknowledging his adulterous intercourse. The damages were assessed at the enormous sum of £20,000, with costs. The evidence in the subsequent divorce proceedings was heard in the Consistory Court of the Bishop of London in early June, and the final decree granted on July 7th. So as to make certain that no spurious issue who might succeed to his property could be imposed on him, Wellesley later introduced in the Lords a private Bill to dissolve the marriage and enable him to marry again. This did not become law until February 22nd, 1810.

Nine months before that event, Paget had been persuaded by his brothers to agree to an arrangement whereby he became, at any rate in the eyes of the world, reconciled to Car, while Char as a temporary measure was made an allowance by him and provided with a house. It seems that Car agreed to Paget's terms, namely that he 'should return home without any stipulations whatever', but the whole transaction is so veiled in mystery, that it is impossible to be sure of anything except that on May 17th Paget returned to his wife and children in Brook Street, and the next day set off with them for Beaudesert. There they stayed for about a week before returning to London.[1]

* * *

While he was still in Devonshire Paget received a further challenge from Cadogan, which this time he accepted.[1]

At seven o'clock in the morning of May 30th, 1809, the two parties assembled on Wimbledon Common. Cadogan's second was a naval captain named M'Kenzie, and Paget's was his friend Hussey Vivian, who had succeeded him as Colonel of the 7th. The weapons agreed upon were pistols, and when the ground had been measured out so that there were twelve paces between the contestants, the seconds directed their principals to fire simultaneously. The statement put out the following day and signed by the two seconds describes what happened then:

'Captain Cadogan fired, Lord Paget's pistol flashed — this having been decided to go for a fire, a question arose whether Lord Paget had taken aim as intending to hit his antagonist. Both the seconds being clearly of opinion that such was not his intention (although the degree of obliquity he gave the direction of the pistol was such as to have been discovered only by particular observation), Captain M'Kenzie stated to Capt. Cadogan that as it appeared to be Lord Paget's intention not to fire at him, he could not admit of the affair proceeding any further. Lt. Col. Vivian then asked Capt. Cadogan whether he had not observed himself that Lord Paget had not aimed at him? To which he replied in the affirmative. Capt. M'Kenzie then declared his determination not to remain any longer in the field, to witness any further act of hostility on the part of Capt. Cadogan. Capt. C. replied, of course his conduct must be decided by his second; declaring at the same time that he had come prepared for the fall of one of the parties. On Capt. M'Kenzie and Lt. Col. Vivian making it known to Lord Paget that as he evidently did not intend to fire at Capt. Cadogan, the affair could go no further, Lord P. replied: "As such is your determination, I have no hesitation in saying that nothing could ever have induced me to add to the injuries I have already done to the family by firing at the brother of Lady Charlotte Wellesley". The parties then left the ground.'

Paget's conduct, as one distinguished historian puts it, was unlike that of 'the typical military libertine of a generation earlier', and the actions of all the persons concerned in the affair were representative of the 'growing regard for the decencies of life' which could be noticed at that date. 'Both the wronger and the wronged man belonged to prominent Tory families, and there can scarcely be a doubt that a few years earlier such an occasion for coarse merriment would have been welcomed by the Whig Press. But the comments of the Morning Chronicle were irreproachable.'[1]

iii

The Earl of Chatham with his sword drawn
Stood waiting for Sir Richard Strachan,
Sir Richard longing to be at 'em
Stood waiting for the Earl of Chatham.

Anonymous jingle

'We are in anxious expectation of more news from the Continent, and conjecture is at work about our own expedition. Heaven knows where it is going. It takes away all the remaining society of London, and is an immense armament. Lord Paget goes with it, which is the best thing that could happen for him after all that has passed.'

Thus wrote Lady Elizabeth Foster (later to become Duchess of Devonshire) to her son,⁴ some six weeks after the duel on Wimbledon Common. Paget had been using all his influence to get abroad once more, even employing his mother to write to Queen Charlotte on his behalf. On July 2nd the Queen replied to her, 'the dear Kg bids me assure You that no application of Yours can ever be disagreeable to him; but that at this Present moment He can not Specify when Lrd Paget's wishes can be Satisfyed.'ˢ He got his way none the less and left London on the 18th, embarking next day at Portsmouth on Charles Paget's ship the Revenge. But up to the time of his landing in Europe, no command had been assigned to him.

The expedition had been preparing in England for a considerable time, but Ministers had not finally decided on its object or destination till the end of June, when they learnt that Napoleon had been defeated by the Austrians at Aspern-Essling. Not only did they wish to do something to encourage the Austrians, but for some time they had been worried by the need for preventive action against the activity of the Antwerp shipyards. Thus a combined military and naval armament, the largest ever to leave the shores of England, was to be directed across the North Sea, under the command of Lord Chatham, Pitt's brother, and Rear-Admiral Sir Richard Strachan. Its objects included the destruction of the enemy ships in the Scheldt, and the drawing away from the Austrian and Spanish fronts of as many of the enemy as possible.

On the evening of July 30th, seven infantry regiments and an artillery battery landed from small boats on the northernmost tip of the Island of Walcheren. After much importuning, Paget obtained command of this division. Little opposition was encountered, and soon most of the other troops were landed. The following day, Middleburg in the centre of the island surrendered, and the advance towards Flushing was continued. The army was now split into three main columns, Paget commanding the central one, which consisted of six or seven infantry battalions, and six guns. The first enemy pickets were met at Koudekerke, and a captain and fifty men made prisoners. Paget then sent his aide-de-camp, Captain Baron Trip, with a party of the 95th to communicate with General Graham's column, which was moving parallel on his right; Trip returned

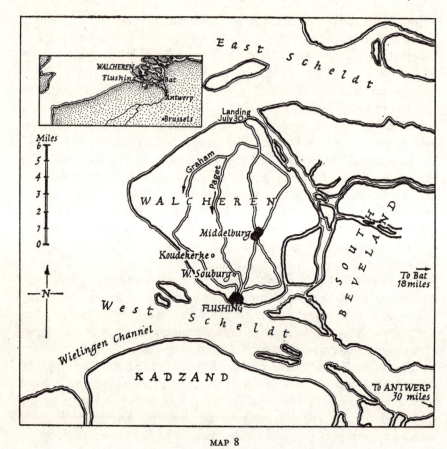

MAP 8

THE WALCHEREN CAMPAIGN OF 1809

with a further forty prisoners. But no serious opposition was encountered until the column had arrived at West Souburg, from where Paget reported,

'The enemy having brought forward a field piece which bore upon a material Picquet, Lt. Col. Johnson with parts of the 68th & 85th Regts. was detached by B. Genl. Rottenburg to attack him, and he succeeded in driving him into the Town of Flushing, close to the gates of which several Prisoners were made. In the course of the day our loss is four Officers wounded, & about 90 men killed and wounded; it has principally fallen upon the Brigade commanded by B. General Rottenburg which, as well as all those engaged, behaved with their accustomed gallantry. About 200 prisoners have been made, and the loss of the Enemy in killed and wounded is considerable.'⁶

On the following day the investment of Flushing was completed.

The French all this time had not been idle; ever since the invasion fleet had been sighted reinforcements had poured into the town; by now the batteries were fully manned, and Flushing was ready to resist a siege. Sir John Hope with eight thousand men had landed unopposed from the East Scheldt upon South Beveland, and by nightfall on the same day he had taken Bat at the extreme eastern tip of the island, within sight of Antwerp. But none of these operations was of much use without the capture of Kadzand, and the consequent domination of the Wielingen Channel and the West Scheldt, since it was only through these that ships could approach Antwerp. The French realized this immediately, for from the earliest moment they had exerted every nerve to reinforce Kadzand, but it proved beyond the dilatoriness of Chatham and Strachan to make the necessary effort to take it, and this was their big initial mistake. While the guns for the siege of Flushing were being brought across Walcheren, Strachan ought to have been forcing the Wielingen Channel with his ships so as to bombard the town from the sea, but all co-operation between the military and naval commanders had broken down, and it was not until the 13th that the bombardment of Flushing commenced. Five days later the Governor surrendered. At long last both the fleet and the army were in a position to join Hope at Bat, but too much time had been wasted, and the enemy was now in force to defend Antwerp.

The awful scourge which was almost to destroy the army had for many days been gathering force. While the troops on Walcheren were waiting for the siege of Flushing to begin, there had appeared the first signs of miasmatic fever. The dykes and drains which criss-crossed the island were the perfect breeding ground for mosquitoes, and the summer was an especially hot and wet one; to add to this, on Napoleon's personal orders, the sluices had been opened during the siege, letting the sea into the ditches, as well as into the trenches in which the troops were living. A week before Flushing surrendered, so many men were stricken that the dead had to be buried after dark without lights 'lest the survivors should see them and despair'.⁷ By August 20th the fever had spread to the troops on South Beveland.

With Antwerp now fully defended and men dying at an increasing rate each day, it became obvious that the expedition had failed most dismally. On the 27th the Quartermaster-General submitted to the lieutenant-generals a paper in which he estimated that there were now 26,000 of the enemy between Ossendricht and Antwerp, and in Antwerp itself, and a further 9,000 or so within a short distance. The effective British force had been reduced to 24,000 men. 'The matter, therefore,' he wrote, 'for consideration, is whether under all the circumstances ... it is advisable to undertake operations, so serious and extensive' as the reduction of Antwerp and the forts protecting it.

The lieutenant-generals, of whom there were six besides Paget, replied that they were of opinion that the siege of Antwerp was impracticable. They were then asked whether they thought any minor objects could be undertaken with advantage, to which they answered that since the siege of Antwerp could not be attempted, 'the success of which could alone accomplish the ultimate object of the Expedition', no possible advantage could result from embarking upon any minor operations.

Thus came to an ignominious end the fourth of the continental expeditions in which Paget had had a share. Walcheren was perhaps the most disastrous of them all, for the casualties from the fever came near to destroying a large part of the British Army, and almost nothing was achieved. It gave Paget no opportunity to distinguish himself, and no further experience with cavalry, but he was fortunate to escape the fever which killed so many of his comrades and permanently disabled most of those who survived it. As regards his chief object in joining the expedition, he had managed to be out of England for only two months.

iv

They write from Scotland (I suppose not seriously) that the Duke and
Duchess of Argyll have invited Lord and Lady Paget to pass the honeymoon all
together at Inverary.

Lord Auckland to Lord Grenville, December 11th, 1810

My Lady and I have just calculated that she has cost me £20,000 for the 1st
divorce, £10,000 for the 2nd, and £1,000 a year for Her Grace [Car] — and I
must admit I find her [Char] a good and cheap bargain notwithstanding.

Paget to Arthur Paget, 1811[g]

Paget returned from Walcheren in the first week of September. For the
next four months he lived ostensibly under the same roof as Car, spending
his time chiefly in Staffordshire and London.

Char, more surprisingly, according to Sir Arthur Wellesley, had been
taken under her husband's protection, two of his children being sent to
live with her. 'I don't', wrote Sir Arthur to his brother William, 'exactly
understand however how her brother [Henry Cadogan] who I suspect
has been the Instrument of bringing this about, can reconcile to his
feelings & notions of Honour, to allow his sister to live & *perform* with
a Man, from whom she has been divorced by the Church; & I conclude
that poor Henry will again be dragged through the Mire, & will marry
this blooming Virgin again as soon as she will have been delivered of
the consequences of her little amusement....' The 'consequences', in the
shape of a baby girl, arrived on March 4th, 1810;[k] but Sir Arthur was
wrong in his other prediction, for Henry Wellesley did not remarry
Char. From Badajoz in November 1809 Sir Arthur learned that the
divorce was 'still to go on in the House of Lords, notwithstanding the
Protection & of course the *Performance*. If the Protection meant no more
than to support her; & to treat her even handsomely & kindly, I think it
right and praiseworthy. But why send her the Children?'

For how long Henry extended his protection to Char is not known, but
it would have been surprising had he done so after the Divorce Act was
passed at the end of February, and it seems that Paget, in defiance of the
'reconciliation', was paying increased attention to her by the end of
December. It would be easy, and probably correct, to assume that the
'reconciliation' was in no way genuine, that Paget and Char had never
abandoned their intention of getting married once they were both free,

especially when it was known that she was pregnant by him, but there is no conclusive evidence on the point.

*   *   *

Early in April 1810, a month or so after Wellesley's Act had become law, Car called in the assistance of counsel and agents, with a view to obtaining her divorce from Paget. In those days, and for many years afterwards, though a husband could obtain a divorce on the ground of his wife's adultery, as Wellesley had done, it was not possible, by English law, for a wife to divorce her husband for the same reason. In Scotland, however, a wife had the same remedy as a husband, and it was immaterial that the initial adultery was committed outside Scotland, so long as the parties resided in that country for forty days. So as to comply with this condition, Paget and Char, some time in April 1810, took a house in Perthshire, he assuming the name of 'Mr Price'. In June they moved to an hotel in Edinburgh, where proofs of Paget's adultery were easily obtained by Car's agents. The proceedings were heard in October before the Commissaries of that city. Two obstacles stood in the way of a satisfactory outcome of the case. First, it was necessary for both parties to swear that there was no connivance. This was overcome only by obvious perjury, for by now the world knew that Car was more or less engaged to be married to the Duke of Argyll the moment she was free.[1] The second problem was that the law did not permit the divorced husband to marry the particular woman with whom he had been proved to have committed adultery. It was necessary, therefore, that Paget should have been detected in bed with someone *other* than Char, and (according to Lady Bessborough), she 'positively refus'd letting Ld Paget domiciliate with any other woman'. This further difficulty was met by the agent and the chambermaids being induced to depose that they had no idea of the identity of the female whom they saw in bed with Paget. This may well have been true, for it was said that Char '(like the Masque de fer of old) eat, drank and slept in a black veil'.

The decree was made absolute in October, and before the end of the year Paget had married Char, first in Scotland, and then, after finding some difficulty in persuading an English clergyman to perform the ceremony, in England. Car became Duchess of Argyll in November, declaring before the wedding ceremony that her good fortune was so great 'that till the business was absolutely over, she should not be able to believe it'. Her mother too was delighted: 'surely', wrote Lady Jersey, 'there is every reason to rejoice, and I am not too sanguine when I think she will be more comfortable than ever. I am out of patience with those who croak, and had more pleasure in pitying her than they have in seeing her happy.' Car told Charles Paget in May 1811 that anything which she had thought happiness in the former part of her life was not for a moment to be compared 'to the superlative degree of bliss which she was now enjoying'.[*]

Lord Glenbervie wrote in his diary that the whole affair had given such great offence in Scotland that there had been a meeting of the Lords of Justiciary at Edinburgh who had entered into some sort of resolution or protest on the subject. It was thought in legal circles that if the Argylls had a son (in fact they were childless) his right to succeed to the dukedom and estates might be challenged, and further that both Paget and Car might be indictable for bigamy under a statute of James I: but in the event nothing came of this.

As a result of these domestic upheavals and marital exchanges, which though today they seem tame enough were considered so scandalous at the time, all the principal parties settled down happily for the rest of their lives. Henry Wellesley married again six years later, pursued a distinguished career as a diplomatist, and in 1828 was created Lord Cowley.[m] The Pagets, as we shall see, appeared to be sufficiently contented for the rest of their exceptionally long lives, though Char was looked upon as a person not fit for intercourse with respectable persons, even long after she had become Lady Anglesey; and the Argylls died, childless, within a few years of each other in the 1830s.

At the end of 1811 Lady Bessborough wrote: 'Ld. Paget's children are all in town in their way from Inverary to Beaudesert; they talk with filial tenderness of Mama Argyll and Mama Paget: Vive la Liberté! ... Without much beauty, without much cleverness, without any one particularly attractive quality that can be defin'd, this same Ly. Paget [Char] is the most fascinating of human beings to man or woman; ... she governs him despotically, and the only very Mark'd Nature of her Character is being over strict in the performance of all Religious duties; ... to see her you would imagine she was innocence itself — how strange!'[n]

It was some time before a reconciliation between Paget and his mother and father took place, and the brothers, sisters, brothers-in-law and sisters-in-law found it very difficult to accept Charlotte.[o] But by 1812 most of the close relations were no longer actually hostile. Lord Galloway summed up the sensible approach to the problem when he wrote to his brother-in-law Arthur Paget in June 1811: 'If your daughter should elope with a man offensive to you, I do not suppose you would speedily be reconciled, and yet I do not suppose you would determine never to be reconciled. Feelings extremely shocked require *Time* to recover, as well as Time to manifest the probable permanent conduct of the other party. ... I can easily conceive Lady Ux. refusing intercourse now, and yet after P[aget] and his Wife have lived long enough together and as amicably and respectably as possible, being disposed to bury in oblivion Present events. ... This is so much the constant practice of the world in *all Extreme Cases* that we must conclude it to be natural, and consequently correct.'

CHAPTER SEVEN

In February 1810 there opened in the House of Commons an inquiry into the Walcheren Expedition. Paget was one of those summoned to appear before the committee; this, however, he eluded. 'I am sorry Paget avoided the Summons of the House,' wrote his brother-in-law Lord Galloway, 'his evidence would have been good, because it would have been decided, and he would have become a little more habituated to the World, which by prolonged Retirement he will dislike to meet again.'[2]

Paget's withdrawal from the world lasted on and off for over five years. From the military point of view he was virtually unemployed between the date of his return from the Scheldt in the late summer of 1809 till the early months of 1815. The reasons for this will appear later. In the meantime he had enough to occupy him, if not satisfactorily, at least fully, for his father had recently entered into his dotage. Old Lord Uxbridge was already unable to walk unaided when towards the end of 1809 he fell down and broke a rib. This accident hastened his decay, which greatly to the distress of the family affected his morals as much as his physique. At about this time he formed what Charles Paget called an 'unfortunate connection' with a young woman, whose identity remains obscure. 'My father', wrote Charles to Arthur, 'fancies that she really *loves* his *person*. He told Edward so. Edward's remark was a very just one & had the effect probably of opening his Eyes more than any argument would have done. He said, "What should you think if Sir David Dundas [then aged seventy-five] was seriously to tell you that a girl of 20 was seriously & truly in *Love* with his *Person*? If you did not laugh at him, should you not be disgusted at the communication?"' Lady Uxbridge's brother, the Rev. George Champagné, tried another approach in a letter 'in which he painted in the strongest light the dreadful situation he stood in: when at his age & infirmity he might so shortly expect to appear before the most

113

awful Tribunal.' This argument was reinforced by his doctor, who described to him 'the many instances which had come within his knowledge of old men being carried off at the very instant of their intrigues without having even a moment to make their peace with their Maker'. This combined assault, at any rate temporarily, seems to have had a salutary effect. After lengthy negotiations, conducted by his agent, John Sanderson, Lord Uxbridge, who had been paying 'this Hellkite' (to use one of Charles's more flattering descriptions) £500 a year, managed to get rid of her for an annuity of £300 for life. What Lady Uxbridge suffered in these last years of her husband's life was summed up by Charles: 'Nothing can exceed ... the most cruel and heartrending situation of our amiable and truest mother. It is much too dreadful to contemplate.'[3]

*   *   *

On March 13th, 1812, Lord Uxbridge died, aged sixty-eight, and Paget succeeded him as the second Earl of Uxbridge of the second creation. More than a year before that event, he had taken over responsibility for his father's multifarious affairs. These he found in an extremely poor way. For a long time old Lord Uxbridge had been living at a rate of expenditure well above that of his income, not chiefly through heedless extravagance, though there were instances of that, but through his absolute determination to attend to business as little as he possibly could. Paget found that estimates of the annual profits from the copper-mines in Anglesey, made many years before, had been highly optimistic, yet all his father's great expenditure on elections, on his various domestic establishments (which included building and improvements), and on generous allowances to poor relations, was geared to those over-sanguine calculations, long since proved false. As early as 1805, Lady Uxbridge, in reporting to her son Arthur that of the £26,000 prize-money awarded to Charles for the capture of four Spanish treasure-ships Lord Uxbridge had immediately borrowed £14,000, declared: 'We are going down hill fast, and unless we can sell Ux. House, I don't know what will become of us. One of the [copper] Mines we have ceased working as it did not pay the Expense, and the other is not so prosperous as it has been.' Asked in July 1811 to buy a new property, Paget replied from Plas Newydd that his father's circumstances were such that it was

'impossible to purchase any thing any where, which will not yield to
him sufficient to cover the interest of any loan he might be obliged

to make in the purchase.... I really live surrounded by too many embarrassments and have too constantly before my eyes the fatal effects of extravagance, of want of calculation of success, of hasty decisions to incur enormous expenses, not to shudder at the probability of still further distresses. Here I am at the very seat of mismanagement and extravagance. Such inconsiderate purchases made, such frauds of some agents, such ignorance of others, such general inconvenience and distress from want of calculating means, that you cd not have taken me at a worse moment to have consulted me upon a point of Finance.'

In an attempt to bring order to his father's affairs, Paget brought in two half-pay admirals, Aylmer and Bentinck, as supervisory agents. This measure, as might be expected, caused discontent in more than one quarter. Sanderson, whom Paget at first much distrusted, but later in life came to rely upon implicitly, supposed himself to be superseded, and was for a time uncooperative; while the brothers, themselves feeling the pinch, were far from happy. 'A Parent', wrote Charles to Arthur, 'in a state of decrepitude which precludes his justly estimating the impoverished state in which he will leave *us* all, and an elder Brother, from whom we have no reason to expect a more favorable state of circumstances, when he comes into the possession of the family property: This is *not* cheering.' To Paget's complaints of his father's and the agents' extravagances, Charles would have liked to have replied: ' "It's very true, Paget, they do swag away — that's certain, but you have had your full share of it, and have lately, that is within these two years cost my father from Thirty to Forty Thousand Pounds [a reference to Henry Wellesley's damages and the allowance to Car], and therefore *you* have no right to complain of *their* extravagances." If, my old Boy, I had said that, I should have said what is true, but no *good* would have been obtained.... Aylmer has absolutely possession of Paget. His opinion of him is that no other man could have retrieved the family from positive Bankruptcy.' Paget thought the family finances 'almost desperate and that nothing but general good management and steadiness can retreive them.... By Sanderson's calculations there will this very year [1811] be a deficit of £11,000.... I wish I could have seen you and Charles.... I would have run down, but I have not *de quoi payer les chevaux de poste — diable m'emporte....* I think we [all the brothers] had better club establishments for a year, hire a barrack, and place ourselves under Graves [his brother-in-law] for instruction. Indeed ... the aspect of affairs is most serious.' In December 1810, Paget was as worried about his own finances as about his father's. 'The more I look into matters,' he told Arthur, 'the more I am convinced that *I* for one have been shamefully plundered. The foolish extravagance and waste that has existed *chez moi*, is amazing.... This sort of thing goes to trifles, which, I am sure till now, I hardly considered as expenses. Who, for instance, wd conceive that a few almonds and raisins dealt out daily to two persons (who by the by never touch them) shd amount to a serious charge?... And so in every other article of Dessert; the habit of my family it seems having been always to make a clean sweep of everything upon the table.'[4]

Though reports current at the time of old Lord Uxbridge's death probably exaggerated the debts which he left behind him, throughout his successor's life there was never a time when large parts of the estates were not mortgaged, nor when he was not spending at least every penny of his income. This, as will be seen, was partly due to the extravagances of his own sons. Yet there was equally never a time, until well into the twentieth century, when it would have been possible to describe the head of the Paget family as anything but a rich man.[a]

*   *   *

On June 17th, 1811, the day upon which Char gave birth to her son Clarence, there was a review on Hounslow Heath of the four regiments of hussars which formed the Hussar Brigade. Charles reported to Arthur that there was

'an immense concourse of spectators. It was truly fine and Paget was quite in his element after it. The Prince and all the Brothers, with all the Staff and Officers of the Brigade, repair'd to the Castle at Richmond, where a most sumptious *dejeuner*, or rather a d——d good dinner, was prepared by Paget's order. It was of the most luxurious style, I suppose about 200 sat down to it, and as Turtle, Fish, Venison of the best quality and quantity was provided; as Champagne, Hock, Burgundy, and Claret, Vin de France and Hermitage was drunk in copious libations; as Peaches, Nectarines, Grapes, Pines, Melons and everything most rare in the dessert way was provided in abundance, it was a feast worthy of the magnificent piece of Plate, which had been (unknown till the moment) *in readiness* to present to Paget by the Prince, the Dukes, and the Officers of the Hussar Brigade.[b]

'Nothing could surpass the effect of the whole day. The Prince exceeded himself in his praises of Paget, and all seemed to unite in the expediency of getting him to serve. In short it was a most flattering day for him.... My father stood it famously, and this morning sent Sanderson to Paget, to desire *he* might have the *Bill* to pay.'[5]

* * *

In March 1814 the Allies entered Paris. On April 5th Napoleon abdicated, and peace at long last came to Europe. While preparations were going ahead in Vienna for the Congress which was to shape the continent's destiny, serious disorders occurred in London. During the first days of 1815 there was introduced into Parliament a Bill to prohibit the importation of corn, except when it had reached a price considered by most consumers as exorbitant. This led to a serious outbreak of anti-Corn Law riots in the metropolis, and to many of the houses of the Bill's supporters being damaged. At the beginning of March Uxbridge (as he now was) was placed in command of the troops in the London district, ready to support the civil power. He took up his headquarters in the Horse Guards, from where he at once communicated with the magistrates, from the Lord Mayor down, with a view to their being on duty at specified points throughout the twenty-four hours. He followed this up by visits to many of them. One reported that at 1.15 a.m. on March 8th 'Lord Uxbridge ... politely called upon me to have a little conversation about the Military.... Much indebted for his Lordship's kindness.' Besides setting up military posts at strategically important points, his chief use of the regular forces at his disposal was, as he wrote some years later, 'merely to cause constant patrols, chiefly of Cavalry, but occasionally of Infantry, to patrol the streets'. It was an extremely busy time for him: the stream of complaints and requests for aid which flowed by day into his office in the Horse Guards, and by night into Uxbridge House, had to be dealt with promptly and personally. There was, for instance, an urgent message from Carlton House about slogans which had been chalked up near all the royal palaces, the Prince requiring 'immediate action to see that they are erased without delay as they occur'. One John Trotter, living in Soho Square, received positive notice on March 9th that his house was to be attacked that very evening: this and others similarly threatened had to be unobtrusively guarded.[6]

Uxbridge seems to have quickly sown a spirit of confidence among the property owners of London, and to have worked well in harness with the magistrates and the constables. Only two complaints of any importance reached his headquarters: one from a law-abiding citizen who claimed to have been injured by Life Guards at the House of Commons, and the other from the Lord Mayor, who though forewarned that the situation made it necessary, deemed it due to the City's honour to complain about military patrols passing through its streets.

The riots quickly subsided, and were soon eclipsed in the public mind by events of quite a different order.

CHAPTER EIGHT

His Lordship is still the Lord Paget of 1808, the same fine and anxious spirit as ever.... He is not only the cleverest cavalry officer in the British Empire, but unfortunately he is almost the only one with a cavalry genius. In this line all he does is peculiar to himself, and wherever he appears he invariably gains spontaneously the confidence of the whole of his profession.

Captain Jones of the 15th Hussars: entry in his journal for June 5th, 1815[1]

NAPOLEON escaped from Elba on March 1st. As soon as the news reached Vienna, the Ministers attending the Congress ceased their wrangling, declared the disturber of their deliberations an outlaw, and pledged their forces to destroy him. In late March the Duke of Wellington left Vienna for Brussels to assume command of the Allied army assembling in Flanders.

Among the problems which at once beset him was the question of the command of the cavalry. It was a matter of importance, for although much of the Peninsular infantry had been hurried across the Atlantic to fight the Americans, a considerable quantity of cavalry (from the nature of the American war not required there) was immediately available for Flanders.

The choice lay between Uxbridge and Combermere. The Duke of York and an influential section at the Horse Guards were for Uxbridge, but Wellington preferred Combermere. In 1809 the chief obstacles to Uxbridge's employment in Portugal and Spain had been his seniority to Wellington, and the awkward fact that he had eloped with Wellington's sister-in-law. The seniority bar had long since been removed, for the Duke had received his field-marshal's baton two years before; and it is unlikely that had Wellington wanted Uxbridge, he would have allowed a scandal now six years old to stand in the way.

From time to time, between 1809 and 1811, efforts had been made to find Uxbridge suitable employment. In August 1811, after being

summoned to the Horse Guards, he had written to tell Arthur Paget
that he was

'not going abroad. Why they sent for me I know not, for the Duke
of York so far from wishing me to serve *under* Lord Wellington
told me, as he had told the Prince [Regent], that altho' he wd not
oppose the measure, yet that he could by no means advise me to it.
The Prince however had a strong desire that I shd serve, until all the
difficulties both publick and private had been represented to him.
This I had no occasion to do, it had been already done, and when I
went to him, I found him fully sensible that no advantage was likely
to result from the unusual measure of waiving my Rank. There was
still another thing that he wished me to do and which in my mind,
and in that of all I spoke to upon the subject, was still more objectionable, namely that of going out to inspect, report upon, and in part
reorganise the Cavalry. This wd really have been too insulting to
Ld W[ellington] and (what is perhaps of less consequence) to all his
Officers of Cavalry. It would imply that both he and they were
ignorant of the management and application of that Arm and do no
ultimate good, for as Edward very justly observed, unless I could
take out with me a parcel of Heads to place upon their Shoulders, all
the Chocolate I might deal out wd avail nothing. This project
therefore is given up.... Altho' it would have been quite ruinous to
me and mine to have stirred at this moment, yet I cannot help feeling
quite distressed that I was unable to overcome all difficulties and to
offer my Services. I conclude however that I shall not be allowed
to remain quiet very long.'[2]

No doubt, throughout his years in the wilderness, Uxbridge himself
was pressing hard for employment: certainly those who felt, with the
Duke of York, that first-class talent was going to waste, were pressing on
his behalf. But until 1815 the 'publick and private' considerations
prevailed.

Apart from all questions of seniority and scandal, it is clear that
Wellington would have always preferred a man such as Combermere for
his cavalry commander. In 1812, after Combermere had been wounded at
Salamanca, Wellington wrote to Torrens, the Commander-in-Chief's
military secretary: 'Sir Stapleton Cotton [as Combermere then was] is
gone home. He commands our cavalry very well — indeed I am certain
much better than many who might be sent to us & who might be supposed

cleverer than he is.' The truth was that Wellington, always sceptical of 'clever' men, much preferred the sound and solid to the brilliant and imaginative. Uxbridge would have alarmed him, no doubt, with his view that a cavalry general should 'inspire his men as early as possible with the most perfect confidence in his personal gallantry. Let him but lead, they are sure to follow, and I believe hardly anything will stop them.' Wellington felt safer with officers who bore in mind his own advice to Combermere, 'that cavalry should be always held well in hand; that your men and horses should not be used up in wild and useless charges, but put forward when you are sure that their onset will have a decisive effect.'[*] Further, Combermere had a long association with his chief, dating from the days of Tippoo Sahib in 1799,[*] and extending through most of the Peninsular War. Uxbridge, on the other hand, had never served under Wellington, and his reputation in the field, high though it was, rested almost entirely on his handling of five regiments of horse under Moore in 1808.

In these circumstances it was natural that Wellington should be loath to have Uxbridge pressed on him in the spring of 1815, when Combermere was equally available. On April 1st Torrens wrote to the Duke that there appeared to be a very general wish that Uxbridge should be appointed. Four days later Uxbridge wrote to his brother: 'I now incline to think I shall serve. It certainly depends upon the Duke of Wellington & as the Duke of Y[ork] tells me that the Prince wishes it so much that H.R.H. wanted to name me at once & that Ministers & Ld Bathurst particularly also urged it, & as Torrens is sent over [to Brussels] amongst other things to take His Grace's pleasure hereon, I conclude then the thing must be so.'[4]

Combermere twice wrote requesting Wellington not to forget him in the arrangement about to be made and the Duke replied on April 7th that he was 'most anxious to have the assistance of all those to whom, on former occasions', he had been so much indebted. 'We shall have, I hope, an enormous body of cavalry of different nations; and I trust that Torrens will be able to make an arrangement which will be satisfactory to you.' Next day Torrens, on his way back to England, wrote to Bathurst, the Secretary for War, that he was in hopes that an arrangement might 'eventually be made for the employment both of Lords Uxbridge and Combermere. Upon this point the Duke has been perfectly fair and reasonable.' No such arrangement was in fact made, and Combermere remained at home. Uxbridge was appointed to the command on April 15th. Torrens, the following day, told the Duke that he had 'given to Lord Combermere a full explanation of the circumstances attending the appointment of Lord Uxbridge, and I have no reason to think that he is dissatisfied with it. [Lord Uxbridge] is in great delight at the prospect of serving under you, and I have little doubt but that he will give you satisfaction.'[5] Wellington, not for the first time, had been overruled by the Horse Guards.[b]

ii

Wellington never, till the Waterloo campaign, had an officer of proved ability in chief command of his cavalry.

                                                    Sir Charles Oman[6]

Uxbridge, with some of his staff, arrived at Ostend on April 25th.[c] His old friend and admirer, Sir John Elley, who had served him in the same department in Spain seven years before, became assistant adjutant-general to the cavalry, and Lord Greenock, assistant quartermaster-general. Major Thornhill (who had served with Uxbridge in Spain), Captains Horace Seymour, Wildman, and Fraser (all of the 7th Hussars), and Captain Streerwitz of the 2nd Hussars, King's German Legion, formed his 'family' of aides-de-camp. Lieutenant-Colonel Sir Augustus Frazer, who commanded the Royal Horse Artillery under him,[d] found Uxbridge 'quiet in business and very decided; this is the true way to do much in a little time'.[7]

On arrival in Brussels, Uxbridge found himself allotted a house in the centre of the city. The Belgian marquis and marquise who owned it had gone to much trouble to provide all his wants and had given up the whole of the ground floor for his use. His sister, Caroline Capel, who was in Brussels with her family, reported that Uxbridge remained only one night in the house, '& took up his residence at one of the Hotels, having made the Lady a very handsome speech for the accommodation he had met with, but declaring that he could not with any comfort take possession of another person's house while it was possible to find lodgings anywhere else. I believe', she continued, 'they were truly sorry to part with him, for his remaining would have kept out others who may not make themselves quite as agreeable.'[8]

His first task after reaching Brussels was to inquire of the Duke what was required of him. 'I place the *whole* of the Cavalry and Light Artillery of the United Army under your command,' he was told; though a few days after this the Duke said, 'The Prince of Orange has begged that the Cavalry of H.R.H.'s nation should remain under his immediate command. I hope you have no objection to this'; to which Uxbridge replied, 'Not the slightest. I am quite ready to act in any way you please.' However, on the morning of the great battle, just as it was about to begin, the Prince of Orange wished him, after all, to take charge of the Belgian cavalry. Uxbridge told the Duke, 'I will do my best with them, but it is unfortunate that I should not have had an opportunity of making myself acquainted with any of his officers or their regiments.'[9]

*   *   *

As the British and King's German Legion cavalry regiments arrived in Flanders, they were cantoned by brigades, seven in number, along the

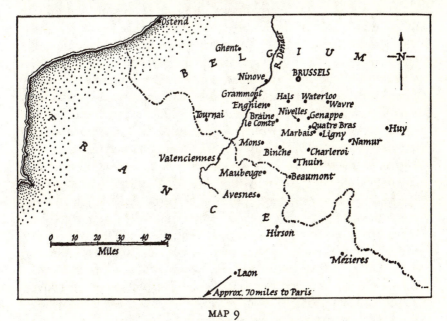

MAP 9

THE WATERLOO CAMPAIGN OF JUNE, 1815

line of the rivers Dender and Haine. The Dutch-Belgian cavalry linked up with the Prussians south of Binche; the 3rd cavalry brigade, consisting of the 1st and 2nd Hussars of the King's German Legion, was at Mons,

under the Hanoverian general, Sir William Dörnberg, who was made
responsible for the collection of intelligence from the frontier. The other
six brigades were quartered in numerous villages covering a large area.[•]
Cavalry headquarters were established at Ninove, sixteen miles to the
west of Brussels.

By the end of May most of the Allied troops had arrived in the theatre.
The armies of Wellington and Blücher now lay in their cantonments on
and behind the Belgian frontier, covering a front of about a hundred
miles from Tournai in the west to Huy in the east, with their line of
contact the great road which runs from Charleroi to Brussels.

On the 29th a grand review of the cavalry was held in the plain of
Grammont.[1] Frazer, who commanded the horse artillery, described the
scene:

'We found on our arrival fifteen regiments of British cavalry, with
six troops of horse artillery, drawn up in three lines on a beautiful
plain on the banks of the Dender. About 1 p.m. the Duke, Marshal
Blücher, &c &c., arrived.... We received the Duke with a salute of
nineteen guns. After going down the lines and inspecting the
cavalry generally, and the horse artillery very minutely, and repeatedly expressing his approbation of our appearance, the Duke
took his station in front of the centre of the first line, and the different
corps passed in columns of half squadrons. It is not possible to
imagine a finer sight. The day was bright and hot, but with a gentle
breeze. We were in meadows with grass up to the horses' knees, in a
country fertile and rich, and well wooded. There were thousands of
spectators, both of military men from all parts of the army, and of
the people of the country for ten leagues round. The review passed
off without a check, an error, or an accident; one could see the cavalry
had fallen into the hands of a master.... His Lordship gave a dinner
to the Duke, Blücher, and all the generals and commanding officers of
corps. Dinner was laid for a hundred. Never was anything better
arranged. His lordship lives in an abbey, the large rooms of which
were well calculated for the princely feast.... Dinner was served
about five: it [consisted] of many courses, all served on plate. An
excellent dessert followed, and the finest wines of every kind flowed
in such profusion that 'tis well if I can this morning write of any
thing but pink champagne. The moment dinner was over, folding
doors behind the Duke opened, and a band struck up "God save the

King". The Prince Regent's and Duke of York's healths followed
that of their royal father; and then Lord Uxbridge gave the Duke,
which was drunk with three times three.'

Numerous other toasts followed, watched by 'ladies and gentry of the
place', Blücher, in a neat speech, giving 'the Cavalry and Horse Artillery'.
After coffee had been served, the Duke was received by a guard of honour
of the Life Guards, and rode back to Brussels, passing under a triumphal
arch which had been erected at Ninove 'with very flattering devices; the
whole town,' wrote Frazer, 'adorned with branches of trees, looked like a
grove, and our troops, wearing the oak-bough of the 29th of May gave
to the whole, additional gaiety.'[10]

*   *   *

By the time hostilities opened the total strength of Uxbridge's cavalry
was about 14,500 sabres, with forty-four guns. There were, in all, thirty-
one cavalry regiments. Of these, six were heavy, and the remainder light:
fifteen British, five of the King's German Legion, and the rest Hanoverian,
Brunswickian and Dutch-Belgian. Of the horse-batteries attached to
brigades, three were equipped with nine-pounders; one, Whinyates's,
with eight hundred rockets as well as its field pieces; one with heavy
$5\frac{1}{2}$-inch howitzers, and the rest with light six-pounders.[11]

In his brigade commanders he was well served. Hussey Vivian and
Colquhoun Grant were old friends: both had served under him in Spain
in 1808; John Vandeleur, at the age of fifty-two, had behind him a distinguished career including three years with Wellington in the Peninsula.
Dörnberg and Colonel Arentschild, the two German brigade commanders, were experienced officers, while William Ponsonby, who commanded the 'Union' Brigade and lost his life in the great charge on
June 18th, and Lord Edward Somerset, commanding the Household
Brigade, had been capable cavalry leaders in Spain.

iii

It was a universal opinion that his lordship was the first cavalry general in the British Army.

Dr Gibney, medical officer of the 15th Hussars[12]

On June 1st Wellington wrote to Uxbridge that he had reason to hope that they would soon be on the move. In the second week of June intelligence regarding Napoleon's secret concentration of the French army on the frontier began to trickle through. On the 12th, Uxbridge communicated to Wellington a report that 'Buonaparte was to establish his headquarters at Laon on the 10th, that the Imperial Guard had made two days' march from thence to the front, and that it was his intention to attack immediately.' Major-General Dörnberg, from the cavalry outposts at Mons, reported on the 13th to Uxbridge: 'The whole French Army it appears is concentrating at & near Maubeuge. The troops near Valenciennes marched yesterday afternoon at 3 o'clock, leaving only their Picquets. The troops near Mezières have passed Beaumont for Maubeuge, and those from Avesnes & Laon march in the same direction. There is', he added, 'a considerable body of Cavalry with this Army, a great part of it was reviewed by General Grouchy near Hirson two days ago.' Lord Hill, who commanded the second Corps, learnt during the night of the 13th at his headquarters in Grammont that the French outposts at Maubeuge had fallen back. This information showed that Napoleon was concentrating to the east, behind Charleroi. Early on the 14th, Marshal Blücher, the Prussian commander-in-chief, received definite news at Namur of the French concentration, and at three in the afternoon of the 15th an officer from Ziethen's Prussian corps at Charleroi arrived in Brussels reporting that the Prussian outposts at Thuin had been driven in. At about the same time Uxbridge arrived in Brussels from Ninove, for that evening there was to be a ball at the Duchess of Richmond's. 'We were just dressed [for the Ball],' wrote his aide-de-camp Wildman, 'when we heard that the Prussians had been attacked in the morning ... and that the enemy had occupied the frontier town of Binch.'[13]

Blücher's liaison officer with Wellington had for some time been urging the Duke to tell him where he would concentrate his army, but the Duke preferred to wait for more definite information from his own outposts at Mons before feeling certain that the real attack was to come from the enemy's left and not along the more direct and usual road to Brussels,

namely that which passed through Mons and Hals on the right. The most
he would do was to order the army to be ready to move without delay,
which he did at six o'clock.[14] The cavalry he had ordered to be collected
that night at Ninove. But just before midnight, while at the ball, the
Duke learnt from Dörnberg that the French had moved away from
Mons, and at about one in the morning of the 16th, as the party sat down
to supper, a messenger announced that the enemy had advanced to
Quatre-Bras, within seventeen miles of Brussels. Wellington then explained the situation to his senior officers, who discreetly left the ball for
their posts, he himself retiring to bed.[h]

Of this momentous day, in the course of which the two great battles of
Ligny and Quatre-Bras were fought, Captain Wildman, writing on the
19th, gives the best account, so far as Uxbridge's actions are concerned.

'[After the ball] where the Duke of Wellington & Lord Uxbridge
had a long conversation,... we mounted and rode back to Ninove,
from thence orders were sent to assemble the whole of the Cavalry
and Royal Horse Artillery near Enghien [25 miles west of Quatre
Bras].[i] There I met Ld. Uxbridge who immediately sent me to Brain
le Comte, and not finding the Duke of W. there, to Nivelles.[j] It was
then about 4 o'clock and I heard a considerable firing in front to
which point I made accordingly and found the Belgic and Dutch
troops engaged in a village called Quatre Bras about 5 miles on the
road to Namur. Two English divisions had been sent for, and I wa
immediately despatched again to bring up all the cavalry and
another British division from Braine le Comte. There I met Lord
Uxbridge & returned with him to the scene of action which began to
grow very warm; our infantry had arrived and the action lasted till
dark when the French were repulsed on all fronts & retired leaving us
masters of the field. This affair was obstinately contested and the
Lancers charged our solid Squares of Infantry several times, and
when repulsed by one, wheeled about and attacked another. The
Guards suffered considerably & the Highlanders received a charge of
the Cuirassiers, repulsed them and destroyed the whole Squadron.
Our cavalry did not arrive till after the action was over which was not
till 10 o'clock at night, except Sir J. Vandeleur's Brigade of Light
Dragoons with which Ld. Uxbridge shewed a front and kept the
enemy's cavalry in check.'[15]

iv

The retreat was conducted with perfect regularity.
Lord Uxbridge[16]

The commander of the cavalry spent the night of the 16th in Genappe
with Wellington. Before it was light some welcome rain fell, but the
morning of the 17th dawned fine, turning later into an excessively oppressive and sultry day. Except for a minor attack by the French soon after
daybreak, all was quiet at Quatre-Bras for the rest of the early morning.
While the Duke spent it awaiting the arrival of Hill's corps to complete
his army, Uxbridge was busy placing and replacing the cavalry pickets.
At about six, the Duke sent off his aide-de-camp, Sir Alexander Gordon,
escorted by a troop of the 10th Hussars, to discover what had happened
to the Prussians at Ligny the previous day. He returned with the news of
their defeat, and at nine a Prussian officer brought the news that Blücher
was in retirement on Wavre. Wellington at once gave his orders for a
withdrawal to the position of Mont-Saint-Jean, a movement corresponding to Blücher's. The infantry, breakfasting first, began to move, and the
cavalry were ordered to cover their withdrawal. Still, to the astonishment
of the Duke, the French made no movement. He thought it 'not at all
impossible that they also might be retreating'. From about ten o'clock
Uxbridge began to form up the cavalry and the horse-batteries in the
positions vacated by the infantry, momentarily expecting to be attacked
by the enemy's cavalry. He placed the hussars in the first line, the light
dragoons in the second, and, some way behind, the 'heavies' in support.[17]

As the last of the infantry cleared the village, the first movements of
the enemy were observed: an enormous mass of French cavalry was seen
to be forming about two miles to the south.k But it was not until nearly
two o'clock that they were observed to mount and advance along the
Namur road, the *lanciers* leading the way. Almost immediately Uxbridge's
advanced pickets on the left and in the centre became engaged. At this
moment, satisfied that his main body had got well away, Wellington left
the conduct of the rearguard to Uxbridge, exclaiming: 'Well, there is the
last of the infantry gone, and I don't care now.' He enjoined Uxbridge to
avoid anything like a serious engagement, and to remain in position as
long as he conveniently could.[18] [1]

As the hordes of enemy cavalry came on, the guns of Uxbridge's
horse-batteries opened fire on them.m The heavy-laden, low-lying clouds

A branch of Weeping Willow gathered at the village of Waterloo, from the tree under which lies interred the leg of the brave Marquis of Anglesey.

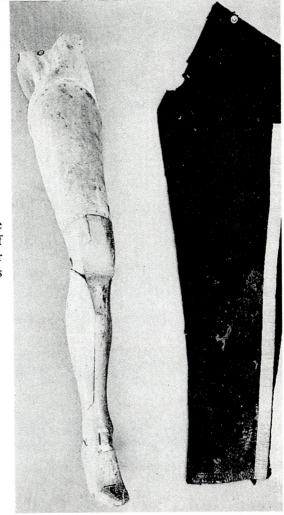

A leg of the Hussar trousers worn by the Earl of Uxbridge at Waterloo, and one of the articulated artificial limbs designed for him by Mr Potts, both preserved at Plas Newydd

An apocryphal meeting between Wellington and Uxbridge after the
Battle of Waterloo

which had been gathering for some hours gave immediate reply: the oppressive calm of the morning was shattered by a tremendous flash of lightning, followed by the first of many rolls of thunder. 'It rained as if the water were tumbled out of tubs', wrote an officer of the Greys. Young Cornet Bullock of the 11th described it as the heaviest tempest he had ever seen. Roads became full of water, and all movement was immediately restricted to a slow walk, except on the paved main road, or *chaussée*, the horses being up to their knees in the fields, which had become 'perfect swamps'.[19n]

Uxbridge now gave the order for the cavalry's withdrawal to begin. On the right (that is, furthest from where Napoleon's cavalry was now coming on) he had placed Dörnberg's brigade, with orders to cross the Dyle and Fonteny rivers to the west of Genappe. In the centre were the 'heavies' (Somerset's Household Brigade and Ponsonby's 'Union' Brigade), who were to retire along the main road through Genappe itself, covered by the 23rd Light Dragoons, with the 7th Hussars as rearguard. The eastern column (that which was nearest to the advancing enemy), consisting of Vivian's brigade, supported by Vandeleur's, was to cross by a small bridge which had been located near Thy. As soon as Vivian (whose brigade was posted at right angles to the Namur road) saw that a part of the French cavalry was attempting to cut him off by a northward thrust, he ordered off his guns: these managed to cross the bridge only just in time. Vandeleur's brigade was drawn up about seven hundred yards behind Vivian's.

'On my arriving within about fifty or sixty yards of Sir J. Vandeleur', wrote Vivian many years later, 'he put his Brigade about and retired, upon which I moved to the ground he had occupied, and directed the 1st Hussars [K.G.L.] to cover the left flank and left front. In this manner we stood some time skirmishing with the enemy, and during which Lieut.-Colonel Thornhill, A.D.C., came from Lord Uxbridge to me to see what we were about. I told him I had enough upon my hands, but that I hoped to get my people all well off, and I sent an A.D.C. to Sir J. Vandeleur to desire he would as fast as possible get his Brigade over the bridge, in order that I might have no interruption in my retreat in case I was hard pressed.'[20o]

Both brigades managed to cross the Dyle with small loss and continued their retreat without further molestation.

The heavy brigades in the centre, meanwhile, made their way along the

E

chaussée, across the narrow bridge, and through the street of Genappe. On the northern side of the town they formed up on the rising ground with the 23rd in their front. During their withdrawal from Quatre-Bras to Genappe the 7th Hussars had acted as rearguard, its rear troop — O'Grady's[p] — successfully retiring in the face of twenty-four French

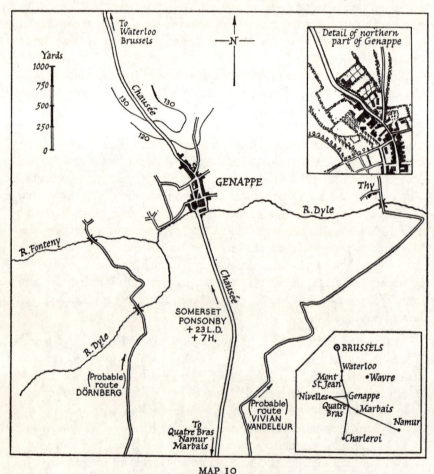

MAP 10

THE RETREAT THROUGH GENAPPE, JUNE 17TH, 1815

squadrons. These had started to advance along the *chaussée* towards Brussels shortly after their comrades to the right on the Namur road. On O'Grady's troop joining the rest of the regiment, Uxbridge warmly praised it for all to hear.[21]

The two heavy brigades now awaited the enemy, the rain streaming down all the while. After a quarter of an hour loud shouting was heard from the massed *lanciers* and *cuirassiers* as they rode slowly into the town. Another fifteen minutes and the leading troop of the *lanciers* (some of them in a drunken state) was seen at the northern end of the narrow, winding street, about to debouch on to the wide *chaussée*. Before they were clear of the jaws of the town, Uxbridge let loose Major Hodge's squadron of the 7th. With a spectacular rush the men and horses crashed into the *lanciers*, who received the charge at the halt, their lance-points lowered. There followed a grim and determined 'seesaw', which was kept up for a considerable time, under heavy fire from the French artillery, Napoleon in person having hurried a horse-battery into position on the north-east of the town. The hussars had a hopeless task from the first, for not only were the *lanciers* tightly jammed between the last few houses on either side of the street, making it impossible for their flanks to be turned, but the sabre-play of Hodge's men was comparatively ineffectual against the length of their opponents' lances. Further, the Frenchmen were quite powerless to escape from the fury of their attackers, however much they wished to, for piling up behind them, massed as thick as the horses could stand, were the men of their succeeding squadrons. The leaders of the opposing squadrons were both cut down, and many others killed or wounded, before Uxbridge ordered the squadron to disengage.[q]

The moment the *lanciers* perceived that they had held the English cavalry in their first charge of the campaign, they started in pursuit, shouting 'En avant! En avant!' As they came on, Uxbridge, left alone on the road within fifteen yards of the enemy,[22] rode up to the 23rd, according to his own account, and ordered them to advance.

'My address', he wrote, 'not having been received with all the enthusiasm that I expected, I ordered them to clear the *chaussée*,[r] and said, "The Life Guards shall have this honour", and instantly sending for them, two squadrons of the 1st Regiment [of Life Guards] . . . came on *with right good will*, and I sent them in to finish the Lancers. They at once overthrew them, and pursued into the town, where they punished them severely.[s] Having thus checked the ardour of the Enemy's advanced guard, the retreat was continued at a slow pace, and with the most perfect regularity. Assuredly this *coup de collier* [sudden effort] had the very best effect, for although there was much cannonading, and a constant appearance of a disposition to charge, they continued at a respectful distance. The Royals, Inniskillings, and Greys manoeuvred beautifully, retiring by alternate squadrons, and skirmished in the very best style; but finding that all the efforts of the Enemy to get upon our right flank were vain, and that by manoeuvring upon the plain, which was amazingly deep and heavy from the violent storm of rain, it only uselessly exhausted the horses, I drew these Regiments in upon the *chaussée* in one column, the Guns falling back from position to position, and from these Batteries, checking the advance of the Enemy.'

In 1852, answering a correspondent's question, Angelsey, as he then was, wrote,

'the moment the Squadrons of the Rear Guard halted and fronted, those of the Enemy invariably avoided a collision, and the retreat was conducted at a walk. The Artillery however on both sides were occasionally at work, and our Congreves Rockets were pitched into their Squadrons with good effect. We were received by the Duke of Wellington upon entering the position of Waterloo, having effected the retreat with very trifling loss. Thus ended the prettiest Field Day of Cavalry and Horse Artillery that I ever witnessed.'[23]

*   *   *

That night Uxbridge slept at Waterloo, but before he went to bed he consulted Vivian upon a subject that was weighing heavily on his mind. According to Sir William Fraser, he said to Sir Hussey,

'I find myself in a very difficult position. A great battle will take place tomorrow. The Duke, as you know, will not economize his safety. If any accident happens to him, I shall suddenly find myself Commander in Chief. Now, I have not the slightest idea what are the projects of the Duke. I would give anything in the world to know the dispositions which, I have no doubt, have been profoundly calculated. It will be impossible for me to frame them in a critical moment. I dare not ask the Duke what I ought to do.'

Vivian advised him to consult Count Alava, the Spanish general, whose friendship with Wellington led to his being attached to his staff during the campaign. Uxbridge at once went to him and found that Alava agreed that the question was a serious one, but suggested that it was for Uxbridge himself to tackle it. Alava therefore went to the Duke and told him that Uxbridge wished to see him. Uxbridge then explained to the Duke 'the motive of his visit with all the delicacy imaginable'. The Duke listened to him to the end, without saying a single word, and then asked: 'Who will attack the first tomorrow, I or Bonaparte?' 'Bonaparte,' was the reply. 'Well,' continued the Duke, 'Bonaparte has not given me any idea of his projects: and as my plans will depend upon his, how can you expect me to tell you what mine are?' The Duke then rose, and putting his hand on Uxbridge's shoulder, added, 'There is one thing certain, Uxbridge, that is, that whatever happens, you and I will do our duty.' The two men then shook hands, and Uxbridge retired to sleep.[24]

V

> Oho, my boy! this is but child's play to what *we* saw in Spain.
> *Captain Mercer of the Royal Horse Artillery*[25]

Allied headquarters that night were in the small whitewashed houses that lined the street of Waterloo. On the door of one of these was chalked up the name of the commander of the Allied cavalry. It was something to be sufficiently senior to rate a roof over one's head. For the troopers bivouacked in the fields near Mont-Saint-Jean, the memory of that night's discomforts remained vivid for years to come. The infantry, who had arrived at the position some time before the cavalry and in many cases before the worst of the rain, were comparatively well off; but for none were there rations or drinking-water, and such fires as the limited supply of firewood made possible were soon extinguished by the downpour. The tall standing crops had been trampled under foot by the horses, and the ground was ankle-deep in mud. Many of the men slept at their horses' heads with one arm passed through the reins, and a restless night they had, for they were constantly woken by their mounts taking fright at the lightning and thunder.

Sunday morning, June 18th, dawned dull and overcast, but the rain had ceased. Soon the sun shone through to reveal, as Lieutenant Hamilton of the Greys wrote in his Journal, 'a miserable looking set of creatures — covered with mud from head to foot — our white belts dyed with the red from our jackets, as if we had already completed the sanguinary work,

which we were soon about to begin'. At first light Uxbridge went forward
to visit the cavalry outposts. As he mounted his horse he remarked to the
Duke of Richmond and his fifteen-year-old son, who had ridden out from
Brussels, 'We shall have sharp work today.' Between ten and eleven
o'clock the cavalry brigades left their bivouacs for the positions assigned
to them.[26]

Wellington, being inferior in numbers, especially in guns, had decided
to give battle in the position of Mont-Saint-Jean, on the clear understanding that Blücher would come to his aid with at least one Prussian
corps. The Duke expected it on the battlefield at midday: as it turned out,
the first Prussian did not come into action until nearly half past four.
Napoleon, believing Blücher, after his defeat at Ligny, to be retiring
north-eastwards on to his own communications, intended to destroy
Wellington by a massive frontal attack, and to sleep that night in Brussels.

The two armies now faced each other from opposing ridges across a
gently sloping valley, the distance between them being nowhere much
more than a thousand yards. Each army presented a front of about three
miles, bisected by the Brussels-Charleroi *chaussée*: the Allies at the crossroads just north of the farm of La Haye Sainte, the French at the inn
known as La Belle Alliance. Wellington, who had long marked the
position of Mont-Saint-Jean as a favourable one, chose his ground with
his usual skill. The Wavre–Braine l'Alleud road, along the north side of
which he had placed his army, was for a part of its length sunken; to the
west of the *chaussée* it averaged about six feet in depth, while to the east
it was lined on both sides by thick and straggling hedges. Further, and
more important than this hidden obstacle, the incline behind the ridge hid
his troops from the enemy's until they were right on them: for instance,
only the headdress of the Allied cavalry sitting on their horses behind
the ridge could be seen from any part of the French position.[27] Napoleon's
army, on the other hand, was prominently displayed on a forward slope,
and, when the smoke allowed, Wellington was able throughout the battle
to gauge the Emperor's intentions by observing his troop movements.

The extreme left of the line was occupied by Vivian's brigade, with
detachments to the east to give warning of the approach of the Prussians.
Next to Vivian's was Vandeleur's and between it and the *chaussée* there
were five infantry brigades, all of them concealed behind the sunken road
except Bijlandt's, which had placed itself by mistake on the forward slope.
To the right of the *chaussée* was Alten's infantry division, and in and
around the semi-fortified château of Hougoumont the Foot Guards, with

Maitland's brigade holding the hollow road towards Braine l'Alleud. These joined hands with Chassé's Netherlanders, who held the extreme right in Braine l'Alleud itself. Behind the Foot Guards was Grant's brigade, with one squadron of the 15th Hussars thrown out to cover Mitchell's right flank, and behind Alten's infantry were the brigades of Dörnberg and Arentschild. Between the farm of Mont-Saint-Jean and the central crossroads were placed the 'heavies', Somerset's Household Brigade to the right of the *chaussée* and Ponsonby's 'Union' Brigade to its left. Behind them and around the farm itself were three brigades of Dutch-Belgian cavalry in reserve, and the Cumberland Hussars.

As was Wellington's custom, the front of the position was covered with infantry skirmishers, and most of the guns were placed just behind them. In front of the central crossroads, holding the farm, orchard and gravel pit of La Haye Sainte, were four hundred infantrymen of the King's German Legion under the valiant Major Baring.

vi

Well, Paget, I hope you are satisfied with your cavalry now.
Wellington to Uxbridge, after the charge of the heavy brigades[28]

Just before midday Napoleon launched a part of his left-hand corps against Wellington's right at the château of Hougoumont. This was intended to be a diversionary attack, with the probable object of forcing the Duke to weaken his centre. In the event more and more French battalions were drawn into the fight for the château, which raged all day much as a distinct operation.

At about this time Uxbridge completed his visits to the outposts, and from his central position near the Mont-Saint-Jean crossroads, sent Colonel Thornhill with verbal orders to brigade commanders, 'authorising them to act discretionally under certain limitations'. These, according to Vandeleur, were to engage the enemy whenever they could do so with advantage without waiting for orders.[29]

As soon as he heard the beginning of the attack on Hougoumont, Uxbridge rode over to that part of the line, where he met the Duke. To aid in the defence of the château, he ordered over Bull's troop of horse artillery from its position to the left of the *chaussée*, and to Sir Augustus

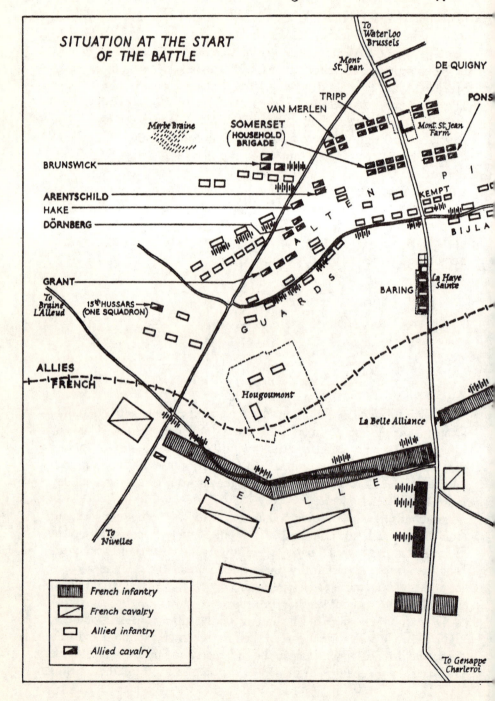

SITUATION AT THE START
OF THE BATTLE

To
Waterloo
Brussels

Mont
St. Jean

DE QUIGNY

TRIPP

VAN MERLEN

PONS

Merbe Braine

SOMERSET
(HOUSEHOLD
BRIGADE)

Mont. St. Jean
Farm

P
I

BRUNSWICK

ARENTSCHILD

KEMPT

HAKE

DÖRNBERG

BIJLA

A
L
T

E

N

G
U
A
R
D
S

La Haye
Sainte

GRANT

BARING

To
Braine
L'Alleud

15ᵗʰ HUSSARS
(ONE SQUADRON)

ALLIES

FRENCH

Hougoumont

La Belle Alliance

R
E
I
L
L
E

To
Nivelles

	French infantry
	French cavalry
	Allied infantry
	Allied cavalry

To Genappe
Charleroi

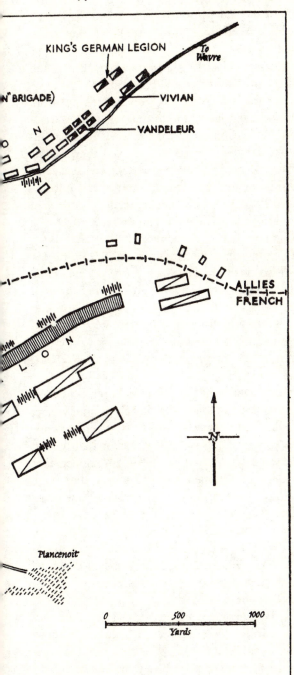

MAP II

THE BATTLE OF
WATERLOO
JUNE 18TH, 1815

Frazer he offered the free use of the other gun troops attached to Grant's and Dörnberg's brigades. He stayed some time watching the initial attacks upon Hougoumont.[30]

While these were going ahead Napoleon had been concentrating enormous quantities of artillery for his first main assault which was to be made by d'Erlon's corps upon the left centre of Wellington's position. His guns were not finally in position, due to the heavy going, until close on one o'clock; then with a tremendous roar they opened up, playing upon the Allied line for a good half-hour before Ney led forward his master's ponderous masses of close-packed infantry, supported by cavalry and preceded by swarms of skirmishers. The western end of this impressive wave struck the breakwater of La Haye Sainte, driving Baring's men from the orchard, eddying round the farm itself, and sweeping into the garden behind it. A supporting regiment of *cuirassiers* then battered down a raw Hanoverian battalion coming up to Baring's aid, and swept up the slope to charge the main British position. Further to the east Bijlandt's mis-placed Netherlanders, not waiting for the blow to fall, fled through the lines, to be seen no more. This crumbling of a breakwater before the sea had hit it left a critical gap in the Allied centre. But Picton was quick to fill the breach by throwing in Kempt's battalions. Pouring a volley into the surging waves of men, Kempt's infantrymen charged with the bayonet, holding them back for a brief breathing-space.

Uxbridge, coming at this moment from the right, recognized at once that the defeat of the raw Hanoverians behind La Haye Sainte, and, worse, the flight of Bijlandt's brigade at the weakest part of the centre, constituted a grave danger. This was especially so as it was clear that behind Kempt's battalions there was no reserve. At this moment it seemed that all would soon be over; certainly the gunners thought so, for they were leaving their guns and hurrying to the rear. One sergeant actually went so far as to spike his gun, rendering it useless for the rest of the day. Without a second's delay, Uxbridge 'galloped up to the Heavy Cavalry', as he wrote many years later, 'and ordered the Household Brigade to prepare to form line, passed on to Sir William Ponsonby's, and having told him to wheel into line when the other Brigade did, instantly returned to the Household Brigade, and put the whole in motion'.[31]

To d'Erlon's divisions, as they advanced across the valley, there had seemed something uncanny about the Allied position, for excepting those in La Haye Sainte and Bijlandt's, no infantry could be seen, and the guns on the forward slope seemed quite unsupported: nor, of course, could

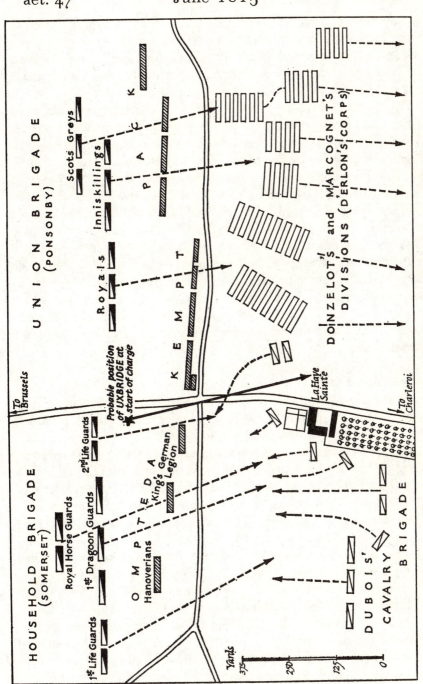

MAP 12: THE CHARGE OF THE HEAVY BRIGADES AT THE BATTLE OF WATERLOO

they see Uxbridge's cavalry: not indeed, until the awe-inspiring moment when, the redcoats making intervals for the 'heavies' to pass through them, the two thousand men and horses of the Household and 'Union' Brigades, Uxbridge himself at their head, poured over the ridge and crashed head-long into their serried ranks.

The effect of this immortal charge was such that in a very short space of time the French columns had dissolved into a mere pack of fugitives. Perhaps never in all military annals has there occurred a more spectacular, speedy and complete destruction of formed infantry by cavalry. Fifteen thousand Frenchmen were flying in wild disorder before six regiments of the finest cavalry the world has ever seen. As the triumphant heavy brigades swept the crowds of bewildered and demoralized men into the valley, they destroyed two field batteries which had stuck fast in the mud while trying to follow up the French attack. At least fifteen guns were so entirely wrecked that they could not be brought into action again that day; two Eagles and more than 2,000 prisoners were taken. Some French accounts say that d'Erlon's disastrous attack cost the French 5,000 men.[32]

The price paid by the British was not low, and Uxbridge must take some of the blame for casualties which were far from light.[11] He later admitted that

'the pursuit had been continued without order and too far.... After the overthrow of the Cuirassiers I had in vain attempted to stop my people by sounding the Rally, but neither voice nor trumpet availed; so I went back to seek the support of the 2nd Line, which unhappily had not followed the movements of the Heavy Cavalry whose horses were now exhausted, and had to receive the shocks of fresh troops.

'Had I, when I sounded the Rally, found only four well-formed Squadrons coming along at an easy trot, I feel certain that the loss the first line suffered when they were finally forced back would have been avoided, and most of [the captured] Guns might have been secured, for it was obvious the effect of that charge had been prodigious, and for the rest of the day, although the Cuirassiers frequently attempted to break into our Lines, they always did it *mollement* and as if they expected something more behind the curtain.

'My impression is that the French were completely surprised by the first Cavalry attack.... These 19 Squadrons pouncing down hill upon them so astonished them that no very great resistance was made, and surely such havoc was rarely made in so few minutes.

'When I was returning to our position I met the Duke of Wellington, surrounded by all the *Corps diplomatique militaire,* who had from the high ground witnessed the whole affair.ᵛ The plain appeared to be swept clean, and I never saw so joyous a group as was this *Troupe dorée.* They thought the Battle was over. It is certain that our Squadrons went into and over several Squares of Infantry, and it is not possible to conceive greater confusion and panic than was exhibited at this moment.

'This forces from me the remark that I committed a great mistake in having myself led the attack. The *carrière* once begun, the leader is no better than any other man; whereas, if I had placed myself at the head of the 2nd line, there is no saying what great advantages might not have accrued from it.'³³

For the rest of his life Uxbridge was haunted by this error. The arguments as to whether the Blues and the Greys were in the first or second line, whether, in fact, any of the regiments had been detailed to act as reserves, are of little consequence; for it is clear that had Uxbridge resisted the temptation to hurl himself at the enemy at the head of the leading squadrons, he would have been able to see to it that there was in fact a second line for him to send in support of the first. But with his nature it was inevitable that he should be in the absolute forefront. None the less, it seems certain that he did in fact intend the Blues and Greys for the second line, and that the brigade commanders expected such an arrangement. The captain commanding the right squadron of the Royals was close to Uxbridge when he ordered the 'Union' Brigade to wheel into line, and he distinctly heard him say, 'The Royals and Inniskillings will charge, the Greys support.' It is also accepted by most authorities that much the same was ordered in the case of the Household Brigade, the Blues being detailed for support. However that may be, it must be remembered that there was very little time for concise orders. Uxbridge had only just ridden from the right at the moment of crisis, and, as Clark Kennedy of the Royals put it, 'had the charge been delayed two or three minutes, I feel satisfied it would probably have failed, for the leading Frenchmen had already gained the crest of the position when the attack was ordered.'³⁴

It was a fearful moment for Uxbridge and his officers when they realized that both brigades had got beyond control: but it was a worse one when they saw that there were no supports to hand. The Greys, with some of the Royals and Inniskillings, not content with cutting down the gunners, drivers and horses of two batteries half-way up the ridge, actually reached and assailed Napoleon's great battery on top of it. As they tried to get back, two regiments of *cuirassiers* and one of *lanciers* fell on them with annihilating effect. Against these a second line would have been invaluable: as it was, only the infantrymen who had followed in the wake of the charge so as to secure prisoners were able to provide any protection to the exhausted horsemen on their return.

In this dire emergency Uxbridge naturally looked to the nearest brigade for succour. This was Vandeleur's to the left. In spite of the discretionary order which he had received at the start of the battle, Vandeleur was tardy in coming to the rescue, due almost certainly to his fear of moving without direct orders from the Duke, under whom he had served long in the Peninsula. However, both Vandeleur and Vivian, who followed him, were able to give some assistance, but not before the cream of the 'heavies' had been lost for ever.[w]

Whatever blame must attach to Uxbridge for leading the charge himself, it cannot be denied that by choosing exactly the right moment to launch it he had so completely smashed an infantry corps and a large portion of its artillery that it was virtually out of action until late in the day and then so reduced in numbers and enthusiasm as to have no major effect on the battle.

vii

The Cuirassiers attacked our Squares of Infantry with a desperation that surpasses all description, but no power of language can ever give an idea of the determined Gallantry and real intrepidity of our infantry....

It is false to state as has been asserted by the ignorant and the mischievous, that our Light Cavalry was unable to contend with that of the Enemy. In no one instance, had they not a decided superiority.[x]

Lord Uxbridge

I've charged at the head of every cavalry regiment, and *they all want spurs.*
Lord Uxbridge to Charles Beckwith[35]

Along most of the front there now followed a lull, though the French artillery never ceased to play. Indeed, as Napoleon brought more guns into action for the next attack, the cannonade reached unprecedented proportions. Anxiety among the Allies as to what the next move would be became intense. Before long a formidable mass of heavy cavalry, perhaps forty squadrons in all,[36] was seen to be collecting under cover of the concentrated artillery fire. Wellington could scarcely believe his eyes, for a frontal attack by massed cavalry on unbroken infantry was almost certain to fail. But Marshal Ney, to whom Napoleon had entrusted most of his cavalry, undoubtedly thought that the British infantrymen were on the point of breaking. When the artillery fire first became really heavy, Wellington had ordered a slight rearward movement, so that his troops could gain some shelter on the reverse slope from the destructive rain of shot: the Marshal had mistaken this for the start of a retreat.

Seeing that Ney intended to launch his hordes of horsemen against the right centre of the Allied line, that is between Hougoumont and La Haye Sainte, Wellington gave orders for the gunners on that part of the front to keep up their fire as long as they could, and then to retire into the squares (or rather oblongs) into which he had ordered the infantry to form themselves.

To draw attention away from his main assault, Napoleon sent two squadrons and one battery of artillery to make a feint attack on the right of the Allied line near Hougoumont. Uxbridge, as he afterwards wrote, at once

'detached Sir C. Grant with three Regiments to fall upon [this] corps of Cavalry, which with nine guns threatened our Right and actually enfiladed our Line. This movement was judiciously executed, 3 Squadrons had actually gained the Enemy's Rear before it was discovered; the guns were precipitately withdrawn, the Cavalry fell back. Sir C. Grant was at the moment of charging, and the annihilation of this Corps was upon the point of being accomplished, when seeing [the main attack] upon the centre of our Position, with the most creditable forbearance, [he] relinquished his prey.'[37]

The main attack now began. The Imperial cavalry, closely packed, came on at their traditional trot, wave after wave of them (twelve successive lines) beating against the immovable squares, sweeping round their sides, and suffering appalling casualties to no purpose. As this valiant tide of horsemen expended itself and began inevitably to ebb, Uxbridge ordered what cavalry regiments he had been able to collect to make a determined counter-attack.[z] This they successfully accomplished, driving the *cuirassiers* clean off the plateau into the dead ground under the southern slope of the ridge. Recovering with amazing speed, the enemy cavalry at once made a fresh assault, but it met with an exactly similar fate. As they again streamed back down the incline, the twice-repulsed squadrons met newly formed comrades ready to renew the attempt: behind these they reformed and, preceded by a terrific cannonade, the fresh led the exhausted — perhaps 12,000 horsemen in all[38] — to a third heroic charge; but their speed was now greatly hampered by the churned-up mud and the dead and dying men and horses which were the legacy of the two earlier attempts. 'The front ranks', says the historian of the British army in a vivid passage, 'were torn to tatters by the Allied artillery as they ascended the slope to the batteries, and when the survivors had passed by the abandoned guns, they were sucked by a dozen channels into the intervals between the squares, where they eddied round them in streams and back-waters, now firing their pistols, now charging resolutely in small bodies, but always beaten off by the steady fire from behind the bayonets.'[39]

Still not sated with defeat, yet another wave of French cavalry threw itself against these rocklike squares of redcoats. As Uxbridge counter-attacked again, the enemy for the fourth time rallied near the bottom of the hill, renewed the assault, and compelled their pursuers to retire behind the infantry. Once again as the attacking horsemen fell back, Uxbridge chased them off the field. Ney repeated these incredibly gallant but uniformly unsuccessful charges again and again: some say that as many as twelve separate attacks were made. On each occasion the British cavalry drove the remnants back to their starting-point, and always under the heaviest artillery fire — for once the French had retired their guns broke forth afresh.

Eventually, seeing that the squares were quite unbreakable by cavalry alone, the enemy began a series of attacks using cavalry and infantry in conjunction. The first of these was held off by the fire of the artillery which Wellington had reinforced from the reserves. The second was temporarily held by a timely charge of the Household Brigade, once again led by Uxbridge in person. This failed to make a lasting impression, for the Dutch-Belgian cavalry, on whose support he depended, not only refused to follow him but, in running away, upset a part of the 3rd Hussars of the King's German Legion. These, quickly recovering order, charged and broke the *cuirassiers* immediately in front of them, but flank attacks forced them to retire almost at once. Uxbridge then called upon the Cumberland Hussars, but found this Regiment even less ready to follow him: without more ado they turned and fled right back to Brussels, where they caused the utmost panic and confusion. 'I have the strongest reason', he wrote, 'to be excessively dissatisfied with the General commanding a Brigade of Dutch Heavy Cavalry, and with a Colonel commanding a young Regiment of Hanoverian Hussars.'[40aa]

An officer who saw Uxbridge at this time, galloping from regiment to regiment and leading several of them on to the charge, observed how the sweat poured down his face while he was thus exerting himself. The same officer wrote home that the commander of the cavalry had had eight or nine horses shot under him in the course of the day. At one moment an aide-de-camp 'was with him when he put himself at the head of a Squadron of Cavalry & charged a solid mass of their infantry. The fire was terrific and destroyed many. The rest would not go on, but he rode on and struck their bayonets before he turned.'[41]

viii

Only one serious misfortune prevents me from saying it was the proudest & happiest day I ever knew. The loss the British army will sustain in the service of Lord Uxbridge must be felt by all, and you may conceive how much more strongly so by me who always admired and looked up to him as an officer and have lately learnt to respect esteem and love him as a man. His conduct the whole day beggars description; his arrangements, firmness and intrepidity surpassed even what had been expected of him, and not in cavalry movements and attacks only, but he frequently rendered the most judicious and timely assistance in affairs of Infantry where any sudden danger was to be apprehended.

Capt. Thomas Wildman to his mother, June 19th, 1815

St Helena, December 2nd, 1815

You have heard I suppose of the ex-Emperor of the French being an inmate of mine at this moment. Knowing how much attached you are to that noble fellow the Earl of Uxbridge (now Marquis of Anglesea) I shall repeat what Napoleon says of him at the Battle of Waterloo. He speaks of the Earl as a very gallant officer and says had he not been wounded, he (Napoleon) certainly would have been taken prisoner by him.

W. Balcombe to Lieut. Williams[42]

The battle had now raged for nearly six hours, and as regards the cavalry three sorry facts clearly emerged. First, nothing could be hoped for from the Dutch-Belgian brigades: they were clearly more of a liability than an asset. Second, the strength, though not the discipline, of the British heavy brigades had been so impaired that they could no longer render much service. Third, the brigades of Grant, Dörnberg and Arent-schild were in little better plight. Thus Uxbridge was left with Vandeleur (whose casualties also had not been small), and Vivian, whose brigade had been the least engaged of the seven. This was the state of the cavalry at the most critical moment of the day. By a desperate effort, and on Napoleon's orders that it must be captured at all costs, Ney at last succeeded in taking La Haye Sainte, the key to the Allied position. He was greatly aided by the fact that Baring, who had so long and so gallantly held the buildings all day, had come to the end of his ammunition. Thus the French had gained the one thing they most needed: a new base at the very centre of the Allied line from which they could shatter it to pieces. For one frightful moment they had before them a completely unguarded section of the Allied line. Had Napoleon himself been present, instead of a mile and a half away holding off the Prussians, all might have been lost. As it was, Ney let the fleeting moment pass, and the gap was closed in time. It had been a very near thing.

During this crisis the remnants of Somerset's Household Brigade, by standing firm and immovable behind the infantry at the vital point of the line, materially assisted in averting disaster. Some time before, Uxbridge had recommended Somerset 'to withdraw his Brigade (who were extended in single file to make a show) from the heavy fire that was kept on them by the Enemy's Artillery. Lord Edward's remark', wrote Seymour who delivered the message, 'was that should he move, the Dutch cavalry, who were in support, would move off immediately. The Household Brigade retained their position until the end of the Action.' Thornhill records that at this moment Uxbridge, 'perceiving that a gallant Regiment of Infantry (which shall be nameless), pressed by the onset of superior numbers, was wavering, galloped to the rally — reminded this regiment of its distinguished name, and that of its no less gallant Colonel, told them who he was, and led them to the charge. They followed him to a man, drove back the Enemy, and maintained their post.'[43]

At about this time the Prussian cavalry at long last appeared on Vivian's left. 'I first sent,' wrote Uxbridge, 'and then being uneasy about it went myself to reconnoitre it. Having happily ascertained that it was a Prussian Force, I immediately withdrew all the Cavalry from the left [i.e. Vandeleur's and Vivians' hussars] in order to strengthen the Centre.'[44] Vivian, with his usual alertness, had forestalled Uxbridge's intention, for as soon as he was satisfied that the Prussians had joined his left,[bb] he suggested to Vandeleur, his senior officer, that their two brigades should move westwards. Vandeleur, typically, declined to move without orders, but this did not stop Vivian from starting off without him. He soon met Uxbridge who led the

'brigade from the left', as Vivian remembered eighteen years later, 'and posted it immediately on the crest of the position, to the right of the road to Genappe, where the 10th and 18th Hussars formed in line, and the 1st German Hussars [K.G.L.] in reserve; the left of the 18th touching nearly to the high road. The moment of our arrival was also the moment of Napoleon's last advance, and the fire to which we were exposed, both of cannon and musketry, was very severe. After having seen my brigade occupy the position he had assigned to it, Lord Uxbridge left me to proceed to Vandeleur's brigade, which had followed mine from the left of the line, and which his Lordship posted on the right and rear of mine to act as a reserve to it. Lord Uxbridge shortly returned to me, and finding the fire still heavy, and the enemy evidently in great force immediately in our front, he asked me whether we had not better advance and charge. The smoke at this moment was so dense on the side of the hill, that it was scarcely possible to see ten yards before us; and consequently, no enemy being visible, I observed, "that as my brigade was in perfect order, I thought it would be advisable not to hazard an attack whereby we might be thrown into confusion, which it would be difficult to repair; that if the enemy appeared on the crest of the hill through the smoke, by a sudden and unexpected charge on them we could, no doubt, drive them back." His Lordship then dismounted from his horse, and advanced himself on foot and unattended down the hill, hoping to be able to see under the smoke and make his own observations. I rode down to him and begged him not to expose himself so; on which he returned, saying he agreed with me in thinking that I had better remain steady, ready to attack if the enemy appeared; and, mounting his horse, he left me to join the Duke, and I saw no more of him during the day. I mention this anecdote not only as descriptive of my position, but in justice to Lord Uxbridge: it will prove to those who imagine that in the management of the cavalry on that day he was at all incautious, (and such I know there are), how little they understand his real character; as a proof of his intrepidity and the readiness with which he exposed himself, it is not necessary; to these qualities every one does justice.'[45]

The arrival of Vivian and Vandeleur at this most desperate moment for the Allies, when, for the third time during the day, it seemed that all was lost, greatly revived the spirits of the harassed infantry.

Then, suddenly, and to the surprise of nearly everyone present except the Duke, the end was at hand. At the moment when Wellington ordered the whole line to advance, Uxbridge is said to have expressed his alarm and to have suggested that they should not go beyond the range of heights originally occupied by the French. 'Oh, damn it!' the Duke is supposed to have said. 'In for a penny, in for a pound is my maxim; and if the troops advance they shall go as far as they can.'[46]

Wildman describes what happened next. The sun had just set when Vivian's hussars

'charged down upon the enemy taking two squares of Infantry and a column of Cavalry in their way. Our Infantry rushed down also; the Prussians closed in on the left. Genl. Vandeleur's Brigade cut up those who were dispersed, and the rout became general. A panic seized the enemy in every direction, and they fled on all sides deserting their artillery throwing down their arms and each man thinking of his own preservation. Our Cavalry & the Prussians joined in the pursuit, the latter continued it the whole night, giving no quarter.'[47]

ix

Here rests, and let no saucy knave
    Presume to sneer and laugh,
To learn that mouldering in the grave
    Is laid a British *calf*.

For he who writes these lines is sure
    That those who read the whole
Will find such laugh were premature,
    For here, too, lies a *sole*.

And here five little ones repose,
    Twin-born with other five;
Unheeded by their brother *toes*,
    Who now are all *alive*.

A *leg* and *foot* to speak more plain
    Lie here, of one commanding;
Who, though his wits he might retain,
    Lost half his *understanding*.

And when the guns, with thunder fraught,
    Pour'd bullets thick as hail,
Could only in this way be taught
    To give his foe *leg-bail*.

And now in England, just as gay —
    As in the battle brave —
Goes to the rout, review, or play,
    With one foot in the grave.

Fortune in vain here shewed her spite,
   For he will still be found,
Should England's sons engage in fight,
   Resolved to stand his *ground*.

But fortune's pardon I must beg,
   She meant not to disarm;
And when she lopp'd the hero's leg
   By no means sought his *h-arm*,

And but indulged a harmless whim,
   Since he could walk with one,
She saw *two legs* were lost on him
   Who never meant to *run*.

Epitaph for the Tablet in memory of the Marquis of Anglesey's leg,
by Thomas Gaspey[cc]

'Just as Sir H. Vivian's Brigade were going down to the charge,' wrote Wildman the day after the battle, 'Lord Uxbridge was struck by a grape shot on the right knee which shattered the joint all to pieces. I did not see him fall & went on to the charge, but soon missed him and perceived Seymour taking him to the rear.' The Duke told his brother William (also on the day after the battle) that Uxbridge was wounded when talking to him 'during the last attack, almost by the last shot'. To Stanhope Wellington explained that he was on the side from which the shot proceeded, and that it passed over the neck of his horse till it reached Uxbridge. The Duke supported him and prevented his falling from the saddle.[48] Writing as a very old man, and thirty-seven years after the event, Uxbridge himself remembered that he was hit 'in the low ground beyond La Haye Sainte, and perhaps $\frac{1}{4}$ of an hour before Dusk, at the moment when I was quitting the Duke to join Vivian's Brigade of Hussars which I had sent for, being the only fresh Corps I had'. In the popular version, Uxbridge exclaims 'By God, sir, I've lost my leg!' Wellington momentarily removes the telescope from his eye, considers the mangled limb, says 'By God, sir, so you have!' and resumes his scrutiny of the victorious field.

Men of a Hanoverian infantry battalion, advancing rapidly behind the cavalry, helped to remove the wounded hero from his horse, and six of them, with the faithful aide-de-camp Seymour walking at their head, bore him from the field. A number of old soldiers claimed in years to come that they had assisted in this 'melancholy duty', among them one with the name of Esau Senior of the Inniskilling Dragoons.[49]

Back at his headquarters in Waterloo, the surgeons who examined the wound all agreed that it would be at the imminent danger of his life to attempt to save the limb. His comment was typical: 'Well, gentlemen,' he said, 'I thought so myself. I have put myself in your hands and, if it is to be taken off, the sooner it is done the better.' He at once wrote a letter to Char, saying that had he been a young single man he might have run the risk of keeping his leg, but that as it was he would, if possible, preserve his life for her and his children. Then, while the surgeons prepared for their task, he put the coming agony quite out of his mind, and conversed at length with his staff about the action, forgetting his wound 'in the exultation for the Victory'. Wildman, who was present at the amputation, tells how

'he never moved or complained: no one even held his hand. He said once perfectly calmly that he thought the instrument was not very sharp. When it was over, his nerves did not appear the least shaken and the surgeons said his pulse was not altered. He said, smiling, "I have had a pretty long run, I have been a beau these forty-seven years and it would not be fair to cut the young men out any longer" and then asked us if we did not admire his vanity. I have seen many operations,' continues Wildman, 'but neither Lord Greenock nor myself could bear this, we were obliged to go to the other end of the room.

'Thank God he is doing as well as possible. He had no fever and the surgeons say nothing could be more favourable.'[dd]

Later that night Vivian looked in, fresh from the pursuit. He was greeted with: 'Vivian, take a look at that leg, and tell me what you think of it. Some time hence, perhaps, I may be inclined to imagine it might have been saved, and I should like your opinion upon it.' Confronted with the gruesome object, Vivian readily confirmed that it was best off, and left his chief to compose himself for sleep.[50]

The owner of the house where the operation was performed, a M. Paris, placed the leg in a wooden coffin and asked its owner's permission 'de placer le membre du noble et intéressant Milord dans notre petit jardin'. Permission was granted, and in due course a weeping willow was planted over the site. M. Paris erected a commemorative plaque, which may still be seen today; upon it these words appear:

'Ci est enterré la Jambe
de l'illustre et vaillant Comte Uxbridge,
Lieutenant-Général de S.M. Britannique,
Commandant en chef la cavalerie anglaise,
belge et hollandaise, blessé le 18 juin,

1815, à la mémorable bataille de Waterloo;
qui, par son héroisme, a concouru au
triomphe de la cause du genre humain;
glorieusement décidée par l'éclatante
victoire du dit jour.'

Some wag is said to have scribbled beneath the inscription:

'Here lies the Marquis of Anglesey's limb;
The Devil will have the remainder of him.'

The wife of the Bishop of Norwich, visiting the house on the first anniversary of the battle, was shown 'as a relic almost as precious as a Catholic bit of bone or blood, the blood upon a chair in the room where the leg was cut off, which M. Paris had promised my lord "de ne jamais effacer" '. When in later years Uxbridge visited the place, it was said that he found the very table on which he had lain for the amputation of the limb, and that by his direction dinner was spread upon it for himself and two of his sons who were with him.[51]

The evening of the day after the battle 'the most perfect Hero that ever breathed', as Seymour designated him, was brought into Brussels on a litter. Also there, with three stabs and a sabre-cut, was his adjutant-general Sir John Elley, who, in speaking of Uxbridge to Wildman, 'cried like a child and said that though he rejoiced that his valuable life had been preserved yet the loss to the British Army was irreparable. His emotion was so great', wrote the aide-de-camp, 'that I was obliged to leave him for his own sake after trying in vain to change the subject.'

The patient soon became restless. 'Lord U.', wrote his niece Georgiana Capel, who was in Brussels with her parents, 'begins to be very fidgetty and tired of his Beds, he has *four* and he is moved about from one to the other.' On June 23rd he was allowed to sit on a couch for the first time, and three days later was dressed and sitting up in his chair as if nothing had happened. On the 25th he was reunited with Char, who had come over to Brussels as soon as she had heard the news of her husband's wound.[••] She had crossed the Channel in the royal yacht, placed at her disposal by the Prince Regent: with her came her son Clarence, aged four.[52]

Within three weeks of losing his leg, Uxbridge was back in London. The Prince Regent, declaring 'that he *loved* him,... that he was his best officer and his best subject', at once made him a Marquess.[53] For the second time in four years his name had changed: by succession Lord Paget had become the Earl of Uxbridge, and by creation the Earl of Uxbridge had become the Marquess of Anglesey.

X

A letter was received this morning at Uxbridge House, dated the 22nd instant, WRITTEN BY LORD UXBRIDGE HIMSELF, by which it appears that his Lordship is going on as favourably as could be wished. June 26th.
The North Wales Gazette[54]

The new marquess made the passage from Ostend to Deal in the royal yacht on July 8th. Next afternoon, exactly three weeks after the great battle, he entered London. As he crossed Westminster Bridge a number of people who had recognized him took the horses from his travelling carriage and drew it through the streets. He entered the Park by Storey's Gate, which though normally reserved for the Royal Family had been specially thrown open so that his carriage by avoiding the pavement might jolt him as little as possible. The triumphal procession, accompanied by numerous pedestrians and gentlemen on horseback, now turned up St James's Street and made its way to Burlington Gardens. On the steps of Uxbridge House he removed his hat to the crowds, thanked those who had conducted him thither, and with the help of his crutches painfully entered the front door. His first caller was Colonel Bloomfield, the Prince's private secretary, sent to inquire after his health and to congratulate him on his safe return. Sir Thomas Lawrence called next morning and found him at breakfast with Char and a daughter, looking in the best of health. On July 10th he was visited first by the Duke of York and then by the Regent, who remained with him at Uxbridge House for an hour and a half. On the 26th he returned the visit, staying at Carlton House for more than three hours.[55]

*   *   *

The months which followed were filled with congratulatory addresses, civic processions and numerous renderings of 'See the conquering Hero comes'. At Lichfield on August 11th twenty thousand people gathered to see Staffordshire's distinguished son receive a richly enamelled presentation sword. On this occasion he entered the city in an open carriage drawn by twenty-four young men. In spite of the rain, which the crowds laughed off as another *Water*-loo triumph, he wore nothing to cover his blue coat and pantaloons and buff waistcoat. Beside him sat Char and, sharing the dickey, his brother Berkeley and his son and heir, now Earl of Uxbridge. The cavalcade was preceded by a buffoon, mounted on a donkey, dressed to represent Bonaparte going to *Hell*-ena. In his speech of thanks, delivered at the Guildhall, transformed for the occasion into a forest of laurel, Anglesey attributed the successful conclusion of the war to the 'persevering resolution of the Prince Regent and his ministers' and the final delivery of Europe from its chains to the skill and vigour with which they united the 'jarring interests of the confederated continental states'. The victory of Waterloo he unhesitatingly ascribed to 'that illustrious and beloved commander', the Duke of Wellington, and to the men who fought under him. 'In that arduous contest,' he said, 'our troops under any other commander must have failed, and with any other troops, under that great chieftain, the struggle must have been unsuccessful. For myself, Gentlemen,' he concluded, 'I had little more than a plain duty to fulfil. With such zeal in my officers, and devotion in my soldiers, I had only to lead them into combat.'[56]

In 1817 on the second anniversary of the battle a massive stone column, over a hundred feet high, containing a spiral staircase, was completed within sight of Plas Newydd. It was erected by the people of Anglesey and Caernarvonshire 'in grateful commemoration of the distinguished military achievements of their countryman'. Six years after his death there was added to its summit a twelve-foot bronze statue showing Anglesey in his uniform as Colonel of the 7th Hussars. From the platform at the base of the statue can be seen a superb panorama of the mountains of Snowdonia.

*   *   *

In the months which followed, Anglesey's stump gave him excruciating pain. It was well into 1816 before the wound was properly healed. 'Your account of Paget is upon the whole satisfactory', wrote his mother to Arthur Paget on April 1st, 'though whilst there is the appearance of another splinter, poor soul! he cannot be without pain. It is quite dreadful what he has gone through.'[57] There is reason to suppose that at first he wore what was known as a 'clapper leg', so called because locomotion was accompanied by a clapping sound; but in due course a limb-maker

named James Potts, of Chelsea, who had invented an artificial leg articulated at the knee, ankle and toe joints, provided him with one of these.
Patented as 'the Anglesey Leg', it was still being commercially advertised
at least as late as 1914. One of those worn by Anglesey is still maintained
in working condition at Plas Newydd. Other relics preserved there
include one of the boots he wore during the battle, his sabretache and a
leg of his hussar trousers, bespattered with the mud contracted on the
plain of Waterloo, on that memorable 18th of June, 1815.

PART II

———————— * ————————

CHAPTER NINE

IN less than a month from his arrival in London Anglesey found himself, not for the first time and certainly not for the last, involved in the affairs of the royal family. The footing on which he stood with the Regent may be gauged by a letter which he wrote to him at the time of the visit of the Allied sovereigns to London in 1814, at the height of the Prince's unpopularity over the treatment of his wife. The Princess's exclusion from all the official festivities in honour of the sovereigns was marked and resented by the public. When they made a state visit to the opera she attended independently, sitting in her own box, applauded by the company, but embarrassing the royal party. It is to this that Anglesey refers in the following letter:

'Sir,
'I will not intrude myself upon you in this time of hurry or take up your time by apologising, but I will at every risk conjure Your R.H. not to lose a single opportunity of shewing yourself in publick. My source of information is infallible & I know what will instantly be said upon Your not riding in the Park today. After what happened at the Opera last night Your R.H. had the game in your own Hand.

155

I intreat you, Sir, at once to put down every attempt at mischief by braving the mischievous and they will at once sink into insignific-ance....

'UXBRIDGE

'If you could even now go, Sir, it would be such a thing!'[2]

Then as long ago as 1804 Anglesey had been the means of patching up a quarrel between the Prince of Wales and the Duke of York. The Duke, as Commander-in-Chief and on his father's behalf, had refused the Prince, who was anxious to distinguish himself in the time of national danger, a higher command than that of the 10th Light Dragoons; there followed a lengthy and acrimonious correspondence between the brothers which was made public. The incident was closed only when the Prince saw that he could make no headway against his brother's determination. 'Paget has brought about a complete reconciliation between the P. and the D. of Y.', wrote old Lady Uxbridge to Arthur Paget, 'and they both thanked him most cordially for having effected it.' Exactly how he managed this feat is not clear, but Lord Malmesbury in his diary says that Paget had mediated between them with great good sense.[3]

A year after the visit of the Allied sovereigns he was called in again: this time as one of a number of the Duke of Cumberland's friends, who were to try to persuade that much feared and most unpopular younger son of George III to leave the country. The Duke's marriage to his cousin, Princess Frederica of Solms, in May 1815 had caused intense embarrassment. A more provocative and unsuitable marriage can hardly be imagined. Not only was this once-beautiful lady thirty-seven years of age, and possessed of a notorious past, but she was twice a widow. Further, some years before, she had been publicly betrothed to the Duke of Cambridge, Cumberland's youngest and more popular brother, whom she had jilted in favour of her second husband, the Prince of Solms. Queen Charlotte, who at first had seemed to countenance the marriage (thus, incidentally, encouraging the Prince Regent to agree to it), soon changed her mind and declared that nothing would induce her to receive her niece and new daughter-in-law. The King of Prussia, Frederica's brother-in-law, had rightly become angry at the insult offered her by Queen Charlotte, and had even ordered his ambassador not to attend the Queen's receptions. For reasons connected with Hanoverian-Prussian relations, England could ill afford at this juncture a breach with Prussia's ruler. Thus it became a great object to the Prince and Lord Liverpool, the

Prime Minister, to bundle the Cumberlands back to Hanover (of which
the Duke was Deputy-Elector) as soon as possible.

At the beginning of August 1815, Anglesey acted as a sort of unofficial
liaison between the Prince and the Duke. A month later, together with
Lord Bathurst the secretary for war, Lord Eldon the Lord Chancellor,
and Lord Lauderdale, an extreme Whig but a loyal friend to the Regent
and his brother, he was busily employed in relieving the general embarrassment (increased by the leakage to the press of one of the Queen's
letters to the Duke) by trying to induce the Duke and Duchess to take
their leave. This he failed to do, for as Lord Liverpool wrote to the
Prince, the Duke's determination to remain in England 'appear'd to be
very fixed, though he had received the strongest representations from the
Lord Chancellor, and an opinion to the same effect from Lord Anglesey
and Lord Lauderdale'. The difficulties attending these efforts are clearly
shown in a letter from Cumberland to Lauderdale, dated November 10th.

'What', he asks, 'would be the result, if ... we were to leave this country? Such a departure would be immediately held forth as a *proof
of conscious guilt* [a reference to his supposed responsibility for the
leakage to the press of his mother's letter] *& fear* of *shewing ourselves*;
you say ... that Anglesey joins you in opinion, I beg you therefore
... to forward this letter to him for his perusal, for he is a man of
such high principles of honor, and so much my friend, he would no
more than you ... wish me to do an act either *disgraceful* or *detri-
mental* to me.'

Anglesey, when he had seen this letter, wrote to Lauderdale on November
22nd:

'Being what His Royal Highness does me the honor to call his
friend I cannot help sincerely regretting that the advice you [Lauder-
dale] originally gave respecting his return to the Continent and in
which I most fully concurred, has not been acted upon.... If you
think the Duke would like to know my opinion, here it is.... I am
truly sorry he is not abroad, because his own concerns would go the
better for it; he would sooner get the money [the Commons had
refused him the customary royal marriage allowance] and the
Duchess would sooner see the Queen. Instead of being degraded by
the step, he would be extolled for it. I heartily regret the publication
of the [Queen's] letter. I wish His Royal Highness could devise the

means of proving that he deprecates the measure. I hope and trust that Parliament will make a suitable settlement, but I think it would be more easily done if he was away. At all events I have no hesitation in saying that I will do all I can in support of it.'[4]

All was to no avail. In April 1816 the Cumberlands were still in England, nor did they finally leave until the summer of 1818.

An instance of Anglesey's influence with the Prince Regent was the part he took in persuading him to yield Princess Charlotte to Prince Leopold in 1816. Archduke John of Austria told Metternich that Castlereagh 'and the honest Marquis of Anglesey' were the chief movers in overcoming the Regent's paternal resistance. Many years later Queen Victoria told Lord Melbourne that Anglesey had spoken to her of his part in this transaction. Melbourne remarked that it might be true, but that he had never heard of it before.[5]

*   *   *

At the end of 1814 Uxbridge (as he then was) had thought himself slighted at not being given membership of some high Order — preferably that of the Garter; but when the Regent wrote to offer him the Bath, on an enlargement of that Order in January 1815, he affected to be offended and indifferent. To his brother Arthur he wrote:

'I cannot disguise from you that I wish I was out of their confounded batch of Stars. I have been so long let alone that I had no other desire but to be so left and the only pretension I really felt was that of not having that given to me which I was well without. But when I saw the P.R. most anxious that I should receive kindly what he professed to think so honourable, I had not courage to disappoint him by any remonstrance but only told H.R.H. that I did *not* come to thank him for the order, but for the very kind and affectionate letter he had written to me. But I will give you *my very words*. They were rather strong! "To tell Y.R.H. the real truth and to speak with perfect frankness, when I first read Your letter I could not help exclaiming, *Damn the Bath*, but when I reflected upon the flattering manner in which you expressed Yourself, upon Your constant attention & I presume to say, affectionate and friendly conduct towards me, I instantly decided that You *must* be the best *judge* of what I *ought* to have & therefore I thought it my duty to present myself here [Brighton]." *He* well knows what I think of the thing itself & therefore is the more pleased at the manner in which I take it. In fact I *abhor* the thing, but am determined to take it kindly of Him & altho' I admit that after reading His letter, appearances are against him, yet I cannot help thinking that Ld Bathurst and perhaps the D[uke] of Y[ork] have run their rig upon *Him* as to the matter of numbering the Knights, & that he has never intentionally deceived me about it, for how can a Man write that you are to be the *very first*, whilst he at the same time knows that you are to be the 50th or whatever number I am? But here is enough upon a foolish point of vanity. Some have the Vanity to like this concern, I have the vanity (& it is equally & perhaps more vain) to dislike it extremely. The short view of the thing is this. If I deserve it at all & *ought* to have it at all (all things considered), I ought to have had it a long while ago.'

What he did not tell Arthur was that the Regent had held out strong expectations to him, when offering the Bath, that the Garter would follow it as soon as a vacancy occurred. Anglesey chose an odd moment to remind the Prince of this. To a letter of condolence on the death of the Prince's daughter, Princess Charlotte, in 1817, he added:

'I feel a most serious scruple in touching upon any subject at this moment foreign to this calamity & as that which I am about to name is personal to myself, I have an additional repugnance in doing so. As however I am strongly assured that it is agreeable to your Royal Highness that I should do so, I no longer hesitate in taking the liberty to express a hope that when an opportunity offers, your Royal Highness will not think me less worthy of the high honor of the Order of the Garter, than when you graciously mentioned to me before that I should have it.'

To this solicitation the Prince wrote in reply a letter typical of his rather florid and confused style.

'I can only assure you that *your having now afforded me* the opportunity of meeting your wishes upon the earliest occasion which may present itself, is *most gratifying to me*, & I cannot help saying that *you ought always* to have been *persuaded* that it was not only my *anxious desire*, but *my intention* to do so whenever *you would put that* in my power: mais je ne veux pas me fâcher avec vous, mon cher ami, car je vous connais trop bien et trop long temps pour cela; vous avez au fond le coeur bien placé, bon et loyal; quant au reste c'est à votre sang, et à la nature que vous en êtes redevable, et ainsi ma foi, c'est plus fort que vous, et vous n'avez pas moyen d'y resister.

'My bile is now all discharged, & therefore I shall take my leave assuring you that I am as you have ever found me, your sincere friend,

'GEORGE, P.R.

'P.S. Remember me in all that is kindest to Lady Anglesea, & those around you, & tho' last not least in love to little Edward [Clarence Paget, now six years old, whose second name was Edward].'

The irritable parts of this letter can perhaps be explained by Anglesey's having importuned Sir Benjamin Bloomfield, the Prince's private secretary, for a reply about the Garter; for the Prime Minister on political grounds wished the Duke of Northumberland to have the next one which fell vacant. Lord Liverpool wrote to Bloomfield that he wanted to discuss the matter with the Prince before an answer was returned to Anglesey, adding 'Lord Anglesey cannot be so unreasonable as to expect an answer from the Prince Regent, before he has had an opportunity of communicating with his confidential servants.' To the Regent Anglesey replied at once:

'Altho' thro' the whole course of my life I am unconscious of having ever deserved the *lash* in any thing wherein your Royal Highness has been concerned, yet I take it now as I am convinced it has been intended, and if this *lenient application upon my back*, has been the means of discharging the little latent bile which your Royal Highness has owned to, & which I have most unfortunately & certainly very unintentionally caused, I feel most happy in having suffered for such a result. I will seize the earliest opportunity that may be agreeable to your Royal Highness of paying my respects at the Pavillion and of assuring you of the sincere attachment and devotion with which I have the honor to remain, [etc.].'

It seems that this letter was also unsatisfactory to the Prince, there being in it no grateful acknowledgment of the intended boon, for only three days later, Anglesey wrote again:

'I should not so soon again have trespassed upon your Royal Highness's time by another letter, if I had not been made aware that in the

The Marquess of Anglesey six years after Waterloo

above: Beaudesert House, Staffordshire, *and below* Plas Newydd, Isle
of Anglesey, in the early 19th century

last I had the honor of addressing you, I had committed the very fault I was so distressed at being thought guilty of.... In fact, Sir, great as is the honor you are pleased to intend for me, I appear to have lost sight *even* to *that* in my eagerness to shew that I had never failed in that attachment to you I have so long professed. Allow me to implore your pardon for this omission and to assure you of my gratitude, and of the pleasure with which I shall avail myself of your kind invitation to the Pavillion.'⁶

At Brighton, doubtless, he was able to soothe the ruffled dignity of the Prince, for on February 19th, 1818, a year before the Duke of Northumberland, Anglesey was elected a Knight of the Garter.

*   *   *

The occasion of Anglesey's fiftieth birthday, on May 17th, 1818, is an appropriate moment for a glance at his ever-increasing family. Mary, the third child of his second marriage, was born on June 16th, 1812, one day short of a year after the birth of Clarence [see p. 116]. There followed Alfred, who, after a short life of thirteen days, died on his father's birthday, a month before the battle of Waterloo. 1816 saw the birth of another Alfred, who survived to become Queen Victoria's Chief Equerry and Clerk Marshal, and the youngest of whose children (the late Lord Queenborough) lived till 1949.

Meanwhile Anglesey's *first* family was growing up. In 1817 his eldest daughter Caroline married, at the age of twenty, the fifth Duke of Richmond, whose mother had given the famous ball in Brussels on June 15th, 1815. Caroline Richmond's first-born, who became sixth Duke, was Anglesey's first grandchild. He was born in 1818 less than a month before Anglesey's seventh son, George, who thus shared with his sister Adelaide (born in 1820) a nephew older than himself. Adelaide was the last of Char's children to survive infancy, though three more were born — in 1822, 1823 and 1825. Each of these died within a few months of birth: since their mother was forty-four in 1825, this is hardly surprising.

In 1819, at the age of twenty-two, Lord Uxbridge, much against the wishes of his father, married the first of his three wives. The bride was the daughter of the famous beauty and novelist, Lady Charlotte Bury, whose *Diary Illustrative of the Times of George IV*, based upon her experiences as lady-in-waiting to Queen Caroline, had a *succès de scandale* when

F

THE MARQUESS OF ANGLESEY
aged 51

published in 1838. Uxbridge's eldest son, Henry, who eventually succeeded his father as third Marquess, was born in 1821. By the time
Anglesey was sixty he had nineteen surviving grandchildren: at his death
twenty-four years later, this number had been more than trebled.

*   *   *

Though Anglesey became a full general in the army in August 1819,
his active military career had come to an end with the battle of Waterloo
four years before. With only one leg and a long period of peace stretching
before him into the future, he would have little enough opportunity for
further distinction in the field. He therefore looked around and soon
began to press for some employment suited to his high rank and un-
doubted abilities. There were certain situations which he felt would suit
him very well. He would not object, for instance, to being viceroy of
India or of Ireland, Master-General of the Ordnance, or even Commander-
in-Chief. Such posts as these were held more directly from the Sovereign
than others, and, at least in theory, were somewhat removed from the
sphere of party politics — a sphere in which he was far from being at ease.
They had the further attraction for him that they did not require constant
speech-making in the House of Lords, an exercise he neither enjoyed nor
was good at. Pressed in 1830 to take a greater part in the Lords' debates,
he declared himself 'wholly unequal to it. Nothing', he wrote, 'is to be
done in this country without a certain share of oratory — I have not a
grain of it. I have no facility of expressing myself — the thing does not
come naturally to me. When I have been forced to utter, it has always
been in misery and in distrust of myself, and that will not do. I am too old
to mend.'[7]

Though speaking seldom, he often attended debates and cast his vote
in divisions, either in person or by proxy. In 1820 he supported the Bill
of 'Pains and Penalties' against Queen Caroline, by which George IV,
newly come to the throne, hoped to divorce his wife on the ground of her
misconduct and adultery.[a] In four divisions on the Bill between August
and November 1820 he was to be found in the lobby voting with the
majority. Brougham's eloquence on the Queen's behalf, which eventually
killed the Bill, had no effect on Anglesey; nor had the hostility of the mob
who, aware of the profligacy of the King, considered his wife a gravely
injured woman. On one occasion Anglesey is said to have been surrounded in the street by an angry crowd who barred his progress till he

should give: 'The Queen!' Complying, he said, 'God save the Queen — and may all your wives be like her!' That something of the sort happened has contemporary confirmation in a letter written on August 20th, 1820, in which it is stated that Anglesey was 'hissed and abused and his two wives rubbed under his nose. Yesterday, *il ne pouvait plus*, so he turned his horse short round and addressed the mob. They shrank away as they generally do when fronted.'[8b]

The Queen's pathetic and ineffective efforts to gain admittance to Westminster Abbey for her husband's coronation on July 19th, 1821, slightly marred that magnificent if theatrical affair. Anglesey, as Lord High Steward, took a leading part both in the ceremony itself, and at the great banquet which followed. In the Abbey he had the weighty task of bearing St Edward's Crown before his sovereign; at the banquet a more demanding exercise awaited him. He was required, coronet on head and staff in hand, to proceed down the full length of Westminster Hall, mounted upon 'a goodly horse trapped and furnished suitable to the occasion', in company with Lord Henry Howard, deputy Earl Marshal, and the Duke of Wellington in the role of Lord High Constable. It was the business of this trio to lead into the hall the procession of Gentlemen Pensioners who bore the first course of the banquet to the royal table. When the dishes had been duly set down, the three horsemen were required to back from the royal presence down the centre of the hall and to leave it by the way they had entered. This difficult manœuvre Anglesey achieved with consummate skill. Sir Walter Scott, who was present, later extolled the exquisite grace with which Anglesey managed his horse, despite the loss of his leg. 'I never saw so fine a bridle-hand in my life,' he wrote, 'and I am rather a judge of "noble horsemanship".' His feat is celebrated by an anonymous epigram:

> Tho' Anglesey's steed with retrograde pace,
>   So delightfully curvets and prances,
> 'Tis before the King's friends he retreats with such grace,
>   His enemies dread his advances.

There now occurred a humorous hitch. 'Lord Anglesea', reported a female onlooker, 'fancied his duty done when the dinner was on the table and did not return, so a herald was sent to say His Majesty could not dine till he came and took the covers off.' This announcement caused Anglesey great distress for, failing to foresee that it would be necessary to dismount in the course of his duties, he had neglected to provide himself with one of his 'walking legs', which were of a different type from those which he wore for riding. He at once returned, still on horseback, to explain in person to the King that he was 'unable to walk with *his riding leg on*'. This produced a great roar of laughter which echoed around the crowded hall, but which turned to gasps of admiration when it was seen that instead of excusing himself from the duty of removing the covers, he bravely dismounted and, supported by his pages and others, moved forward to perform the necessary office. 'He got along very well,' it was observed, 'tho' much more lame than usual.'[9]

*   *   *

Anglesey's political career did not start in earnest until he had reached the age of fifty-eight. In July 1826 the Duke of York was attacked by the dropsy, and towards the end of the year (in spite of a 'broom medicine' administered on Anglesey's recommendation[c]), it was clear that he had not long to live. His death would leave a vacancy at the Horse Guards. To nearly everyone, except the King who thought to do so himself, Wellington's claims to succeed to the office of commander-in-chief were pre-eminent. With the Duke thus promoted, it was likely that the office of Master-General of the Ordnance, which he had held since 1818, would be relinquished. Here was Anglesey's opening.

On December 31st, six days before the Duke of York died, Anglesey, writing in the third person, made it known to the King

'that in the event of the situation of Master General of the Ordnance becoming vacant, he [had] the ambition, (and he trusts it may not be thought other than a laudable one,) of aspiring to fill that important office. The Marquis of Anglesey', he continued, 'has reason to know that his appointment to it, would not be disagreeable to the distinguished corps [the Royal Artillery and Royal Engineers] he would have the honour to command....[d] The Marquis of Anglesey has not applied, nor will he apply to any of His Majesty's Ministers upon the subject.... He is content to make known to the King, this, his anxious desire, and whatever may be His Majesty's decision, the Marquis of Anglesey will be fully satisfied of its justice and wisdom.'[10]

The day after the Duke of York's funeral, at which Anglesey was one of the supporters of the canopy, he had a long interview with the King. He described it to his brother Charles.

'The King offered me [the colonelcy of] the Blues^e & shewed that they were a Corps of distinction, that had been in the hands of the most Illustrious Men &c &c &c. I of course acquiesced in this Character of them, but said I was disinclined to change my Regiment, that the duty would not suit me, & how much soever I was personally attached to H.M. it was not of sufficient importance, of no responsibility & of no patronage. That I was of that Rank in Society, in the Army, & in respect of Services rendered, that entitled me to consideration — that the Ordnance was what the Army in general had long destined me for, & which alone would suit me, & so forth. I cannot trace our conversation regularly as the subjects successively presented themselves. In the course of it I said I knew how ill I played *my cards* if I wanted distinction, but that nothing should tempt me to change my course. To succeed, a Man should attach Himself to a Party & not profess to be a King's personal friend. That a King of England if he was willing, had not the power of selecting those he might prefer. That Ministers could not bear a Man not dependent upon *them* & that therefore every attempt to give *me* distinction was always opposed — Witness the Garter!.... Witness India! Witness Ireland! & so forth!!! I said that two governments (both usually offered to Men of high Rank) had been disposed of without paying the Compliment of offering either to me (altho' in fact I should have refused both), Plymouth & Portsmouth.

'Here the King said that in this He (if any[one]) was to blame. That I might have commanded either, but that he really thought I would not accept either. I answered "certainly not, but the offer might at least have shewn that I was not overlooked".... The King then said a vast number of kind things & declared the pleasure He would have to do any thing that might gratify me. He said "I at first thought of offering you the Grenadier Guards, but then I felt that you would not like to quit the Cavalry for the Infantry." I said *that* would not weigh with me, but as the Grenadiers could only be given for its Emolument (I believe it is from 7 to 10,000 a year) & that however *wanted* by me, It was *not that* which I *sought*, that therefore It was *much better bestowed*! The King added "I thought, too, of the Constableship of the Tower for you — now that is a place of High Honour & little Pay — Tell me whether, if I had offered this to you, with the Blues, you would have thought the two worthy of your acceptance." To this I replied: "that, Sir, would have required consideration. Certainly the two situations offered conjointly, would very materially increase the honor proposed."[t]

'All this & a great deal more having passed, I withdrew, having stated that I thought I owed it to myself, to my family & to very many who looked up to me for patronage, to make this effort to obtain a High Station of trust & patronage — that having failed, I should with perfect composure & satisfaction retire to my retired style of life which suited me perfectly. That I really wanted nothing & that at all events I would never submit to an inferior Station in publick life. That I should be content to remain His Colonel of the 7th Hussars, always ready to serve My Country if ever my Services were worth having, but that most assuredly I would never again offer myself for any employment.'[11]

This revealing letter, besides demonstrating Anglesey's technique with his sovereign, rather confirms the account given in Mrs Arbuthnot's Journal. She reports that the King, after the interview, had complained to Wellington of Anglesey's talking 'in the most lofty way of his pretensions and what the country expected shd be done for him'. The King thought the marquess an impertinent fellow and 'those Pagets a most presumptuous set', and added that it had formerly been said that 'there were in the world men, women & Herveys; now it seemed that there were men, women & Pagets.'[12g]

Three days after the Duke of York's funeral, Wellington was gazetted Commander-in-Chief, but the King asked him to retain the Master-Generalship for the time being. Hussey Vivian told Anglesey that he had heard

'a few days since & *from Authority that I cannot doubt* that a point was made by some of the parties in office not to let you into the Ordnance — They knew your personal friendship for the King — and they feared you would be inclined to give way to his *follies* (this was the word used to me & I am convinced was that which my informant heard) & that your determination to retire from publick life was just what they wished. — *Now I have not the slightest doubt from the Quarter whence this came, that these very sentiments in these very words* have been expressed by certain persons now in power.'[13]

Thus Anglesey's first sustained attempt at gaining high office was thwarted.

ii

Ld Anglesea has taken the Ordnance, *without Cabinet.*... Is not this a signal piece of good fortune? Conceive 'Kill 'em' in Cabinet!
*Lord Howard de Walden [a Canningite, and junior member of the Government],
to Sir Charles Bagot, April 19th, 1827*

Ld Anglesea is I believe to be in the Cabinet.
George Tierney, jun., to Sir Charles Bagot, April 26th, 1827[14]

There matters might have rested, but for the startling events of the spring of 1827. On February 17th of that year Lord Liverpool, who had headed a Tory government for no less than fifteen years, was smitten by a severe paralytic stroke from which he never recovered. For a considerable time before this event his Government had been on the point of breaking up: dissensions within the Cabinet had reached the point where its ultra-Tory and Canningite sections could no longer work in harness. There was conflict between them on each of the three great questions of the day: on Catholic emancipation the Cabinet was divided into 'Protestants' and 'Catholics'; on the Corn Laws the ultra-Tories opposed the changes which the Canningites saw as essential; and Canning's masterful foreign policy did not commend itself to the Ultras. Now with Lord Liverpool's removal from the scene, what little cohesion there had been in the Cabinet vanished. There followed a protracted and intricate series of political manœuvres, the first stage of which ended in victory for the Canningites. On April 10th the King sent for Canning to form an administration. Six of the Ultras (including Wellington, Eldon and Peel) promptly resigned, thereby creating a situation which made it impossible for Canning to form a strong government without admitting at least some Whigs. The replacement of Ultras by Whigs would mean the substitution of some 'Catholics' for some 'Protestants', and to the King, who, like his father before him, had become obsessed with the notion that any further concessions to the Catholics would be a violation of the Coronation

Oath, such an accession of men known to favour the Catholic claims was anathema. Canning tried to overcome this problem by attempting to convince himself, the King and those Whigs and 'Protestants' whom he strove to persuade into serving under him, that the basis of the new Government with regard to the Catholic question would be the same as it had been under Lord Liverpool. To Anglesey, considered by many to be a full-blooded 'Protestant', he wrote 'that it was not to be made a question of Government; and that each individual was to exercise upon it an equal and perfect freedom of opinion and of action'. This was on April 13th, the date on which Wellington's resignation from both the Horse Guards and the Ordnance was accepted. On the same day, Hussey Vivian was the bearer to Anglesey of the King's offer of the Ordnance,[h] and that night Canning told him that he was 'authorized by His Majesty to tender to your Lordship the seat in His Majesty's Cabinet, which was held by the Duke of Wellington in conjunction with that Office'.[15]

In the first days of April, nearly a fortnight earlier, Anglesey had indicated in a letter to Lord Londonderry that he refused to join the party then forming against Canning, thus making it clear that he was 'quite at liberty and quite prepared to do every thing to support His Majesty (for whose kindness he feels most gratefull) & His Majesty's Government'. But he immediately balked at the idea of being one of the Cabinet. 'He feels some alarm', wrote Vivian to Sir William Knighton, the King's secretary, 'at the thought of being obliged to speak in the House, & he is not quite at ease on the Corn question on which his opinions differ from the late Administration in some measure, but His Majesty will no doubt hear all this from himself.... Lord A's dread of being called on to speak is so great that he seems to think he might do better in Ireland [as Lord Lieutenant] than at the Ordnance.'[16]

The Ultras, of course, affected to consider him a traitor. Londonderry thought him 'a sad exhibition of defection', and wrote to Mrs Arbuthnot: 'That HE should have so lost himself, I deplore. I always thought him *high-minded*.' In the Lords on May 2nd Londonderry said that he did not envy Anglesey the 'tottering seat to which he had attained — for convinced he was, that that noble Lord's triumph would be but momentary — and thought that he would have acted much better than by accepting it, in reconciling the breaches, if any there were, between two illustrious individuals [the King and the Duke]. Then he would have stood on higher ground, and in a better position, than he did at present.' Anglesey's reply was characteristic. He was bound, he said, 'by no conditions; he was in every respect free as the air he breathed'. Whether in or out of office, he felt it 'his duty to support the Throne'; that he considered the King 'to be fully at liberty at any time to form what administration he might think best suited to the wants of the country. If, therefore, any arrangements

The Ordnance going off & relieving guard

Anglesey is shown bestride the cylinder of 'the Regent's bomb', holding a rein attached to the jaws of the bronze monster. On the bomb sits Wellington, holding his Field Marshal's baton, and saying, 'I've done the state some Service — but no more of that.' A winged figure of Fame flies after the Duke holding out a laurel wreath. Anglesey's left leg (he in fact lost his right one) terminates in a cork transfixed by a giant corkscrew. Behind is the Horse Guards.

'The Regent's bomb', a giant mortar (or bomb), was uncovered on August 12th, 1816, the Regent's birthday, on Horse Guards Parade. It was a gift from the Spanish Regency in memory of Wellington's victory at Salamanca, after which battle it had been abandoned by Soult, who had used it to bombard Cadiz from the unprecedented distance of three and a half miles.

more conducive to the public good than those which now existed could be entered into, he should retire from office with the most perfect good humour.... With respect to the insinuations which had been thrown out', he said 'that he should not condescend to explain them away; but if he thought it right, he could show that he had pursued a course in diametrical opposition to that which had been insinuated.'[171]

As soon as Wellington heard that he was to be succeeded at the Ordnance by Anglesey, he wrote offering every information and assistance in his power, 'both now and whenever you may think proper to call for it, to enable you to conduct the duties of the office; and I will use any influence that I may have with those [in the department] who have determined to quit their offices in the existing crisis to remain with you, till you can fill their situations to your satisfaction.' He added, characteristically, 'there is one thing which however I must tell you even at this moment; and that is, that you will find it necessary that the offices at the Board [of Ordnance] should be filled by men capable of doing their business.' Anglesey replied next day, 'I gladly and gratefully accept your kind offer of assistance until I am fairly in my stirrups.'[18]

In the meantime Canning was proceeding with the lengthy and involved task of cabinet-making. His chief problem, as he told Anglesey, was on the one hand to reconcile the King to a government in which 'the members of the Cabinet favourable to the Catholic question will considerably outnumber those who hold the opposite opinion', and on the other to persuade those Whigs with whom he must coalesce to be content with a further postponement of that question.[19]

Whether Anglesey would accept the proffered seat in the Cabinet or not was one of the factors considered by Lord Holland, the great Whig luminary, in deciding whether his party should take the hazardous step of 'union with Canning's Government'.

'It is not clear', wrote Holland to George Tierney on April 23rd, 'whether Anglesey is in the Cabinet or not, but if he is there, he is so against his wishes and remonstrance, at the earnest solicitation of the King, and with the full acquiescence of Canning after he had told the latter that he disliked being there, that he concurred in scarce any part of Canning's policy, that to say the truth he had never in his life *had any great fancy for him*, and that he accepted a seat in the Cabinet directly from the King, thought he was there to serve and obey, and did not consider himself as personally or politically connected with his colleagues further than as serving the same Sovereign!!!'

Holland went on to say that the Duke of Devonshire, with whom

Canning was negotiating, was to ask whether Anglesey was definitely to be in the Cabinet or not, and if he was, whether he had in fact accepted the seat against his will and as a result of pressure from the King. Holland then inferred that 'confirmation of such details' might influence Devonshire's mind or conduct, though how much he could not tell. On April 27th Anglesey and Devonshire had a joint audience of the King. Canning's private secretary makes it clear that Anglesey had not finally made up his mind by that date. 'It just depends on his vote on Corn, on which he entertains some doubts.'[20] Exactly what his views on the Corn question were is obscure, but in the next few days he was able to satisfy himself and Canning on the subject, for at two o'clock in the afternoon of April 30th he went with the rest of the Cabinet to St James's to kiss hands and be sworn of the Privy Council. On May 1st he was gazetted Master-General of the Ordnance *with* a seat in the Cabinet, and on the following afternoon, Wellington handed over the office to him.

iii

I hear that the King said the other day, 'I shall keep the command of the Army in my own hands till my friend Arthur recovers his temper'.
                                        Duke of Rutland to Lady Shelley, May 9th, 1827[21]

The weeks which followed saw Anglesey busily engaged in the duties of his new office, and in acquainting himself with the business of the Cabinet. Towards the end of May he became involved in the attempts which were being made to induce the Duke of Wellington to resume his post at the Horse Guards. The Duke's resignation as Master-General had been inevitable since the seat in the Cabinet which went with it made it a political appointment, and it was clear that he could not serve politically under Canning; but he had resigned as Commander-in-Chief because he considered himself (with some justice) rebuked and insulted by certain parts of Canning's letters to him of which the King had approved.

The King, on May 21st, had written to his 'dear friend' a conciliatory letter in which he said 'the command of *the army* is still open, and if you choose to recall that resignation, which it grieved me so much to receive, you have my *sincere* permission to do so.' But the Duke was adamant. Nevertheless a number of his friends and others sought, some for the country's sake, some for his, and others for their own, to persuade him to reconsider. Anglesey was employed by Canning to sound the Duke as to 'what reparation he required'. For this purpose he spent two hours with him on May 26th, but Wellington declined to talk about the subject, except to say, according to Mrs Arbuthnot, that 'those who had given the offence might make the proper reparation, that it wd be impertinent of him to suggest any thing'. Anglesey, however, still would not give up. On June 1st he wrote the Duke a long letter ('I am unauthorized by any one to communicate with you') in which he went over the familiar ground once again pointing out that the King in a most affectionate letter had proved his confidence in him; and that Canning had 'over & over again declared' that no rebuke was intended, adding,

'You, unless I have unaccountably misunderstood you, are very desirous of resuming the command of the Army, provided this can be effected without compromising Your Honor.

'Surprized that I should have taken so different a view of your position & [of] the correspondence of which we have so often spoken, from that which you appear to take, I have again read the letters over & over most attentively,¹ and after the most serious deliberation, I cannot discover that there is anything at which to take offence.... What then prevents a reconciliation? — A simple straight forward explanation would effect it. — It could not fail. — But to accomplish an explanation, it is necessary that what is objected to, should be accurately defined. — This I have not been able to ascertain, but if I was once in possession of that, I should entertain some hope of effecting an object so truly desirable.'

The same day that this letter was written, the Duke (misunderstanding, it is said, the wishes of the Canningite Huskisson) introduced and carried in the Lords a 'wrecking' amendment to the Corn Bill. Since Wellington had been a member of the Cabinet when that Bill was drafted, and had not then objected to it, his behaviour was not unnaturally taken as further indication of his hostility towards the Government. This decided Anglesey that further remonstrance would be a waste of time, consequently he refrained from sending his letter. 'About 10 days afterwards however,' he later wrote at the foot of it, 'I shewed it to the Duke & told him why I did not forward it. I could make no impression upon him & from that moment, I considered reconciliation as hopeless.'²²

iv

Lord Ellenborough tells me you made a most sudden appearance at Kingston
Hall, no doubt with a Communication to the Duke from the King.
Sir Hussey Vivian to Anglesey, August 19th, 1827[23]

The tragic death of Canning on August 8th, at the age of fifty-seven,
though it solved the problem of the Duke's employment, created many
fresh ones. The administration which four laborious months had brought
into being was suddenly deprived of its leader. 'It is impossible', wrote
Mrs Arbuthnot in her diary, 'to guess what the King will do, whether he
will attempt to go on with the present heterogeneous mass or have recourse
to his old Ministers', by which she meant the Ultras. But the King soon
made up his mind. It was too early for him to go crawling back to those
who, in his view, had deserted and attempted to dictate to him less than
four months past, so he called on the pliable and weak leader of the
Lords to form a new government. Lord Goderich (Disraeli's 'transient
and embarrassed phantom') was told to make it as like its predecessor as
possible. The King informed him that he had made up his mind not to
add any more Whigs to the Cabinet, and that he did not wish it in any
way to look like a Whig administration. Such a thing would be in direct
opposition to his principles. He insisted that at the age of sixty-five he
was not going to put these aside to satisfy the crotchets of individuals.
'These observations', he concluded, 'arise from what passed in conversation with Ld Anglesey.'[24] Thus it seems that Anglesey played an important
part in determining the King's views on the new administration. He
certainly did so in the new and successful attempts which were now made
to bring Wellington back to the Horse Guards.

On August 15th Anglesey left London with two letters for the Duke,
one from the King and another from Goderich. 'He travelled without
stopping,' wrote Palmerston (still, after eighteen years, Secretary of
State for War), 'arrived at some country house in the west [Kingston
Lacy Hall in Dorsetshire] where the Duke was staying, about three in the
morning, found the Duke in full uniform, just come home from a fancy
ball, obtained his immediate acceptance, and arrived with it at Windsor
while we were sitting in Council' on the following day.[k] 'Lord Anglesey
said to us, "Well, gentlemen, I have done what you sent me to do. I
have brought you the Duke of Wellington's acceptance as Commander-
in-Chief; and by God, mark my words, as sure as you are alive, he will

trip up all your heels before six months are over your heads" ': a prophecy
which was pretty well fulfilled. 'Before the six months were well over,'
wrote Palmerston, 'the Duke was in, and our heels were up.'[25] 1

v

Believe me, the [Whig] Party has made a great sacrifice & it ought to be
appreciated — Now do not set me down as a Whig. You know indeed that I am
not one. I am most anxious that that most odious & absurd Line of Demarcation
of Tory & Whig should be obliterated & now is the time.
Anglesey to Goderich, September 6th, 1827

My dearest Papa,
   I was very much gratified the other day, by being told by Princess *Leiven*
(who is not apt to pay compliments) *how much* you are liked by *yr colleagues.*
She said 'Absolument on l'adore, on regrette seulement qu'ils ne pensent pas lui
garder en Angleterre, aussi bien que de l'envoyer en Ireland.' This I thought a
very pretty little compliment.
Jane, Countess of Mount Charles, to Anglesey, August 31st, 1827[26]

Goderich's administration, though strengthened by the return of the
Duke to the Horse Guards, was still an inherently weak one. Anglesey
told the Prime Minister that the King was sowing the seeds of discord and
disunion and preparing the way for a relapse into ultra-Toryism. The
members of the Lansdowne section of the Whigs, which had joined
Canning's Government in the summer (thereby causing a split in their
party), had loyally carried on under Goderich; but the King's insistence
upon the Tory, John Charles Herries, as Chancellor of the Exchequer,
and the Prime Minister's watery concurrence, so sickened them that
Lansdowne tendered his resignation as Home Secretary. The King
appealed to him to stay at his post from a sense of duty. 'Though I have
enough of Whiggish heresies about me,' wrote Lansdowne to Anglesey,
'to think that such appeals ought not *always* to be successful, I have
thought it not inconsistent with my public duty to acquiesce on the
present occasion, reserving it to myself hereafter to press for Holland as
soon as the proper occasion arises.' Here was the chief bone of contention
between Lansdowne and the King — indeed between Goderich and the
King too — for it was generally agreed that the addition of Lord Holland

would much strengthen the Government. 'Lord Lansdowne and his friends', wrote Anglesey to Goderich, 'have shewn much temper & good taste, & I have not the least doubt that if the King is allowed to become better acquainted with them,[m] His Majesty will soon reconcile himself to the idea of letting in the man [Lord Holland], whose introduction they have most at heart, & whose honesty & integrity, aye, and whose moderation I will vouch for. Let him in and then you will be strong indeed.' In August Anglesey had spent much time trying to wean the King from his antipathy towards Holland but to no effect: the King remained adamant.[27]

In this uneasy manner the Government tottered on its way,[n] until, in December, Goderich recommended verbally to the King the pressing need to include Lords Holland and Wellesley (Wellington's eldest brother), and then wrote tendering his resignation if the recommendation was not adopted. To this letter he afterwards added, without the knowledge of his colleagues, a declaration of his incapacity in any case to continue in office. This, he asserted, arose from personal and domestic circumstances and was assumed by the King to be an actual resignation. It was not in fact accepted until January 8th, 1828. In the interval the King sounded Lord Harrowby as a successor to Goderich, but he, from reasons of declining health, put that arrangement out of the question. Had it been a feasible one, Anglesey would have been pleased, believing, as he told Lansdowne, that Harrowby had firmness and decision and that he would have been favourably disposed towards Lord Holland. But Anglesey's fear of a return of the ultra-Tories did not blind him to the opposite danger. 'In strengthening the Government from the Whigs, of whom', he assured Lansdowne, 'I am not the least afraid, permit me to observe that there would be infinite mischief in having it looked upon as a purely Whig Ministry. In fact neither the King nor the Country would stand it.'[28] [o]

Lyndhurst, Huskisson and others wanted at this time to represent to the King the true state of affairs, namely how near its end the Government was, and how fatal it would be if, through failure to strengthen it, an Ultra administration succeeded it. They considered it essential that whoever carried out this mission should be accompanied by Anglesey, and he himself wished to go, but in the event a bad attack of the tic (facial neuralgia) prevented him from doing so.[p]

Disraeli, at first hand from Lord Chancellor Lyndhurst, gives a delightful account of affairs at this stage.

'Nothing', he wrote, 'can give an idea of the scene under Goderich. No order at the Cabinet. A most ludicrous scene. Nothing ever done. Anglesea sitting with a napkin round his head from the tic, but the only one who seemed to exert himself. As they went home Lyndhurst said to a colleague, "This can never last." In a few days Goderich sent for Lyndhurst to Downing Street — walking up & down the room in great agitation, wringing his hands and even shedding tears. Told Lyndhurst that he [Goderich] must resign. Lyndhurst tried to reason with him, but no avail. Resigned the next day. George IV sent for Lyndhurst & asked what he was to do. Lyndhurst said there was only one thing. "Send for the Duke of Wellington." '[29]

Mrs Arbuthnot asserts that Goderich advised the King to send for Anglesey, 'who he knew would recommend *Whigs* (the turncoat!!). Instead of that, the King ... sent for the Duke.' If this is true, it seems that Anglesey was, for this brief moment of his career, on the threshold of No. 10 Downing Street. He believed it himself, for in February he told a Staffordshire neighbour in confidence, and not a little complacently, 'that during the late disagreements in the ministry, he was solicited strongly by the leading men to become Prime Minister in preference to the Duke of Wellington, and which would have gratified the King.'[30] However this may have been, the King sent for the Duke on January 9th, and commissioned him to form a government.

vi

You have ensured the esteem and regards of us all by the frankness and the manliness of your character and conduct upon all occasions.
Goderich to Anglesey, January 9th, 1828

I could now answer for it that Ld Anglesey would be well received by the Catholics as Lord-Lieutenant if he would take any one occasion to declare publicly that he is *not* our Enemy. I mean by this merely a disclaimer of enmity, even without any pledge whatsoever of friendship.
Daniel O'Connell to the Knight of Kerry, June 24th, 1827[31]

For Anglesey the dissolution of the Goderich administration posed some difficult questions. In the first place the atmosphere of inefficiency, intrigue and personal wrangling suited him ill. He despised his colleagues from the heart. He was reported as saying that they were a set of confounded fellows, who didn't know what they were at. He disapproved of all they did and absented himself constantly from the Cabinet.[32] Secondly, and of far greater importance, more than a month before Canning's death, he had been designated to succeed Lord Wellesley as Lord Lieutenant of Ireland. He had left neither the King nor Canning in any doubt that this was the post he most coveted. Some time in early July the appointment was positively settled. Wellesley, however, wished, for financial reasons, to remain in Dublin until the end of the year.[q]

On August 27th, soon after he had brought Wellington back to the Horse Guards, Anglesey expressed on paper the predicament which faced him. In a letter to Arthur Paget (which in fact he never sent, doubting, as he wrote at the foot of it, if he 'should be justified in so far opening himself, even to a brother'), he complained that he was

> 'full of fears and doubts. Supposing His Majesty to relapse into Ultra Toryism of which I have little doubt, He will still think me bound to stick to Him & will hear of no difficulties, & fancy that everything is to bend before Him. His new, or rather his renewed friends [the Ultras] will — to do them justice — do their best to relieve me from my dilemma. They will gladly set me free.... But His Majesty is not as easily disposed of and I anticipate a tough job with Him. My determination is not to serve in any exclusive administration & above all things not to go to Ireland in leading strings. Upon the character of the [Irish Lord] Chancellor and upon that of the [Irish] Secretary who may be appointed, must depend my conduct. The more I look to that country and the more I become acquainted with its whole state & organization, the more formidable do I think the undertaking of governing it & if it was proposed to me to go there with Mr Peel for instance as Home Secretary, with such a one as Lord Manners for Chancellor, & with Mr Herries for Irish Secretary, I would say, "Give me 2000 or 3000 men & odious as the Service would be, I will as a soldier only do my best to preserve order & to keep down Rebellion, but *civilly* to govern the Country in conjunction with such hands, is more than I will undertake." Now this is a serious crisis of my life.'[33]

In resolving the crisis — in making up his mind as to whether he could bring himself to serve under Wellington — Anglesey had not only to consider the King's attitude (the likely accusations of 'desertion' and appeals to 'sense of duty to the royal person' which would arise should resignation be decided upon), but also certain vital questions affecting policies and personalities. If the members of the new Cabinet were too exclusively Tory, Anglesey would not wish to support them, not only on general grounds, but also because then he would be expected to close his mind to the Catholic question. On this great issue there was a variety of views among his contemporaries as to the exact sentiments of the prospective Lord Lieutenant. The most diehard of all Protestants, the Duke of Cumberland, thought Anglesey as diehard as himself. 'By your having appointed our friend Anglesey to the Ordnance', he had written to the King in June 1827, 'you have shewn publicly, the purity and *staunchness* of your sentiments upon the *great* question.' Similarly, when in December it looked as if Herries and Bexley, two of the most Tory of Goderich's ministers would resign if Lord Holland were brought in, Lyndhurst wrote that he would 'be left, with the exception of Lord Anglesey, alone in the Cabinet as to questions connected with the support of the Church and the Protestant interest'. Yet in April Sir Charles Bagot had asked a friend: 'Would Lord Anglesey do for Ordnance, or would his wheel-back about Catholics be a disqualifier?' The confusion arose because in the first place it was assumed by many that anyone as close to the King as was Anglesey must share the royal view that the smallest concession to the papists was a violation of the Coronation Oath, and in the second because the votes which he had cast in the Lords from time to time seemed contradictory. In fact, he had long taken a liberal view and had never accepted the exaggerated Tory stand on Catholic emancipation. As long ago as 1807 he had been uncertain about the merits of the question, but while George III still reigned he was certain that emancipation was inexpedient. 'No man in his senses,' he told Arthur Paget in that year, 'after Pitt's failure with the King upon the subject, can have hoped for one instant that His Majesty (who is very likely, by the by, to be driven out of *his* senses by the discussion) would permit the measure to be adopted.' In four divisions in the House of Lords (in 1817, 1819, 1821 and 1822), he had voted with the minority in favour of some degree of removal of Roman Catholic disabilities.[34] But in May 1825, when Lord Colchester moved to postpone consideration of Lord Donoughmore's Roman Catholic Relief Bill on second reading, Anglesey was his seconder. In his speech on that occasion he explained why.

'Since I have had a seat in Parliament', he said, 'I have ever approached this perplexing and intricate subject in painful doubt. . . . I have been desirous, on the one hand, to do what was kind, liberal, and generous by the Roman Catholics; on the other hand I have never for a moment shut my eyes to the fact that in supporting their claims I have been assisting in breaking down a very important barrier that our ancestors felt the necessity of throwing up round the Constitution of the Church and the State.

'I had hoped, my Lords, that the change of circumstances, in this lapse of time, might justify the measure. I had hoped, too, and expected, and really did believe, that for every concession made — every advantage granted to that body, a corresponding spirit would have manifested itself of conciliation, of kindly feeling, and of good fellowship towards their Protestant fellow-subjects — towards this Protestant State.

'My Lords, I have been disappointed in these expectations.... It now appears to me that Catholic Emancipation is not that which they alone seek, but that nothing short of Catholic Ascendancy will satisfy them.

'Here, then, I feel it my duty to quit them. Here I take my stand. If there must be a trial of strength (and we are daily told that six millions of people are not to be resisted: that they will take by force that which they cannot obtain by representations) — I say, my Lords, if the battle must be fought, I would fight it in the best position I could find; and I can look to none so good as that in which we at present stand.'

'It grieves me to be compelled to pursue this course, thus to express myself. Whilst I *could* doubt I have given the benefit to the petitioning party. But, my Lords, I can no longer doubt. Recent events forbid it and that which I would willingly have conceded to the prayer of a petition, I must now refuse to threats and attempts at intimidation [reference to the activities of O'Connell's Catholic Association, founded in 1824]. Still, my Lords, I profess to be, and I really and sincerely am, friendly to the Catholics; — that is to say, I would gladly relieve them from all their disabilities. I would willingly place them upon a footing of perfect equality, in respect to political power, with the Protestants. But, my Lords, it must not be at the expense of the Protestants, — and therefore, until some plain, clear, decided, unequivocal guarantee can be offered for the perfect security, the undisturbed possession of the existing Establishment and Protestant security, I cannot consent to any further extension of political power to the Catholics.'[35]

In March 1827 Lord Holland had gone to great pains to convert Anglesey to the straight 'Catholic' line.

'I think', he wrote, 'that you agree with me that sooner or later a full participation in the political rights of his Majesty's other subjects must be conceded to the Irish, among whom the Roman Catholics form so large a majority. But you have taken fire at the insolent and foolish speeches of the Demagogues — You cannot brook the notion that they should imagine that they had carried their point, in itself a reasonable one, by intimidation. To deprive them of that triumph you are disposed to refuse them (& not them only but the vast majority of those of their faith who are quite guiltless of such extravagances) what you otherwise consider as their just rights.... The reasonableness of the request not the manner of asking it should at all times be the real motive for granting anything to large bodies of men — But the request does not become unreasonable because the manner of asking it is somewhat offensive — Moreover the longer this boon is refused, the more offensive the manner of asking it is likely to become. If granted hereafter, it will probably have more the appearance & the reality too, of being extorted by force than it would now — In short we should make up our mind to grant it with as good a grace as we can *even now* or be prepared for all the consequences of refusing it for ever — What they may be I really shudder to think — confiscations, ruin, massacres, carnage in the field & murders on the scaffold form a dreadful picture....

'Surely, surely it would be hard on millions to suffer because their orators lacked judgement, taste, temper or honesty.'

In reply Anglesey reiterated much the same sentiments as he had expressed in his speech two years earlier, adding that to grant emancipation under duress

'would be nothing short of holding out a premium upon Violence, Outrage & Rebellion, for if the Claims of the Catholicks are to be admitted, standing as they do in their present menacing posture, there is but one course that the disaffected throughout the Empire will hereafter pursue whenever they fancy they have a grievance; & let their discontent proceed from political feelings or from agricultural or commercial distress, or from whatever cause it may, Combination, Intimidation, Insult, Violence, *Bullying* will be the universal line of conduct. This risk *I* dare not run. I prefer a present danger, the extent of which I can in some measure calculate, to a more distant one, of the force of which I can know nothing but apprehend every evil....

'Now for all these dangers & difficulties, I do think remedies might be found.... Find me some plain, clear unequivocal guarantee for the quiet possession of the existing [Protestant] Establishments & you shall have me with you *Tooth & Nail*....

'I should despair of reconciling the *Ultra* Anti-Catholicks to *any* arrangement, but I think that very many of those who oppose an unconditional surrender to the Clamorous Summons that is now made, would gladly receive the Catholicks upon terms, & these terms once settled & dictated, I should be sanguine as to the result.'[36]

Since April 1827 the Irish Chief Secretary[a] had been the Hon. William Lamb, later to become Lord Melbourne and prime minister. In September, Anglesey had told him that he rejoiced to know that he should have with him a man whose views upon the Catholic question appeared to be identical with his own.[37] But would Lamb be retained in the new Government? By whom would Wellington replace him, if he went? What was to be the attitude of the new administration towards emancipation? Only when these questions were answered would Anglesey himself know what to do.

CHAPTER TEN

Previous to his departure for Ireland, [Anglesey] had taken the utmost pains minutely to inform himself of the real state of Ireland. A sort of domestic or friendly committee of the most distinguished political characters of the day sate upon the subject. He listened, — he treasured up, — he planned for himself a rule of future conduct.... His intentions of governing in a sense very different from those who had preceded him, were frankly and warmly avowed. In these intentions he left England. He was not long in Ireland before he realised them.

Sir Thomas Wyse, 1829[1]

TWELVE days elapsed before Anglesey heard from Wellington, who then told him that he had just completed the list of members of the new Government (which he enclosed[a]), and that it was the anxious wish of the King, himself, and Peel, that he should remain as Lord Lieutenant. They hoped too that the state of his health would soon enable him to proceed to his post.

Peel took the earliest opportunity after his appointment as Home Secretary to express the hope that neither his own appointment nor the recent change in the Government would induce Anglesey to relinquish the trust he had undertaken. 'I was in a private station', he wrote, 'when I heard that it was destined for your hands — and I cordially rejoiced — (at that time from very disinterested motives) — in the selection which had been made.' To this handsome letter Anglesey replied that if the system which he had prescribed for himself in carrying on the administration of Ireland met with the Duke's and Peel's approbation, he would not shrink from the arduous undertaking. He was fortified by the fact that Lamb, after seeing Wellington, had expressed himself satisfied that it was intended to conduct the government of Ireland 'upon the most rational, sensible & liberal footing'. Further, Huskisson, Palmerston, Dudley and Grant, all of them 'Canningites', had consented to serve under the Duke; so had Melville and Ellenborough, neither of them Ultras. The remaining members of the Cabinet were certainly 'Protestants', though the arch-Ultra Eldon feared that some of them were 'very loose'.[2]

183

Anglesey's talks with the Prime Minister and Home Secretary were satisfactory to all three, and he being sufficiently recovered from a severe attack of the tic, the necessary arrangements were at once set in train for his journey to Dublin. March 1st was fixed upon for the state entry.

On February 21st he took leave of the King at Windsor. In the room at the time of the interview was Lord Mount Charles, a Lord of the Treasury and Anglesey's son-in-law. According to him, the King said 'God bless you, Anglesey! I know you are a true Protestant', to which the reply was, 'Sir, I will not be considered either Protestant or Catholick; I go to Ireland determined to act impartially between them and without the least bias either one way or the other.'[3]

*   *   *

For at least six months past Anglesey had been preparing for the task ahead. From the moment the rumour of his appointment got abroad, a ceaseless stream of applications poured in on him. With John Sanderson, his faithful chief agent, and Lieut.-Col. William Gosset, who had followed him from the Ordnance as private secretary, he spent many hours penning polite refusals to requests for posts and patronage of all sorts. By the beginning of December his 'family' had been agreed upon: the corps of aides-de-camp, six or seven in number, was headed, as it had been at Waterloo, by his old friend, Colonel Thornhill, and included the indispensable Baron Tuyll.

The Household of the Lord Lieutenant of Ireland was modelled in miniature on the King's: it included a Chamberlain, a Master of the Horse, a Comptroller, and a Steward. There were four Gentlemen-at-large with salaries of £150 a year each; two Gentlemen of the Chamber at £200, and an Assistant Gentleman Usher who was unpaid. A very important member of the Household was the Physician. Dr de Courcy Laffan had for some time past been Anglesey's personal doctor, and now on his appointment as viceregal physician, he was made a baronet upon the Lord Lieutenant's recommendation.[4] The degree of nepotism practised by Anglesey was not excessive. He made his son Uxbridge, now thirty-one years old, Steward of the Household; William Paget, his second son, twenty-five, Captain of the Dublin Yacht; his brother Berkeley's son, Frederick, one of his aides-de-camp, and his cousin Lord Forbes, Comptroller. Lord Forbes, with his excellent Dublin contacts, was most helpful from the start. As early as August he had written from Paris that he was making inquiries about wine; but Anglesey replied that he was determined to buy all provisions in

Dublin, and this he did, starting with an order for six thousand pounds'
worth of wines and liqueurs from Messrs Sneyd and Company.[5] Forbes
knew, too, all about the Lord Lieutenant's Church patronage. 'The
average of livings which are at the disposal of the Lord Lieutenant
annually, is *15*', he wrote. The chaplains to the viceroy — there were
thirty-one, 'but you can have as many or as few as you choose' — were
merely honorary appointments entailing 'on you only to hear one
sermon in the year and to give one dinner to each unless you should wish
to see more of the Clerical part of your establishment'.

There was the important question of liveries.

'I do not conceive', wrote Forbes, 'that you require any Livery
richer than that which your servants now bear, unless you might
choose to give the upper servants a dress coat for particular occasions.
The manner in which Lord Wellesley affects Royalty [he carried to
Dublin the unsurpassed pomp which he had practised twenty-five
years before as Governor-General of India] is quite beneath your
character, and would render your life very miserable.... The Line
you propose to adopt is much more dignified and it has one great
advantage, that it enables you to judge for yourself of the manners
and character of the people you are sent to govern — if an absurd
affectation of state is kept up you really could form no opinion for
yourself, and must see through the medium of others, and misrepresentation on every subject and occasion is what renders the
Govt of Ireland difficult to a Lord Lieutenant.'

The question of which tradespeople to 'appoint' was an important one
too. 'I am applied to', wrote Forbes, 'by tradesmen of all descriptions in
Dublin to name them to you — it is an advantage to them to be enabled
to say they are employed by the Lord Lieut.' He thought that to make the
selection judiciously, without reference to religion, would be a means of
giving a favourable impression of determined impartiality. 'You will
wonder that political feeling should be mixed up in the choice you are to
make of your Taylor, &c, but unfortunately so it is in Ireland.' As to the
domestic staff at Dublin Castle, which numbered about sixty,[6] Forbes
strongly advised the new viceroy from what he heard of Lord Wellesley's
establishment, 'not to have any servant who had lived with *him* — the
system of Plunder was ruinous and they would not only practice it
towards you but would also corrupt your people.'

During the greater part of the year the Lord Lieutenant lived in the

Viceregal Lodge at Phoenix Park, but for the Dublin season he occupied
apartments in the Castle. Forbes found that these were 'filthy beyond
description' and immediately set about renovating them. He also had a
bath installed in Anglesey's dressing-room. He found neither the Lodge
nor the Castle at all comfortable, though the public money laid out on
them had been enormous. 'I think that I have suggested to Lamb a plan
by which we shall be able to check it for the future, and he is most
anxious to cooperate.'

Many another detail of a similar nature had to be settled. To a minor
one, Anglesey referred in a letter to Lamb. 'One thing I already know
requires (& you have given me proof of it) instant reform & that is The
Government Ink.'[7]

ii

I am not one of those who anticipate evil from the administration of Lord
Anglesea. I believe at least that he will come over with the intentions of discharging his functions for the benefit of all; but we ought to recollect that he will
be surrounded by the worst men that ever poisoned the ear of authority.
Daniel O'Connell to the Catholic Association, February 23rd, 1828[8]

To understand the situation in Ireland in 1828 it is necessary to go back
thirty years. When in 1796 a French fleet had appeared off Bantry Bay, the
latent seeds of revolt, engendered by centuries of English tyranny, had
taken hold in Ireland: by 1798 they had produced a large-scale rebellion
which swept like a tornado through the land, just at a time when England
was fighting for her existence against a revolutionary force in France
which had arisen from conditions in some ways alarmingly like those of
Ireland. Though the rebellion was put down, England certainly could not
risk such another, for the invitation to a French invasion which it offered
was altogether too attractive: and such an invasion, if successful would
spell disaster for Britain. Ireland, therefore, as R. B. McDowell, one of the
ablest of modern Irish historians has put it,

'had to be tranquillized and secured, and the obvious solution to the
British Cabinet seemed to be a union with Great Britain which would
reassure the protestant minority, permit it to adopt a generous
attitude to the catholic majority, render Ireland a safe field for
British investment and enable it to participate in British prosperity.

It was a drastic remedy but a wartime atmosphere sometimes has a stimulating effect on legislation, and although in Ireland the union was fiercely fought over, it slipped through the British parliament after a few languid debates.'[9]

The 1801 Act of Union meant that direct responsibility for Ireland was concentrated in London. During the American wars she had been given parliamentary independence; by the Union she lost it, and the House of Commons at Westminster had the doubtful gain of a hundred Irish members. Because of the penal laws against Catholics, all the members of the Irish Parliament had been Protestants, while at least five-sevenths of the population of the country were Catholics. Further, the Irish Parliament had been, in effect, a tool of the administration and of the Dublin Castle bureaucracy, about two-thirds of its members being place-holders or pensioners, yet it had given a semblance of independence to the country. By the Act of Union, Ireland, from being in some degree a separate part of the Empire, became incorporated as an integral part of a United Kingdom. Though the wartime need for this was apparent, once peace had come in 1815 the political and economic disadvantages were no less clear. The two countries were so very different. The political system, which barely managed to cope with an era of industrial expansion in England, was wholly unsuited to the very different needs of a backward agricultural community in Ireland.

The chief political effect of the Union during its first quarter-century was the emergence of Catholic emancipation as a major issue at Westminster. Most of the penal laws against Roman Catholics had been removed on both sides of the Irish Sea in the last thirty years of the eighteenth century, but exclusion from Parliament and from the highest government and legal posts still remained in Ireland. In Britain, the issue in no way dominated political life; in Ireland it was overriding. In Britain, religious controversy had long since disappeared from the forefront of men's minds; in Ireland it was still the mainspring of political and social life. In Britain, the Catholics were a small minority; in Ireland they were a large majority.

When the Portland Whigs joined Pitt's wartime coalition in 1795 the Whig Lord Lieutenant, Fitzwilliam, had shown himself ready to support Catholic emancipation. This had so alarmed the King, the vested interests and Protestant opinion generally, that the viceroy had been hastily recalled. It had been Pitt's firm intention six years later to combine

Catholic emancipation with the Union (indeed, his subsequent resignation was due to his being prevented from doing so), but the obstacles to it which had obtained in 1795 persisted in 1801. They were still there in 1828. The most potent of them was the 'conscience' of the King. George IV said that 'his father would have laid his head on the block rather than yield, and that he was equally ready to lay his there in the same cause.'[10] Both father and son fervently believed that to grant full rights to their Roman Catholic subjects would be to betray the solemn oath which they had taken at their coronations. There existed a similar if less strong feeling among the English people — a vague but ingrained dread of 'popery' — a notion that if Catholics were admitted to the highest counsels of the State, they would contrive to overthrow the Constitution with the help of foreigners. To this lingering legacy of the Gunpowder Plot the forces of reaction gave powerful shape. The increasingly vigorous Irish agitation which centred in the Catholic Association, formed by O'Connell in 1824, served to foster the fear expressed by Anglesey in his speech the following year that nothing short of ascendancy seemed to be the Catholic aim.

By the time Anglesey went to Dublin, the second great obstacle to the granting of emancipation, though less virulent than it had been in the past, was still a factor to be reckoned with. It consisted in the Protestant monopoly of all the chief posts in Ireland. It was not to be expected that a tiny minority holding all the lucrative jobs should welcome the flood of competitors which emancipation would release. The strongest resistance of all was put up by the bureaucracy of the Castle; and it was these permanent officials who advised the Lord Lieutenant. Chief among them was William Gregory, who had been Under-Secretary for upwards of fifteen years, serving four viceroys and four chief secretaries. To Anglesey he had been represented as an '*Arch* Jobber. A man who has the Press at his command — a determined intriguer. False as hell. A violent Anti-Catholic — a furious Tory — and quite ready to betray the secrets of any one whose confidence he obtains. It is misery', wrote the new Lord Lieutenant, 'to feel that you have a spy in your camp & I intended to make a point of having him removed.'[11] Lamb, however, was sufficiently satisfied with him, and Gregory was not replaced until the end of 1830 when Anglesey made his removal a condition of acceptance of the Lord Lieutenancy under the Whigs.[b]

Anglesey's predecessor, Wellesley, had been viceroy since 1821. He was a mild supporter of Catholic emancipation, but in view of the attitude of the King and of Lord Liverpool's Government, had had to content himself with a conciliatory and impartial administration. When Canning succeeded Liverpool in 1827, Wellesley's hopes for a more liberal policy soared: so did the Catholic leaders'; and when Canning died, they did not despair, for Goderich's cabinet was no less predominantly pro-Catholic. But on Wellington becoming Prime Minister and Peel Home Secretary, they were despondent indeed.

*   *   *

The social and economic state of the country in 1828 was as unhealthy as could be. The secret societies and persistent agrarian crimes, which had made necessary so many years of coercive government, were rampant. Their causes, since the Parliamentary Committees of 1824 and 1825 had brought them into the open, were known to all. Chief among these were the system of rack-rents, the oppression of tithe-proctors and a host of middlemen, the perpetual absenteeism of the great landowners, and the lack of public spirit of the squireen class. The Irish labourer was paid half, or less, what his counterpart in England received; there was massive unemployment aggravated by an ever-growing population. An Oxford professor of history has put it succinctly:

> 'The peasantry chiefly depended for food upon potato patches of which the rents, owing to reckless competition, ranged as high as £10 an acre; ... these holdings were continually being sub-divided to such a point that the produce, even in good years, barely sufficed to keep the tenant and his family from starvation.... It was necessary to encourage the investment of private capital in Irish industries; to drive the people into new employments by means of restrictions upon sub-letting; and, until these employments developed, to encourage emigration as a counsel of despair. But capital would not migrate to Ireland while agrarian crime defied repression. The difficulty of repression was due to the general mistrust and hatred of all constituted authorities.'[12]

It was this mistrust and hatred of the constituted authorities which lay at the bottom of all Irish problems. For the landlords, the police, and the magistrates, were, in the eyes of the people, the instruments of Protestant tyranny, and until this largely justified view of them was removed, there could be no breaking of a circle which was as tragic as it was vicious.

*   *   *

Anglesey arrived at a time of comparative calm. The usual series of agrarian outrages continued, particularly in Tipperary, where more than fifty people were on trial for murder, but there was nothing exceptional by Irish standards. At the end of March he could declare that the monthly reports from the Provinces were not alarming. 'I was rather amused with one of them', he wrote to Lamb. 'It begins "all is perfectly quiet here" & then the two first acts recorded are: 1st, an atrocious murder; and 2ndly, a violent Riot by 7 persons who beat the Police & terribly injured one of them!!!'

Throughout the years of his two administrations, Anglesey never lost sight of the social and economic evils which beset the country, nor of the urgent need to remedy them. From Peel and Wellington he got precious little help: from Grey and Melbourne, hardly more. He came up against that blank wall of misunderstanding which rendered futile each successive government in Ireland. The Whigs were scarcely better than the Tories, both parties steadfastly believing that the policy of *laissez-faire* which seemed to work in England ought to work in Ireland too. The idea of state interference and assistance was anathema to the rulers of Britain. How often had liberal Englishmen appealed from the Castle to Whitehall in words similar to Anglesey's: 'The people of Ireland want proof that their interests are attended to & that they are to be improved by other means than mere acts of Parliament!'[13]

Soon after his coming to Dublin, Anglesey pressed upon the Home Office four immediate remedies for Irish troubles. Direct interference on the part of Government to encourage manufactures in the South, especially by means of a guarantee against malicious damage to factories; the repeal of the import duty on coal; the financing of road-building through the inaccessible districts; and the building of police barracks. A paltry £10,000 was advanced for road-building in Tipperary, but almost nothing else was done, however strongly and often Anglesey might urge the need. Holland, expressing the Whig point of view, gave little encouragement. Nothing would effect any good 'till the Great [Catholic] Question is decided', he wrote, 'unless indeed you can devise some contrivance to prevent their getting children, which is not I think a reformation very much in *your* line, and would be as little to the taste of the teacher as the scholars.'[14]

iii

Between one and two hundred packages were landed yesterday, from the *Commerce* steam boat, from Liverpool, belonging to the Marquis of Anglesea — one very long and large package was marked 'Cocked Hats'.[c]

Irish newspaper report[15]

On his way to Holyhead Anglesey stopped off at Beaudesert. He had not been gone two hours on the road from there, when a messenger arrived in haste from Lamb, announcing that the new governor of Ireland had made a false start. He had set off without his Commission or his official instructions, thinking that Peel had already sent them on to Dublin. In fact, it was legally necessary for the Commission to pass the Great Seal, and for Anglesey to be 'named' in person at a meeting of the Privy Council. Nevertheless a way was found to avoid the necessity for a return to London, and after some delay he proceeded on his journey possessed of the proper papers. 'It would afford great matter for observation', wrote Lamb, 'if you were to arrive in Dublin without your credentials.'[d] 'I must acknowledge myself', Anglesey replied, 'to have been a little flippant in the premature departure. But we Hussars are ready fellows and neither *old age* nor pain seem to correct me.'[16]

On February 28th the new viceroy arrived off Kingstown in the steam packet. That night he spent aboard the viceregal yacht. Next day, amid all the traditional splendour of the landing, the ships dressed overall, the troops lining the pier, the gun salutes and the rockets, he was rowed ashore wearing his plain blue coat and round hat. The rumour had been believed that he would enter the capital in a full suit of armour borrowed from the Tower of London, but the sight of their new governor in the clothes of a private gentleman, decorated only with the ribbon of the Garter, impressed the crowds lining the route of the procession more than any knight in shining armour. What delighted the horse-loving Irish even further was his exquisite horsemanship.

In the Council Chamber of the Castle, the lengthy process of installing a new Lord Lieutenant took the best part of the afternoon. When the oaths had been administered and the Sword of State received, the Lords Justices invested him with the collar of the Order of St Patrick as Grand Master: the State Trumpeters sounded their trumpets, the ordnance in the Park fired three rounds of twenty-one guns and the infantry on College Green answered with a volley. 'I had a very hard day's work', wrote

Anglesey next day. 'It all went off vastly well, & as there was nobody to give me a dinner, I gave an impromptu of 30 covers to all the Bigwigs. I was a good deal fagged, & had much pain, but I was not interrupted in the proceedings.'[17]

*   *   *

From the first weeks of his residence in Dublin Anglesey established himself in the hearts of the inhabitants. Each day, when his health allowed, he rode through the city in the plainest of clothes, a single equerry in attendance.[e] 'The rank of this illustrious Nobleman', remarked one newspaper, 'is not marked by "pomp and circumstance", nor is it swelled by groups of pageant Nobles, or squadrons of dragoons — no factitious aids are necessary to his station, character, or fame.' On St Patrick's Day he wore a large shamrock in his hat, at which he repeatedly pointed, much delighting the crowd assembled outside the Castle.[18]

Besides his lavish hospitality, the wide range of guests asked to partake of it,[f] and his encouragement of local trades, two of his actions had an especially conciliatory effect upon the Catholics. In reply to the Address of Welcome of the Dublin Corporation, an exclusively Protestant body, he referred to the wartime deeds of 'the sons of this generous land', which, as the Catholic press was quick to point out, being a compliment to the Irish people was an indirect censure on the Orangemen. Then he refused to attend a dinner of the notoriously Orange Beef Steak Club until they renounced politics, which they duly did. These actions did not go unnoticed in the Catholic Association. O'Connell declared that 'the tone and temper produced by the Marquis of Anglesea was the best forerunner of an event [Catholic emancipation] which must soon occur.'[19]

iv

Oft have I seen, in gay, equestrian pride,
Some well-rouged youth round Astley's Circus ride
Two stately steeds — standing, with graceful straddle,
Like him of Rhodes, with foot on either saddle,
While to soft tunes — some jigs, and some *andantes* —
He steers around his light-paced Rosinantes.

The Marquess of Anglesey as Lord High Steward at the Coronation
of George IV, aged 53

The Marquess of Anglesey was recalled from the Lord Lieutenancy of Ireland for his advocacy of Catholic emancipation in the winter of 1828-9. He defended his conduct in the House of Lords in May 1829

So rides along, with canter smooth and pleasant,
That horseman bold, Lord Anglesea, at present; —
Papist and *Protestant* the coursers twain
That lend their necks to his impartial rein,
And round the ring — each honoured, as they go,
With equal pressure from his gracious toe —
To the Old medley tune, half 'Patrick's Day'
And half 'Boyne Water', take their cantering way,
While Peel, the showman in the middle, cracks
His long-lashed whip, to cheer the doubtful hacks.

Ah, ticklish trial of equestrian art!
How blest, if neither steed would bolt or start; —
If *Protestant's* old restive tricks were gone
And *Papist's* winkers could be still kept on!
But no, false hopes — not ev'n the great Ducrow
'Twixt two such steeds could 'scape an overthrow:
If *solar* hacks played Phaeton a trick,
What hopes, alas, from hackneys *lunatic*?

If once my lord his graceful balance loses,
Or fails to keep each foot where each horse chooses,
If Peel but gives one extra touch of whip
To *Papist's* tail or *Protestant's* ear-tip —
That instant ends their glorious horsemanship!
Off bolt the sever'd steeds, for mischief free,
And down, between them, plumps Lord Anglesea!
Thomas Moore[20]

When in 1824 O'Connell and Sheil had founded the Catholic Association in Dublin, with the object of forwarding the removal of the Catholic
disabilities, it had been harmless enough; indeed they had often found
difficulty in assembling a quorum for its meetings; but their institution of
the 'Catholic Rent' had quickly transformed it into a potent, nation-wide
organization. Every Catholic, rich or poor, was asked to contribute.
Each parish had its collector, closely supported by the priest, and although
the minimum subscription was fixed at no more than a farthing a week, by
the end of the year over £2,400 a month was pouring in from all over the
country. The membership of the Association itself rapidly increased, and
its debates in Dublin, which aped those in the House of Commons,
became one of the sights of the capital. The public was admitted at a
shilling a time, and the press reported the proceedings. The Government
sent shorthand writers but always failed to find a pretext for prosecutions.

G

This was no matter for surprise since the speakers were some of the finest lawyers at the Irish Bar, an institution which attracted the best brains in the country.

Lord Wellesley in Dublin and the Cabinet in London had soon become alarmed at the power which the Association wielded, especially through the 'aggregate meetings' which were held all over the country to endorse the policy of the Association. In 1825, therefore, Goulburn, the Irish Secretary, had introduced and passed a measure designed to suppress the Association, and one of the first questions of policy with which Anglesey was faced was whether or not to recommend a re-enactment of the Goulburn Act, which was due to expire in July 1828. In a long and able memorandum to Peel, Anglesey summed up the questions to be considered. First he asked whether 'any law *can* be framed that shall effectually suppress the meetings? 2ndly. If it is determined to attempt to draw up *such* a bill, is there reasonable ground to hope that the legislature will pass it? 3rdly. What effect will the reagitation of the question have upon the Roman Catholics & indeed upon the whole population?' To the first two questions he believed the answer to be a negative. An effective Bill, which Goulburn's had not been, would be too harsh to satisfy the Commons: a lenient one would continue to be evaded by O'Connell, who had already made good his boast that he would drive 'a coach and six' through Goulburn's Act (chiefly by adding to the title of the Association the word 'New'). Anglesey's only fear was that the Orangemen's processions and meetings, which had also been suppressed by Goulburn's Act, would again be held. But he firmly recommended that the Act should be allowed to expire without notice. If this was agreed, it would be important to use the common law to the full, supported by 'that excellent Establishment, the Constabulary Force'. His advice was taken, but not without the initial opposition of the Prime Minister.

'I have just seen the Duke of Wellington,' Lamb told Anglesey, 'who by the way has contrived to tumble out of his Cabriolet, upon his face, his hands being entangled in his Cloak & so totally unable to save himself — he has cut & bruised his nose & forehead a good deal, but nothing worse.... I was sorry to find ... that his mind was a good deal impressed with the idea of its being necessary to renew the bill.... I stated to him strongly my opinion that the bill could have no other effect than to produce useless & unnecessary exasperation.... He looked staggered & with that air, which he always has, of

a man very little accustomed to be differed from or contradicted,
& changed the subject.'[21]

*   *   *

In April and May there occurred two events of the widest consequence
so far as Catholic emancipation was concerned. The first was the repeal of
the Test and Corporation Acts. These Acts which had been passed in
Charles II's time stipulated that every person before holding any office
in corporations, or any place, civil or military, under the Crown, was to
receive the sacrament according to the rites of the Church of England.
Though the Acts were not rigorously enforced, there were numbers of
staunch Dissenters who suffered under them. The Government in the
House of Commons resisted the motion, but in the Lords it was carried
by forty-four votes. The Duke of Wellington, to the surprise of many,
did not oppose the repeal, and it became law before the end of April.
Anglesey thought he saw that the Duke was altering his course a good
deal in politics. 'It is time he should', he wrote. 'If he will act by the
Catholics as he has done by the Dissenters, all will go well. If he does not,
I wish he would come and govern Ireland himself.' But the hopes of the
pro-Catholics were set too high. Wellington's agreement to the repeal
stemmed less from liberal sympathies than from expediency, for he saw
that a clash at this time between Lords and Commons might well have
been fatal to the continued existence of his Government. Anglesey's
general appreciation of the feeling at Westminster led him to advise
caution. 'I do most anxiously hope', he wrote to Lamb, 'that no attempt
will be made this year to put on the Catholic Question. Give people a
little time to gulp what has been done for the Dissenters, & they will be
ready next season to swallow more. If they are forced this year, they will
choak.'[22]

The second event took place on May 8th, when the annual debate in the
Commons on the Catholic claims ended in a majority of six in their
favour. This was the first time in the life of the 1826 Parliament that there
had been a majority in favour of the Catholics: it showed which way the
wind was blowing. When the Lords debated the resolution on June 9th
and 10th, though it was lost by forty-four votes, the Catholic hopes raised
earlier were not dashed.

'Nothing', wrote Holland to Anglesey, 'could be better for the
cause ... than the tone, temper and argument of the debate....

I think the general intention and spirit of our Great Commander's speech was good and he conveyed to my mind that he *wished at least* to bring the great question to some amicable adjustment.... To talk his and your professional jargon, I do believe he wishes to occupy the high ground and is not without hopes that by manoeuvre or by capitulation he may reach it, but whether he would risk a real battle to attain it may be more doubtful.'[23]

V

I am in a distressing dilemma. All *my* friends are walking off, I hardly know why. Yet all are requiring *me* to stay behind. To have a Rear Guard is very well, if you can count upon support, but when quite abandoned, it alters the case.

Anglesey to Arthur Paget[24]

At the end of May there occurred one of those political crises which start from ridiculously small beginnings and end with consequences of the largest importance. The Commons were discussing whether the franchise of East Retford should be transferred to Birmingham (which was under-represented) or to the hundred in which the borough was situated. Huskisson, the Colonial Secretary, and Palmerston voted for the former, the rest of the Government front bench, including Lamb, for the latter. Such a division of opinion was a very minor matter, and could not reasonably be considered a threat to the government. Huskisson, however,

'went home', as Lamb told Anglesey, 'under feelings of strong excitement, and being apprehensive that his vote would probably be remarked upon by his colleagues next morning, determined to be beforehand with them, & wrote a letter to the Duke of Wellington ... in which in certainly rather short & abrupt terms he expressed that if his vote was thought a breach of that understanding to act together which usually existed between Ministers, he placed his office at the Duke's disposal. This letter was marked private and confidential. The Duke ... treated it as an absolute resignation & immediately laid it before the King. Huskisson upon learning this from the Duke, wrote to him to explain that he could not have intended it as a resignation or as a letter to be submitted to his Majesty, because in the first place it was marked "private and confidential" & in the second that there were in it none of those expressions of duty and attachment which it is always customary & fitting to employ upon such occasions towards the Sovereign.'

The Duke stood firm. There followed an acrimonious correspondence in which he maintained that he had received a definite resignation, but indicating that Huskisson if he wished could retract it. To Lord Dudley, who interceded on Huskisson's behalf, Wellington declared, 'there is no mistake, there can be no mistake, and there shall be no mistake.' Huskisson held that he had never sent in his resignation and therefore could not retract what did not exist. Having tried to secure an audience of the King, which was resisted, there remained nothing for him to do but deliver up the seals of the Colonial Office. In short, the Duke had taken the opportunity to rid himself of the remnants of the Canningites, for most of them, including Lamb, resigned with Huskisson. Lamb said that it had always been a maxim with him that it was more necessary to stand by one's friends when they were in the wrong than when they were in the right. Anglesey laid all the blame on the Prime Minister. 'He certainly *snapped* at the opportunity given to him', he wrote to Holland.

For Anglesey, there was posed for the third time in less than a year the question as to whether or not he should stay at his post. A few days before he heard of the rumpus in London, he had warned Lamb that in Ireland there would be disturbances of a most dangerous nature if Wellington parted with the liberal section of his Government. 'I for one', wrote Anglesey, 'shall beg that they will choose some other Governor to administer the affairs of this country, for I never will stay here to act with an anti-Catholic cabinet.' He was assured by Wellington that there was to be no change of policy — but that, of course, largely depended upon who was to fill the vacant cabinet posts. He cast about for good advice. Lamb recommended him to stay at his post, so as to show that even with an anti-Catholic government in London, an exclusively Orange one in Dublin was not thought prudent or practicable. Holland thought that he would only be justified in resigning if 'another Lamb' could not be found to become Chief Secretary.⁸ The person Anglesey would have preferred above others was Sir George Murray, his son-in-law, who was Commander of the Forces in Ireland, but that admirable man was now taken to fill Huskisson's place at the Colonial Office. The Duke proposed the twenty-nine-year-old Lord Francis Leveson-Gower, later to become first Earl of Ellesmere and a close friend of Wellington's. Anglesey, though he had no personal objection to him and knew him to be a moderate in support of the Catholic claims, was persuaded that it would not be a good appointment. He agreed, nevertheless, to make the best of it and to remain at his post as long as he could do so 'with a fair prospect of rendering effectual service'. As soon as Lord Francis was appointed, Anglesey wrote to tell him of the objections he had had to his appointment. 'Being myself young in official life, altho' old in years, I felt that I wanted a practical man of business — one of more experience than either you or I possess, but I beg you to believe that as we are thus thrown together, I will act with you with as much cordiality and goodwill, as if the appointment had originated in me.'[25]

vi

> The Chief Governor of Ireland at this crisis of Irish History was ... a brave and distinguished soldier.
>
> *Sir R. Peel*[26]

Among those who resigned with Huskisson was Charles Grant, the President of the Board of Trade. To fill his office Wellington brought in Mr Vesey Fitzgerald. In those days it was necessary for a Member to seek re-election on appointment to a government office. A by-election therefore had to be held in County Clare, the seat for which Fitzgerald sat. Under normal conditions this would have been little more than a formality and Fitzgerald, a well-liked man and certainly no anti-Catholic, would have been re-elected without trouble. Anglesey, however, was quick to warn his correspondents in Whitehall that since the liberal elements of the Government had left it, political conditions in Ireland had worsened. On the very day that he gave this warning, the Catholic Association voted £5,000 of the Catholic Rent to support a candidate against Fitzgerald. Before the end of the week over £14,000 had been subscribed towards the election fund. Since no Roman Catholic could *take his seat and vote* in the House of Commons without swearing the Protestant oath, though there was no legal bar to his being *elected*, the Association at first cast around for a pro-Catholic Protestant to fight the election. But in this they failed, for Macnamara, the man they chose, at the last moment declined to stand,[h] and so it came about that O'Connell himself, the most Catholic of Catholics, took the bold step of putting himself up.[i] This caused the greatest excitement all over Ireland, and led to one of the most dramatic electoral events in parliamentary history. Though a number of the more wealthy Catholics as well as some of the Catholic bishops thought it unwise to contest Clare, their influence with the agitators, and indeed with the parish priests, was much less than Anglesey had hoped. From the moment it was known that O'Connell was to stand, the Lord Lieutenant was 'inclined to think he would be returned.... The novelty of the attempt, and the very surprise at it, may set in his favor.'[27]

O'Connell had no time whatever for canvassing. He arrived in Ennis, the chief town of Clare, at two in the morning of nomination day, June 30th, and polling was to begin next day, but his supporters had prepared the ground well. Word had gone forth from the altars of the chapels that the whole male population from the ages of fifteen to eighty was to gather in Ennis. It was estimated that as many as thirty to forty thousand men and women, with one hundred and fifty priests at their head, assembled in the town: and it was costing as much as six guineas to obtain a bed for the night. Baron Tuyll, Anglesey's faithful aide-de-camp, who was on the spot, described for his master the scene on the first day of the poll. 'Everything', he wrote, 'is *perfectly quiet*! Thousands and thousands of people were marched into the Town this morning by Priests, and returned to their *bivouacs* this evening in the same good order in which they entered it. No army can be better disciplined than they are. No drunkenness, or any irregularity allowed. O'Connell is called the Irish Washington & Bolivar; and people, instead of saying "God be with you", say "O'Connell be with you". The children in the street sing "Green is my Livrey" and "the Liberty Tree".'

How out of the ordinary this election was can only be realized when it is remembered that the 40s. freeholders, that is, the numerous small tenants to whom the franchise had been granted at the end of the eighteenth century, were in normal elections driven to the polls like cattle, and that the threat to evict them if they did not vote for their landlord's nominee was a very real one. This fate in fact awaited a number of them in County Clare. 'Between their Landlords and their Priests', wrote Tuyll, 'they are certain to be sufferers in the end, and they seem to feel it. Some were actually seen crying whilst polling.' It was only the intimidating organization[J] set up at Ennis by the priests that procured their votes for O'Connell in such large numbers (the figures at the close of poll on the fifth day were: O'Connell, 2,057; Fitzgerald, 982). Priests were stationed all over the town. 'They harangue, and *preach Rebellion*', wrote Tuyll, 'everywhere, and threaten to withhold all Religious Rights from those who vote for Mr Fitzgerald. Every coach brings fresh importations of them from every part of the Kingdom.'[28]

Fitzgerald was much alarmed. 'No words', he wrote to the viceroy, 'can give you an adequate picture of our state. Rebellion would be much better and more safe.... I confess I cannot help thinking our means of preserving the peace to be extremely inadequate.' But Anglesey had taken full precautions. As a result of a secret visit by Tuyll to a meeting of the Catholic Association earlier in the year, which had become known and made much of by the press,[k] he had been sent by Anglesey into honourable banishment upon a tour of inspection of the constabulary, and as soon as it was known that there would be a contest in Clare, the viceroy had taken advantage of his aide-de-camp's presence in the area to cause a strong muster of the force at Ennis under the pretence of inspecting them. At the same time there was encamped outside the town a military force sufficient to keep the peace and to ensure freedom of election.[29] [1]

For the Lord Lieutenant himself it was an anxious time. Lamb (who had not yet been succeeded by Leveson-Gower) and Doherty, the Solicitor-General, the member of the Irish Government with whom Anglesey was most intimate,[m] were in London, and he felt very isolated without them. To Lamb he wrote, 'Now if I had had you here, I might have left the civil concerns with you, & gone a soldiering myself which is my natural vocation.' To Holland he wrote, 'I am, as you may guess, in high force; I believe I ought to be very much frightened & worn down by the weight of responsibility but somehow or another I cannot help thinking that everything will shake right.' And so it did, for on July 5th Tuyll reported that the election was peacefully concluded, with O'Connell the new Member for Clare. 'I have made up my mind,' Anglesey told Holland, 'or nearly made it up, to believe that this will be a very delightful termination of this odious question. Probably at the next general election the returns will be chiefly Catholic. And what then? Why', he continued with considerable prescience, 'they will be as subservient & in a very little time as eager for everything that is good (*for their pockets*) as the present proprietors of good things!'[30]

* * *

While the issue at Ennis was still undecided Anglesey had written a letter of the greatest importance.

'Such is the power of the agitators', he told Lord Francis, 'that I am quite certain they could lead on the people to open rebellion at a moment's notice.... I believe their success inevitable — that no power under heaven can arrest its progress. There may be rebellion, you may put to death thousands, you may suppress it, but it will only put off the day of compromise, and in the meantime the country is still more impoverished and the minds of the people are if possible still more alienated, and ruinous expence is entailed upon the Empire. But supposing the whole Evil was concentrated in the Association, and that if that was suppressed, all would go smoothly, where is the man who can tell me *how* to suppress it? Many, many cry out that the nuisance must be abated, that the Government is supine, that the violence of the Demagogues is intolerable, but I have not yet found one person capable of pointing out a remedy. All are mute when you ask them to define their proposition. All that even the most determined opposers of emancipation say is, that it is better to leave things as they are than to risk any change. But will things remain as they are? Certainly not. They are bad, they must get worse, and I see no possible means of improving them but by depriving the demagogues of the power of directing the people. And by taking Messrs O'Connell, Sheil, and the rest of them from the Association, and placing them in the House of Commons, this desirable object would be at once accomplished....

'I abhor the idea of truckling to the overbearing Catholic demagogues. To make any movement towards conciliation under the present excitement and system of terror would revolt me. But I do most conscientiously, and after the most earnest consideration of the subject, give it as my conviction that the first moment of composure and tranquillity should be seized to signify the intention of adjusting the question, lest another period of calm should not present itself.'

Lord Francis at once communicated this letter to the Duke, who showed it to the King. The Prime Minister's only comment was that he could not see his way through the difficulties which impeded a final arrangement.

In the face of this, Anglesey's duty was to keep hammering at the door for all he was worth. 'Now is the time, or never', he wrote.

> Notwithstanding the present frightful aspect, I would venture my life that I could even now settle the question upon terms which would satisfy *all* the Catholics, and *all but* the Ultras of the Protestants. If the King and the Government would decide upon settling the question & would confide in me, I should have no fear of the result. I feel confident that I could ensure such tranquillity for a time, as would take away from the measure all appearance of its being the result of fear, & that in a few months Ireland would assume an entirely new aspect.'[31]

To his brother Arthur, Anglesey opened his mind. He was sure that his energetic representations would produce a deep effect even upon the King, who was so seldom told the truth. But he feared that the Prime Minister had not the nerve to let the viceroy play his hand, that the Duke was temporizing and vacillating. Nearly three weeks later Anglesey wrote to Charles Paget that he had 'no doubt that the Premier will try to do everything without me, altho' he takes his cue from me, & I doubt', he wrote, 'if he will be as readily trusted as I should be.'[32]

vii

> The first step of all is to reconcile the King's mind to an arrangement. Till that should have been done, I should deceive myself, by talking about it at all.
> *Wellington to Anglesey*[33]

In this uneasy state the situation rested, as summer turned into autumn. That it had been radically transformed by O'Connell's election, that Catholic emancipation was now the only alternative to large-scale revolution, which might well take all the resources of the Empire to quell, seemed clear to nearly everyone on both sides of the Irish Sea. Yet neither Wellington nor Peel would give the slightest indication that he was aware of the position. But aware of it in fact they were. Before July was out, the two statesmen had come to the conclusion that Catholic emancipation could not much longer be delayed. For Wellington this meant the start of a long and well-prepared seige of the King's conscience.

For Peel the change of policy seemed to point to resignation, though he promised to support the Government wholeheartedly in the measure after his retirement from office, which was to take place only after the King had been won over.[34]

The greatest secrecy regarding their change of front was observed by the Prime Minister and the Home Secretary: the only other member of the Government made privy to it was the Lord Chancellor. No one else, not even those most closely concerned with the government of Ireland such as Anglesey and Lord Francis, was to be given an inkling of what was afoot. Peel felt it his duty, as he confessed twenty years later, to conduct the correspondence with Ireland without the slightest reference to the settlement of the Catholic question. Consequently all that Anglesey received from him in reply to his urgent representations was the cold assurance that the advisers of the King would continue to direct their most serious consideration to the whole state of Ireland and determine some time before the commencement of the next session what advice to offer the King and Parliament.[35]

The viceroy meanwhile tried to discover from Lord Francis the Duke's real sentiments and ulterior objects. 'It will not do', he insisted, 'to be hanging on much longer on uncertainties.' But Lord Francis was just as much in the dark himself,[n] though unofficially convinced that the question would be settled next session. 'If', he wrote to Anglesey, 'you wish for a bet on the subject, though I am no sporting man myself, I could procure you at Crockford's any odds you please in favour of this result.'[36]

On August 1st, the Duke wrote for his Royal master a lengthy memorandum giving a picture of the situation in Ireland. He concluded it with these words:

'We have a rebellion impending over us in Ireland, ... and we have in England a Parliament which we cannot dissolve, the majority of which is of opinion, with many wise and able men, that the remedy is to be found in Roman Catholic emancipation.... Whatever the King and his ministers may think of the chances of pacification which Roman Catholic emancipation would afford, it is the duty of all to look our difficulties in the face and to lay the ground for getting the better of them.'

In reply the King gave his full permission for the Duke to go into the question with Peel and the Lord Chancellor, adding that for the moment he pledged himself to nothing. Two days later, the King, angered by the viceroy's conversion to emancipation, sent for Wellington to propose to him that Anglesey should be removed from his post. The Duke thought his presence there very inconvenient, but was afraid his removal would be found to be still more so. The Premier, as he wrote to Peel, told the King that it would be impossible to make public 'the real causes of dissatisfaction with [Anglesey's] conduct, some of which are personal; and that the measure would be liable to much misrepresentation, and might do mischief.' With this the King and Peel reluctantly agreed.[37]

What the Duke held to be the real causes of dissatisfaction with the Lord Lieutenant's conduct were not entirely fictitious. First, having decided that emancipation was the only solution to the troubles of Ireland, Anglesey had resisted (and undoubtedly correctly), so far as he could, all attempts by the Government in London to launch prosecutions against leaders of the Association; second, he had consorted a little too freely and often with men such as Lord Cloncurry,° who were certainly enemies of the Establishment; third, he had not, perhaps, shown enough indignation with Tuyll for attending the meeting of the Catholic Association; and fourth, he was possibly insufficiently guarded in his conversation. There may have been a grain of truth in Wellington's exaggerated complaint that the Lord Lieutenant had been 'repeatedly heard to say that his hands were tied up by ministers, otherwise he would do everything that was wished'.[38p]

Wellington, of course, had only to confide his intentions to Anglesey to put an end to these embarrassments, but that was not the Great Commander's way, and after all it could not be expected that he should place his confidence in one who was a Canningite, and in the eyes of the Duke's Ultra friends, such as Londonderry, a traitor to the party.

That Anglesey suspected what was going on regarding his personal position, though with the emphasis wrongly placed, is shown by his comment to Holland of August 4th:

'I am assured that great efforts are making to decry my Government & that the King's *secret* advisers are busily engaged in poisoning His Mind with regard to my measures & conduct.... If they succeed & if H.My. & his advisers have nerves to try a contrary course, I have little doubt that they will have the house about their ears. I feel that I am conferring a favor upon *them* by remaining, — and not *they* upon me by keeping me here.

'I am disposed to think that the Duke of Wellington would

willingly adjust the question, but that he does not know how to set
about it. I feel confident that I do, but he has not nerves to put
himself into my hands, & to open his heart to me.'[39]

viii

*Lord Anglesey begged that when I got back to London, if I was able by any means
whatever to pick up what were the intentions of the Government, I would write him
word.* The Lord-Lieutenant of Ireland begging a private gentleman to let him
know if he could find out what the Prime Minister meant upon a question deeply
affecting the peace and welfare of the country, which that Lord-Lieutenant was
appointed to govern, and upon which question he was every week stating to
the Government the opinions he himself entertained — a strange instance of the
withholding of that confidence which, for both their sakes, ought to have existed.
Lord Palmerston's journal [1829][40]

Tension between Whitehall and the Castle steadily mounted during the
last months of the year. Once confidence had been lost, relations between
the two governments deteriorated with increasing speed. Every action
which the viceroy took or failed to take acted as a further irritant to
Wellington and to Peel. The less their intentions were communicated to
Anglesey and the more coldly formal their letters became, the greater
was the stimulus to his sense of angry frustration.

*   *   *

At the end of July O'Connell asked for an audience of the Lord
Lieutenant, ostensibly to engage him to set up a commission of inquiry
into a case of murder.

'I have no doubt however,' wrote Anglesey to Peel, 'that Mr O'C
has other objects. It has been considered whether I should receive
him, & universally agreed that I ought not to object. It will be my
business to be very patient, very guarded, but not severely reserved,
& whilst he is endeavouring to penetrate me, to try if I can make any
thing out of him.

'I give you the information in advance, as I am aware that this occurrence may, & probably will be insidiously commented upon. To guard as well as I can against his misrepresentations, I shall take care to have a witness present.'[q]

Anglesey thought the meeting a success. The great agitator's manner was respectful and gentlemanlike, and when the viceroy stressed his determination to put down insurrection from whatever quarter it might come, O'Connell '*humbly* offered *his best assistance*' in preserving the peace. He also listened to a lecture on the unwisdom of personal attacks on Wellington and Peel, and the need to conciliate the Duke, upon whom it rested to determine whether a measure of relief should be proposed or not. Though Peel at the time saw no reason why the Lord Lieutenant should not see O'Connell, this interview was one of the matters covertly complained of in the acrimonious correspondence which later in the year took place between Wellington and Anglesey.[r] Another was the Lord Lieutenant's firmly stated scruple about recommending an Irish List pension for the Marchioness of Westmeath. This lady, a daughter of Lord Salisbury, described by Henry Fox as a pretty little vixen, married Lord Westmeath in 1812 but was soon after judicially separated from him. She was a close friend of Wellington's and of the King's. It cannot be denied that Anglesey was in the right, for as Greville said, though the Duke 'does not love jobs, Ly. Westmeath's pension can hardly be called anything else.'[s] '*If*', Anglesey replied to the Duke's request, 'I may consider the allotment of a pension of £400 to the Marchioness of Westmeath as an order of the King, His Majesty's Commands shall be instantly obeyed, but I could not bear that it should stand as an act of mine.' Lord Francis was wholeheartedly with the Lord Lieutenant in this matter, and supported him in agreeing not to send the usual, formal recommendation from the Irish Government.[41]

In the same period, Peel became incensed at the Lord Lieutenant's failure to inform him that the Irish Yeomanry had *not* been disarmed. Anglesey replied that the newspaper reports to that effect (which were the cause of Peel's worry) were so absurd that he did not think it necessary to contradict them; adding, perhaps a little too sarcastically, 'It is not easy to foresee what importance may on your side of the water be attached to the idle & frequently mischievous reports that are put forth here.'[42]

* * *

Meanwhile, as was to be expected, things did not stand still in Ireland. In early September Anglesey calculated upon a quiet winter. He could imagine, he told Peel, 'nothing less inviting than a rebel bivouac during a long dreary winter's night. Therefore it appears probable that you will have time to legislate before we begin to fight.' Yet before the end of the month he was forced to admit that there had been a rapid and alarming change. The number of meetings and processions, and the attendance at them, increased rapidly, especially in the counties of Tipperary, Limerick and Clare, and the priests were for the first time clearly losing control of the people. In more than one instance in mid-September they had interfered and remonstrated in vain. Just as menacing as the Catholics were the Orangemen. Anglesey reported that great numbers of them were anxiously looking for an opportunity to draw blood.' 'Regardless of the danger to their brethren in the South', he told Holland, 'the northern Furies would willingly set on.'[43]

What the viceroy now proposed for the consideration of the Cabinet was that a proclamation should be issued giving the people 'full notice of the illegality of such assemblies, and warning of the risk they expose themselves to by attending them'. But he pointed out that such a proclamation would be useless 'without a fixed determination to enforce it, and to disperse the meetings if they should take place after the notice given.' He therefore asked for reinforcements. Wellington was prompt to oblige. Without delay six infantry and two cavalry regiments were ordered to be ready to embark for Ireland.[u] 'I must say you do not do things by halves', wrote Anglesey. 'Why, you have placed at my disposal troops enough to control the Brunswickers and the Association even if they should coalesce and combine to make war upon me!' To which came back the typically Wellingtonian reply: 'Of course we placed at your disposal every available soldier we had; and if the insurrection had not been checked, we should have called out all the resources of the empire to put it down.'[44]

ix

Lord Anglesey and Lord Francis Leveson Gower have no notion how much they increase my difficulties with the King by their unwillingness to carry into execution the measures necessary to show that the government will preserve the peace of the country.

Wellington to Peel

'For God's sake,' exclaimed a witty Irishwoman to Lord Anglesey, 'don't make yourself so much beloved by us all: do something unpopular, that you may be left here a little longer.'

'The Times'[45]

It had been the normal practice in the past when a proclamation was issued by the Government of Ireland, that it should be signed by as many Privy Councillors as could be brought together for the purpose, but in this case Anglesey decided to issue it in his name alone. His official reasons for this were the need for speed and the availability of only a small number of Privy Councillors, none of whom would have lent it much weight. The Duke suspected that his real reason was a wish to avoid having it signed by the Privy Councillors who would most probably be found in Dublin and the neighbourhood, who 'being the old servants of the Crown are Brunswickers and Orangemen!' Anglesey told Melbourne four years later that the few Privy Councillors available would have attached ridicule rather than importance to the document. Wellington and Peel were furious with him, and let him know it.[46]

Even before the proclamation was issued the meetings in the South ceased. Palmerston says that the Association leaders

'were delighted by a hint which they received from Lord Anglesey, through Parnell and Spring Rice, that these meetings could not be permitted, and that he *must* put a stop to them, and only wished that the Association would themselves anticipate him; and they accordingly issued their proclamation a few days before his came out. The effect of the *two* — and *one* would have been sufficient — was magical; and all popular demonstrations from that time ceased on the part of the Catholics, though not entirely on that of the Orangemen.'[47]

The Lord Lieutenant was now much pressed to prosecute the Catholic leaders for their inflammatory speeches and breaches of the peace. Jack Lawless, a prominent member of the Association, who had just completed

a tour of agitation in the North, was in fact arrested, but Anglesey skilfully avoided wholesale prosecutions, such as the King and the Prime
Minister demanded. Wellington wanted the prosecution of everybody
that could possibly be prosecuted. 'These prosecutions', he wrote to Peel,
'will tend to put the Protestants in better temper with the Lord-Lieutenant,
and when he shall find himself embarked in the same cause with them, and
finds them in good humour with him, he will probably treat them better
than he does.'[48]

Some days before the issue of the proclamation, Anglesey, who had
been secretly in communication with persons in the confidence of the
Association leaders, once again returned to his paramount duty of pressing
on the Duke and Peel the urgent need for settling the Catholic question.
Under the heading 'most private & most confidential', he wrote to the
Duke:

'I have been long doubting if I should communicate with you upon
certain information I have, regarding the question of Catholic
Emancipation, for, as you have never named the subject to me, I have
had a delicacy in introducing it. Upon full consideration however, I
deem it essential that you should know what I know; and as I have
not the slightest desire to dive into the secrets of your mind upon the
subject, & in fact do not require any answer to this communication, I
feel convinced that good may arise from it, whilst it is thus impossible
that any harm can result from giving you the information.

'I have known for a considerable time, & a recent communication
has strongly corroborated the fact, that the Catholic Question may be
adjusted at this moment with more facility (upon as good terms, &
with as little opposition on the part both of the Bishops & of the
agitators), than at any other period. I have reason to feel confident
that ... there would only be that sort of resistance by the Agitators,
that a French garrison which is most anxious for terms makes to
save its honor. How far such an arrangement would be palatable to
the Protestants, you are much more competent than I am to judge of;
but I am bound to state my opinion that even amongst the Protestants
there is a conviction that things can not remain as they are, & that
many of those who were formerly very violent, would be glad to
acquiesce in moderate concession to the Catholics, provided the
40s. freeholders were abolished.

'Pray bear in mind that in making this communication I am not in the slightest degree attempting to advocate the cause, but that I feel it to be an indispensable duty to put you in possession of all I know.'[49]

X

The Beau [Wellington], according to custom, writes atrociously, and his charges against Lord Anglesey are of the rummest kind. Lord Anglesey in his answers beats him easy in all ways.

Mr Creevey to Miss Ord

Lord Anglesey is gone mad. He is bit by a mad Papist; or instigated by the love of popularity.

Wellington to Lord Bathurst[50]

The approach of winter brought on a series of bad attacks of the tic. These, coupled with the tension and irritation of his situation, caused the Lord Lieutenant to consider whether he ought not to retire. Holland's advice, which as ever weighed heavily with him, was clear as to principle, if of little help as to timing. 'No man', he wrote, 'but yourself would have been able to keep the Measure open for decision so long. When the time approaches where that can be done no longer, you must insist on decision or retirement. It is difficult not to say impossible for your best friends here to ascertain that time — It is one of the painful circumstances of your arduous situation that on that point you must decide yourself.' Arthur Paget's advice went further. However badly Wellington and Peel might behave, he hoped that Anglesey would stand by the Irish to the last moment, leaving to the King and Government the odium of recalling him. 'I should not', he wrote, 'deprive them of that additional benefit.' Nor were they in the event deprived of it. By the second week in November, the acrimonious correspondence between the two heads of Government, which led before the year was out to Anglesey's recall, was under way.[51]

There were two sparks which lit the fuse. First, Anglesey's decision, after careful consultation with the Irish Lord Chancellor, not to remove from the magistracy O'Gorman Mahon and Tom Steele, two prominent members of the Association, though desired to do so by Wellington and Peel; and, second, his staying at the house of Lord Cloncurry, who immediately afterwards attended a meeting of the Catholic Association.

'What do you say', asked the Duke of Dean Phillpotts, his Protestant mentor, 'to the Lord-Lieutenant, the Lord Chancellor, the Chief Secretary, and their families, going to Lord Cloncurry for the Curragh races? A traitor!' The Duke's pompous and querulous rebuke upon these two subjects drew a detailed defence from the Lord Lieutenant of Ireland. What had happened in the case of O'Gorman Mahon, he explained, was that the High Sheriff of Clare had called a meeting with the object of forming a Brunswick Club, to which Mahon, whose intention was to oppose the project, had been refused admittance. The High Sheriff had called out the military on his own authority, fearing that the meeting which he himself had convened, and of which he was to be chairman, might cause a riot — 'a good specimen of Ireland', as Palmerston put it! No disturbance in fact took place, but as the detachments were dispersing, Mahon remonstrated in unmeasured terms with their commanding officer. The Irish Law Officers came to the conclusion that this breach of decorum was not indictable. 'Upon what ground then', asked Anglesey of the Duke, 'would the Lord Lieutenant have stood, if he should have determined upon the dismissal of Mr Mahon? If *his* conduct was censurable, what was that of the High Sheriff? I do not repent of the decision to which I came, I think it was just, & I am sure it was expedient.' As to the case of 'Honest Tom Steele', who was said to have adjured his listeners *by their allegiance to the Catholic Association* to be tranquil, Anglesey informed the Prime Minister that no action could be taken, as the imputed words had never even been deposed to! The Duke's anger that the King's representative should have stayed in the house of one whom he so unjustly considered a traitor, met with a spirited defence.

'When I went to [Lord Cloncurry's] house,' protested the viceroy, 'all I knew of him was that he was an active & intelligent Magistrate, an ardent lover of Ireland, an indefatigable supporter of her interest, & a zealous friend to Catholic Emancipation. During the time I was at his residence, I learned his earlier history — that he had been strongly suspected of Jacobinism at the commencement of the French Revolution; that he had been arrested upon suspicion of being implicated in O'Connor's treason; that he had been liberated for want of proof, but that he had subsequently been sent to the Tower during the suspension of the Habeas Corpus Act; from whence he had been again liberated without trial, & therefore I have a right to suppose without guilt.'

As to Cloncurry's attendance at the Association, Anglesey explained that his only purpose in going had been to suppress, if possible, one of the most pernicious resolutions that could have been passed, namely that which introduced the 'non-intercourse' system, by which Catholics all over Ireland were to boycott Protestants.[52v]

In answer to this carefully worded and good-tempered vindication[w] from Dublin, the Duke returned a further lengthy letter of complaint, covering much the same ground. He added that he considered this painful correspondence to be of a private nature. At this the Lord Lieutenant jibbed, reserving to himself, should it become necessary for his justification, the right to make public use of the correspondence, the subjects dealt with being chiefly of a public character. This attitude determined Wellington, as he told the King, to put an end to the correspondence as being quite useless, and very unbecoming. 'I am convinced that the best measure that I can adopt is to discontinue to write to His Excellency; and to see whether he will alter his measures in consequence of my suggestions.'[53]

The most acrid parts of this remarkable correspondence were Anglesey's accusation that he had up to that moment been left entirely in ignorance not only as to the Prime Minister's intentions towards Ireland, but also as to his sentiments in regard to the Lord Lieutenant's policy; and Wellington's gratuitous gibe that Anglesey was quite mistaken if he supposed that he was the first Lord Lieutenant who had governed Ireland with an impartial hand.

It was clear that a rupture could no longer be avoided. On Christmas Eve Wellington brought his correspondence with Anglesey before the Cabinet, and obtained their consent to the viceroy's recall. The King's agreement was given with alacrity, and Anglesey was duly notified on December 30th. The following day he informed his household that they should prepare for his departure in a fortnight's time.[54]

From London, Princess Lieven told her brother in Russia that the sudden recall of the viceroy had much disturbed the metropolis. 'You know', she wrote, 'that it was the Marquess of Anglesey who occupied this post, the noblest and most honourable of men in England.'[55]

xi

When M. de Talleyrand heard that Lord Anglesey was recalled he saw at once that the Duke had determined on conceding the Irish Catholic claims, and that he did not mean anyone else to have the credit of the concession.

Lord Palmerston[56]

On December 4th Dr Patrick Curtis, the Roman Catholic Archbishop of Armagh, who was in his eighty-eighth year, had written a long letter to the Duke, entreating him for the good of all parties to come to a decision on Catholic emancipation without further delay. Curtis had been of service to Wellington during the Peninsular War: as rector of the Irish College at Salamanca, he had given much vital information about the movements of the French. A government pension had resulted, and a commendation from the Duke in which he described him as an honest, loyal man, who behaved well throughout the war. In his reply to the Reverend Doctor, the Duke made an unequivocal statement (without so much as marking it 'confidential', and the like of which he had never thought fit to vouchsafe to the viceroy), declaring that he was 'sincerely anxious to witness a settlement of the Roman Catholic question; which by benefiting the State would confer a benefit upon every individual belonging to it. But I confess', he continued, 'that I see no prospect of such a settlement.... If we could bury it in oblivion for a short time, and employ that time diligently in the consideration of its difficulties on all sides (for they are great), I should not despair of seeing a satisfactory remedy.' That this extraordinary letter should almost immediately have become public knowledge ought not to have surprised anyone conversant with the ways of the Irish post office at that date, particularly as it was franked by the Duke himself. Curtis in his reply declared that its contents reached the public from the post office before the letter reached his hands.[57]

On December 22nd, Richard Sheil, one of those to whom Curtis had shown the Duke's letter let the Archbishop know that Anglesey wished to see it.[x] In consequence the Archbishop sent him the original. Anglesey's first words on reading it are believed to have been: 'Well, I hope and am inclined to think that it looks well for the cause.' He then considered what he should do. There were two alternatives before him. Either he should complain to the Home Secretary officially that the Prime Minister was engaged in a clandestine correspondence with the Catholic Primate behind the Lord Lieutenant's back, or, as he put it, 'follow His Grace's example'.

He did not hesitate long. The next day he wrote a letter to the Archbishop which showed that he had decided upon the latter course.

'*Phoenix Park, December 23d,* 1828

'Most Rev. Sir,

'I thank you for the confidence you have reposed in me. Your letter gives me information upon a subject of the highest interest. I did not know the precise sentiments of the Duke of Wellington upon the present state of the Catholic question. Knowing it, I shall venture to offer my opinion upon the course that it behoves the Catholics to pursue. Perfectly convinced, that the final and cordial settlement of this great question, can alone give peace, harmony, and prosperity to all classes of His Majesty's subjects in this kingdom, I must acknowledge my disappointment on learning that there is no prospect of its being effected during the ensuing Session of Parliament. I, however, derive some consolation from observing, that his Grace is not wholly averse to the measure; for, if he can be induced to promote it, he of all men will have the greatest facility in carrying it into effect. If I am correct in this opinion, it is obviously most important, that the Duke of Wellington should be propitiated; that no obstacle, that can by possibility be avoided, should be thrown in his way; that all personal and offensive insinuations should be suppressed; and that ample allowance should be made for the difficulties of his situation.

'Difficult it certainly is, for he has to overcome the very strong prejudices and the interested motives of many persons of the highest influence, as well as to allay the real alarm of many of the more ignorant Protestants.

'I differ from the opinion of the Duke, that an attempt should be made to "bury in oblivion", the question for a short time. First, because the thing is utterly impossible; and next because, if the thing were possible, I fear that advantage might be taken of the pause, by representing it as a panic, achieved by the late violent re-action, and by proclaiming that, if the Government at once and peremptorily decided against concession, the Catholics would cease to agitate, and then all the miseries of the last years of Ireland will have to be re-acted. What I do recommend is, that the measure should not be for a moment lost sight of; that anxiety should continue to be manifested, that all constitutional (in contradistinction to merely legal) means should be resorted to, to forward the cause, but that, at the same time, the most patient forbearance, the most submissive obedience to the laws, should be inculcated, that no personal and offensive language should be held towards those who oppose the claims. Personality offers no advantage; it effects no good; on the contrary, it offends, and confirms predisposed aversion. Let the Catholic trust to the justice of his cause, to the growing liberality of mankind. Unfortunately, he has lost some friends, and fortified his enemies, within the last six months, by unmeasured and unnecessary violence. He will soonest recover from the present stagnation of his fortunes, by showing more temper, and by trusting to the legislature for redress.

'Brute force, he should be assured, can effect nothing. It is the legislature that must decide this great question; and my greatest anxiety is, that it should be met by the Parliament, under the most favourable circumstances, and that the opposers of Catholic Emancipation shall be disarmed by the patient forbearance, as well as by the unwearied perseverance of its advocates.

'My warm anxiety to promote the general interests of this country, is the motive that has induced me to give an opinion and to offer advice.

'I have the honor, &c

'ANGLESEY'[58]

By Anglesey's direction, this letter appeared in the *Dublin Evening Post* on New Year's Day, that is two days after he had received his official notice of recall.[y] The immediate result was a formal order from Peel commanding the Lord Lieutenant to return to England at once, and to place the government of Ireland in the hands of Lords Justices. Soon after receiving this order, Anglesey was described as very smiling and glorious, but angry, and declaring that he would do just the same again if he had to choose his line of conduct.[59]

To Arthur Paget he revealed his reasons for making the letter public.

'I shd tell you', he wrote, 'that the letter to Curtis was entirely private. I did not even direct it myself; & I made Gosset explain that it was confidential. It was to pacify the public mind that I consented to its being put forth. It was thus: they dreaded the consequences of the first ebullitions upon hearing of the Recall. Persons came to me in dismay. The Association was to meet the next day. The most violent Resolutions would have been adopted. The whole Country would have been in a blaze.

'*I* could not address the public. *I* could not communicate with the Association. It struck me that the advice contained in that Letter, which was complimentary to the Duke, admonitory to the Catholics, friendly to their cause, altho' in some respects perhaps not quite palatable as conveying a censure for unnecessary violence, yet holding out hope & shewing the warmth & sincerity of a sincere advocate — it struck me, I say, that the exhibition of this letter might have a good effect, & I really saw no other mode of conveying my sentiments.

'The effect as you will have seen was most powerful & effective.'[60]

This was no exaggeration. The resolutions passed next day at the Association's meeting were far from inflammatory, and included one which enjoined all Catholics to submit themselves to the guidance of so enlightened a Lord Lieutenant. Similar exhortations from their leaders appeared in the press. These, together with Anglesey's restrained conduct during the days which preceded his departure, had the most salutary effect. Throughout Ireland there reigned an unprecedented tranquillity.

*   *   *

The day of Anglesey's departure is memorable in Irish history. At ten in the morning of January 19th, he left Phoenix Park for the Castle. There for two hours he received and replied to Addresses, and held his farewell levée. At noon, in brilliant sunshine, he quitted the Castle, preceded by representatives of the Dublin parishes bearing banners of white silk bound with mourning black. He was dressed in his usual plain blue body-coat[z] and check trousers, with the Star of the Garter gleaming on his breast. The route to Kingstown was lined with hundreds of thousands of people, many of them wearing crape in their hats; nearly every house was draped with the same material. The procession of carriages which followed was over three miles in length.

'There was something in the whole sight', wrote Char to her husband, from Phoenix Park that night, 'which never can be described or felt again. Such a mixture of wretchedness and *exultation*

as I did not conceive possible! To see *you torn* from a populace,
from a Nation which perfectly adored you, & for no fault but that of
having won their hearts! ... You have no idea of the magnificence
of the procession — The string of Carriages lasted for an hour after
you had pass'd & in such dead silence it moved along that it was
much more like a grand funeral than what it was! There was no jok-
ing amongst the lower orders. My Maid here is an Irish woman &
she was walking amongst the lower orders, & she says that there
was not one smile nor scarcely a word uttered amongst them, when
even at *Funerals* these *lowest* orders will have their little jokes & fun,
and she heard several say "There he goes with those dear Children
who are as brave as himself — look at them riding in such a
throng." '

Before embarking, Anglesey made a short speech declaring that the
affection shown him by the people of Ireland would ever be deeply
engraven on his heart, and advising them to persevere in that constitutional course which would establish in their country that happiness, unity
and prosperity which he was so anxious to promote. Accompanied by his
brother Charles and his sons William, Alfred and George, he then
stepped into his barge. As he did so, tumultuous cheers and shouts of
'Farewell to Anglesey' caused his eyes to fill with tears, while Alfred and
George (aged twelve and ten) were moved to audible sobs. As he was rowed
round the harbour so as to give the crowds a last sight of him, each ship,
with yards undressed, thundered out its salute. Lady Cloncurry reported
to Char that the scene at Kingstown after he had left 'was beyond all
description — Not a dry eye from the highest to the lowest. The Duchess
of Leinster & all the great Ladies as well as the lower orders cried most
dreadfully.' When the Lord Chancellor arrived back at Phoenix Park, he
too burst into tears.

That night in Dublin the people 'prov'd', as Char put it to her husband,
'their devotion to *your advice*, for *positively* you might have heard a pin
drop in any of the streets, nor has a drunken Person been seen.'[61]

xii

Now as to Anglesey. To his wise, firm, good-tempered and impartial administration, the Government and the Empire owe the power of passing the measure as a boon and not as an article of capitulation.... He comes home full of just resentment and anxious to vindicate himself from the aspersions of having committed a breach of duty. But he finds the measure he had recommended, and for his promotion of which he was censured and to all appearances punished, openly patronized by Government. He immediately suppresses his personal grievances, supports the measure with all his might and main, and labours as much as if he was himself the Minister to reconcile the Irish to those parts of it which are calculated to offend them, and which he himself disapproves of but acquiesces in as the price of the measure.... If this be not magnanimity and patriotism, I know not the meaning of those words.

Lord Holland to Henry Fox, March 1829[62]

On January 15th, four days before Anglesey's departure, leading members of the Cabinet dined with the King at Windsor, and at that dinner he consented to the opening of the Catholic question. The King's Speech, read on February 5th, recommended legislation to suppress the Catholic Association, and a review of the laws which 'impose civil disabilities on His Majesty's Roman Catholic subjects'. The Suppression Bill received the Royal Assent on March 5th, but over the Relief Bill the King gave the Duke infinite last-minute trouble. On March 2nd he threatened to abdicate. Two days later he refused to contemplate any alteration in the Oath of Supremacy, accepted the resignations of Ministers and then, only a few hours before Peel was due to open the debate in the Commons, begged them to continue in office and to go ahead with full royal sanction. On April 13th both Bills received the Royal Assent.[aa]

'How fortunate for the Catholics', wrote Anglesey while the bills were in progress, 'that the ministers did not bite at my proposition to adjust the question for them! I could have obtained much better terms (as they would have been erroneously thought to be) for the Protestants. I therefore rejoice that things are as they are. Notwithstanding a few trifling and silly points, which give the appearance of the measure being adopted against the grain, I do think [the Relief Bill] is a handsome production, and must please the Catholics.'[63]

In the Lords, Anglesey did his best to get the Suppression Bill thrown out. 'You are,' he told their lordships on third reading, 'about to confer a great boon on the people of Ireland. You are about to perform an act of grace; let me implore you not to allow [it] to be preceded by an ungracious act.' He pointed out that the Act could have no effect upon the Catholic Association as that body had already voluntarily liquidated itself.[64] In considering how it might affect other societies, he asked,

'What generated the Brunswick clubs? There is not a noble Brunswicker present who will not at once say, the Catholic Association. They professed to establish themselves in opposition to the Catholic Association, and for the purpose of supporting the government.... I give full credit to the Brunswickers for the loyalty of their intentions, but I, for one, having been at the head of the Irish government when they were formed, beg leave to say that I could not give them my thanks for their efforts, for I felt that I had ample power, and had no occasion whatever for their assistance. On the contrary I only felt that I had an additional nuisance to control. But, my lords, as these clubs grew out of the Association, so they will perish with its dissolution.... Let me implore your lordships, then, to set aside this bill and pass at once and rapidly to the measure of relief.'[65]

*   *   *

It had been Anglesey's intention to bring on, as soon after his return as possible, a debate in the Lords, in the course of which he could vindicate his conduct; but as soon as it was learnt that emancipation was to be granted he agreed to defer it until the Acts had been passed. For the purpose of the debate he required the King's permission to quote his correspondence with the Duke; thus on the day after his arrival in London he begged for an audience. This to the surprise of almost everyone was immediately granted.

'The Duke', wrote Mrs Arbuthnot indignantly, 'thinks it highly improper of the King to have received Lord Anglesey so immediately & before he had reported his arrival in London to any of the Ministers, more particularly as Ld Wellesely was in London for months before the King wd. see him. The King', she continued quite accurately, 'was more eager than any one to recall Ld Anglesey, ...and the Duke said he had no doubt wd., in private to Lord Anglesey, say he had done all he could to save him but in vain.'

Exactly what happened at the audience is not clear. Wellington learned from the King next day that Anglesey had 'blustered & bullied', but had not received permission to make use of the correspondence. This the Duke was quite prepared to believe was a royal lie. It put him in an awkward position during the debate (which did not in the event take place until May 4th), for he was then obliged to admit that although he had been authorized to state that Anglesey was *not* permitted to read the letters, there might have been a mistake, and that Anglesey himself might consider that he *was* so permitted. In the debate Anglesey replied that he had stated to the King what had been his conduct and policy while in Ireland, adding:

> 'I did not believe his Majesty had seen all my letters, but only extracts, or he could not have derived the impression of my conduct which I thought he had imbibed. He said that he had seen them. I, however, placed in his Majesty's hands copies of them, which he was graciously pleased to read at the moment, and then, on my request to that effect, to tell me that he saw no violent tone in that correspondence, and that I might use them all in any way I pleased for my vindication, and also any other documents which I thought proper to call for. His Majesty was graciously pleased further to say, upon my observing that I could easily omit those passages in which the Royal Name was introduced, that he had no desire for such omission.'

It seems clear from this categorical statement that the King had said one thing to the Duke and another to the Marquess, as was so often his way when confronted with personalities stronger than his own.[66]

Coming of necessity so long after the recall, the debate of May 4th caused less interest at the time than if it had occurred three months earlier. The speeches of Anglesey and the Duke contained lengthy extracts from the correspondence, but nothing new emerged. As early as January 13th, Anglesey had confessed to Holland that there was one thing in which he was not wholly borne out in his assertions.

> 'I mean that', he had written, 'wherein I tell the Duke that I am left in ignorance of his intentions & of his opinion of the policy I had pursued. In the latter I am certainly correct. In the former *not*.... He does tell me *something* of his views, but he certainly does not give me that sort of information of which I could make use in regulating my style of intercourse with the influential men.'

On this point Wellington scored slightly, on all others Anglesey had the advantage. The most acrimonious part of the debate came at the end when the Duke raised the question of royal permission to quote from the correspondence. At 10 o'clock in the evening of the debate, Anglesey wrote a note to Holland, from Uxbridge House.

'Some of my friends here tell me that the D. of W. was so offensive & personal & gave me so nearly the *Lie direct*, in regard to the King's giving me leave to use the letters in my vindication that they suppose I must call upon him for a more *private* explanation. I own they surprized me, for I was not aware of anything beyond what an Angry Man says in a bad cause. I am the least pugnacious of animals & should think it amazingly ridiculous that he & I should run a tilt, but as we must keep up certain forms & fashions, I am ready even to do as I am bid. Do tell me if you think there is anything that requires further notice.

'I am not the worse for the Field Day.'

Holland agreed that no duel was called for, and nothing more was heard of it. Anglesey's sons, Alfred and George, who were just starting their first term at Westminster School, stayed up late to hear their father's speech. Anglesey commented that it was 'well they did not rush through and attack the Duke with their little fists!'[67]

This was the low-water mark in relations between the two old soldiers: before long their friendship revived, until by the Duke's death twenty-three years later, it had become warm and constant. In 1849 Anglesey wrote to his son Clarence: 'Of Wellington you well know my attachment, amounting almost to adoration. You know too what sturdy battles I often fight for Peel. But these two *are* not the men *they were*. They have had the wisdom to discover that what they might have thought desirable, was no longer attainable or rather *re*tainable and they are steering their course accordingly.'[68]

*   *   *

Twenty-three years after his recall, full disillusionment had set in. In 1851, sad to relate, Anglesey was writing to his old friend Cloncurry, 'the main evil [in Ireland], I now feel quite certain, lays in the Religion of the People. Its intolerance, its restlessness, its ambition is a total bar to all prosperity in that unhappy country.'[69]

CHAPTER ELEVEN

Thank God, my parliamentary and official duties are now over; and I have ascertained beyond a doubt that I am not fit to fight with thorough-paced politicians, so I shall leave them to their dirty work.

Anglesey to Cloncurry, May 7th, 1829[1]

THE tension of the last six months left Anglesey tired but robust. The usual painful bouts of the tic continued, but the rest of 1829 found him well enough to indulge his two favourite relaxations. Large shooting-parties assembled at Beaudesert in season and much of the summer was spent at Cowes.

At the end of May he attended a military review in honour of the visiting French princes, at which the Duke of Wellington fell from his horse. This unfortunate occurrence was ascribed to the top-heaviness of the extravagant Grenadier cap which the King had introduced and which, in a high wind, was apt to overbalance its wearer. As Wellington fell almost literally at the feet of the Duke of Cumberland, the Ultras, who could not forgive the Prime Minister for selling the pass over Emancipation, thought it an excellent omen. At the state ball which followed, the King was reported as saying to Anglesey: 'Why Paget, how came you to be so clumsy as to fall before the foreigners? Was it the want of your leg?' to which the reply was: 'I did not fall, sir, nor should I, even if I had to wear a high cap.' 'Bravo,' exclaimed the King, 'that's the best thing I ever heard.'[2]

*　　*　　*

Family scandals intervened at this time to disturb Anglesey's peace of mind. Two months after his return from Dublin his fifth daughter, Agnes, married the eldest son of Sir John Byng, the commander-in-chief in Ireland. A few days after the wedding reports appeared in the newspapers to the effect that the newly-weds had already separated. It was insinuated in some, and boldly stated in others, that the bride, previous to her marriage, had had an affair with the Earl of Erroll, son-in-law of the Duke of Clarence and Mrs Jordan, and a member of the ex-viceroy's household. It was said that she had refused to consummate the marriage, had confessed her guilt to her husband, and had been deserted by him three days after the wedding. This scurrility was traced to a Mr Gerald Callaghan, lately Member of Parliament for Dundalk, a strong convert to Orangeism. This gentleman, against whom the Byngs brought a libel action in August, denied that he was the author of these reports, but admitted that in a letter to a friend he had repeated rumours which had come to his ears, and that 'from foolish credulity he had been made the dupe of declarations against the character of Lady Agnes' which he now believed to be utterly false. The same letter is believed to have contained a reference to another rumour, namely that Anglesey had sanctioned his daughter's intrigue with Lord Erroll in order the better to carry on his own with Lady Erroll! The case was never tried, for Callaghan made an abject apology, which included a disclaimer as to his ever having been influenced by political feelings towards any of the parties concerned. Though there was absolutely no truth in the rumours of a separation (for it was easily established that the couple had been living happily together ever since their marriage), for five months from the first newspaper reports the widest publicity was everywhere and by every means given to the libel. By the Brunswickers it was taken up as a convenient method of discrediting the ex-Lord Lieutenant's family, and by the Catholics to demonstrate their venom towards Callaghan. To the Paget and Byng families it gave nothing but pain. It is an ironical fact that at the time of the libel action, Lady Agnes was in her second month of pregnancy. It is a fact, too, that her marriage turned out to be a particularly happy one. The Byngs were very popular in society: a typical comment upon them is that of Georgiana, Duchess of Bedford, who found them 'amiable and lively people'.[3]

*   *   *

The Graves affair, which came a year later, caused a far greater sensation. On February 7th, 1830, Lord Graves, for many years a Lord of the Bedchamber to the King and afterwards Comptroller of the Household to the Dukes of Sussex and Cumberland, committed suicide as a result of the alleged infidelity of his wife with the Duke of Cumberland. His wife was Anglesey's youngest sister Mary, who in her day had been a considerable beauty, and is said to have been the first lady to dance a waltz in London; but now in her forty-seventh year, the mother of twelve children, a grandmother many times over and forced to wear spectacles, it is hard to believe that even the Duke of Cumberland was seriously enamoured of her. For some months she had been living apart from her husband: he had rooms in Hanover Street, and she a 'grace and favour' residence at Hampton Court. Whether this was a temporary arrangement occasioned by Graves's limited income and large family which prevented his keeping up a proper establishment, or whether they were in truth estranged, it is impossible to say. Whatever the facts, the gossips had noticed that Cumberland was paying Lady Graves particular attention in the summer of 1829, and by the following January the story was all over London that Graves had discovered his wife in the arms of the Duke. The print shops quickly filled with every species of scurrilous caricature: the anti-Tory newspapers regaled their readers with columns of squalid gossip. Cumberland, by no means for the first time in his career, was left in no doubt as to his being the best hated man in Britain. This obscene campaign had not lasted three weeks before Lord Graves could bear it no more; he cut his throat from ear to ear with a razor.

The inquest was held the morning after the death and seems to have been conducted a little hastily. Only three witnesses were called: his servant who had found him dead, the friend in whose house he was lodged, and Anglesey's doctor, Anderson, who had attended Graves for the first time only four days before he killed himself. It transpired that his servant had been sent off with a letter to Lady Graves from her husband a short time before the fatal act; but the contents of this letter, though believed to be of a most affectionate character, were never before the coroner's court. The jury returned a unanimous verdict of suicide in a sudden fit of delirium.

Cumberland strenuously denied that he was in any way the cause of Graves's death. He claimed that Graves had called on him in a perfectly friendly way only two days before the tragedy, and in that same week in company with Lady Graves had driven out to the Duke's house in the country. Cumberland told Lord Eldon that forty-eight hours before the suicide he had been

'a full hour at my friend Anglesey's, who received me just as ever in the most friendly and usual manner. Had Lord Anglesey', he wrote, 'had the slightest idea of anything of the sort, he certainly

The Marquess of Anglesey with his dog 'Nep' shooting blackcock from
horseback on Cannock Chase, aged 61 (see p.296)

The Duke of Wellington and the Marquess of Anglesey. Caricature
sketch by George Cruikshank (1792-1878) about 1829

would not have been so perfectly friendly and amicable with me as he was, nor could he have entered so fully with me on political subjects as he did. So much was his manner perfectly the same, that it so occurred during our conversation, something was talked in which his sister's name was mentioned, and so we talked just as if nothing had occurred, so that I feel perfectly persuaded that *he* at least never had had any such impression on his mind.'

The Duke's friends pressed him either to institute proceedings for libel, or to make a statement in the Lords. He refused to do either. 'How can I get up', he wrote, 'and state all these particulars? It appears to me that Lord Anglesey, the head of his family, might put an end to the whole, by either calling openly on me, or my being seen publickly with him.' What action, if any, Anglesey took to help the Duke, does not emerge, but three months later Mrs Arbuthnot averred that Cumberland was still carrying on with Lady Graves and that her children had left her in consequence.[4]

*   *   *

Eighteen-thirty, a year of revolution abroad and economic distress at home, saw the agitation for Parliamentary Reform reach new heights. But in its first months, attention in political circles was largely centred on the health of the King. Partial blindness in February was followed by a steady decline in the succeeding weeks, and it soon became clear that his death was only a matter of time. Since in those days the sovereign's demise was followed by a dissolution of Parliament and a general election, political activity became intense. The aspirations of the Whigs soared, for not only was Wellington's Government increasing in unpopularity daily, but the Duke of Clarence, heir to the throne, was thought to be rather more of a liberal than his brother.

Anglesey, acutely aware that neither the country nor the Commons would much longer tolerate a Government which had set its face sternly against Reform, tried at this time, through personal contacts, to weld the leading men of the Opposition into a strong team ready to grasp the reins as they fell from Wellington's hands. He became one of the chief means of liaison between the 'official' Whigs — Grey, Holland, Brougham, Melbourne and others — and the followers of Canning and Huskisson. On May 3rd Croker, a junior member of Wellington's Government, admitted

H

that if 'to the Whigs were to be added — by the mediation of Anglesey and Carlisle — Goderich, Grenville and Seaford, Huskisson, Palmerston and the Grants, they would have a very strong Government.'⁵ª

In these days, while his brother wrestled with death at Windsor, no one was more active than the Duke of Clarence himself. He came constantly to London from his accustomed retirement at Bushey; he indicated to Wellington that he would wish to keep him as Prime Minister, and he established political contacts in all directions. But if Clarence was active, so were others. The Tory Lady Jersey, for instance, forced herself on the Duchess of Clarence, though they had never been on terms of intimacy. 'The Duchess', wrote Croker, 'received her very coolly, even to the extent of expressing some surprise at a pleasure so *new and unexpected*; but that', he continued, 'is perhaps not so surprising as Anglesey's having gone down to the Duke of Clarence. He, I dare say, did not intrude so cavalierly as the Countess, and indeed I have heard that Lord Erroll [Clarence's son-in-law] arranged the interview.'⁶ This was quite correct, for Anglesey kept a detailed record of what passed.

'In the course of May, (I think it was in the early part)', he wrote, 'Ld Erroll frequently called upon me & always told me how much the Duke of Clarence talked of me, how much he respected me, how he regretted I was not employed, that I was not at the head of the Army, or in Ireland, &c &c. He told me that the Duke often complained that he had no one to consult & advise with & so forth. This induced me to express myself pretty fully as to the line of policy & of general conduct H.R.Hss ought to pursue. Lord E., forcibly struck with my remarks, ... asked me whether if H.R.Hss wished to see me, I would call upon him. I said most certainly provided I was at liberty to say in case the interview was spoken of that it was not of my seeking but took place at the express command of H.R.Hss.'

In due course the meeting was arranged. Anglesey described what took place.

'The conversation', he wrote, 'was at first rather constrained, and neither chose to begin upon serious matter. The Duke (I really believe from shyness) soon got into some very mild, light & frivolous subjects, which, as they were by no means what I came to discuss, I contrived to stop, & at once entering into grave matter,

I began by expressing how much I had been flattered by the assurance of his good opinion & his anxiety to converse with me &
craving his permission to express myself fairly & openly. I proceeded
to give my opinion at considerable length upon the situation he was
about to be speedily placed in & the course H.R.Hss ought to pursue.
I observed that Kings & Princes had disadvantages to which their
subjects were not liable — that they rarely, if ever, heard the truth —
that they were surrounded by courtiers & flatterers who only told
them what would be agreeable to hear, & hence they little knew
what the public thought & expected of them. I would speak out, if
I was to speak at all, & in this H.R.Hss having encouraged me, I
proceeded thus:

'The Public looks with considerable alarm to your ascending the
Throne — people think you will be wild — unmanageable — full of
prejudices & arbitrary — Now I have always maintained a contrary
opinion & I now assert that if Y.R.Hss is surrounded by proper
persons & honest men, you are about to enter a career that will
enable you to be the most popular and the most constitutional Sovereign that ever filled the Throne. You will commence under every
advantage & if you profit by it your reign will be a prosperous & a
brilliant one — You follow a Court the most sombre & melancholy
that ever was known, for the King with all his love of pomp,
& his taste for magnificence — for the Arts — for brilliant society,
together with his powers for shining under such circumstances, has
shut himself up & withdrawn himself from the Public Eye, & that
too at a time when the most profuse expenditure has been carrying
on, by which the Public have in no respect profited & for which
ample grounds have been laid for the most heavy & just complaints
on the score of extravagance.

'Your R.Hss must bear this in mind — You must keep a brilliant
Court — you must have regular periodical Levees & Drawing
Rooms — You must go not unfrequently to the Theatre — without
making yourself too common, you must nevertheless frequently
show yourself amongst your subjects — Your habits of life have been
economical & with these habits you will have ample funds for a
splendid Court — for creditable acts of liberality, without preying
upon the pockets of the people — The People are truly loyal — They
love their Kings — They are really Monarchical & will be ever
ready to maintain the fair splendour of a Court — They will never

refuse reasonable demands to uphold the dignity of their Kings, but they will always grumble at & resist profusion & extravagance —Let it be a fixed rule, whenever any thing is wanted for Palaces, or for any legitimate expences to lay the claim fairly before the Public — let Estimates be made, & if they are scrupulously adhered to, there will never be a complaint uttered, & the money will be cheerfully voted & paid — But I have omitted to state the first maxim to adhere to, & if not forgotten, will avoid endless trouble, misrepresentation & complaint — Make a solemn determination *never to promise any thing to any body* — However determined you may be to grant the prayer of a petition or request — *never promise* — note down your intention — grant the prayer — bestow the boon — when the convenient time arrives, but *promise nothing* — I speak of the eminent advantage of such a resolution from the experience of *my own short reign* [in Ireland] — every one immediately about me & serving under me fully knew of this rule & they were always fully able to meet those who ventured to assert that they had received a promise, by a peremptory denial of the fact.

'Your R.Hss. stands in a very peculiar situation on account of your children — It will require much discretion to provide fairly & handsomely by them, without bringing them too prominently before the public eye — with your economical habits & ample means you will easily provide for them without burdening the public, yet in time & by degrees, they may attain situations of trust & respectability, to which no objection will be made, but (looking at a picture of Charles II which was in the room) I observed that we were not living in times when that Monarch could be taken as a Model with impunity.

'I strongly impressed upon H.R.Hss that with discretion & moderation in such like matters he would soon win the Nation & that the less it was inclined at this moment to hail with joy his occupation of the Throne the more Easy & effectual would be his conquest over their mistaken notions of his character.

'I said that he was most fortunate in his consort — that she was universally well spoken of & that the advantages of a female Court after so long an absence of any thing of the sort, were incalculable.

'I observed that his profession [the Navy] would be an advantage to him in the public eye — that it was the favorite profession of the Nation — that he should however avoid all undue preference & deal out honors & favors as fairly & as equally as possible, making no distinction whatever, but in real worth & merit.

'I ventured to caution H.R.Hss against all frivolities about dress & deeply regretted the many complaints to which the King had rendered himself subject, & the ridicule to wh. he had so much exposed himself, by the frequent changes & expensive appointments he had established in the army (I more particularly dwelt upon this subject because I had reason to believe that H.R.Hss himself meditated some great changes in the clothing & equipment of the Navy & Army).

'I urged the most extreme caution in increasing the Peerage, showing how the operation weakened both the Houses of Parliament, by bringing the most influential persons out of the lower House, to be lost in that of the Lords, at the same time that undue increases of the numbers of the upper House weakened its weight & influence in the Country.

'I observed upon the propriety of a King visiting periodically the various parts of his dominions, & that he should hold Courts from time to time at Dublin & at Edinburgh.

'All this ... was fully, freely, candidly stated, most kindly taken & in general cordially agreed in.

'I then said H.R.Hss would have a most difficult card to play in the choice of His Ministers, & his decision respecting the dissolution of the Parliament — I stated that it probably would not be adviseable to make any immediate change, but I could not disguise from H.R. Hss my conviction that the Ministry as at that time constituted could not long hold its ground — That it was a very weak one & at the same time the most unconstitutional one that ever existed — that it held the King in complete thraldom whilst it was dictated to itself by a small body in the House of Commons, that was enabled to throw over every Measure the Government proposed. I said H.R.Hss was too well acquainted with the constitution to attempt to establish a power beyond the just prerogative of the Crown — That the day was gone by when such an attempt would be for even a day tolerated, but that at the same time, a King disgraced himself by allowing any Minister to usurp a dictatorial power & that that was in effect the present state of the Government & I most sincerely hoped H.R.Hss would not submit to such degradation....

'H.R.Hss ought to come to a clear understanding with the

present Ministers before the dissolution of Parliament — He might choose one of the following Courses:

'1st Offer his confidence to the Ministers as they stood, & leave it to them to attempt to carry on the Government upon its present basis if they chose to make the trial;

'2dy Require that they should strengthen themselves by offering to share power with the most independent & influential Men of the several parties;

3dy To announce his intention of calling other men to form an entire new administration.

'I did not offer the least advice as to the best course to pursue but impressed the necessity of a candid & explicit declaration on the part of H.R.Hss to the then Ministers of his intentions previously to the dissolution of the Parliament.

'In the course of the conversation I certainly very freely expressed my opinion of the inefficiency & incapability of the present Government — I pointed out ... their perfect determination to hold their places by a suppleness of conduct that was dishonorable & disgracefull & (in consequence of an observation that *I* might go to Ireland or to the Horse Guards with perfect independence) I took the opportunity of saying that altho' I would not say that if others in whom I could trust & place confidence, were introduced into the Cabinet, the mere personal hostility of the D. of Wellington & of Mr Peel to me & their very offensive & unjustifiable conduct, would not be an insurmountable Barrier to my acting with them, still that nothing could tempt me to hold any office whatever whilst the Cabinet remained as at present — the D of Clarence immediately said "I don't wonder at you — By G-d, except myself you are the worst used man that ever was." ...

'I also urged the many inconveniences to which the King had been subjected & wh. the public suffered for, by his personal prejudices & dislikes — I mentioned His Majesty's particular objection to Lords Grey & Holland amongst many others — the D of Clarence declared to me, he was free from all such feeling — He thought indeed Ld Holland a *wild* politician, but he spoke very favorably of Ld Grey. Notwithstanding this declaration I certainly detected H.R.Hss in some pretty strong prejudices & I was most sorry to find that he ... was violently anti reform, & a bitter enemy to free trade.'

This astonishing memorandum is here reproduced almost *in toto*, for besides revealing Anglesey's lack of inhibitions, his supreme self-confidence, and his determination to speak his mind, it goes a long way to explain why George IV and his brother both feared and respected him. Here is a subject-to-be giving advice to his prospective sovereign, with complete frankness, without the smallest reservations, and not without wisdom and common sense. Self-interest is there, but subordinate throughout to honesty and truth.

ii

Poor Lord Anglesey is dying of the tic douloureux.
Mrs Arbuthnot[8]

Towards the end of February, Anglesey had retired to bed with a very severe cold. This brought on the worst attack of the tic that he had ever experienced. Intermittently throughout March, April and May he was in considerable pain. In the last days of May, his condition had so far deteriorated that the doctors gave strict orders for the patient's mind to be kept disengaged from all agitating subjects. By the beginning of June Anglesey thought that the end was at hand, for he wrote at this time a long letter to Uxbridge, which began: 'As I do not think this state of things can last very long, I must have a word with you my dearest Henry.' He went on:

'I wish I could talk to you, but that, you know, I am unequal to. I cannot say what a real source of comfort it is to me to think that you ... will prove yourself an affectionate Father and Protector to all my dear children & that Lady Anglesey may with confidence look to you as a warm friend, supporter and defender. You cannot imagine the immense load of anxiety and of apprehension from which I am relieved by a conviction that she and they will be safe in your hands. When I think of the delightful situation in which I leave my dearest children — Car [Richmond], Jane [Conyngham], Augusta [Templemore], Agnes [Byng] — all united to men who independently of their own merits, have that of appearing to be sensible of and to appreciate theirs (and in my mind these are great indeed for 4 more excellent women in their respective ways do not exist) — for them, I

say, I do not undergo a moment's uneasiness — They deserve to be
happy — may God bless them and make them so. Then comes my
dearest little Georgy. How can I but be happy in her prospects —
she is so composed and constituted that, in every individual who
knows her, she is sure to find a friend and a home everywhere.
She is safe. You know her, I need say no more. God bless her.
[Georgiana married Lord Crofton in 1833.] — But what must I say
of my wretched, my unfortunate William! Alas! Alas! There is a
source of severe misery and apprehension. What is to become of that
unfortunate youth? The pangs he has cost me have been tremendous.
I had a singular affection for him — with none of my children did I
ever take more pains than with him to win him to my affections, to
soften a certain rigidity of temper I early discovered in him and
which no pains — not volumes of good advice have been able to
remove. But alas! Alas! other sad qualities have latterly broken
forth, or rather burst upon me, that I am shocked — appalled,
alarmed. Where there appears to be an absence of all principle of
honour (alas! I say again) of *truth*!, what can be expected? I shudder
to think of it. After hours, days, weeks, aye, months of reflection,
and of consultation and advice, I came to the dire resolution, as well
for the sake of him as of others, to make him feel the weight of his
own follies and dishonorable conduct, always, however, holding out
the hope that if he reclaimed, my warmest affections were to be
regained, and I now tell you that if he really and sincerely repented
and altered his course and lived within his means, I meant to make
these means again equal to that of his brothers and sisters, notwithstanding the shameful debts he incurred and the dreadful manner in
which he was in the habit of providing for his extravagances. I mean
by this to say that independently of the fortune he has already
dissipated, I would have again started him with his original fortune,
namely £10,000. God grant that he may reform and entitle himself
to this indulgence and may God bless him.

'I come now to the other dear children — the 3 dear girls Emily,
Mary and Adelaide. Whilst their mother lives I have not the slightest
fear for them, but they may benefit immeasurably by your kind
protection and attention even during her life, and afterwards you
must, you must, my dearest Uxbridge, use your best exertions to
befriend them in every way — in fact to become an affectionate
substitute for their lost parents. I own I have much solicitude about

them. [Emily married Viscount Sydney in 1832; Mary, the Earl of Sandwich in 1838; and Adelaide, her mother's nephew, the Hon. F. W. Cadogan in 1851.] And now for the dear boys, Clarence, Alfred and George [at this time 19, 14, and 12 years old respectively]. Properly guided they have sense and cleverness and amiability enough to push forward well in the world. But they will sadly want good monitors and watchful care and parental advice and for all this I look confidently to you. Assist and protect and advise them and do not let any little angry effusions at your attempt to control them irritate and induce you to abandon them. They are dear good boys and are worth saving. As for poor Lady Anglesey, she I know will conduct herself as a woman of sense and of the strictest propriety, and I have for some time cherished the fond belief that you are sensible of her merits and will stand by her and be kind to her. She will have the sense not to sorrow too much at my loss, for she must have too long and too painfully, witnessed my frightful sufferings not to derive some sort of consolation from my release. For the sake of all and for religion's sake I have struggled desperately to support myself, but I have never satisfied myself that I have done enough. So much for my beloved family — God knows how sincerely I love, how devotedly I am attached to them all, and how well I know they all love me to excess — God bless and protect them all.

'Nor must I omit to mention all my brothers and sisters, who have been always all kindness and affection for me. And for the world in general (say what they will) there is much more of good and kind feeling in it than is generally allowed.

'If I were to begin ennumerating friends, I should never end. This I will say, that I have been favoured with having a set of the most affectionate and devoted that every attached themselves to man. Thus you see, if I die in misery and frightful suffering, I die at least in charity and good will towards all men. I have written rapidly and in pain. I cannot bring myself to read over again, so make me out as you can. I dare say Char will like to read this and so will Sanderson. This Sanderson is an honest treasure — do not abandon him. I have done something for him, as I recollect, but not so much as I would if I had not hoped that he would continue to be helpful to you. I have a high opinion of Beer [the under-agent], keep him. But take my word you must cut down the establishments. Begin quietly — It is easy to increase — it is most difficult to diminish expense. I have long meditated the latter, but the way I have been drawn forth into public life and a thousand other things that you will not have to contend with, have marred my plans.... I believe you should sell Uxbridge House — It will only lead you to useless expense. It is too large for you and I am sure a much smaller residence and snugger concern will suit you better. There is an enormous weight of debt. Dorsetshire and Somersetshire cannot pay it. Don't touch Ireland — that country *must* rapidly improve in value — Dorsetshire and Somersetshire, although rich, are troublesome, unsatisfactory properties. If they affront you in Wales, I do not see why you should not sell there if you can do it advantageously, but as long as Caernarvon and Anglesey behave well, stick to them. Parliamentary interest without any view to jobbing is respectable and useful. For this reason retain Milborne Port [in Dorsetshire]....

'Of my servants I can say little. I believe they are a good set.... Maritta is absolute perfection. I do most anxiously and strenuously recommend him to my dearest Char as her Factotum. Let her have any coach she likes and the fly and her ponies and phaeton, or if she prefers them, the 2 Norwegians. For the carriage I would recommend John to her.

'I have written till I am quite tired and must leave off. I dare say I have omitted much, but you will no doubt gather my general wishes from what you find above. And now may God Almighty bless and protect you and support you all. Say a kind word from me to everybody, for heaven be praised, I die in perfect peace and charity with all men, loving my dearest family to distraction, and have a love and regard for my many friends who would *many many* of them go to the world's end for me.

'God Bless you all.
'A.

'I should like this to be read to my dearest Char — also to Sanderson. Indeed, I leave to your discretion to show it to those who *really* love and are deeply interested about me — omitting such parts as purely connected themselves with the property.'

It will be seen from this letter that Anglesey's mind was much exercised as to the future of his second son, William, for whom he entertained 'a singular affection'. William's tragic career was to cause his father acute pain and embarrassment for many years to come.

At the age of fourteen he had entered the Navy; by the time he was twenty-three (in 1826), he had reached the rank of post captain. In November 1827, he had been appointed to command the *Royal Charlotte* yacht at Dublin, upon the appointment of his father as Lord Lieutenant. Nine months earlier he had married Fanny, daughter of General Rotten-burgh, who had served under Anglesey at Walcheren in 1809. To this unhappy union, on various grounds, not least that the bride had no fortune, Anglesey had refused his consent; but this had not deterred William, who went ahead in defiance of his father's remonstrances. From this turning point in his career he launched himself, ably seconded by his wife, along the road to ruin, which was to lead him to a debtors' prison and eventually to permanent exclusion from Britain.

William's debts first became serious enough to engage his father's attention soon after their return from Ireland. In March 1829 Anglesey had warned him of 'irretrievable ruin' if he did not keep within his income, especially as his salary of £1,000 a year as commander of the viceregal yacht had ceased. Four months later his debts had mounted to such an extent that he thought to put pressure upon his father to get them paid. The method he chose was to state to William Lowe, the family solicitor, his intention of giving up his seat in Parliament — (in 1826 he had succeeded his uncle Charles Paget as Member for Caernarvon) — so as to surrender himself as a debtor, Members of Parliament being immune from arrest for debt. Anglesey was disgusted by this shabby trick, but saw that there was nothing for it: 'he has me in his clutches', he told Lowe. 'I must now save him from prison ... you must make the best arrangement you can.' William agreed to make a list of his debts, but a month later all that Lowe received was a letter which said: 'Dear Sir, my debts amount to £20,000. Yrs. truly, William Paget.' Shown this insulting missive, Anglesey exploded: 'I will *not* pay them. I do not believe it. The thing is impossible.' It was not until a full list was later dragged from William that his father for the first time saw the full infamy of his son's behaviour. William had made 'solemn, deliberate and repeated' assertions to his father that he would leave Ireland free from all debts in that country, yet this mammoth list included numerous and long-standing debts incurred in Dublin. Anglesey was horrified. 'I have been kept in entire ignorance of his conduct and general character,' he wrote to Lowe, 'but this thunder-stroke having set me to enquire, I am shocked, disgusted, shamed, at all I *hear*! What a catalogue of meanness — of shuffling shifts — of prodigality — of selfishness, does his list of debts exhibit!' The faithful Sanderson, who was with Anglesey at Beaudesert when the full extent of William's deceit was first revealed to him, declared that he had 'never seen Lord Anglesey's feelings more strongly excited than they have been by recollection of the manner and confidence with which Lord William has, at different times, represented himself as free from all pecuniary incumbrance, and those feelings are not abated upon observing that, with the disclosure of the real facts, there is scarcely an expression of regret at the infliction of the deep distress which he could not but know such conduct would occasion, or on account of the injustice done by it to every branch of his family.'

Anglesey now decreed that a sum, equivalent to his son's patrimony of £10,000, should be put in trust (Sanderson and Forbes being among the trustees) for the payment of his most pressing debts. This sum could only be raised by a loan secured on certain of the landed properties. At the same time Anglesey decided, in his generosity, to increase William's allowance, so that he should have a reasonable income on which to live over and above his naval half-pay. The conditions imposed upon him were that he was to go abroad, but not to a capital city, until such time as he should again obtain active employment in the Navy; to sell his carriages and horses, and to give up certain of his less desirable associates. Anglesey's chief concern was that the Irish tradesmen should be paid in full. He could not bear that they should suffer: 'they are poor & would naturally confide in Ld. Wm. considering his situation.... As for the fools of this country [England], if they choose to give him credit, they must suffer.' The Irish creditors, expressing their respect for the ex-Lord Lieutenant, went so far as to say that they would be satisfied with a payment of 10s. in the £1; but Anglesey insisted that they should be paid in full and before any other creditors.

While the trustees set about their laborious task, Anglesey was anxiously wondering how to obtain for William further naval employment. 'What can I do?' he asked of Sanderson. 'How can I go and ask for employment for a man whose character is not to be depended upon ... ? Could I, if he were a stranger, recommend him at the Admiralty? No, I could not, and would not, and if ever I apply *for* him, I will speak openly *of* him, and throw myself and my family, and this degraded young man, at the mercy of the Admiralty.' Whether Anglesey made application or not, is not clear, but in December 1829 his son was appointed to command the *North Star*, 28 guns, and in April 1830 set sail for the West Indies. Before that voyage took place he once again threatened to vacate his seat, relinquish his new command and take the benefit of the Insolvent Debtors' Act, declaring to Lowe: 'A fig for Lord Anglesey's favor and protection!!!'

Now, in June 1830, as has been seen, his long-suffering father was ready 'independently of the fortune he has already dissipated, to start him off afresh with his original fortune, namely £10,000', should he really and sincerely repent of his past, and reform for the future. Alas, that was not to be; but for the moment William was far away and the thorn in Anglesey's flesh was temporarily withdrawn.[10]

*   *   *

Later in June the spectre of death began to retreat from Anglesey's bedside. On the 28th Sanderson found his master much better, and ten days later he was off to Cowes in an advanced state of convalescence.[11]

While Anglesey was convalescing, the King was sinking fast. In the early hours of June 26th he died.

iii

The accounts from Ireland are very bad. They want a man of energy and determination who will cause the law to be respected and impartially administered. If Lord Anglesey was there, it is very probable these outrages would not have taken place, but no one cares for such a man of straw as the present Ld. Lt.
Charles Greville, July 1829[12]

The results of the general election which followed the King's death came as no great surprise. The obscurities of the parliamentary situation were much the same after as before it, for Wellington's had been a minority government from the moment it introduced the Catholic Relief Bill in 1829.[b] There was indeed an increase in the number of Reformers in the Commons and there was further proof of the unpopularity of the 'party of the Duke's', but he carried on much as if nothing had occurred. As was his way, he compromised not one jot: he had set his face against even the mildest measures of Reform, and scorned to avert his defeat, which was bound to come sooner or later, by a single change of policy or personnel. None the less there were those who tried to shore up the crumbling edifice on his behalf. In late October Anglesey was pressed (by whom it is not known) to lend his support to the Administration. In a rough draft dated November 1st, he wrote:

> 'I have no particle of feeling of *personal* hostility to the Duke of Wellington. I think he acted unwisely by me, perhaps unkindly under all the circumstances, but I know how he was urged on & pressed, & I have always made full allowance for that.
>
> 'I am attached & bound to no party. I am perfectly independent of all.
>
> 'If the Duke's views on politics & upon the state of the Country corresponded with mine, I wd not have any difficulty in acting with him, but I am entirely certain they are so totally different, that I should be an eternal incumbrance, rather than an aid to him. I have a thorough conviction that nothing but a most extensive Reform — that nothing but a total change in the whole system of governing the Country — of raising the supplies — of collecting the Revenue — can save it from Revolution.° ... Judge then, if the Duke and I could attempt to act together with any prospect of benefit to the Country. We should differ too about the course to be pursued in regard to Ireland.'

As this draft shows, Anglesey was in the process of developing very radical economic views. Three years later he was telling Lord Holland that he believed in a property tax. 'But I would not stop here', he went on. 'I would pay *the* [National] *Debt*. Coute qui coute, I would pay it; and after each of us giving up our half of what we possess to accomplish it, we should live with more ease, and be enabled to have more luxury and splendour than we now enjoy, and the People would be in comparative affluence.'

When it was clear that he would not join the Cabinet he was urged to give the Government the support of his name by going to the Horse Guards or the Ordnance. 'I contended', he wrote, 'that I was worth nothing but for the character I bore, & that if I accepted a situation from a Government whose acts I disapproved, I shd not strengthen that government & only lose my own character.'[13]

* * *

The blow fell on November 15th, when more by accident than design the various groups in the Commons combined at last to beat the Government, not as might have been expected on a motion for Reform, but in a division upon the Civil List. Wellington himself thought his defeat due to two events: the concession of Catholic emancipation and the July Revolution in France, where the people had risen against the foolish despotism of Charles X and his chief minister, Polignac. Charles X was allowed to abdicate, and fled to England. From Cowes on August 18th Anglesey wrote to Holland:

'Charles X with all his miseries around him arrived in this place last night.... They are in 2 fine American Merchantmen under the American Colours, but with a red Flag at the Mast Head, pierced with white, with the letters C.C. in it. Does that mean Charles Capet? I have been in some little embarrassment as to what I should do. Having been so very intimate with the unfortunate & foolish man formerly, he having been constantly at my house during his first misfortunes [during the Napoleonic Wars], I should not upon any other spot on the Globe but here, have hesitated to wait upon him — partly from former intimacy — partly because we cannot help leaning to & pitying misfortune under any circumstances, but here I happen to be the King's Officer, being nothing less than *Captain of Cowes Castle*!!!a & I had some little fear of compromising this important Character & offending William the 4th & his Master the Duke. However Heart overpowered Head, and so I have been to pay my respects to fallen Majesty en bourgeois, not as Governor of this Fortress. The poor man looks surprisingly well considering age [he was 73] & circumstances, & talked all the nonsense upon the state of things, that you, who are so well acquainted with those of the ancien regime, can well imagine. It was too much to hear in silence & too absurd to allow to pass without observation so I fairly told him all I thought & I assured him that there was scarcely a rational man in this Country who did not clearly foresee the consequences of the conduct that he had been led to pursue.... He has written for leave to land in this Country.... In default of this, he requires to be allowed to reside in Hanover, if not permanently, at all events until he receives an answer from the Emperor of Austria, to whom he has applied for an Asylum.... I said I calculated upon his going to Naples — but it is clear he does not think that Country safe from Revolution, nor indeed Spain, nor the Low Countries, & I took the liberty to add (but of course in as delicate a way as I could) that with the present enlightened views of Mankind, no Government would stand that attempted to act in opposition to public opinion. I did all I could to dissuade him from his desire to reside in England, by assuring him that there is a particularly strong feeling throughout the Country in favor of the People of France, & that consequently they will look upon him with a very evil eye.

'The poor man talked much nonsense about legitimacy & (will you believe it?) positively thinks that there will be a reaction & that the Duc de Bordeaux [son of the Duc de Berry; chosen by Charles X to succeed him] will be loudly called for!!!'[14]

*   *   *

'AN IN AND AN OUT'
Anglesey and Wellington
November, 1830

On the day following the Government's defeat, the King sent for Lord Grey the leader of the Whigs, and commissioned him to form a new administration. 'In this fearful undertaking', wrote the new Prime Minister that evening to Anglesey, 'I look anxiously to your assistance'; and two days later: 'The King received the notification of your acceptance of the Office of Lord Lieutenant, and of Mr Stanley's of the [Irish] Secretaryship, with expressions of the greatest satisfaction and pleasure — nothing could be more cordial.'[15] As the slow process of distributing the portfolios went ahead, Anglesey rejoiced to see Holland made Chancellor of the Duchy of Lancaster, Lamb (who in 1829 had succeeded his father as Lord Melbourne) Home Secretary, and his old friend Lansdowne, President of the Council.[e]

CHAPTER TWELVE

I assure you every hope for Ireland rests on you.
Lord Brougham to Anglesey[1]

NEARLY two years had passed since Anglesey's recall: and now he was to return to Ireland. The social and economic state of that country had altered little, but politically the scene was very different. The Protestant Ascendancy had done its best to negative the benefits of Emancipation;[a] Anglesey's successor, the Duke of Northumberland, whom the Irish nicknamed 'Sugar of Lead' — 'sweet and heavy' as Forbes explained to Anglesey — was a nonentity, and Hardinge (one of Wellington's 'yes-men') managed in a short spell as Chief Secretary to make a number of influential enemies. The most important development had been the launching of O'Connell's great campaign for Repeal of the Union — or, in other words, Home Rule — not, in the event, to be achieved for nearly a hundred years. Here was something very different from Catholic emancipation, which after all had been conceded only on the ground that the Union of the two countries made such a measure a safe one. In the minds of many Englishmen, agitation for Repeal of the Union was akin to treason. There could no more have been a majority for it in either House of Parliament in the 1830s, than for, say, a 40-hour working week; but O'Connell's personal authority among the Catholic peasantry was such that he had them massively behind him in his new crusade. From the moment he announced his object, he changed the political face of Ireland. Before 1829 the chief division had been between Catholics and non-Catholics; now it was between Unionists and anti-Unionists. Large numbers of Catholics of the better classes, till recently his devoted admirers, as well as many moderate Protestants who had wished him well in the past, now shed their allegiance once and for all.

No one realized this fundamental change more clearly than Anglesey.

With Plunket, Sheil, Cloncurry, Blake and many another he had kept up a regular correspondence on Irish affairs. He had twice called upon O'Connell after his maiden speech in the House of Commons and congratulated him most warmly upon it; but as early as April 1829, Anglesey was trying to dissuade him from Repeal agitation. To Pierce Mahony, an influential Dublin solicitor, who, though a Protestant, was a close adviser and friend of O'Connell's, he wrote:

'You can have no idea of the alarm that is excited upon this subject. It is not, believe me, from any apprehension that the separation could ever be effected, but from the certainty that the attempt would infinitely injure the *mooter* of the measure, & that it would very much shake the confidence of the public in those who have so warmly advocated the cause of the Catholics. They will at once cry out, See the effect of Emancipation! Look at the first act of the great agitator! What may we not expect from the admission of such men into the Legislature.... There really would be no end to the mischiefs that would ensue, and all to no purpose whatever, for I am as certain as I am of my existence that the establishment of a separate Parliament is utterly & entirely out of the question. You may state this to O'Connell if you like.'

Later in the year, similar advice from the same source was flatly rejected. O'Connell said that he was as much politically bound to devote his energies to effect a repeal of the Union, as he was in conscience bound to subscribe to the doctrines of the Roman Catholic Church.[2b]

It so happened that only a week before the fall of the Government, Anglesey was asked to present in the Lords a petition from the parish of Grangegorman advocating Repeal. He decided after some days of consultation and thought to write a letter for publication in the Irish press. In it he said that he was reluctantly compelled to decline giving the petition his support. 'To me it is, indeed,' he wrote, 'a heavy sacrifice to decline to obey the call, but thoroughly convinced, as I am, that the prosperity of Ireland depends much upon her close union with Great Britain, I do most ardently wish that the agitation of the question of separating their legislatures may not be urged.' He concluded by stating his view that in 'separation there would be ruin for Ireland, irrevocable weakness for England, in short total eclipse of the power and glory of the British Empire.'[2] Here was an unequivocal statement which can have left no one in any doubt as to Anglesey's views as a private gentleman. Within a week of its publication, he was no longer in that capacity.

ii

I heard yesterday a story concerning Lord Anglesey and Mr O'Connell, which is really very good, and amused the King amazingly. Lord Anglesey met O'Connell, and the latter said, 'Believe me, my Lord, there is nothing personal in my manner of acting, yet I will leave no stone unturned to break the union of Ireland.' 'Nor have I anything personal towards you, sir,' replied Lord Anglesey; 'still, if I can have you hanged, you may depend upon my doing it.' It surely is enough to kill one with laughing; I think Lord Anglesey was quite right.

Duke of Cumberland to Frances, Lady Shelley[A]

THE RETORT COURTIOUS (Anecdote in the Chelmsford Chronicle)

Before leaving for Dublin, Anglesey had much to do. Almost his first action was to dislodge William Gregory, who had been Under-

Secretary since 1812. This was a wise move, for Gregory had come, over the years, to be identified with all that was most exclusive and illiberal at the Castle.[c] In his place Anglesey put his private secretary, Sir William Gosset, whom he described as 'honest, zealous, indefatigable, industrious to a degree. The public cannot have a better or more efficient servant.'[d] This change commended itself to O'Connell; but not so another and more controversial appointment, namely the confirmation of Doherty in the post of Solicitor-General, for Doherty, though once a friend of the Liberator's, was now his bitter foe. A first-class debater and a moderate lawyer, he had lashed out at O'Connell in the Commons and elsewhere with devastating effect, and this was never forgiven him. On this one appointment alone, O'Connell decided without a quaim to obstruct the new Government. Anglesey had not, in fact, been responsible for the arrangement. 'I know', he wrote to Melbourne on December 4th, 'that Doherty's remaining where he is is unpopular; but I had nothing to do with it. I was asked [by Lord Grey], Did I object to him? I said, No. I said I had liked him whilst I was in Ireland, but it is utterly false that it is through my influence that he was kept.[e] It is not, however, meant to keep him where he is. He and Joy must both go to the Bench; and I am making some arrangements that cannot be objected to. Yet there is no pleasing everybody.'[f] To Holland he declared, 'I am almost ashamed to acknowledge that the very appointment most cried out against was settled with the view of doing a kind act by O'Connell, by removing *his Master* (for so Doherty certainly was in the H. of Commons) from under his nose; yet the ungrateful man turns round & grumbles at it, as of a deep grievance. He has really almost worn down my patience (& now-a-days I can command a good deal).'[g]

Before the offending appointment was announced, O'Connell declared himself very favourably disposed to the new Government, and particularly towards Anglesey, but as soon as it was public knowledge he reversed his position and left London for Dublin,

'with more mischief in hand', as Anglesey told Cloncurry, 'than I have yet seen him charged with. I saw him yesterday [15th December], for an hour and a half.[g] I made no impression upon him whatever; and I am thoroughly convinced that he is bent upon desperate agitation. All this will produce no change in my course and conduct. For the love of Ireland I deprecate agitation. I know it is the only thing that can prevent her from prospering; for there is in this

country a growing spirit to take Ireland by the hand, and a determination not to neglect her and her interests; therefore I pray for
peace and repose. But if the sword is really to be drawn, and with it
the scabbard is to be thrown away — if I, who have suffered so much
for her, am to become a suspected character, and to be treated as
an enemy — if, for the protection of the State, I am driven to the dire
necessity of again turning soldier, why then I must endeavour to
get back into old habits, and live amongst a people I love in a state
of misery and distress.'⁶

*   *   *

Two days before Christmas Anglesey made his second entry into
Dublin. At first O'Connell had agreed that a procession to meet the
returning viceroy should be prepared. Then, even before he knew of
Doherty's appointment, he had come to think it safer for the anti-
Unionists not to accord the Lord Lieutenant any glorification. Doherty's
retention changed this negative approach to a hostile one, and Anglesey
began to receive from his friends

'various kind and even affectionate letters, warning me', he told
Cloncurry from Beaudesert, 'of what I may expect, and suggesting
to me the landing where I am not expected, and proceeding quietly
and secretly to Dublin. They might just as well propose to me to
consent to mount a balloon for the purpose of seeking the moon!
No! No! I will land at Kingstown, and will proceed unostentatiously
to the Castle. Let no friend of mine come forward and mix himself up
with my *unpopularity* (what a term for *me* to make use of amongst
Irishmen!!!).... I am anxious to see the thing. It will be curious
enough to contrast the first days of 1829 with the last days of 1830
— and the whole change of sentiment to be upon the *plea* of a solitary
law appointment!'

'In respect to health', he told Melbourne from Holyhead, 'I still just
hold my head up, but I am sadly threatened. I pray for a good day on
Thursday, when, please God, I will put a very ungrateful people (or
rather let me say, a deluded People) to shame, and show them that I ride
the same pace through an affectionate, as through an insulting crowd.' As
it happened, the State entry was a tame affair. Cloncurry rode at the head

of the procession, and except for spasmodic cries of '*Dirty Dog*herty', the large crowds were mostly silent.[7]

*   *   *

The prodigious power of O'Connell was never better demonstrated than by the success he had in inflaming the people into a state of near-insurrection by the time of Anglesey's arrival in Dublin. On his very first day the viceroy wrote that he believed an early and vigorous inter-ference would be necessary to prevent the enormous and frequent meet-ings which were threatened, and for the first and last time he admitted that rebellion in Ireland seemed inevitable. Within forty-eight hours (on Boxing Day) he had put forth the first of the many proclamations which he was to issue in the next few weeks. He had a copy of it placed on O'Connell's breakfast table just before notices announcing a great procession of all the trades through the streets of Dublin were to be stuck up throughout the city. O'Connell at once issued a handbill telling everyone to obey, as if the order of the Lord Lieutenant was to derive its authority from his permission. The notices were withdrawn and the procession cancelled. Two days later, on his daily ride through the streets, Anglesey fell in with a large multitude attending another meeting of O'Connell's. 'I had not time for reflection', he wrote to Grey. 'If I had turned back, the probability is that I should have been followed and insulted: so I kept my course. The people opened out for me to pass, with the most perfect respect, and evinced quite as much enthusiasm as I ever witnessed. Having passed on, when I got to a bridge across the Liffey, I desired the vast numbers who were following me, to stop, that I might pursue my ride. Not a man crossed the bridge.'[8]

Grey, meanwhile, was urging him to find some way of stopping O'Connell by legal means. He did not have long to wait, for on January 14th there was published a letter from O'Connell recommending a run on the banks. This and other actions at last decided Anglesey. 'I am just come from a consultation of six hours with the Law Officers,' he wrote to Char, who had not yet joined him from London, 'the result of which is a determination to arrest O'Connell, for things are now come to that pass that the question is whether he or I shall govern Ireland.'[9]

'The popular excitement', wrote one commentator, 'reached white heat when the news became known that O'Connell had just been arrested in his own house.... Mr Farrell, an old peace-officer, accompanied the

constables, and on the plea of an attack of gout expressed a desire that
O'Connell should ride in a hackney-coach. "I am very sorry for your
gout," was the reply, "but since the Lord-Lieutenant has chosen to arrest
me as if I were a common housebreaker, I think it right the whole city
should know it — I must therefore walk." ' At first O'Connell thought of
allowing himself to go straight to prison, but, afraid that the people
might break out unmanageably, he determined instead to give bail,
entering into securities for £2,000. Anglesey believed, with that self-
confidence which never deserted him, that since the time had now come to
fight it out with the arch-agitator, there was no one better able to do it
than himself. 'I do believe I am the *Man*,' he told Holland, 'for I know the
rogue to a turn. — *His new title for me is "Anglesey the Liar" — Good!*'
The Cabinet, after initial hesitations, fully approved of the arrest. Every
sort of legal expedient was now brought into play on O'Connell's behalf
to put off the case — and with eventual success, for in fact he was never
brought up for trial. But the chief reason for this was that the political
situation had suddenly undergone a radical change.[10]

On March 1st, 1831, the Government outlined its scheme for Parliamentary Reform. The secrecy which had been observed in its preparation
made its far-reaching provisions seem even more staggering than they
actually were, and the effect on O'Connell was extraordinary. 'I did not
believe', he declared in a public letter while still awaiting trial, 'a Ministry
which confided the affairs of Ireland to Lord Melbourne, Lord Anglesey
and Mr Stanley capable of bringing forward any other than a delusive
plan of reform. That Ministry has nobly vindicated itself from these my
suspicions.' He at once offered the Government his full co-operation, and
for the time being ceased seriously to agitate for Repeal. Although, in the
event, Reform as applied to Ireland was far from satisfying to him, he at
first threw himself into the Parliamentary fight for it in England with
great effect, bringing much-needed aid to Ministers. This being the case,
they were glad enough to allow him to escape trial, the Law Officers
agreeing that the dissolution of Parliament in April precluded further
proceedings in the case.[11]

This marked the end of the most bitter phase of warfare between
Anglesey and O'Connell, though the contempt which the 'Tribune'
entertained for the viceroy died hard. 'Anglesey is hare-brained; he
knows nothing'; 'I wish that ridiculously self-conceited Lord Anglesey
were once out of Ireland'; 'Lord Anglesey can meddle in Irish affairs only
to spoil them'; 'he excites only compassion'; 'that crazy Lord Anglesey';

THE TINKER.

arly in 1831 the Marquess of Anglesey issued a number of Proclamations designed to curb
Daniel O'Connell's agitation for Repeal of the Union; these did not have the desired effect.

'that egregious ninny'; 'the harsh, virulent, proud, ... good-for-nothing, palavering ———— Anglesey. His name is Scoundrel.'[12] These were some of the denunciations which occurred in his letters over the next three years. How unfair they were the student of Anglesey's copious correspondence with Ministers will at once observe.[h] Undoubtedly O'Connell would have retracted every one of them if he could have known how hard a fight the Lord Lieutenant put up for measures of real value to Ireland; how desperately he strove to lessen the impotence imposed upon a well-meaning Government in London by the ignorance and apathy of a Parliament preoccupied with English affairs.

Anglesey bore O'Connell no lasting ill-will. Though in 1839 he could still fulminate against his behaviour earlier in the decade and call him an 'egregious cheat' (see p. 299), by 1844, when the 'Liberator' was once again facing trial, Anglesey's parting words to Pierce Mahony, after a dinner in Uxbridge House, were: 'I greatly regret any differences between me and O'Connell, and let him know that I sincerely wish him success, and if I had power I would exert it on his behalf.'[13]

iii

Real distress is a fearful ally to traitorous agitation.
                                        Anglesey to Grey[14]

No Government in the nineteenth century ever started its career with better intentions towards Ireland than Lord Grey's. From the first moment of its existence the Cabinet was resolved to get things done to improve the state of that wretched country. Spring-Rice, the Secretary of the Treasury, announced that nineteen bills were in preparation for curing Irish ills. But O'Connell was sceptical: he dismissed them all with the one word 'fudge!' During the first long interview with the viceroy, he had asked, 'What will you do for Ireland?' to which Anglesey had replied, 'Everything.' And so he would have, had he possessed the power. The irony of the situation was that nearly everything which O'Connell thought necessary to benefit Ireland, with the exception of repeal of the Union, was being actively and persistently pressed for by the Lord Lieutenant he so much execrated. Within a few days of O'Connell's arrest Anglesey wrote, 'Now see what has happened. Protestant, Catholic, Banker, Merchant, Bar, Church — all have rallied to me. You cannot conceive the altered state of the public mind. It is truly magical. Now send me money to employ the people without a moment's loss of time. Then pass quickly a few popular Bills; — particularly relax the Coal Bill, & finally, pay the Priests; and I promise you shall never hear more of O'Connell or any such fellow.' The repeal of the duty on sea-borne coal was effected immediately, but the payment of the Catholic clergy, on which Anglesey from the start placed heavy emphasis, was never achieved. The reason for this was simple. To attempt to persuade an English Parliament that the State should actually support the priesthood of Rome anywhere in Britain was politically impossible. Yet Anglesey's chief ground for wishing to do so was the desire to lessen the potency of the priests' hold over the people and vice versa.

'Some persons', wrote Anglesey in early 1831, 'are of the opinion that the people are under the control of the Clergy. Others assert that the Clergy being dependent upon the people for their bread, readily bend to their inclinations. There is some truth in both statements. What weight the Priest really has with his flock it is difficult to determine. Much must depend upon the character of each individual priest, but there cannot be a doubt that a People who *pay* their priest must have a very strong tie upon him. Therefore until the Priest is paid by the Government, no Government can depend upon either Priest or People.'

The truth of this was of course seen by the agitators and the priests themselves; hence there was opposition to the payment from those quarters as well as from the forces of Anglicanism. No wonder Anglesey had to admit before his first year was out that the time was not yet ripe for paying the priests.[15]

The most pressing need was the provision of money for public works, so as to alleviate unemployment, and though Grey hopefully set aside on paper an initial grant of £500,000, this was soon whittled down to loans of negligible value. Neither the Treasury nor Parliament was sufficiently confident of a return for its money if spent in Ireland, and here was one of the chief causes of Ireland's continuing troubles. Capital would only follow tranquillity; but tranquillity could only be achieved by the injection of capital. It was a vicious circle which never resolved itself. In

Stanley, the Irish Secretary, later to desert the Whigs and become Tory Prime Minister as fourteenth Earl of Derby, Anglesey had at first a firm ally so far as material aid was concerned. Indeed the Irish Government was a strong team. Had it been less inhibited it would have done much for Ireland. But as it happened, for the next two years both Parliament and people across the Irish Sea were so preoccupied with the Reform Bill and the crises which accompanied its progress to the statute-book, that the crying needs of Ireland were more than ever relegated to the background.

iv

The King's conduct is most cheering. Oh! What should we have done without him! I shudder to think of what might have been. However, *we*, at least, should not have been principal actors in that contingency. We should merely have been passengers, and probably should have been upset.
Anglesey to Holland, May 23rd, 1831[16]

Anglesey was delighted with the ministerial plan of Reform.[1] For some years he had been an ardent Reformer, though by Reform he was bound personally to lose considerable parliamentary influence and patronage. Six months earlier he had written:

'I want reform, temperate, but deep and general, and not the least reason for wanting it is, that I prefer the monarchial state, and am an aristocrat. But then aristocracy wants reform,[1] for I believe it to be the most powerful of the three estates, and what I take to be right is that no one of the three should be too powerful for the other two. We must contrive to get a government that shall rule by public opinion and the confidence of the people, and that shall at once, and manfully, cease to carry on their measures by the power of patronage, influence, and intrigue. This I firmly believe to be practicable; but where is the man who has the nerve and vigour to undertake it?'

In Grey the country thought that they had found the man.

The strength of the opposition to Reform was formidable: how formidable had yet to be tested; but Grey from the very start was prepared for defeat, if not in the Commons then in the Lords, and it was his intention, when that happened, to go to the country. He asked Anglesey whether, under existing circumstances in Ireland if the Government should be beaten he was prepared to face a dissolution. The answer was an emphatic 'Yes'. Whatever the risks (and he did not, in fact, fear election riots), Anglesey thought they should be faced in an attempt to save the Empire from revolution — which he felt would inevitably occur if Reform were not carried.[17]

At the end of March the Bill's second reading in the lower House was carried by only one vote. This meant that in committee the Bill would almost certainly be whittled down to unacceptable proportions. Grey was despondent, for the only alternatives before him when that happened were dissolution or resignation, and to the former the King positively objected. When nearly a month later a wrecking amendment was carried on the committee stage of the Bill, the Cabinet at once recommended a dissolution. At first the King stuck to his scruple, but by the following day Grey and Brougham, the Lord Chancellor, had worked on him successfully. The state of Ireland had been one of the King's strongest reasons for objecting to a dissolution, but, as Melbourne confided to Anglesey, 'the authority of your letters, in which you state that such a course would be safe in Ireland at the present moment, was urged to the King, and was much relied on by him in the expression of his assent.'[18k]

The amazing scenes which were enacted when the dissolution took place have often been described. It is enough here to recall the sudden decision of the King, for tactical reasons, to go down to the House of Lords in person; the impotent rage of the Tories in both Houses, and the enthusiastic mob which cheered their monarch on his return to the Palace with: 'Well done, old boy! Served 'em right.'

V

It is the overgrown, ill-grown House of Lords that has been long tending to our troubles.

Anglesey to Grey[19]

The result of the general election which followed the dissolution and occupied the early summer was a resounding majority for the Government. The slogan 'The Bill, the whole Bill and nothing but the Bill' had triumphed. In Ireland the elections went off quietly, and the perfect good humour of the people amazed the Lord Lieutenant. In Parliament the Government at once proceeded to introduce the second Reform Bill. This they carried with sweeping majorities in the lower House. As for the Lords, it was certain from the start that they would fight the Bill to the last ounce of their strength. Before the elections had got under way, Grey's mind was already working on the possibility of creating peers, the very last of constitutional resources, so as to overcome the adverse majority expected in the upper House. In the first place he would advance only the eldest sons of peers (it was agreed that Uxbridge should be among them), so as to avoid a permanent enlargement of the House of Lords; at the same time, for the same reason, Anglesey was asked to select suitable Irish Lords for United Kingdom peerages which would enable them to sit in the House. He also went to great pains to persuade doubtful peers and bishops to declare themselves for Reform, and, just as important, to urge the known Reformers to take their seats so that they could vote when the time came. There was one English peer to whom Holland begged Anglesey to write, for he had heard that a word from the Lord Lieutenant was necessary 'to secure his politics, and sure to do so'. This was the Earl of Harrington, who, as Lord Petersham, had given his name to a greatcoat, to a ribbon and to a snuff mixture. 'As I once,' explained Anglesey, 'at the earnest request of the late King, engaged [Lord Harrington] to cut off his whiskers and his beard, which His Majesty himself had been unable to effect, I may surely hope to persuade him upon the subject of the support of Reform and the King's Ministers, which, compared with the grave matter of whiskers and beard, is one so insignificantly trivial.' He failed none the less, for Harrington remained neutral on Reform, his name occurring in none of the subsequent division lists.[20]

The first trial of strength came on October 7th, when the Bill was thrown out of the Lords by a majority of forty-one. On September 3rd, Grey had asked Anglesey for his opinion as to what should be done in just such a case. The reply was clear.

'I would not hesitate', Anglesey averred, 'to make Peers to any extent, and I would boldly avow my motive; I would say, "This is done to carry the Reform Bill." The People will be with you. The King is for Reform — the Lower House is for Reform — The Ministers are for Reform, & *as such*, were called upon by the nation, and selected by the King.

'If we considered ourselves only, we should instantly retire from office upon defeat. There is not a doubt of it. But we should have to answer for such a step to the King and to the People. And in whose hands should we throw them? In those whose measures and whose conduct would effect revolution and ruin in 6 weeks. This is my dread.'

So vital did Grey consider the Lords' debate, that Anglesey was brought over from Dublin to record his vote. He attended the Cabinet meeting next day, Grey not wishing to come to any decision as to the next step without his advice and concurrence. The decision taken was to prorogue Parliament, so as to enable a new Bill to be brought in when it reassembled. This it did on December 6th, against the wishes of Grey and Palmerston, who would have preferred a January meeting. Anglesey wrote from Dublin that he approved of the early meeting,

'*if* you are prepared with the Lords. It is called for, and will tend to pacify the public mind. But *are* you prepared? If you cannot carry the Bill, ruin ensues. If we are beat without every possible effort having been made to carry the Measure, all confidence will be withdrawn from the Ministers, and the King will lose his strength, — and then what is to happen? You must not — You cannot resign, unless the King absolutely refuses you the full means of carrying your object. I deprecate an increase of the Peerage; we are already too numerous; but I see no safe means of averting the evil.'[21]

The passage of the third Bill through the Commons was even more triumphant than that of its predecessor. On March 23rd, 1832, it passed its third reading by a majority of 116. During the three-and-a-half months it took to reach that state, the popular excitement, the house-burning, the riots in many parts of England, which had succeeded the first rejection of the Bill five months before, continued unabated. Meanwhile, in Whitehall the great question of the creation of peers was being anxiously debated. At the beginning of the year Grey went down to Brighton to discuss the matter with the King, who agreed in principle to a considerable creation, yet would not commit himself definitely as to numbers. But as the time for the battle in the Lords drew near, the Prime Minister seemed to waver. In mid-February he told Anglesey that he was 'desirous, if possible, to avoid a creation of Peers; which nothing but absolute necessity could justify; more especially as, in resorting to that expedient, fifty, at the very least, would be required to make the King safe.'[22]

For some time the Prime Minister had been conferring with Lords Harrowby and Wharncliffe, the leaders of the 'Waverers' in the House of Lords — men who, though strong opponents of the measure, had, it was thought, at last seen that resistance to it was both hopeless and dangerous. 'They are confident', wrote Grey on February 17th, 'of having sufficient numbers to carry the second reading, but they cannot give a specifick detail of names pledged to support them.' Anglesey, in reply, sounded a clear note of warning.

'The "Waverers" ', he wrote, 'will not themselves deceive you as to the number of converts but may *they* not be deceived by others? There are very interested and very treacherous & very unprincipled men amongst our Compeers, who are ready to sacrifice every thing — Country, Honor, Constitution — all to recover power which would lead them to the scaffold in a month. *I* would not trust their professions. *I* would make Peers, to make my game certain. You will want them even after the Reform is obtained. Remember what you have against you in Our House. Remember what has been placed there within the last 40 years. Remember, too, that you have many interested old Whigs, Carnarvon for instance, sore with the loss of Borough, & the like. All this must be permanently faced, or the machine will go to pieces.... You are bound to put yourself beyond all hazard. There is a good deal of apparent presumption in writing this. I am a politician of very short standing and of like experience, but I have thought deeply upon the subject. I feel it strongly, & I know you will receive it kindly.'[23]

By March 13th Grey had decided to fight the battle of the second reading without a creation of peers, particularly as the King had refused him in January the right to make the necessary number. 'I may be mistaken in my calculations, but I feel certain of success,' he wrote. 'My personal responsibility is tremendous: but I must stand the cast.' The event proved him to have decided aright, for by the defection of Wharncliffe and the other 'Waverers' the second reading was carried by nine votes. Anglesey, who had again come over from Dublin specially to do so, voted in this division.[24]

Before he returned he was received by the King, whose original

'Good morning to you Daniel' – 'Will I nat get lave to spake?'
In January 1831 Anglesey arrested O'Connell, who was given bail in
the sum of £2,000 (see p. 248)

The Marquess of Anglesey as Colonel of the 7th Hussars

intention to yield to Reform as an unpleasant necessity had recently undergone a change, as a result of the influence of those about him. He complained bitterly to Anglesey of the manner in which he was beset and
persecuted by the Queen and his brothers and sisters, and said there was
not one among them who was not violent in political feelings. Anglesey
also saw the Queen. He told Grey that she was more gracious than he
could have expected.

> 'I expressed to the King *very strongly indeed*', he wrote, 'the perni-
> cious consequences that resulted from her known abhorrence of
> reform & of the present system of Government, & that the evil
> effect of his being constantly & exclusively surrounded by the Old
> Tory faction was beyond calculation. He freely admitted all this, but
> said, "What can I do? They are not my choice. The Queen will have
> them. In short, I lead the life of the damned." '

One of the objects of the interview had been to persuade the King to
prevail upon Lord Mayo, the husband of one of Queen Adelaide's
ladies-in-waiting,[1] to pair with Anglesey so that the Lord Lieutenant
could return to his duties rather than hang about in London waiting to
cast his vote in the committee debates which were about to begin.[m]
'My good Lord,' said the King, 'I could do this with pleasure but [Mayo]
is such an obstinate old blockhead that I can make no impression upon
him.' None the less the King did, in fact, persuade Mayo, and Anglesey
returned at once to his post.[25]

*   *   *

The celebrated crisis of May 1832, known as 'The Days of May',
began when what amounted to a wrecking amendment was carried in the
Lords on the 7th of that month. The majority in favour of it, which
included the 'Waverers', whom Anglesey had so rightly mistrusted, was
thirty-five. He thought it the most fortunate event that could have
happened. 'Better, far better, is this defeat by 35, than a weak, unwilling
majority. Oh! It is glorious. Of course,' he told Holland, 'I write under a
conviction that an ample supply of Peers is to be made. I cannot tell you
what spirits I am in about it.' But three days later he was angrily admitting
that his speculation had been a bad one: he had calculated too much on the
firmness of the King. Faced at last with the two alternative of creating

I

sufficient peers or accepting the Government's resignation, William IV had chosen the second. Anglesey raged. 'The King deserves to be deposed', he wrote. 'He has deceived his servants, & unhappily it is in the Blood to do so. What did George the 3rd? What did George the 4th? I *suspected* him, yet I could not quite make up my mind to the conviction of his treachery. Still it is for the interest of the State that he should not be unmasked, & therefore we must screen him.'[26]

Anglesey wrote at once to the King asking to be relieved as soon as possible. 'My dread', he confided to Stanley, 'is that the King will find the impossibility of forming a Ministry — that he will be forced to again ask for our services, & that I shall still have to govern this ungrateful people.' This is exactly what happened, for though Wellington was sent for to try to concoct a Tory government which would undertake to pass a very slightly modified Reform Bill, that redoubtable statesman failed in his efforts. That he should contemplate the task at all was more than most men could stomach. Anglesey could not conceive how he could be so foolish as to take the course he did, without at least being certain of successfully forming a government. To Lord Grey, before Wellington's attempt had failed, Anglesey wrote, 'A firm administration *cannot* be formed. *Your* Bill will not be accepted from other hands, nor can I blame the people. What confidence can they place in men, who for the sheer desire of place, are ready to sacrifice principle!' The Duke's defence, so typical of him, was that he must do whatever the King might command. He was as much averse to Reform as ever, but he considered that no embarrassment of that kind, no private consideration, ought to prevent him from making every effort to serve his sovereign. But Peel, whom Wellington suggested as Prime Minister, refused to be the instrument for carrying a measure to which he was so bitterly opposed. Others who were approached felt likewise. It was already probable that the Duke would fail, when a debate in the Commons clearly showed him that that House would have nothing to do with any Reform Bill which might be brought in by a Tory administration. This being the case, he resigned his commission. The King then had no alternative but to recall his late Government. Anglesey was sure that Grey would be unable to refuse. 'But you will be employed', he warned him, 'in shielding a suspected King, instead of being protected by a popular one.' Grey, of course, would agree to resume the reins only if the King consented to the full creation of peers. This, at last, he could no longer avoid. 'The battle is won for the moment', wrote Grey, 'but I am far from thinking that our difficulties are over. Our adversaries are actuated by a degree of fury that knows no bounds. It is really hardly safe to sit amongst them; and if my blood had been as hot as it once was, I should have been shot myself, or shot some of them before this time.'[27]

'All's safe and restored,' Holland told Anglesey. 'The King agrees to give us full powers. All's well that ends well — Wellington has slunk off to Strathfieldsaye — So let him go. The Tories, in the midst of their railings, seem to me to intend waiving their opposition and letting us go on without any immediate or violent exercise of the power [of creating peers].'[28n] In this Holland was right, for most of the anti-Reform peers followed the ducal lead and slunk off, leaving the House of Lords to pass the Bill without an untoward addition to its numbers. On June 7th the Bill at long last became an Act.[o]

In Dublin, when it was thought that the viceroy would retire on the fall of the Government, the excitement was immense. There was talk of illuminating the city, and he was assured that at least 30,000 people were enrolled to attend him to Kingstown.[29] Had he in fact left Ireland at that moment it might have been in a blaze of popularity nearly as great as in 1829. For his own peace of mind and body, and for the good of his contemporary reputation, this would have been preferable to continuance in office, since the purely Irish problems with which the Government was confronted were already proving too much for it. Before two years were out the greatest of them had been the cause of its fall.

vi

No one who does not live in Ireland, & who, living in it, does not inquire deeply into the real state of this population, can conceive their destitution & misery. It is frightfully oppressed & degraded. It suffers injury & insult & oppression & exaction that no other people upon earth would stand, & my only astonishment is that Ireland is not in open rebellion.

If the Tithe question turns out well, if we can manage to feed the really destitute poor, & to employ a very fine population, we may yet conquer both factions, but we must be prompt in measures of relief.

Anglesey to Grey, December 19th, 1831[30]

'Tithe, tithe, tithe!!! Think of Tithe!'

To this adjuration from the Lord Lieutenant, the Irish Secretary replied that the question of tithes could not be brought on in the 1831 session of

Parliament with any chance of success, for the Tories would be afforded the cry of revolution in the Church following revolution in the State.[31] The exasperation which such a situation inspired in Anglesey was a reflection of what the majority of Irishmen felt at this time, for O'Connell and his demagogues, soft-pedalling on Repeal until Reform was achieved, had temporarily turned their attention to the state of the Established Church in Ireland. And what a good case they had! When it is considered that even in Protestant England at this time there was complaint at the payment of tithes to a Church whose bishops in many cases and incumbents in some had forfeited the respect of the tithe-payers, the injustice of the system in Ireland appals. For there the burden of maintenance of the Anglican clergy fell on Catholics and Protestants alike:[p] of the former there were at least six million, of the latter less than one million. Sydney Smith stated a common case when he wrote: 'On an Irish Sabbath morning, the bell of a neat parish church often summons to worship only the parson and an occasionally-conforming clerk, while, two hundred yards off, a thousand Catholics are huddled together in a miserable hovel, and pelted by all the storms of heaven.'[32]

The grievance had existed from the reign of Elizabeth, when for the first time obligatory payment of tithes was rigorously exacted; its removal, like Catholic emancipation, had been intended by Pitt at the time of the Union, but nothing had been done. In recent years the extensive increase in the population, leading as it had to the further subdivision of holdings, made the weight of the impost intolerable. The starving peasant of the Southern counties, already largely dependent on his potato garden for his meagre subsistence, was forced to give up a substantial proportion of his produce, or, under the Composition of Tithe Act of 1823,[q] an equivalent sum in money. If, as often happened, the miserable peasant could not pay, whatever he might possess which approximated to the value of the unpaid tithe was impounded. 'I have seen the cow, the favourite cow,' wrote one commentator in 1812, 'driven away, accompanied by the sighs, the tears, and the imprecations of a whole family, who were paddling after, through wet and dirt, to take their last affectionate farewell of this their only friend and benefactor at the pound gate.'[33] In the first quarter of the century similar scenes were becoming increasingly familiar throughout the South. By the end of the 1820s organized resistance to the payment of tithes, resulting in riot and bloodshed, was extending alarmingly.

From the system of tithe collection there had grown up an army of corrupt and greedy agents, known as tithe-proctors. The activities of these and a host of other middlemen not only inflamed the peasantry, but were extremely inefficient. By the time Anglesey started to grapple with the problem, it often cost more to collect the tithes than their value when collected. Moreover, a considerable number of the Anglican clergy were subsisting at a very low level. Clearly something had to be done, and done urgently.

An important aspect of the tithe question was the relationship between landlord and tenant. Anglesey was convinced that there existed 'to a most frightful extent, a mutual and violent hatred between the Proprietors and the Peasantry. In general the landholders are harsh and unkind to the people. They treat them scornfully.' In fixing rents the actual value of the land for productive purposes was seldom the criterion, and though, in assessing what the rent should be, the landlords should have taken into account the amount which the tenant would have to pay in tithe, this was rarely done. But the situation was complicated by other factors.

'The great body of the Irish gentry of moderate fortune', Anglesey discovered, 'are much distressed. Their estates are mortgaged, and to provide for their immediate necessities, they take the highest rent they can obtain. As there are no Poor Laws, and scarcely any work for the *people*, it is with these an affair of life and death to obtain potato ground, and for this there is the greatest competition, and they promise a rent that they are utterly unable to pay.... Few however of the gentry have much land over which they have much control. Much of it is under long leases, and it is usually those who hold under such leases who are the most oppressive. Their exactions and their cruelty are frightful. For land for which they pay from 10s. to 25s. an acre, they very frequently exact £4 and £5 for the ordinary purposes of agriculture, but for potatoes, from £8 to £11 (!!!), to obtain the rent for which, they usually drive their cattle, and seize the potatoes in the ground. Another cause of misery and distress, & consequently outrage, is the indiscretion with which many of the large Proprietors attempt to rid themselves of a vast population by ejectment at once, instead of doing it gradually. They then form large farms of Pasture Land, and it is this practice which induces the ejected peasantry to go about in immense bodies to turn up these pastures.'[34]

* * *

As important as the problem of tithes was the whole question of the Establishment of the Protestant Church in Ireland. It was widely felt that apart from the obvious fact that there were too many Anglican clergymen for too few Anglican souls, the number of sees and the value of the bishops' incomes were disproportionately large. The annual income of the Church amounted to £750,000, and out of this sum twenty-two archbishops and bishops were receiving £150,000. Absentee clergy and the scandalous system of pluralities were other causes of complaint. Anglesey gave Grey an instance. 'Will you believe', he wrote, 'that at the moment when this violent stir is making about pluralities, non-residence & the like, the Bishop of Down should have given to his Brother, the Archdeacon — who has I believe, 2 or 3 fat livings — a dispensation for *3* years, not on account of ill health, but merely to live for his pleasure in Jersey, where he has procured a living or Cure!!!'[35]

Anglesey believed that with good management the whole Establishment ought to be able to live off the ecclesiastical lands alone, and that while the bishops and clergy were amply paid by actual possession of property, the very name of tithe should be abolished.

When the Government in the midst of its other occupations came to consider what should be done, it found itself, as so often in Irish affairs, ground between two powerful bodies of extremists. In the Lords there was the High Church party and in the Commons O'Connell and his 'tail' — the one determined to resist any meddling with the Establishment, the other to be satisfied only with radical solutions. These would have been effective obstructions in themselves, but added to them were dissensions in the Cabinet, which were reflected in the differences which grew up between the Lord Lieutenant and the Irish Secretary. Twelve years later Anglesey told Lord John Russell that Stanley and he had scarcely agreed upon a single point with regard to Ireland, and that it had been much the same with Melbourne.[36]

As early as April 20th, 1831, Anglesey began to think Stanley 'a little tainted' upon Irish church and education matters. As the months went by this distrust grew, helped on by Stanley's manner in dealing with Irishmen, which was aloof and unsmiling. But when he read one morning in the papers that the Irish Secretary had given notice of increased penalties, including transportation, in the annual Bill for the registration of arms, Anglesey exploded. Not a word of the proposal had reached his ears. 'Oh! I could be angry', he told Holland, 'only I never permit myself to be so.' He was disgusted that the very first Bill brought in for Ireland was a penal one, when others of an exactly contrary character had been promised. 'In this', he complained, '*I* shall suffer, and most innocently upon my honor.' It turned out that Grey, Holland and Althorp had been equally left in the dark. The Arms Bill, said Grey, had come upon them like a clap of thunder. None of the Cabinet except Melbourne had had the slightest previous intimation of it, and Melbourne was suspected of being negligent in not bringing it before them. The Prime Minister at once protested against the transportation clause and other objectionable features, and in these respects the Bill was altered.[37]

So the incident ended, but suspicion of Stanley and Melbourne grew fast in Anglesey's mind. Nor was this to be wondered at, for Melbourne from time to time gave up Ireland as a hopeless case. 'I have for a long time thought', he told Anglesey, 'that we shall either lose Ireland, or hold her by means of the Protestants, and I hardly know which alternative opens to us the most melancholy and appalling prospect.' Anglesey would have none of that. 'The bare mention of governing Ireland by means of the Protestants', he retorted, 'horrifies and appals me. This I declare, that I will not be the man to attempt it.'[38] As to Stanley, his views on church questions were fundamentally different from Anglesey's. He was devotedly attached to the Establishment on religious grounds, believing that the clergy supplied the country with the benefits of a resident gentry; and above all he would never agree, if he could help it, to the diversion of the Church's income to secular purposes. It was chiefly on this that he fell out not only with Anglesey but also with a good part of the Cabinet.[r]

The King's Speech at the opening of Parliament in December declared that something would be done in the matter of tithes, and Melbourne followed it up with a Select Committee of Enquiry, the time-honoured method of postponing action. By the middle of January 1832, Anglesey had completed a comprehensive plan of Church and tithe reform. It was the result of a long series of consultations within his 'inner conclave'. This now contained Cloncurry, Blake, and Dr Sadlier (a future Provost of Trinity College, Dublin). Plunket, the Irish Lord Chancellor, and Blackburne, the Attorney-General, gave the scheme their full support. Its first recommendation was that tithe composition should be made compulsory, and this point was agreed by all, an Act to that effect being passed on August 16th. It went on to recommend that the State should take over the revenues of the Church; from these it was to pay all the Protestant clergy their present incomes, less four or five per cent for collection of the cummuted tithes, thereby guaranteeing to them a secure but slightly reduced income in exchange for the present very uncertain one. It reckoned that a surplus of £350,000 would then be left for other purposes. This in the first place would be held in trust for the benefit of the Protestant Church whenever the extension of its creed should require more churches and fresh endowments, but there would be enough, too, when the time was judged ripe, to pay the Catholic clergy, which it was thought could be handsomely done for £120,000. Any further surplus which remained was to be used, along with a poor-rate, to provide for the indigent and unemployed.[39] This was, of course, the revolutionary part of the plan.

Though bold and extensive, Anglesey's scheme did not recommend a reduction of the total number of bishoprics; nor did it touch upon the thorny question of the recovery of arrears of tithes. On this last point Anglesey had already made it clear how strongly he felt that any coercive measure to achieve it must come after, or at the worst at the same time as, whatever ecclesiastical reforms were decided upon. This was exactly what Stanley persuaded Grey and the Cabinet *not* to do. 'It is the opinion of many,' wrote the Prime Minister, 'and particularly of Stanley, that before we proceed to any permanent measure, we should vindicate the authority of the law as it now exists.' Anglesey was indignant when he learned that a savage bill to enforce the payment of arrears was to be introduced. 'Why', he asked Holland, 'act severely upon an odious system that you are about to alter? Is it not exactly like hanging a man for forgery upon the eve of taking away the capital punishment?' But the Stanleyites won, for on June 1st the Tithe Recovery Act was passed. Anglesey found himself 'carrying at the point of the bayonet, an odious measure' against which he had strenuously protested. By October he was despairing.

'It comes to this,' he told Holland, 'if you cannot stir up your courage to the sticking place, and force the timid of the Cabinet to adopt the whole Church scheme, and then to force it upon the King and upon the Lords, it were better, at once, to throw up the reins of Government; for to attempt to keep peace in Ireland whilst Stanley's Church prejudices are acted upon, is utterly hopeless. . . . I foresee the very worst consequences from our perseverance in bad measures, and from our dilatoriness in adopting good ones. I have appealed to you all round — To Grey, to Brougham, to Melbourne, to Stanley — even to you — and I make no converts.'[40]

1832 passed with virtually nothing done beyond the Committee of Enquiry. Anglesey had to call for more troops and was in daily fear of large-scale insurrection. Things got so bad at the beginning of 1833 that there had to be passed a 'Coercion Bill' (Palmerston called it the most violent ever carried into law), which combined the provisions of past Insurrection Acts with martial law and the suspension of Habeas Corpus. It was rushed through both Houses, the Government gaining large majorities at all stages. 'It is a real *tour de force*,' wrote the Foreign Secretary, 'but then it is to be followed by remedial measures, and there is the difference between us and Metternich and the Pope; we coerce as they do, but then we redress grievances as they do not.' This was in fact what happened, for on February 12th, 1833, Lord Althorp introduced his scheme for the Reform of the Church of Ireland. It was a far-reaching measure, incorporating many of Anglesey's ideas, but in some ways going further still, for it proposed to abolish ten of the twenty-two bishoprics.[8] The Orangement and High Church Tories were aghast, but O'Connell welcomed it with open arms. So did the Lord Lieutenant. 'Now I see', he told Holland on March 9th, 'that you are about to act in the true spirit of real statesmen, and that you are vigorously preparing to take the only means by which the extraordinary power usurped by O'Connell and his Demagogues can be wrested from their hands.' The combination of the promise of Church reform and the certainty of the Coercion Act enabled the viceroy to report at the end of April 'a phenomenon which is probably not to be found in Irish Annals. In this day's reports there is but one outrage, and that a trifling one, throughout all Ireland!'[41]

However, on the Committee stage of the Irish Church Bill, Stanley, though he had now left the Irish Office, carried an Amendment which removed what many (and certainly Anglesey) considered its most important clause. On the grounds that the Bill would not pass the Lords in its present form, Stanley did away with the idea of diverting the revenues of the supressed sees to non-ecclesiastical purposes. 'What a mess you are making of it', complained Anglesey to Holland. 'For my part I am *désorienté*. I know not where I am, or what you mean. You had last year, a plain, simple comprehensive measure laid before you, which you might then have carried (for then you were more powerful than you are now), & which would have given general satisfaction. The State, the Church, the People would have been gainers. Now I hear of no party that is likely to be pleased.'[42]

Even with this important amendment, it looked as if the Church Bill would be ejected by the Lords on its second reading. In this crisis, prompted by Holland and with Grey's warm approval, Anglesey wrote to the King.

'Your Majesty's advisers', he explained, 'are now encountering the same embarrassments which they last year experienced & from which they were relieved mainly by Yr. My's firmness & decision. They are in the same uncertainty as they were in respect to Parliamentary Reform; ... the same dependence upon actual waverers, altho' real enemies, & ... nearly the same & much more unreasonable impatience for a creation of Peers in those who support Your Majesty's Government....

'As the House of Lords is now constituted, there is not the smallest doubt that without Your Majesty's powerful & ardent & instant interference to avert the coming crisis, the Bill must be lost, & Your Majesty's present servants must withdraw.... But will those who may succeed them have the slightest chance of stability? The preponderance of radical Members in the new parliament will secure to them the power, as they will certainly have the will, of exacting from the new administration much wider measures than they have any hope of carrying with Yr Majesty's present servants.

'[As to Ireland] with a Ministry composed of men who are now designated as the Tory or Orange or Conservative Party, there is not the slightest chance that a House of Commons will suffer the continuance of the [Coercion] Bill, & most assuredly with a Government so constituted, Ireland would not be ruled without doubling the present Military Force, & which no Parliament will vote.'[43]

In his reply the King hoped that the crisis had, for the moment, been averted. He took credit to himself for having rescued his Government and the country by the unreserved and unequivocal expression of his sentiments, by which he meant that he had let Wellington and the Archbishop of Canterbury know that he was decidedly in favour of the Irish Church Bill.

'But', he continued, 'willing as is His Majesty to meet the Marquis of Anglesey with reciprocal confidence, he does not scruple to say that the Monarchy and the Country must suffer from the recurrence of such embarrassments and that means ought to be found to secure the Government, after they shall have escaped from this difficulty and have struggled thro' this Session, from the risk attendant upon the agitation of any and every question which may be brought into the House of Lords, and to secure the Country from the evils of a consequent collision between the two Houses of Parliament.'

He wanted, he said, to avoid exposing the sovereign to the resignation of one Government while the formation of any other that could carry on the business of the country was hopeless; and he vehemently agreed that the creation of peers was objectionable. His solution would be a coalition: what he called a combination of respectable parties. But as Holland pointed out to Anglesey, the royal 'notion of coalition or rapprochement is an illusion. It neither can be, nor if it could would it strengthen either party, but weaken both. We should lose the people, and they the most formidable and, faith, I think the most respectable of their aristocracy.'[44]

In the event the crisis was averted, for Wellington and other Tories absented themselves from the division on the second reading, thereby allowing the Bill to scrape through.

The Government staggered on, depending for its existence largely upon the unwillingness of Wellington to upset it, but the division within its own ranks on Irish matters grew, until, in 1834 (nearly a year after Anglesey had left it), Grey could cope with it no longer. On his resignation the King tried out upon Melbourne, who was generally agreed to be the best man to succeed Grey, his favourite project of a coalition, but Melbourne refused such an impossible task, and the King had to be content with the continuance of a purely Whig administration. Thus came into being the premiership which, outlasting the life of the King, so skilfully launched his young niece upon the era which was to bear her name.

vii

In so far as the education of the lower classes is concerned it may, I think, now be set down that the victory over bigotry has been achieved.

Lord Cloncurry, in 1849[45]

The great questions of Reform and the Irish Church stand out as the most important in Anglesey's second administration, but there were multifarious lesser tasks which he tackled in those three crowded years.

One of the first was to diminish the number of sinecures with which the Irish government was saddled, and to reduce salaries and pensions to realistic proportions. Strongly supporting the recommendations of a Select Committee of the Commons, he started with his own emoluments, which were cut by one-third, bringing them down to the £20,000 a year which they had been in 1784.ᵗ The saddest reform of all was the gradual extinction of the State Musicians, whose establishment dated from 1662. They were appointed by the Lord Lieutenant during pleasure, and now it was intended to abolish them when the existing interests lapsed.ᵘ Music provided by private enterprise flourished none the less, as is shown by Anglesey's injunction to Stanley in September 1831 to provide himself 'with another Governor for Ireland. I can not separate myself from *Paganini*, and mean to follow his fortunes in some humbler situation. We are all mad about him.' The great violinist's Irish tour had been almost as successful as his fabulous English one, during which he was said to have made a £17,000 profit.⁴⁶

Of greater consequence than minor financial reforms were Anglesey's numerous remedies for the social and economic evils which beset the country. A Poor Law, in principle the same as that of England, but without some of its drawbacks, he thought inevitable. Though Poor Laws were not in fact introduced till 1838, many of his ideas upon them were adopted at that date. His pressure for their adoption was continuous, as was his insistence upon direct state aid for the aged and infirm, but little enough was done in his time. As to local government, a number of reforms, too tedious to go into here, were effected at his instigation. They succeeded for the most part in increasing efficiency and lessening corruption.

*   *   *

Perhaps the most important of all the measures to which Anglesey made contribution was that which affected education. In 1830 the few regular educational establishments which existed in Ireland were almost exclusively under Protestant control: to all intents and purposes the mass of the people received literally no formal education whatever. The small number of attempts which had been made in the past to create a system of education which could cater for all religious denominations had invariably failed. Without exception the schools, not long after their founding, had degenerated into proselytizing institutions which no Catholic parents would allow their children to attend. Large Parliamentary grants were made each year to some of these exclusive establishments, and seldom was public money more inefficiently or more corruptly used. The only Catholic establishment which received a Parliamentary endowment was the famous College of Maynooth, attended by students intended for the Catholic priesthood.

Since 1814 an annual grant had been made to a body known as the Kildare Place Society. This had been formed on a non-denominational basis chiefly for the dissemination throughout Ireland of useful books, and for the maintenance of schools which practised the reading of the Bible 'without note or comment'. Like so many similar non-sectarian enterprises in Ireland, it had quickly fallen into the hands of Protestants, and the question of renewing the grant for 1831 was the spark which set Anglesey off in quest of a solution on a national scale. Cloncurry tells how the seed of the great National Education System was planted.

'The war between the Bible-forcers and Bible-burners', he wrote in his memoirs, 'continued to rage with such fury, that it became at length evident to all men, that until it should be forcibly quelled, there could be no chance of accomplishing the great object of a general and liberal education of the people.... The most obvious expedient for at once removing the bone of contention, and applying the bounty of the public to its proper use, was to place the responsibility of administering the education fund upon the executive government, and to remove all control over it from any self-constituted and irresponsible body.

'This plan I pressed upon the attention of Lord Anglesey, and at length it was adopted. Mr Stanley was ... at first much disinclined to the measure. It was indeed the subject of an anxious discussion the very night before he left Dublin, to attend parliament, that session. There dined together on the occasion, *en petite comité*, Lord Anglesey, Lord Plunket, Mr Stanley, Mr A. R. Blake, and myself; and when we parted, at two o'clock in the morning, it did not seem that the united arguments of the party had produced any effect upon the Chief Secretary. The Church and the Protestants, both of England and Ireland, he said, would not stand the withdrawal of the grant from the Kildare-place Society, and the substitution of a project for united and merely secular education. I presume, nevertheless, that the seed did not fall upon stony ground, as it was but a few weeks afterwards when the plan was broached by Mr Stanley himself; and during that session, a grant of £30,000 was made "to enable the Lord Lieutenant of Ireland to issue money in aid of schools, and for the advancement of education." '[47]

Anglesey was delighted with the board which was set up to administer the annual education vote. 'It is admirably composed,' he told Holland, 'I have attended it twice to set them a-going, and I am very sanguine that it will work admirably.' The members of the board, mostly selected by Anglesey, were the cream of the liberal-minded. The pleasant and respected Duke of Leinster was its first president, and he presided over two representatives of the Establishment, two Catholics, and two Presbyterians. Their greatest achievement was to work in complete and fruitful harmony. Success was immediate. Anglesey assured Melbourne in March 1833 that the Board worked admirably. 'The Commissioners have already in actual operation 497 schools, which are attended by 69,648 children. This has been accomplished within little more than 12 months. The Commissioners have made grants towards the building of 93 more schoolhouses, which will be attended by 17,242 children. They have also applications before them for 217 additional schools. It is impossible to say how many of the children are Protestants or Catholics, as no questions are asked by the Commissioners, but of the 807 applications, 783 have been signed by Protestants and Catholics conjointly.' The chief obstructionists of the system, the Lord Lieutenant discovered, were the non-Catholics of the North, who did all they could to injure and impede the liberal instruction which the new schools were calculated to establish, and which was becoming very popular. In spite of this the system quickly proved a triumphant success. In its first decade 3,500 schools attended by over 400,000 children came into being. Anglesey was justly proud of the part he played in bringing into being one of the least spectacular but most successful benefits ever conferred by an English Government on the people of Ireland.[48]

*   *   *

Among other measures for which he was in part responsible was an Act which created Lords Lieutenant for the counties of Ireland on the same basis as in England. This sprang in part from his constant desire to give recognition and responsibility to resident landowners; but the difficulty which he experienced in finding suitable men for the posts was intense. An example was the County of Limerick. 'These', he wrote, 'are the Peers of Limerick, all having good property in it:

'Massey	—	} Opposition.
Carbery	—	
Courtenay	—	!!!
Clare	—	Jobber and Absentee.
Dunraven	—	Jobber.
Limerick	—	Arch-jobber.
Cloncurry	—	Does not reside in [the County].'

He asked the Prime Minister to choose from these a suitable Lord Lieutenant![49]

Yet another enterprise was the starting of the *Dublin Times*. During his first administration he had been worried by the lack of an Irish newspaper which could hit back at the critics of his government. He therefore gave every encouragement to the formation of this new daily paper. 'I believe I may call it my paper,' he told Grey, 'for I went deep into my purse to set it a-going.' Though its circulation never began to compare with that of its rivals, the influence which it exerted for the two years of its existence was not negligible. The O'Connellite *Pilot* often referred to Anglesey as 'editor' of the *Dublin Times*, and was sufficiently needled by its contents to complain, after it had been alive only a few months, that 'the beloved Anglesey has the inestimable satisfaction of having, amongst his other gifts to Ireland, bestowed upon us a newspaper to which the slanderous, pasquinading, ribald, and obscene [*Dublin Evening*] *Mail* is dignity, decency, and patriotism itself.' In October 1833 the paper announced that as the Whigs were firmly established in power, its labours could be terminated. E. J. Littleton (who became Irish Secretary in 1833) later claimed that it was he who had put an end to them, because the paper was doing more harm than good.[50]

*   *   *

In the use of the armed forces for quelling disturbances, Anglesey created a number of mobile columns which could be transferred from one part of the country to another in the shortest possible time, thereby gaining economy in the employment of the limited number of troops which could be spared from England, itself racked by constant disorders. With the army at his disposal he was very satisfied. 'It acts', he wrote in 1831, 'with vigour, with union, with calm discretion. It acts always under the guidance of a legal adviser, — and when peace is restored, whatever unhappy scenes may have occurred, the actors in them are separated. And it is to be particularly remarked, that the Irish people, although they fear, they really respect and like the soldiers.'[51] This was in some measure due to the excellence of the Commander-in-Chief, his old friend, Sir Hussey Vivian.

viii

I am really too suffering an object not to snatch eagerly at the chance of relief in a more genial climate.

Anglesey to Holland, August 12th, 1833[52]

From the end of 1832, Anglesey's health had been getting steadily worse; by mid-July his sufferings were perpetual. To Holland he wrote: 'I am never for a moment well. The pain is sharp, acute & ever threatening at the slightest movement of the muscles of the face to bring on paroxysms, and thus I am really dragging on a miserable existence. Everyone is calling upon me to try the more genial, the more steady, and the drier climate of Italy. Tell Lord Grey that I would die here, rather than embarrass him. . . . If you take the decision of strengthening the Government by fresh men, my post must be considered an advantageous one to have in hand.' On hearing November 1832 that Lord William Bentinck's health necessitated his giving up the Governor-Generalship of India, Grey had suggested to Anglesey that he might like the situation. He had replied that the object nearest his heart was to live quietly at Beaudesert, if he was well enough. Otherwise he wished to go to Italy. 'But if Ireland wants me', he declared, 'I stay at all hazards. Or if it is decided that I could live and work in India, I would not hesitate to go.' Since the consensus of medical opinion was against a sick man of sixty-five being sent to India, the question was dropped.[53]

It was not only Anglesey's ill-health which had prompted the Prime Minister's offer: it had also been aimed at putting an end to the intolerable situation which now existed as a result of the disagreements between the Lord Lieutenant and the Irish Secretary.[v] Creevey well illustrates the pass to which their relationship had come.

'Let me give you', he wrote to Miss Ord, 'a specimen of the manner in which our great men govern us. Lord Anglesey said to Duncannon at Dublin: "Mr Stanley and I do very well together as companions, but we differ so totally about Ireland that I *never mention the subject to him*!" Anglesey then showed Duncannon a written statement of his views respecting Ireland, which he said he had sent to Lord Grey. Duncannon says nothing could be better, and he asked him why he had not addressed it to the Cabinet. — "Oh," said Lord Anglesey, "I consider myself as owing my appointment exclusively to Lord Grey, and don't wish to communicate with any one else." When Duncannon talked to Grey on the same subject, Ld. Grey said he was apprehensive of offending Stanley by laying these opinions of Anglesey's before him. Now which do you think of all these gentlemen deserves the severest flogging?'[54]

The storm broke on January 13th, 1833. On that day Grey wrote to the Lord Lieutenant that he had long perceived that there was not that confidential and friendly union between the viceroy and Stanley which their respective situations required. Anglesey at once expressed his readiness to fall in with whatever course would best suit Grey.

'I shall be content', he replied, 'to be recalled, or I will resign, or I will wait until you can make an eligible arrangement. I own I have often thought that I am not well placed here. I cannot sit at ease, and occupy a critical and responsible situation, without thinking for myself, and giving my opinions after I have maturely formed them, and I never do give them without the most anxious consideration. I have sometimes felt that I was perhaps not sufficiently satisfied with the ordinary functions of a King's Representative, by confining my exertions to the mere execution of orders received. I am by no means certain that such would not be the safest and the wisest course. I fear there is no medium between that and the alternative of a Governor so entirely possessing the confidence of the Government, that his views should be instantly adopted and carried into effect. I cannot expect such general confidence. I do not feel myself entitled to it. (From you, indeed, I have received it to a most flattering extent.) Yet I do most devoutly wish that such a Governor were found, for until that is the case, Ireland will not be effectually governed.

'You may do with me what you please, and account for my withdrawal in any way that may best suit your purpose.'

Grey was full of admiration and gratitude for so noble a reaction: so was Holland. 'Never', he wrote, 'was anything so handsome. I can assure you without affectation your letters make tears come in my eyes from sheer admiration. It is so unlike others and so like yourself.'[55]

To overcome the difficult situation which faced him, Grey now considered removing both Stanley and Anglesey from Irish affairs and giving them other posts in the Government. But Anglesey did not think that he could be of use anywhere else.

'I know pretty well what I can do,' he wrote to Holland, 'as well as what I cannot do; and, at the risk of boring you, I will make my confession. In situations where I have to control & to command, and to decide, and to act from my own notions, and upon my own responsibility, I can do well enough. I certainly have a facility in establishing an influence and an ascendency over people, and of winning them to me a good deal. I cannot persuade them that I am clever, for I am not so, and I never attempt it, but they know I am honest, and disinterested, and therefore it is, that notwithstanding all the untoward circumstances of the times I have obtained a certain power over this country, for those who do not love me are more or less afraid of me, and both parties know that I would seize by the collar, and shake, the first of them who fairly committed himself within my clutches. Now this is all I am good for. But all these qualities are thrown away in a Cabinet. I cannot debate in the House; and at Council, although I may have judgment and penetration and forethought, and take a right view of affairs, I have not the power of expressing and explaining them, but I can vote as well as the best of you, and there you shall have me, for I cannot conceive the possibility of my not going with you *con amore*. Now here is a picture of an artist by himself. I have seen many portraits thus painted, but I never saw one that was not flattered, and I have taken a similar liberty — that's all.'[56]

In the result, Stanley went and Anglesey stayed. Lord Durham, the Lord Privy Seal and one of the most brilliant members of the Cabinet, overwhelmed by disease, bereavements and dissatisfaction with the toughness of the Stanleyites, resigned in the middle of March. He had been one of those who particularly welcomed Anglesey's appointment[57] and had all along advocated conciliatory measures for Ireland. His antipathy towards Stanley and the measures he was able to force upon the Cabinet had

proved too much for him. Grey persuaded Goderich to exchange the
Colonial Office for that of the Privy Seal, and transferred Stanley from
the Irish Office to the Colonial, where the West Indian slave question was
causing almost as much trouble as the Irish Church.

'I have proposed to the King', Grey informed Anglesey, 'that Hobhouse should succeed Stanley as Irish Secretary, of which His
Majesty approved without hesitation. This therefore makes all further
changes on your side of the water unnecessary, and we all feel the
importance, I should rather say the absolute necessity of your remaining to carry the [Coercion] Bill.... For your own credit, and for
the good of the country, I look with equal anxiety and confidence
to your quelling the spirit of insubordination and violence which
has so long prevailed and to so alarming an extent in Ireland, and to
your delivering over the Government to your successor, whenever
the period of your retirement shall arrive, in a better state than it has
been in for a great length of time.'

Anglesey, though he did not know Sir John Hobhouse, accepted him
without demur, and continued at his post, riding, as he put it, 'at single
anchor'. Hobhouse, however, within a few weeks resigned from the
Government on a matter of taxes, and thus never got into his stride. He
was succeeded by Anglesey's old friend and Staffordshire neighbour,
E. J. Littleton, later to become Lord Hatherton. Their views on Irish
matters coincided completely, and Anglesey's last four months in Ireland
were the first in his four years there to be marked by real harmony
between the Irish Office in London and the Castle in Dublin. 'There
never was in Ireland', wrote Littleton, 'a Chief Secretary whose principles
will bind him more entirely to his Viceregal Master than mine will me to
you.' But Anglesey lamented to his new colleague that he found himself
in a very awkward position.

'There is a most pernicious interregnum. Old laws remain which it
is well known are about to be abandoned or materially altered,
whilst those which are about to be substituted are still in embryo....
The Irish Government is literally between two fires. In the House of
Lords it is accused of supineness, of such culpable forbearance in
not *firmly* enforcing obnoxious laws, as amounts to a virtual approval
of their infraction, whilst in the House of Commons ... all those
who have to talk to save their seats, represent it as encouraging &

executing acts of oppression. I daily read the assertion of falsehoods and misrepresentation of facts which astound & disgust me. The principle upon which I act is very simple. It is to cause the law as it stands to be respected, but only to be enforced in as mild and for-bearing a manner as possible, but you must never keep out of view that as long as a law exists, so long it is the imperative duty of the Government to cause it to be executed.'

Littleton saw the Lord Lieutenant's difficulty clearly.

'It is very hard on you', he wrote, 'that your situation obliges you to be silent towards the public, and leave it to be believed that the narrow and futile measures that have hitherto been proposed with respect to Irish Tithes (and the Church Bill is now not quite exempt from that character) show the limits of your courage in legislation as regards that system and perhaps some others.'[58]

*   *   *

By the end of August Anglesey reported that as a result of the threat of the Coercion Act the state of the country had so wonderfully altered that he no longer hesitated to give up the helm. This, with feelings of profound relief, he was able at last to do before September was out. To succeed him he recommended Lord Wellesley, whose successor he had been in 1828, and on September 6th he wrote, as he told Grey, 'to hurry the little Magnifico, for my Ladies are sadly afraid of being stopped on this side the Alps'. He had decided to spend the winter in Italy, and he wished to get there as soon as possible. Holland wanted him, on his way to Italy, to bear a compliment to the young Queen Maria, whom the Government had just succeeded in establishing on the throne of Portugal. 'You cannot get to a genial climate more rapidly', he wrote, 'and nothing would in the eyes of Portugal or indeed Europe manifest the importance we attach to her restoration more than a salute from such a great gun as you.' Anglesey was gratified and flattered.

'Your suggestions', he replied, 'are made in the true spirit of a real friend. I will tell you what are my feelings upon the subjects. When I quit Ireland, I have no fancy for any other public employment of a permanent nature. Certainly the going upon an extraordinary mission to compliment the little Queen might not be an undesirable, and perhaps it might appear to be an honorable close of my public career; and it would show to all the world that I separated from my colleagues with mutual feelings of attachment and regard. Such will indisputably be the case, whenever we do separate; but if there be really an intention of sending some one to Lisbon, and I be the chosen person, would not that entail upon me the necessity of returning to England to report the result of the Mission to the King? Now, my object is to spend the winter in Italy. There is a chance that Rome may suit my constitution....

'A thought', he concluded, 'this moment flashes across me. Supposing your vision of an Embassy to Lisbon to be realized, and supposing that my return to England were not necessary, might not a Frigate convey me from thence to Naples or Civita Vecchia?'[59]

Nothing came of this project, and by the beginning of October, Anglesey and part of his family passed through London on their way across Europe to Rome.

From that city, in January 1835, when on the fall of the Government it looked as if Wellington might be called on once again to pass a measure of which he had long been an opponent, Anglesey, in bitter mood, wrote to his brother Arthur:

'It is a singular coincidence that I have been twice recalled from Ireland for enforcing political opinions which in both instances the D. of Wellington has adopted or is about to adopt. I urged the Catholic Claims. I drove him into a corner from which he could not escape, and the Tories recalled me with affront. With a subsequent Whig Government, I (from a conviction of its absolute necessity) so inconveniently and vehemently urged the measure of a total and radical reform of the Irish Church, which that Cabinet, with a false delicacy, I think, towards Stanley, would not adopt, that it was thought adviseable to separate us, and I was again recalled, altho' I must admit in a far different (that is to say) in a very flattering and even affectionate manner. Finding that I could no longer keep Ireland quiet after the outrageous Bill brought in by Stanley (and against my advice) for the collection of tithes, without an extension of Power, I was most reluctantly compelled to call for the Coercion Act, fully determined however to use it most sparingly, if at all. It was granted, and it acted like a charm, and I never put it in force. Now that measure wd have been quite unnecessary, if instead of passing Stanley's Tithe Bill, they had manfully adopted mine. [There follows an exposition of his tithe and Church reform plan.] I wanted to take all these good things *in trust* for the Protestant Church, to be used, in the mean time, for the benefit of the state generally. There was the rub. It was there that the shoe pinched, and my friends had not the courage to act upon the suggestion put forth and almost prepared in the shape of a Bill. Well, I frightened them, and I was recalled.'[60]

PART III

--- * ---

CHAPTER THIRTEEN

Alas! Alas! It is a heartrending reflection to make, that my later days are most severely and grievously embittered by my two eldest sons.
Anglesey to Lord William Paget[1]

ANGLESEY'S future employment was one of the subjects discussed at a Cabinet meeting on September 2nd. With his state of health in view, some sort of special mission or governor-generalship in the Mediterranean area was proposed. 'The leaning of Palmerston's mind', wrote Holland from the Cabinet room, 'is perhaps more to a permanent Embassy than would be convenient to you.' This was certainly true, for Anglesey was in no mood for further official commitments. Thirteen years were to elapse before, at the age of seventy-eight, he again accepted any sort of office under Government. At this moment his mind was set upon a well-earned holiday, not only because he was physically and mentally tired, but also for reasons of money. When he had first gone to Ireland a friend had assured him that in point of finance the Lord Lieutenancy would prove an excellent thing for him. 'The late Duke of Portland,' he was told, 'who was no bad judge of expense, magnificence, &c,' believed that 'a man might very well lay by the *whole* of his private fortune ... but even this must require time, for the outfit will be very expensive.' Anglesey's first term of office had not fulfilled this last condition, for it had endured but twelve months, while his second administration had started, as we have seen, with a considerable cut in the Lord Lieutenant's salary; his experience, therefore, was not that of the Duke of Portland. Nor was his pecuniary position improved by the excesses of his elder sons, which at this date were already reaching alarming proportions. An extended sojourn abroad would provide the opportunity to close down his expensive establishments at Beaudesert and Plas Newydd, and this he was able to effect; but the other major economy which he had

279

in mind, namely the sale of Uxbridge House, fell through for lack of a realistic offer.[2]

As soon as he had put these and other matters in train, he set out to accomplish his immediate object, which was to reach the health-giving sun of Italy as speedily as possible. At times on the journey through Europe he was very ill indeed, but his doctor, Sir James Murray, who accompanied the party, reported to John Sanderson that his patient's health improved the farther south they went. In Paris they stayed three days, and he was well enough to indulge in some strenuous sightseeing; besides tours of the picture-galleries, palaces and monuments, he went out to Fontainebleau to inspect the table at which Napoleon had signed his abdication. From Paris by 'a bad road in bad weather' they made their way to Lyons, and then across the Alps to rest two days in Turin.

'From that', wrote Murray, 'we passed Alessandria & came to a glorious place, Genoa. Here we rested two days admiring the golden palaces & ancient splendour of the native town of Colombus & of its deliverer Doria — Groves of oranges, lemons, and every hot house tree & shrub & fruit and flower luxuriating the sides of the sunny hills of Genoa. At industrious Lucca we stayed a day, & three at fair & rich Florence. . . . Nothing can exceed the enthusiasm with which you view the Venus de Medici, the works of Praxitiles & of Canova in the glorious & renowned galleries of Florence.'

It took them exactly a month from their arrival in Calais to reach Rome. The doctor's enthusiasm ran riot.

'It would be vain', he declared to Sanderson, who was at Plas Newydd, enveloped in the wintry mists of North Wales, 'to attempt describing to you the feelings which swell the heart on viewing the Tiber & its bridges, the seven eternal hills. . . . Your Soul expands with delight as you march through the Capitol & hold high converse with the 12 Caesars & their successors. . . . Modern Rome is transcendent, St Peter's would detain you a willing investigator for a year; the Vatican, the Campidolum, the hundred princely & ducal Palaces with their heavenly collections of inestimable statuary & old paintings, the three hundred adorned Churches & the gay & varied admirers & adorers from every clime & country, but most from our own, render Rome one of the finest things on the face of the world. . . . The climate, transparent air, blue & cloudless sky, &

the warm, genial & silent air ... all add interest & benefit to a City which you cannot but love. Lord Anglesey is out every night with some Duke or Ambassador or Prince; he is quite well & happy & had not one pain since he arrived at celestial Rome.'

Anglesey had had his horses sent out from England, and the whole party took daily rides to view 'the splendid historic & classic spots in & around the Eternal City. The Ladies, as well as Lords George and Alfred,' wrote Murray, 'enjoy it much & are all very well: nothing could suit Lord Anglesey better.' By the middle of February, nevertheless, he was thinking of home. To his brothers he confessed that he would be most happy 'if the wished moment should arrive when I could safely and prudently return ... altho' this is more than a bearable way of passing the time, for it is even a pleasant one, yet there can be nothing like Home, and altho' the Mediterranean may be very good cruizing ground and Naples and Castelamare a very good station, yet Cowes and our own Channel are good enough for me.'[3]

*   *   *

On March 3rd, at the invitation of the Pope, Anglesey went to the Vatican for a private audience. The only other person present was the Hanoverian chargé d'affaires, who made a record of what passed.[4] He set the tone of the discourse by introducing the visitor as one 'who enjoyed the unlimited confidence of the King'. Anglesey then said that he 'most willingly acceded to the Pope's wish for the audience', and assured him of the esteem in which he was held by the King and his Ministers, and their interest in the good of his reign. 'The Marquis then cordially told the Pope that he proposed to work on his opinions.' This he proceeded to do, without too much reserve, fully aware that Gregory XVI was one of the most illiberal of Popes, wholly out of sympathy with the smallest measure of political freedom, whose very election had caused a revolution in the Papal States, and whose rule continued to depend upon Austrian armed force.

'I fear,' he told the Pope, 'that in view of the friendly terms now existing between England and France, Your Holiness does not think too favourably of the King's Government, imagining that the King and his Ministers are supporting democratic ideas at the expense of the aristocracy, having regard to the fact that France upholds and spreads a so-called liberalism which, one must admit, often leads to revolution. But I flatter myself that Your Holiness will deign to give up this point of view after hearing my explanation upon the *apparent* agreement of French and English policy.'

At this point the Pope, according to the Hanoverian chargé d'affaires, evinced 'a curiosity as eager as it was sceptical'.

'If,' continued Anglesey, 'Your Holiness considers the fact that the King's Cabinet consists, for the most part, of individuals brought up on aristocratic lines, you will hardly believe that this Cabinet — not to mention the august person of the Sovereign himself — has any intention of demeaning the aristocracy; Your Holiness, too, would hardly attribute such an intention to myself. But the British people too have their rights, and know it. One must admit that the aristocracy has abused its power. One has to make sacrifices sometimes to maintain one's position. The King knows of the rights of his people, and does not wish to put a brake on their liberty: his people know how to guard their liberties. The King's Government, keeping a watchful eye on the march of progress, sees what is right and necessary for the people, it is aware of their wishes and tries, if these are legitimate, to forestall them by making concessions before these are demanded — though naturally they take every care to avoid the appearance of having been forced to grant them through fear.'

Here the Pope interrupted to say that his own experience showed that concessions were immediately followed by further demands, to which Anglesey replied that the English people were shrewd enough to know where their interests lay, and that experience had taught them to use their liberty wisely. 'Because of this,' he went on, 'and he is proud of it, the King is very dependent on his people.' As to Anglo-French relations, Anglesey explained that it was

'entirely so as to watch over, to moderate and to restrain the spread of principles and maxims dangerous to all Kings, that the Government of England took on the task of influencing French policy. Here lie the source and the motives of the friendship concluded between England and France: *it is not a question of liberalism, but of the need to restrain their excess of progress*. Thus the Government of England is working also for the good of the Holy See itself. The

King admires and respects legitimacy quite as much as Your Holiness can admire it; he sincerely wishes to see, I am inwardly persuaded, the Holy See preserved; I hope that His Majesty will prove this by accrediting a permanent British representative to this Court.'

The Pope expressed himself pleased with the British Government's attitude towards the Catholics, and spoke of his high regard for the King, but declared that he saw no evidence that his Ministers were favourably disposed towards the Holy See, and that they had complained of his not keeping his promises regarding reforms. This accusation he attempted at length to refute. He went on to deprecate the British habit of protecting 'propagandists and revolutionary societies from France and Italy', and grumbled about British ships giving asylum to political criminals. To this Anglesey replied that every good contained its own evil: British liberty sometimes sheltered criminals, for in England all individuals of any nation were guaranteed inviolability. He carefully avoided getting drawn into a controversy about the promised reforms in the Papal States, and contented himself with reiterating his belief that the Pope had no enemies in the Cabinet.

He then touched upon a delicate matter.

'In the talk that followed', wrote the chargé d'affaires, 'Lord Anglesey was unable to hide a certain patriotic jealousy of the help given to the Holy See by Austria, and smilingly asked the Pope whether one day that country would quit his states altogether. The Pope assured him that, having no other power over his people than moral force, he had till that time been unable to do without Austrian soldiers. But, he added very seriously, "I have never ceased to have the firmest confidence in the good faith of the Emperor, and I am quite sure that at my first request he would withdraw his troops, and would not keep one *palme* of my land...."

'The audience finished as it had begun, by protestations of mutual personal esteem. His Holiness assured the Marquis, in particular, that all reports from Ireland had sung his praises, and the Holy Father jokingly begged him, on his return to England, to champion the *povere Papa*.'

*   *   *

In mid-April Anglesey moved his family and entourage from Rome to Naples, there to await the arrival of his yacht from England. The beauty of the place quite exceeded his expectations.

'I am enchanted', he told Arthur Paget. 'Probably *the Element* [the water] has *not* a little to do with it, but I admire Vesuvius, which smokes and spits a little to please us, and altogether the *locale* is certainly charming. I am now looking out in earnest for the *Pearl*.... At present I am not in force. The fact is *Italian weather is a humbug* and March is (barring Fogs) as bad at Rome as in London. I fancy this place more. The Scene at least is superb, and if it be too cold to go out, one may at least sit and enjoy it behind the windows *à l'abri du vent*, and with the benefit of Sun, whereas at Home every house is constructed and placed so as to have as little as possible of that very agreeable companion.'

By the end of the month he still delighted in Naples. He told Cloncurry that he enjoyed it as much as his health permitted him to enjoy anything. 'The *Pearl*', he wrote, 'is arrived, which is a great resource. Vesuvius seems to be tired; he is going out fast.... What a gay, lively people, and what a busy town. At Rome, every other man was a priest: here the priest is superceded by the soldier — a favourable change in my eye, particularly as the troops are very fine.'

When the sailing season was past, he sent *Pearl* back to England, and returned to Rome for the winter. In late November, he was 'suffering as usual', but hoped, he told Arthur, 'to find this place agree with me better than Naples. The journey has been against me, as there has been much rain and damp, but the temperature is high & I have not yet thought of a fire.... By the by,' he added, 'what good cooks the Neapolitans are. I have a very good one, but alas! "tis all lost upon Maud!" The utmost extent of my eating is a little macaroni, spinage & *compote de pommes*, with which, however, I quite keep up my condition, altho' I sleep little & wake constantly & in pain. A pleasant life truly!... It so happens that I have an Italian who is perhaps the *best* Valet de Chambre that ever was. But he has not one word of English.'[5]

While he was writing this letter he heard of the fall of the Whigs, and the temporary assumption of the government by the Duke of Wellington. 'What a frightful event!' he wrote. 'I tremble! What infatuation! Personally I am indifferent, but I really tremble for my country! I may be mistaken, tho' I cannot but fear that the exasperation of the People will be so great at the return of Ultratoryism, that the Commons House upon a dissolution, which must be had, will be a mass of Radicalism, & then God knows what may happen.... God grant, however, that I may be a false prophet & that all may go well. Sir R. Peel was here, I understand, but an express took him off yesterday.'[6a]

*   *   *

While he was in Naples there had opened a new chapter in the history of Anglesey's unceasing search for an effective alleviation of his painful malady. None of the numerous conventional remedies to which he had been subjected ever since the symptoms had first shown themselves seventeen years before had had the slightest effect. Nor is this to be wondered at, for even today, in the 1960s, no cure has been found for the tic douloureux. As early as 1830, when Anglesey believed himself to be on the point of death, the new German curative method known as homoeopathy had been brought to his notice. In April of that year his first wife's brother-in-law, the diplomatist Lord Ponsonby, had written to advise Anglesey to give the system a trial, adding that it was being cultivated with extraordinary success in France and Italy, and that he himself was being treated under a doctor who had studied under its founder, the aged Dr Samuel Hahnemann. This remarkable man of medicine, whom Sir Francis Burdett described to Anglesey a year or two later as 'more like a God upon earth than a human being', had an increasing number of disciples among unorthodox medical men in the cities of Europe. One of these was the Neapolitan, Dr Giuseppe Mauro, whom Anglesey consulted in May 1834.[b] Mauro's first action was to write to his revered master at Köthen, near Leipzig, asking for advice. In doing so he described his distinguished patient and his symptoms. He told Hahnemann that he found Anglesey a strong, energetic man with a gentle and charming character, even-tempered and sedate, not easily irritated, patient and persevering, 'but he appears to despair of ever being cured.' Only the right side of his face was affected, the pain extending from the corner of the mouth and the chin, up to the eye socket and as far back as behind the ear. During an attack the outer skin would become so sensitive that on being touched it felt as if something red-hot were singeing it, and the acts of speaking and swallowing became difficult in the extreme. North and east winds and sudden changes in the weather generally provoked severe bouts of pain. These were always accompanied by an irregularity of the pulse and acute constipation. During a bad attack Anglesey would writhe in silent agony, burying his head in his hands, the torment coming in spasms every three or four minutes, over a longer or shorter period. Hahnemann's reply to Mauro was to send off some medicines (which took three months to reach Naples) and to write personally to Anglesey stressing the need for continual outdoor exercise above all else.

In September, Sir James Murray was replaced as Anglesey's personal physician by Dr Dunsford, an English disciple of Hahnemann's. He at once took over the correspondence with Hahnemann, but soon came to the conclusion that as soon as it was possible to cross the Alps, Anglesey and his party should take up residence for a period in Köthen. Consequently, at the end of April 1835, Anglesey, accompanied only by his son Clarence, Dr Dunsford and two servants, arrived within hailing distance of the great Hahnemann himself. The reason for taking Clarence, who was now a young man of twenty-three, was that he too was in need of medical assistance. His complaints were venereal, and Hahnemann refused to prescribe for him without a personal examination. What success Hahnemann had in Clarence's case is not known, but after a month's treatment at Köthen, Anglesey seemed to be well on the way to a cure. This happy but impermanent state of affairs was brought about by a very careful application of the homoeopathic system. At that date the doctrine that 'likes should be treated by likes', which is its essence, was completely revolutionary. The fact that homoeopathy utterly rejected the weapons commonly used against disease, such as bleeding, mercurialism and purgatives, ensured that 'every Apothecary', as Lord Ponsonby put it, 'must be its determined foe.' But Hahnemann had had extraordinary successes in curing diseases which had quite baffled the conventional remedies, and in Anglesey's case, by experimenting with selected medicines and meticulously noting their effects, he managed to reduce the frequency and violence of the attacks very considerably over a period of several months. This partial success may well have been due less to the drugs than to the cessation of the debilitating remedies hitherto employed. For instance, Hahnemann told Dunsford that it was 'never necessary or useful to lessen the amount of blood because it always means a lessening of energy and those forces whose reactions are all the more beneficial the more they are kept intact.' This *diktat*, and others like it, though universally accepted today, sounded like treason in the ears of the orthodox practitioners of the 1830s, but their application was clearly the chief basis of Hahnemann's success. Anglesey was so impressed by what seemed a miraculous cure, that he gave Dunsford permission to publish an account of it. In this were detailed the various medicines tried and their effects; Anglesey was pictured as having 'recovered the stoutness, the vigour and the activity of a young man. For several months he has not felt the coming on of the tic, and he has such confidence in homoeopathy that no relapse can lessen it.' Though this last statement was an exaggeration, Anglesey was certainly grateful to Hahnemann for giving him the longest periods of freedom from pain he had ever had. It was said that he looked ten years younger and wherever he went praised the miracles which homoeopathy had wrought in him. By June 1835, when he had returned to England and re-established himself at Beaudesert, he felt that his sojourn abroad had well served its purpose: what he called the 'wretched nerves' of his face were at last quiescent, and he knew once again the blessing of uninterrupted sleep.[7]

*   *   *

Later in the year, the idea of some sort of public employment was again in the air. Lady Cowper, for instance, told Princess Lieven on September 25th that Anglesey was very much annoyed at not obtaining the Admiralty in place of Lord Auckland, who had gone to govern India. If there was any truth in this, Lord Melbourne's letter of the following day, offering Anglesey the Government of Gibraltar, may have been a sop. 'It is', he wrote, 'one of the best military situations which the Crown has to bestow — the salary has been settled ... at five thousand pounds yearly, it being understood that the Governor is not hereafter to be absent from his post. It has struck me that altho' very improbable it is not quite impossible that you might be willing to accept of this appointment.' The reply was not bereft of asperity:

'*Beaudesert, Sept.* 27, 1835

'Dear Melbourne,
    'I have received your letter of yesterday.
    'I am not prepared to spend the remainder of my life at Gibraltar, & moreover (if even residence were not the condition), having no taste for a sinecure, I have only to thank you for the offer & to decline it.
    'I remain, dear Melbourne, faithfully yours,
                                'ANGLESEY'[8]

*   *   *

Soon after his return from abroad, Clarence Paget had become seriously ill with a supposed abscess on the lungs. After months of suffering, his life was almost despaired of when as a last resort it was suggested that the patient should be taken to consult Hahnemann once again. It was no longer necessary to go further than Paris, for by this time the great man had been driven from his native Germany by the antipathy of his orthodox brethren. The main difficulty was how to make the expedition from England without killing the patient before he completed it. The problem was overcome in an interesting manner.

'Fortunately,' wrote Clarence in after years, 'the King ... remembered there was a luxurious old bed travelling-carriage in the royal coach-houses, which had carried his brother, George IV., and he kindly placed it at the disposal of my father. Into it I was put, more dead than alive, and we got across to Calais, and from thence by easy stages to Paris.... Dr Hahnemann was immediately summoned — a little wizened old man of seventy [he was, in fact, over eighty], not more than five feet high, with a splendid head, and bent double — with him his wife, a remarkably intelligent French woman, who was very plain, and much younger than the doctor. He gave one the idea of a necromancer.[c] He wrote down every symptom, examined me all over, asked ever so many questions which I had scarcely strength to answer, and took up his gold-headed cane to depart. My father hung upon every word, but could get nothing from him. He came next, and next day, and after about the fourth visit he suddenly exclaimed in French, "The doctors have mistaken the case; it is not an abscess on the lungs, but an abscess on the liver, and I will cure him in three weeks." '[9]

From Paris Anglesey wrote almost daily to Char, who, being ill herself, had remained in London.[d] His account differs slightly from his son's, but it confirms the view that Hahnemann saved Clarence's life.

Clarence, his younger brother George (now aged seventeen and a cornet in the 1st Life Guards), Dr Dunsford and Anglesey arrived at the Hôtel de Westminster in the Rue de la Paix on January 12th; Hahnemann visited them the following evening. 'He spent more than an hour here', Anglesey wrote after he had gone. ' ... He examined & questioned [Clarence] & us with great & intense interest and minuteness, having carefully looked at the expectorations & [of] these he distinctly & very authoritatively said "Ce ne sont pas les poumons, qui sont éffectés — Cela à

The Duke of Wellington aged 72 (see p. 300)

The Marquess of Anglesey, aged 74, *and* 'On the terrace at Beaudesert' aged 83

rapport au foie!' — I never was more rejoiced than when I heard this fiat, for I believe the Liver is a much more controllable organ than the Lungs. ... The Old Boy came himself, which is an immense favor, & he will come again.... *I* have not yet entered for any thing into his thoughts — He reserves me for the day after to-morrow when I go to him. He merely complimented me upon my looks, & appeared quite astonished & pleased at my pedestrian atcheivements [*sic*].'

In the midst of his anxiety for Clarence, Anglesey found himself plunged into the Paris Season, and the object of much attention. He informed Char that he had

'seen Ld Granville & Ld Hatherton & Edward Ellice & Greville & *Old Sugarloaf* & I know not who besides, & all the Ladies have announced their intended visits to me.ᵉ I saw too Ly Cadogan [the wife of Lady Anglesey's first cousin] & Ly Kenmare. In short London is in Paris.... Greville has been very active in getting us apartments. They are not brilliant, but they are clean. I wish you could come here per *Balloon*. Of course this will be practicable in a few years — Yet hardly in our time.... Is there nobody here to write you all the gossip of Paris? You know how unequal I am to it. Ly Cadogan did not cease for half an hour to tell me of *their* miseries about a projected marriage. I tried to guess who the Parties were, & beat about the bush, but to no purpose. At length it came out that Ld Chelsea & Miss Wellesley were the Persons, & I was compelled to acknowledge that I had never heard one syllable of the matter, nor of the young Lady's former attachment to Lord Graves which she detailed to me.ᶠ All of which ignorance, or (as she probably thought) stupidity, seemed to fill her with amazement.'

A postscript written next morning told Char that the mere sight of Hahnemann had had a magical effect on Clarence, who was at that very moment eating a hearty breakfast. His pulse rate had been reduced from 120 to 90. The result of Anglesey's own visit to Hahnemann next day was that the great man had said of him '*que j'avance à la guerison....*'

Anglesey's social activities included dinner at the Tuileries with King Louis-Philippe and his family. 'They were most gracious', he told Char, '& said very flattering things & talked much of Emily [Anglesey's first child by Char, born in March 1810, who had married Lord Sydney in 1832]. She had here *le plus grand succès*. If I am in tolerable trim to-night

& Clarence goes to bed comfortably, I may perhaps go to a Ball at the D. de Broglie's for 5 minutes, just to make my bow, & also to a dress Ball at the Queen's to-morrow. I dine with Talleyrand on Monday. I walked between 7 & 8 miles yesterday. Hahnemann is astonished. – The King took me thro' all his alterations at the Tuilleries & insists on shewing me all he is doing at Versailles. There is plenty to occupy me, but I pant for home, yet I will not leave Clarence.... Tuyll is here & at my devotion. He is a great resource. He walks with me.'

On January 25th Anglesey announced that Clarence was gaining ground, and that he was getting into spirits about him. So converted was he to homoeopathy, that he was recommending Hahnemann to all his invalid friends in Paris. 'Ly Belfast is seriously taking to homoeopathy.... Mrs Ver-Ver-Verschoele is also taking to it by my persuasion. Dr Bankhead who was at Rome & who says he has watched me for many many years, expresses his astonishment at me. He says I am 20 years younger. However, *this* I know – I am truly grateful ... for extraordinary relief.'

As Clarence recovered, so did his father's spirits. As for George, he was having a wonderful time. One night he danced till five in the morning, 'after having been to the opera with me', wrote Anglesey, 'till past 12.... I got there about the middle of the first Act of Norma – It was exceedingly well given. Grisi & Lablache were excellent, but the Prova! Oh the Prova! I never laughed so much at any thing in my life. Liston has not greater powers of *Comicality* & then in addition to this, the musick is delightful. I shd like to hear it every night for a year. Give me the Buffo Operas – they beat the Serious out & out. These are heavy and uninteresting. The other is piquant & enlivening. The House was in a Roar. I certainly think Lablache the very best actor as well as singer that I ever heard.'[8] There follows a description of a second dinner at the Tuileries, which gives an amusing idea of life at the Court of *le Roi citoyen*:

> 'I am bound to say that Their Majesties & their family are most agreeable Personages. Of course I was punctual to a minute, but the Queen & Princesses were already there. The King soon appeared, but we had to wait a little for our Ambassador & Lady, & the D. & Duchess of Sutherland.... There might be about 36 at table. I was desired to take in the Princess Clementine. She is a very pretty & agreeable Person; perfectly conversable & at her ease with very good manners & the most goodnatured countenance. In general at a *great*

dinner, I can never get anything that I can eat, but here if I had ordered it, I cd not have had it more to my taste. Every thing was wholesome & *homeopathic* but good, & this is high proof of a good cuisine. It is curious to see Kings & Queens carving large Dishes & helping all around them. Her Majesty had *en partage*, the most enormous Turbot I ever saw & then a not less monstrous Turkey & the King laboured away with appropriate skill & success at a prodigious Boar's Head, which from a large infusion of Truffles & other excellent things I was obliged to decline, altho' it was much & graciously recommended. The dinner was by no means formal & really agreable. The Dining Hall is of vast dimension, in length at least & height, & dinner over, in spite of its slippery Floor I reconducted my little Princess & landed her safely upon the warm & comfortable carpets of the Drawing Rooms. Their Majesties then conversed with me a long while.... George got on very well between two French Ladies of the Court for a short time, but soon she whom he brought in to dinner (a very handsome woman of a certain age — the widow of one of the Marshals & *Dame de Service* to the Queen), was taken with so violent a migraine that she was obliged to bolt, & the Lady on the side of George going out to assist her, he was left next to me, but completely isolated, his two flanks having been thus left open by the retreat of his fair neighbours & thus for the remainder of the dinner he was spared the exertions of his French.'

'Did I tell you', he asked a few days later, 'that the day I dined at the Tuilleries, the King got hold of an Irish Green Tabinet, embroidered with Shamrocks & this, he said, he had had made in a great hurry to receive the Viceroy!!! They are a very amiable family.... There are lots of young Princes, one in the Navy just going to sea, others in the uniform of private soldiers with worsted Cord or Lace &c.'

The early days of February found Clarence rapidly gaining strength. 'You know', wrote Anglesey, 'all our Doctors thought that a Southern Climate was indispensible & that until he could reach one, he must be shut up in rooms of high temperature. He was moreover kept low, & wine would have been considered poison. Old Hahnemann on the contrary by no means wants a warm atmosphere. He recommends exercise in all weathers, gives as much nourishment as Clarence can take & gives him wine & water. George is rather a wreck. He is seldom in bed before

4 or 5, & looks as yellow as a guinea. I think he will not be the worse for a little Barrack Discipline.'

The rage at this time in Paris was to attend the trial of Fieschi, a Corsican adventurer who in the previous July had shot at the King with an infernal machine, killing Marshal Mortier and many others.[h] Anglesey got tickets for Clarence, George and himself. 'One day', he wrote, 'is quite enough, just to see the style of proceedings & the Ruffians.' Fieschi was executed a few days later.

Though Char was told that her husband's existence was one of 'mere vegetation', Anglesey did not waste his time in Paris. He visited the Panthéon, 'a very grand building begun by Louis 13th. It is inscribed "Aux Grands Hommes, La Patrie reconnaissante" & in the vaults are placed the tombs of some good warriors & some precious *Gueaux* [vagabonds]! We then visited Notre Dame, which after Rome, ne valait pas la peine — Chemin faisant, we looked into the *Morgue* where we saw *only one* body (for a wonder) exposed for recognition. The man was said to have hanged himself.'

Anglesey's last letter from Paris, dated March 7th, announced that Clarence was making wonderful progress, that Hahnemann had forbidden him the playing of cards 'on account of excitement', but that he thought well of the case, and that Anglesey himself was coming home being 'sick to death of this place'.[10] [i]

After the season at Cowes, Anglesey returned to Paris, there to meet Char, who had spent the late summer taking the baths at Marienbad. They stayed in Paris well into the winter, once more partaking of the benefits of homoeopathy under Hahnemann. While there, Anglesey resumed relations with Louis-Philippe, who had just survived a further attempt upon his life. The King, in renewing the previous year's offer to show his distinguished guest the museum at Versailles, said, 'You need not be afraid, my Lord, my carriage is bullet-proof.'[11]

*   *   *

Anglesey and Char were back at Beaudesert in time for Christmas 1836. But before the year was out, Anglesey was again plagued with the affairs of his second son, William. To understand the sequence of events, it is necessary to go back five years, to the early months of 1831, when Anglesey's struggle with O'Connell was at its height. In January of that year, William had returned to England in his ship the *North Star*, which it will be remembered had taken him to the West Indies in December 1829. At Portsmouth, by his own desire, he was tried by court martial. The charge against him, which concerned the suicide of a ship's boy, was not proved, and William was honourably acquitted.[j] But as he stepped ashore from the flagship after the trial, he was at once arrested for debts incurred before his departure fourteen months earlier. Anglesey in Dublin, apprised of both events, burdened by business of 'weighty and pressing importance ... upon which probably the fate of Empire depends', ordered Sanderson and Uxbridge to deal with the matter as best they could. 'Can it be', he asked Sanderson, 'that this arrest is a measure concocted by that Old Rogue the father in Law [General de Rottenburgh] ... & also perhaps by Willm? Alas! Alas! You know too well what grounds I have for suspicion. Nevertheless I will not act upon it.... As for the money, it is cruel, really cruel that I shd be so harassed, but what can I do? Is he to remain in jail? — Every personal & public consideration is to be taken into account. We hang by a thread — If it breaks, this country [Ireland], perhaps England is gone. It is frightful to think how much now hinges upon *my* Character, & unfortunately, *mine* is in some respects implicated in those of my family.... Here, too [in Dublin] I shall be ruined in finance, but if I relax, the whole machine will go to pieces.'

To William he wrote a letter which studiously avoided any reference to his arrest.

'My dearest William,
'I write to express my most cordial satisfaction at your most honourable acquittal & my entire approbation of the manly course you pursued in demanding a Court Martial, after having been subjected to two Courts of Enquiry, both most honourable to you. [See note j, p. 384.] Still the present Board of Admiralty cd only act as they did. Had I been 1st Lord, I should have done the same.

'I rejoice then sincerely in the whole proceeding & I never had a doubt of the result myself because I know that your system of discipline is *human* at the same time that it is firm.

'I seize with avidity this opportunity of entirely forgiving you. I will utterly banish from my thoughts all occurrences with respect to your conduct upon those matters, upon which I have had such reason to be most seriously offended & severely angry. I say I entirely forgive & I will endeavour totally to forget all, but the return I ask for this, is that you shall pursue your future course thro' life with principles of the firmest integrity, honor & strict prudence. I have explained to you often my total inability to incur further expences on your account. What I have already done for you has greatly distressed me & I owe to my other children rigidly to act upon the principle I have laid down in regard to you.

'God bless you.

'Most affecy. yours,

'ANGLESEY'

Uxbridge, by paying £500 to satisfy immediate creditors, managed to secure his brother's release, and by the end of February William had put to sea again, out of harm's way.

In 1833, on quitting his command, he went to reside abroad, first in France, then in Brussels, all the while continuing to live well above his means. For a time he served as a volunteer in the unofficial British Auxiliary Legion in Spain which had been raised to fight for the Queen Regent against Don Carlos; from that employment he returned to England in November 1836. Immediately upon arrival, he again allowed himself to be arrested and sent to the Marshalsea debtors' prison with the object (as before) of declaring himself an insolvent debtor. His father was adamant that this should be prevented. 'To take the benefit of the Insolvent Act', wrote Anglesey from Paris, in January 1837, 'is so atrociously horrible — so cruelly unjust towards his dupes, that I am horrified at the idea.' He had no choice therefore but to pay what was necessary for his son's release from prison. This he did under conditions rather more stringent than those which had been imposed in 1830. Eventually William took his family to settle in Pau in the south of France, while Thomas Beer, who had succeeded Sanderson as Anglesey's chief agent in 1835, assisted by Lord Templemore (Anglesey's son-in-law, in whose business acumen he placed great trust) was left to deal as best he could with a host of creditors.[12]

Each fresh crisis in William's affairs (and as will be seen this was not the last or most anxious of them) heralded for his long-suffering father violent recurrences of the tic. Now, in January 1837, he was attacked so badly that for long periods he was completely incapacitated. With this unhappy relapse any hope of a cure by homoeopathy or by any other means seemed to have vanished for ever; and so it had, though the search for more effective means of mitigating the pain continued unabated. In the early 'forties Anglesey tried the fashionable Water Cure which had just been introduced from Germany. For parts of every year until his death, he would go off to the newly opened establishment at Malvern, and there submit himself to what, in those early days of hydropathy, was a very rigorous regimen. 'This treatment', he wrote to a fellow sufferer in 1846, 'is of very great service to me, and has the effect of keeping the bowels in perfect order without any aid whatever.' In answer to another cry for help two years later, he said that hydropathy, together with 'a regular plain diet and much air and exercise', kept him in excellent general health. Comparing the relative merits of homoeopathy and hydropathy, he on the whole gave a preference to hydropathy; but he was fully convinced that nothing would ever effect a cure, 'at least in a long rooted chronic complaint as mine is'. That this was unhappily true is attested by the fact that for the rest of his life he remained what he had been ever since 1815 — a national invalid, whose recurring indispositions were regularly reported in the newspapers. From these reports it is clear that he was never long without fearful visitations, some so excruciating that for days on end he was forced to shut himself away to wrestle in speechless torment with his unconquerable foe.[13]

ii

We are now at the dawn of the reign of a Princess interesting from her exalted virtues, her great acquirements and accomplishments, her peculiarly gracious and fascinating manners, — particularly interesting from her extreme youth.... I cannot conceive any combination of circumstances more calculated to revive in the nation a spirit of chivalry that has been so long dormant, to draw forth a fervent attachment to the Throne, an ardent devotion to the Sovereign who fills it, which certainly have not been the characteristics of the times in which we have lived.

Anglesey's speech at the Waterloo dinner of 1838[14]

King William IV died, in his seventy-second year, on June 20th, 1837. Anglesey was not present at the young Queen Victoria's celebrated Privy Council meeting early that day; but on the next, he was sworn in at the meeting which followed the Proclamation ceremony. Had he looked from the windows of St James's Palace into the quadrangle that morning, he would have seen in the front line of privileged spectators the burly figure of his old antagonist, Daniel O'Connell, who attracted much attention to himself by constantly waving his hat, and cheering most vociferously.[15]

At the Coronation next year, Anglesey was one of the four Knights of the Garter who held the golden canopy over the Queen at her Anointing. His daughter Adelaide and his granddaughter, Caroline Lennox, were two of the Queen's train-bearers.

*   *   *

Lady Cowper, who was one of many who stayed year after year at Beaudesert for the winter house parties, found the place 'delightful and magnificent.... We have been driving in an open carriage round the Park and Chace [Cannock Chase],' she told her son in November 1838, 'Lord Anglesey showing off all its beauties (and himself) on a Prancing Horse à la Portière — and to be sure he is a wonderful man of his age or any age even putting aside the consideration of all he has gone through — such a figure and such a graceful seat.' Three years later she was astonished at his shooting prowess. He 'rides a pony', she wrote, 'and kills everything that gets up within reach of his gun, either before or behind him'. There is at Plas Newydd a charming painting of him shooting at a blackcock from his pony, with his dog 'Nep' masking the bird. This was painted for Lord Deerhurst (later eighth Earl of Coventry) by Richard Barrett Davis in 1830. In recommending Davis to Anglesey, Deerhurst wrote, 'If his stay for a day or two in the house should be necessary, the steward's room, I understand ... is his abode!'[16]

Miss Horsey de Horsey, who became the second Lady Cardigan, remembered with delight the Christmas parties in the 1840s. 'Louis Napoleon [while in exile] was a frequent visitor', she wrote. 'He used to ask me to sing Schubert's "Adieu" to him every evening; perhaps it recalled some memory of happier days.... When he was asked one evening how he liked the house, he replied "J'aime beaucoup Beaudesert, mais — (turning to Lady Desart [a fellow guest]) — encore plus la belle Desart".[k] Our amusements were very simple ones. After lunch we walked over Cannock Chase, and those ladies who did not care for walking, rode sturdy little ponies. We returned to tea, and after dinner there was music, cards or dancing. We thoroughly enjoyed ourselves and nobody was bored.' Greville, on the other hand, when he stayed at Beaudesert early in 1838, found it 'a dreadfully idle life ..., *facendo niente*, incessant gossip and dawdle, poor, unprofitable talk, and no rational employment'. He mentions that Lord Brougham, whose bitterness at being excluded from the Government was at this time mounting to a frenzy, had stayed there for a week. 'He, Lord Wellesley and Lord Anglesey form a discontented triumvirate, and are knit together by the common bond of a sense of ill-usage and of merit neglected. Wellesley and Anglesey are not Radicals, however, and blame Brougham's new tendency that way. Anglesey and Wellesley both hate and affect to despise the Duke of Wellington, in which Brougham does not join. They are all suffering under mortified vanity and thwarted ambition, and after playing their several parts, not without success and applause, they have not the judgement to see and feel that they forfeit irretrievably the lustre of their former fame by such a poor and discreditable termination of their career.'[17]

This is an interesting sketch of three old men out of office (Brougham was sixty, Anglesey sixty-nine and Wellesley seventy-eight), but not quite an accurate one, at least so far as Anglesey was concerned; only four days after Greville's entry in his Journal, Anglesey wrote to Brougham upon his speech in the House of Lords on the Government's handling of the insurrection in Canada. He found the speech

'irritating, teazing, sarcastic and insulting.... I grieve at this, because it tends to no good. It may help to displace the present men; and, if I thought there was a prospect of obtaining better, I should not object to this, but seeing no chance of this, knowing, indeed, that we might go farther & fare worse by falling into hands of high Conservatives, or mischievous Radicals, I deeply deplore that you must now be ranked amongst the most determined enemies of the Government. I know what wrongs, and slights and neglects you may justly complain of, but I would have *you* above all hostile feeling on that account.'

Anglesey wanted Brougham to do what personal mortification would never allow him to do, namely to try 'to guide or lead these people to a course of justice, firmness and decision. Now', he continued, 'this will not be effected by persiflage and sarcasm.... For my part I cannot, I grieve to say, sail in the same boat with you; and I feel confident that our good & able and excellent friend Lord W[ellesley] will view your course in the same way that I do. It is most distressing to me that such talent, such amazing powers as yours should not be available for the public service — that you will not suppress private feeling for public good.' He did not want the ex-Lord Chancellor to support the Government 'in their errors, but to point them out with moderation, and in such a way as to bend them to your purpose instead of irritating and thereby confirming them in their mistaken course.'[18]

All this good advice was in vain, and shortly afterwards, the new-found friendship, which had led to a frequent exchange of letters between the two men, went into a decline. In March 1839, at the height of his rage, which amounted to virtual derangement, Brougham wrote to Anglesey one of his numerous raving epistles. It starts: 'As you are one of the very few adherents of the present feeble & ridiculous Govt. & connexions of the present small & very exclusive if not very select Court, for whom I feel any respect ... ' After pages of vituperation and self-praise it goes on:

'With respect to my positively refusing to give up my own judgment & principles to humour either one class or another — either to suit a ministry or O'Connell (the general idol & master of you all, tho' you are all maltreated by him and all are ashamed of him nearly as much as you all dread him & his tail) as to suit even the views of the Liberal party when I happen to differ with them — that I assuredly will not do.'

With great restraint Anglesey replied that he had been amazed by Brougham's letter.

'I have indeed as you say mistaken you— I certainly thought that all I had from time to time said to you in the most kindly, friendly and perhaps too playful manner, in regard to your political course, would have been taken in the sense in which I intended it.... Having mistaken you upon that point, I may possibly also have mistaken you upon the general tenor of your public career — You *may* be the most prudent, the most discreet, the most popular man in the Kingdom.... You *may* perhaps be best serving your country by placing yourself in the most determined attitude of hostility to the Court and to the Ministry, recklessly following up your principles without the smallest regard to whether the universal propagation of them shall shake the monarchy or not &c &c. All this may be so, but I must be permitted to doubt it. So much for yourself — I am ready to acknowledge myself wrong.... I knock under. But why do you, in your turn, fall upon poor insignificant *me*?'

Referring to Brougham's passage about O'Connell, Anglesey asked:

'Can you really, in your sober senses, have addressed this to me? Impossible. Why, you know as well as any man that I ever set that man at defiance — that I prosecuted — convicted and should immediately have sent him to prison, had *you* not (as you boast of having done) dissolved the Parliament, by which that egregious cheat escaped the punishment he deserved....'[19] [1]

* * *

Though he did not agree with all that Melbourne's administration was doing, Anglesey remained on good terms with its members. There is a record of the Prime Minister dining at Uxbridge House in early June 1838, and no evidence that friendly intercourse was ever interrupted. When in May 1841 Wellesley wrote to announce that he had withdrawn his support from the Ministry, Anglesey replied that he regretted it for he was certain that no government could be formed from any other party which would be able to carry the country through its difficulties, and 'that no other course of policy than that contemplated by the present Ministers, can be pursued without involving this great community in deep distress.'[20]

Ten days before the Coronation, at the Waterloo anniversary dinner at Apsley House, Anglesey, in proposing the Duke of Wellington's health, took the opportunity of commending him for taking what he thought the right course with regard to the Government. He spoke of

'the noble, the generous, the disinterested, the truly patriotic conduct of the noble Duke in his Parliamentary career. At the opening of the session this country was involved in difficulty, and under very considerable embarrassment; the spirit of faction had crossed the Atlantic; the demon of discord was abroad; one of the most favored and interesting of our colonies [Canada] was in revolt. The noble Duke saw this, and seemed at once to decide that it would require all the energies of the mother country to crush the Hydra at its birth. Accordingly, whenever any measure was brought forward tending to support the dignity, to uphold the honor, and to secure the integrity of the Empire, the noble Duke invariably came forward and nobly supported those measures. But the noble Duke did not stop there: spurning the miserable practices of party spirit, he upon many occasions offered his sage and solid counsel to a Government which he had not been in the habit of supporting. Gentlemen, I declare to you that this conduct has made a deep impression on me. It appears to me that this is the true character and conduct of a *real* Patriot; such conduct is, in my estimation, beyond all praise.'

Anglesey told Lord Tavistock that when he sat down after making his speech the Duke squeezed his hand hard and long, saying, 'I cannot tell you what pleasure you have given me.'[21]

This speech marked the beginning of the warm friendship which was to grow up between the two old soldiers, and to last till the Duke's death fourteen years later.

In 1840 Anglesey asked 'a very great favour' of the Duke. He had been, he said, on the point of making the request many years earlier, 'when certain political events which have long passed and are forgotten, disabled me from naming the subject to you. I am most anxious', he wrote, 'to possess a full length portrait of you.' At Beaudesert there was 'an excellent and most prominent place for so valuable an article.... I believe you possess one of me by Lawrence: if I could have yours by the same master, I should prefer it, but I fear that is not attainable.... 'm Wellington answered at length and most civilly, considering his reputation for abruptness in the matter of giving sittings for painters: 'I am much flattered by your desire to possess a portrait of me; and you may rely upon every exertion on my part, that you should have the best that can be painted at present.... I am not aware of any one of Lawrence's now to be sold.' The Duke thought John Lucas the painter 'who has made the best portraits of me since Lawrence [who had died in 1830]. I have got Lawrence's portrait of you. It is not one of his best performances, but certainly better than could be painted by any artist at present.' To Lucas the Duke wrote at once, 'The sooner you make your design of this picture the better.... Of course I will give you any sittings that may be necessary.'[22]

iii

I have Russia under my Lee.
Anglesey to 'Char'[23]

At the end of 1838, Anglesey had become disturbed by what he considered the menace of Russia. He had corresponded a little with

Melbourne upon the subject, and rather more with Palmerston. On November 21st he wrote to the Foreign Secretary:

'May I, without indiscretion ask this simple question. Are you (having brought down upon Turkey by a very judicious Treaty, and wise junction of Stopford's fleet with that of Turkey, the vengeance of Russia) fully prepared to stand by the Sultan at all hazards? If you can answer me that satisfactorily, & by a single monosyllable, you will take a great weight off my mind and shall have my best wishes and ardent support. If you cannot, I will not, I promise you, betray your disavowal, but you must expect my decided hostility.'

To this, Palmerston replied that he did not doubt that Russia was not well pleased but that she must restrain her anger at the Turkish and Austrian treaties, and the junction of the English and Turkish fleets, 'for they furnish her with no just pretence even for remonstrance, much less for any act of vengeance.' He went on:

'What we are prepared to do, in cases that have not yet arisen, it would of course not be fitting for an individual member of the Govt. to say; but let me beg of you to keep your hostility in reserve, till you find us doing or omitting to do things, the commission or omission of which will in your opinion justify such hostility. I do not believe that Russia is at all prepared to volunteer a war with England; and I believe that England may be able to carry all her important objects, without volunteering a war with Russia.'[24]

It goes without saying that Anglesey was not entirely satisfied with this reply. He determined to go and see for himself. Some years previously the Grand Duke Michael of Russia, in the course of a visit to Britain, had stayed at Plas Newydd as Anglesey's guest. It was probably on this occasion that his host was invited to pay a return visit to Russia. In 1830 he had made inquiries of Prince Lieven, the Russian Ambassador in London, as to whether that summer would be a suitable moment to take advantage of the invitation;[25] but, though the Prince gave an affirmative reply, other things intervened to prevent the visit taking place. It was not until nine years later, in June 1839, that Anglesey set off in the *Pearl* yacht for a visit to the Emperor Nicholas I. With him he took, as well as his horse, his three youngest sons, Clarence, Alfred (a lieutenant in the 'Blues'), and George (now a full lieutenant in the Life Guards). Though Clarence and George were destined to fight the Russians in fifteen years' time, and their father to live to see the start of the Crimean War, in the glorious summer of 1839, all was *couleur de rose*. Two accounts of the visit survive, one in Anglesey's letters to Char, and the other in Clarence's journal, quoted in his autobiography.

The *Pearl*'s arrival at Cronstadt was at once telegraphed to the Emperor at Peterhof, who dispatched, as Anglesey told Char, 'a steamer, attended by a sixteen-oared Row Boat', with an admiral aboard, to bring his distinguished guest to the Imperial birthday dinner and ball that night. But Anglesey and his party had already hired a steamer of their own to take them to St Petersburg. 'So we missed our Emperor for that day,' wrote Clarence, 'but I spent my next evening with the Empress and the Emperor, Autocrat of all the Russias, *Czar* of Muscovy, and God knows what besides!' Arrived at the Hôtel de Paris (where Clarence might have fancied himself in England, except that his legs 'itched famously with bug and flea-bites innumerable') Anglesey wrote home:

'Here we are, my dearest Char, after as fine a passage as ever was made, having been actually at sea only 9 days and ten hours, and the *Pearl* has astonished them all! I have left her at Cronstadt, there not being water for her further up. Yesterday about 6 leagues from Cronstadt, a Russian Squadron of about 9 sail laying at anchor, we passed within about 6 miles of them. There were 3 Admiral's Flags. I rowed into the Harbour last night and this morning. The Emperor is at Peterhof and, between that Palace (which looks upon Cronstadt), and this latter place, the water is studded with Pennants, there being a few frigates, some Corvettes, and lots of Royal yachts.'

Anglesey noticed the magnificence of the city, thought its palaces very fine and the large numbers of droshkys incredible. The British Ambassador, Lord Clanricarde, was in the country, so that plans for the party were vague; 'but this I know', wrote Anglesey, 'that I have not the least fancy for Moscow. What I *hope* to do is to assist *a little* at the approaching Fêtes, to see the garrison of St Petersburg and go to sea when the Emperor takes out his Fleet.'

The following day was the anniversary of the battle of Pultowa. Having heard that the Emperor had sent 'an *Admiral* with his own steamer' to convey him to the great commemorative display, Anglesey, who had earlier declined to attend the ceremony ('for in truth I was fagged, and hardly equal to it') changed his mind, and 'started at ½ past 4 (the Boys did *not* keep me waiting!) in 2 carriages with each 4 horses *abreast*'. On arrival at Krasnoi Selo, they found that the Emperor had provided a horse for Anglesey and a carriage for his party to take them to the Imperial quarters near by, where he was encamped with 40,000 men.

'The Grand Duke Michael first arrived and immediately pounced upon me — talked over his visit to P[las] N[ewydd] and showed great interest about you all. I was then presented to the Duke of Leichtenberg, who is, in a few days, to marry one of the Grand Duchesses. The Emperor then arrived and never allowed me for a moment to quit his side, excepting during the Religious part of the ceremony, until the parade of the day had concluded.'

Clarence described the scene in detail:

'The infantry formed three solid masses, composed of the three divisions of guards on three sides of a square, in the centre of which, on an elevated platform, stood the priests and choristers at the altar.
  'Harsh sounds of "To arms!" announced Nicholas, and he came galloping through the camp, surrounded by a brilliant cortège of generals. As he went to the head of each division of the hollow square, he said Russian words, meaning, "Good morning, my children!" and a loud, wild and enthusiastic exclamation from the division conveyed, "Good morrow, Emperor!" How wild was that sound from twenty-nine thousand throats — all, I verily believe, adoring this remarkable, soldier-like & brave man.'[n]

Anglesey recounted for Char what followed:

'There was Grand Mass in the centre of the Army.... The day was beautifully serene, and so warm and still, that I did not suffer from being bare-headed nearly an hour. The chanting was beautiful — the voices imposing — magnificent. This being over all would have concluded but H.I.M. was pleased to give me a specimen, in small numbers, of various regiments of *Asiatic* Cavalry, and they caracoled and played about us and skirmished and fired at marks at full speed with great skill and address. It was very interesting and amusing. The Emperor enquired most kindly and particularly about you, and all my children, and seemed to know everything about everyone. He was most anxious in his enquiries about Jane ... he had heard of Car's good looks, and talked much of Emily's beauty.

... He remembered Georgiana — in short he seemed to have forgot nothing. I presented Clarence, Alfred and George to H.I.M. and he expressed great pleasure at seeing them. He reminded me that I had long promised this visit, and hoped it would be a long one. This obliged me to express my regret that I could not prolong my stay beyond the month.... In truth nothing could have been more gracious and flattering than my reception.... Tomorrow I am to dine at Peterhof. As it is a small family party, the Boys are not to go — but, of course, they will assist at the Fetes which commence after the marriage, and then the manoeuvring of the Army will take place, and He literally said that he would put them entirely at my disposal. All this is very fine and flattering, but, long before it is over I know how I shall pant for a little quiet and repose. I am at least 10, and I might say 20 or 30 years too old for it all. It is now ½ past 10 at night and I am writing without candles! But I must stop and go to bed, having been up since half past 2!'

Apartments at the Peterhof were provided for the party, into which they now moved, the Imperial family being at 'the Cottage, a very delightful little residence a mile and ½ from the Palace'. At four o'clock Anglesey dined with them 'and a more amiable and agreeable party, not the whole circle of my acquaintances could furnish.' At seven o'clock 'the Emperor mounted the Box and took the reins of a caleche. I was commanded to sit by the Empress. There were about 8 carriages ... occupied by the dignitaries of the Court and the Boys amongst them. We took a very beautiful drive thro' the extensive Park and shady woods, which are laid out with great taste. We finished the drive at a remarkably nice Palace (upon a moderate scale) of the Empress! Her M. took great pleasure in showing me every part of it. We then had tea, and finally supper, and retired before 12.' Next morning the Emperor showed off five hundred of his own remount horses, and then having

'sent as an impromptu for the 1st Cuirassiers of His Guard (who made a long march for the purpose), he took command of them (they are *His own* Regiment). I *never* saw anything more perfect.... Alfred and George were astonished, and I think a little jealous! This done, the Emperor went on to the Camp of about 4,000 cadets, whom he inspected.

'This is a mass of nobles of from 8 to 16 years old, who are destined for commissions in the various services. There is a *tenue*, an order, a method and precision in all this, that is very striking. They marched past as well as Veterans, and then having dismissed, the Emperor dismounting, called them all around him, and I never saw a more joyous or apparently affectionate group! He talked to them and seemed to give them my whole history, showing my Order of St George [Russian Order conferred on Anglesey after Waterloo, by Nicholas's brother and predecessor, Alexander I], when they pressed around me, stared, felt my leg, and gave that hollow, deep monotone sound which amounts to our "hurrah".'

After dining with the Grand Mareschal ('at ½ past 3'), Anglesey and his sons embarked with the Royal family 'in a steam boat, where there was tea, coffee, and fruits, and landed near another Palace of the Emperor, upon one of the Islands of this most singular place, where we all dispersed to our respective abodes.'

On July 12th Anglesey wrote: 'Today is — Dieu Merci! — one of repose'; but three days later he was writing: 'We are living in a perpetual state of parade … and uniform and bustle.' At the wedding of the Grand Duchess, the Empress was 'naive and delightful — ditto the Princesses'; there were Fêtes, with superb fireworks, and further inspections of regiments marked by 'a coquettish rivalry between Their Majesties about their respective Corps'. After the exhausting day of the wedding, they 'went to the Bal Paré. The Winter Palace is magnificent. The ladies were all in Russian costume. The men superbly dressed, and of all nations — Chinese amongst others. The dance is entirely confined to the Polonaise, which, as you know, consists in walking with a lady on your hand round the room to musick. This was an immense one, perhaps 150 feet long. In spite of all remonstrance' Anglesey was 'compelled to fall into the column' having been singled out 'by the handsomest woman here'. The Empress sent for him too, and as he says, he 'really did a good night's exercise. This promenade lasted more than 2 hours.' After the ball nine hundred people sat down to supper. For a man of seventy-one with a wooden leg this was pretty good going, particularly as the heat was 'excessive and oppressive to the highest degree. We all agree that it far exceeds Naples. … The fact is that the sun is so very short a time below the Horizon that the Earth has no chance of cooling.' Anglesey now strove, but in vain, to give up his place at the next day's 'Spectacle au Théâtre en Gala' for one of his sons; and he tried, too, to be firm about leaving on August 1st, though he much feared that he should 'be compelled to give up 10 or 12 days more, for the Emperor is bent upon shewing me His Army and also the Fleet, and H.M. is really so kind in every way, that it is almost impossible to resist his wishes.' The days that followed were comparatively quiet; there was the launching of a warship of a hundred-and-twenty guns, followed by two more balls. On the day after the second of these, they returned to Cronstadt and sailed through the Fleet in the *Pearl*.

'We landed the next morning to attend the Fêtes of the following day. We sat down to dinner about 200, in grand costume at 4 o'clock. All dispersed then until ½ 7, when we reassembled at the Palace where operations began by a Polonaise, through an immense suite of rooms and through a crowd which appeared perfectly impenetrable. All the men were in Dominoes and with hats or caps on.... The heat was excessive, and how Her Majesty stands it, who is very thin, and weak, and ailing, I cannot conceive, but she has an elasticity and vivacity that carries her thro' everything. About 10 o'clock, when there probably was not a dry rag (male or female) in the Palace, we sallied forth in open carriages (there having been about 3 hours of the most incessant thunder, lightning and heavy rain) to view the illuminations. These open carriages, of which there were, I think, 27, and which are called "Lignes", hold 6 or 8 persons sitting back to back in the manner of the Irish cars, but upon 4 wheels, and extremely long traces. To describe the extreme splendour and magnificence of this wonderful display of brilliant light, diversified in most beautiful and symmetrical fountains of amazing power, throwing the waters to an immense height and extent, thro' endless avenues opening occasionally into large circles and then again into immense squares, and oblongs, each surpassing the former in brilliancy — is much more than I can undertake to do. I can only give you some idea of the extent of it by telling you that we were nearly 2 hrs. in the carriage, never standing still and sometimes trotting. About 1 o'clock I got to bed, highly delighted, but really tired almost to death.

' ... Today (25th July) we attend the Emperor at 10 o'clock on board his steamer. H.M. made an inspection of the Fleet, and we visited several ships. Upon going on board the frigate which bears the Flag of the Admiral who commands the Fleet, the Russian Flag was hauled down and the Austrian replaced it, upon which a salute was fired from every ship, which including his yachts, of which there are about 8, may be stated at about 40 sail. This was in honour of the Arch-Duke Albert of Austria who arrived 5 days ago. We dined on board the steamer and landed at 6. An invitation was sent to drink tea at a Maison de plaisance of the Empress, but, after visiting the ships, having also been in every nook and corner of the dockyard and arsenal of Cronstadt I have been obliged to excuse myself.'

Anglesey's next letter to Char tells of 'the superb crash' made by the two thousand instruments of the forty regiments of guards, during the ceremonial beating of the Retreat. Clarence describes it in detail:

'On the arrival of the Emperor the whole struck up the National Anthem in front of his tent, and the assembled multitude took off their hats and crossed themselves.... One might have fancied one-self among the legions of trumpets at the last day; but the strains seemed to produce little or no effect on the minds of our Russian companions, who were chattering the whole time. Perhaps, like other things, even music may become tiresome, although I can hardly conceive that. Imagine a Strauss waltz played in exquisite time & tune by fifteen hundred horns, and that on a lawn on a charming evening!'[26]

Of the following morning's mounting of the guard, Anglesey wrote:

'It was not intended to have had a grand manoeuvre, but upon my mentioning, after guard mounting "I must soon take my leave," His Majesty without saying one word to anyone else, instantly gave the signal of alarm and the whole camp was under arms and scurrying to their alarm posts with the utmost speed. Some Regiments of Cavalry at the advanced Posts had to ride 7 miles to come in. In proof that this was entirely an impromptu, and unpremeditated, I must tell you that I was almost too late at guard mounting from having been detained at the window of my quarters whilst these Regiments of Cuirassiers marched past which had had a long field day, and they had again instantly to turn out, and I doubt if they had time to feed their horses. The Emperor commanded himself. The manoeuvres lasted 6 or 7 hours and I am bound to declare that it is impossible to imagine a finer body of men and horses, a more perfect intelligence, quickness and precision in all the movements, or any officer more completely master of his business, than this same very extraordinary man. I left the field in delight.'

There followed two days of Fleet inspections and, in the evenings, 'teas and suppers at different cottages ... in fact, if not Palaces, at least country residences upon a magnificent and impressive scale.' Aboard one of the ships was the Grand Duke Constantine 'who is to be, or is, Grand Admiral, but whom they buffet about like any common midshipman.' A cruise with the Fleet, a stay at the ambassador's country house, breakfast with the Empress, who gave him a malachite paper-weight, and a visit to the farm of Tsarskoe Selo — ('such cows! — such cream and butter, such perfect cleanliness. Oh! How jealous, darling, I could be') — after all these activities and yet more reviews, one each of the artillery and the cavalry, and finally one of the whole army, it is not to be wondered at that the poor man complained of suffering and declared that he could only 'with much difficulty and risk hold on'. The Imperial ladies visited the *Pearl*, wrote all their names in Anglesey's prayer book, and took, as souvenirs, 'the Empress ... an excellent ... Atlas lately published, that I, luckily, brought with me, Olga the Army and Navy List bound together ... and Alexandrine the Red Book.'

Having been for two mornings on horseback at four o'clock, the time at last arrived for the honoured guest to take his leave.

'It really was quite overwhelming: Upon finally taking leave and kissing Her Majesty's hand, and asking Her commands for England, she said "you must send me your picture" "and me one!" "and me one!" said each one of these captivating Ladies and finally the Emperor laid *his* injunction to me to send Him one! Thus I have 5 prints to provide of my ugly old visage, and where to get them, I really don't know, but get them I must. Have you any? I never see them in the Print shops, and I know not what is become of them. At last the Empress gave me 3 most cordial embraces and the most hearty squeezes of the hand, and I backed out and shut the door, but, in a moment out His Majesty bolted to *take care of me* down the stairs....'

Clarence, Alfred and George were induced to allow their father to go home alone, while they continued the endless round of balls and reviews which ceased only when a grand scale re-enaction of the battle of Borodino brought the summer to a triumphant end. Anglesey's lonely voyage home was extraordinarily rough. 'Nothing but the *Pearl* so handled could have done it,' he wrote. 'Now you know I am not very nervous, but I do own that I passed many of these hours rejoicing that the 3 dear Boys were not with me!'[27]

iv

Lord Anglesey, then in command of the Blues, once remarked, 'I hear in the Blues every officer has a sobriquet. There's Nutmeg, Jos, the Giant, Shaver, and, I suppose, shortly they will give me one.' 'Why, bless you,' replied his son, Lord Alfred, 'they've called you Old Peg ever since you had the regiment!'
Montague Guest in Memorials of the Royal Yacht Squadron[28]

The new reign saw an immediate increase in the number of Paget relations who were courtiers. At the time of the Coronation, for instance, no less than five — two of Anglesey's sons, two of his sons-in-law, and one of his nieces — held positions at Court. This was all part of Melbourne's assiduity in surrounding the new sovereign with none but Whigs. 'It is with a mixture of aversion and contempt', wrote Greville, 'that people read in the Court Circular of ... the Ladies Eleanora and Constance Paget [daughters of Uxbridge] tagging after the Queen, on foot, on horseback or in the carriage, 6 days out of the seven.' Between the accession and Anglesey's death, at least twelve of his close relatives were members of the Royal Household. The same influence was felt in the services. Melbourne told the Queen that he was quite alarmed at the number of Pagets in the Navy, which he thought belonged 'more exclusively to the Aristocracy than the Army'.[29]

The Queen's journal in the early years of her reign gives some revealing pictures of the Pagets at court. A few days before the Coronation, for instance, she 'made Lady Mary Paget sing after dinner, which she did beautifully, two songs before the gentlemen came in, the pretty one from *The Ambassadrice*, and one by Alari; Lady Adelaide [Paget] accompanying her in the last. The gentlemen then came in.... They, particularly Lord Anglesey ... insisted on *my* singing; which I did, but literally shaking with fear and fright....'[30]

Anglesey's sixth son, Alfred, with whom gossip decreed that the Queen was in love, became an equerry in 1837, and spent the rest of his life at court, later becoming Chief Equerry and Clerk Marshal, relinquishing these posts only at his death fifty-one years later.° In the newspapers of the late 1830s and early 1840s he figured fairly often as a lovesick swain. He was said to have worn the Queen's portrait over his heart, and even to have hung her miniature round the neck of his dog.³¹ Uxbridge started the reign as Lord-in-Waiting and two years later became Lord Chamberlain. Though the scandalmongers said that he went so far as to provide a place in the Royal establishment for a mistress (his predecessor and brother-in-law, Lord Conyngham, had installed *his* mistress as housekeeper in Buckingham Palace), he seems to have given satisfaction, until replaced by a Tory after the General Election of 1841.

In 1842 a case was brought against him by seven individuals who had lent him money in return for annuities. These he had failed to pay, and the case was decided against him; but not before Anglesey had been dragged in as a witness. When he had been called and duly sworn, he was given a seat on the Bench in deference to his disability, and examined as follows:

MR JAMES: I believe, my Lord, you are the father of the Earl of Uxbridge?
THE MARQUESS: I believe so. (*A laugh*)
MR JAMES: Now, in 1838, where was the Earl of Uxbridge residing?
THE MARQUESS: Upon my life, I'm sure I can't say.

Further questions as to his son's establishment were followed by a final one as to what property Uxbridge owned, but this was successfully objected to by defence counsel, and Anglesey's ordeal was over.³²ᴾ

Uxbridge and his wife at once retired to the country, leaving his father to foot the bill. Thomas Beer, the chief agent since Sanderson's retirement in 1835, found it necessary, in 1842, to advise Anglesey to borrow at 4½ per cent the £60,000 necessary to pay the debts of his son and heir (mostly incurred upon the turf), so as to avoid further usurious loans; but he pointed out that what had already been paid towards Uxbridge's and William Paget's debts in recent years was causing an annual deficiency of £3,500. This might be overcome by letting Plas Newydd, putting down the Burton-upon-Trent establishment (the Abbey there was kept as a sort of shooting-lodge) and reducing stable expenses. If, however, wrote Beer, Uxbridge's present debts were to be paid, sales of property would have to be effected, 'and these very advantageously. To go abroad, therefore, appears at present the only alternative, having the sole view of living within present means; and returning home must depend upon sales being effected; and even then ... to live upon the lowest scale of expence.'

Ways and means of avoiding this course were in fact found, but it was no wonder that the Queen heard from her Prime Minister 'a very bad account of Lord Anglesey's affairs. His case is a hard one', wrote Melbourne, 'for these pecuniary difficulties are owing to the extravagance of others, and by no means his own.'[33]

*   *   *

The Queen was ever filled with admiration for Anglesey as a horseman. One afternoon when she met him in Hyde Park, he rode beside her for a considerable time. 'He rides so well,' she wrote that night, 'so gracefully, it is quite wonderful; and he rode a beautiful horse.' At a military review in 1838 she could have 'cried out not to have *ridden* and been in *my right* place as I ought'; but she was advised against doing so on account of the great crowd. 'Lord Anglesey (who had command of the day, looked so handsome, and did it beautifully and gracefully) regretted much I did not ride.'[34]

Over the years Anglesey had come to be regarded as the great arbiter in matters of military and civil equitation. 'We consider Your Lordship', wrote the colonel commanding the cavalry depot in 1840, 'as our supreme judge ... but unfortunately are not so often within reach of nor guided by your advice as would be desirable for the cavalry.' His views on all aspects of horsemanship were clear and decided; when, for example, he was asked in 1850 to subscribe towards a steeplechase, he replied that with all his love for equestrian exercises and whatever might lead to the improvement of horsemanship and the breed of horses, he considered 'the practice of Steeple Chases highly objectionable'.[35]

*   *   *

Anglesey was brought a step closer to the person of the Queen when, in 1842, he was persuaded to exchange the Colonelcy of the 7th Hussars for that of the Blues. This entailed attendance at Court as Gold Stick-in-Waiting, a duty shared by the colonels of the three regiments of House-hold Cavalry. The vacancy had been caused by the death of Lord Hill, the Commander-in-Chief, and Wellington (who had once again assumed the supreme command of the Army), now offered it to Anglesey. It was not the first time that the approach had been made, for George IV, it will be remembered, had offered him the Blues in 1826, and he had turned it down.�q This time he was still not very anxious to accept. In a letter, which in the event was never sent, he asked the Duke whether in his view refusal could be considered by the Queen 'an improper indifference to the honor of being brought as Gold Stick, in occasional attendance upon Her Majesty? Or — Would my not being removed to the Blues put you to even the slightest inconvenience by subjecting you to applications that might embarrass you? In either case I cheerfully go to the Royal Horse Guards, but if neither of these cases would occur, then a Service of 45 years in the 7th would make me lean to remaining as I am.' His son-in-law George Byng, writing from Woburn, where there was assembled a house party of some thirty-five Whigs, 'all good men and true', expressed their fear that the Blues might 'fall into the *Tory* hands of Lord London-derry'. There was much concern, he said, that their party had no representative at the head of any of the Household regiments, 'and consequently the Whigs are unwilling to ask & probably unable to obtain, an entrance into that Service for their sons and relations.' But before this letter was written, Anglesey had already placed himself at the Duke's disposal.³⁶

The break with the Hussars was a painful one. Lieutenant-Colonel Whyte, who had served twenty years under his chief, declared that it was 'indeed a black day for the 7th.'

> 'None', he wrote in forwarding his last report, 'can know as well as I do, perhaps not even Your Lordship, how entirely to your example, your influence and your care, we owe the good feeling and the harmony that have always pervaded the corps. The Regiment will doubtless retain its character for discipline and long feel in every branch the good principles your long guidance has engendered; but the spell is broken.... The day is past, when the intimation that such was Lord Anglesey's wish, could produce, in every party *cordial* acquiescence, and dissipate any dissatisfaction.... The accumulated love and reverence of five and forty years cannot be replaced — the power that protected us, and filled our ranks with gentlemen is gone — and I feel that with Lord Anglesey, the individuality of the old 7th is departed; I need not say how bitterly I regret it.'

This touched Anglesey to the quick. 'I had not need of this searching probe,' he replied, 'for I was already suffering deeply at this sad separation.'³⁷

* * *

In May 1838, after enjoying nearly a year's respite from the affairs of his son William, Anglesey had generously offered to relieve him of responsibility for the education of his eldest son, Billy, then aged nine, provided he was given complete control over the boy. This was readily accepted by his parents, who, it will be remembered, had settled in Pau, at Anglesey's direction, in 1837. Billy was duly placed in a school of his grandfather's choosing, and all seemed to be going smoothly, when, in August 1839 William broke the most important of the stipulations which had been negotiated in 1837 by returning to England. This action was taken ostensibly to make it known that he had separated from his wife (a separation of short duration, as it turned out) and to find himself employment either in the Navy or elsewhere. The real object was an attempt to get money out of his father with which to pay new debts incurred at Pau, to which place he could not return without being arrested by his creditors there. In effect he succeeded in this, for in February 1840 Anglesey decided to make a grand effort towards reconciliation with his erring son. To this end he convened a family council at Uxbridge House. Besides William, there were present his wife, his uncle Berkeley, his sister Agnes's husband, George Byng, and his two younger stepbrothers Clarence and Alfred. Thomas Beer kept a minute of the meeting, which opened by Anglesey explaining that he had assembled such members of the family as were near at hand to bear witness to what he had already done, and what he now intended to do for William; that the occasion was a most solemn one, for, without there resulting from it a complete reform on the part of his son, he would be totally discarded. William's past career was reviewed at length, beginning with his improvidence, as a second son who was incapable of economy, in marrying a woman without fortune. Anglesey pointed out that his son's name was so bad at the Admiralty that when his uncle Charles had offered to take him to the West Indies as his Flag Captain, Their Lordships would not hear of it; that it was only out of consideration for Anglesey himself that William's name was retained in the Navy List. He then recited the various sums of money which he had had to raise to pay his son's debts since 1830. The total was £26,916, a sum which represented his patrimony three times over. On top of this he was still receiving as an allowance the interest from the original patrimony. What right, asked Anglesey, had he to expect to have his extravagance fed at the expense of his brothers and sisters? He then came to his proposals for the future. He would increase William's allowance by £100, which would give him an income of £780; he would pay his debts at Pau, and would try to obtain some sort of employment for him, though this would be difficult to achieve. He then said, ' "and now William I will take you by the hand once more" — which his Lordship did most kindly, and kissed him — saying then — "I freely forgive you all your past conduct in the hope you will yet prove worthy of my affection and regard." ' Thus ended the family conclave. William and Fanny returned at once to Pau; but not for long. By the end of October 1840 he was back in London, attempting to gain his father's permission to return from France, on the grounds of the instability of that country 'and the possible emergence of forces stronger than the King, Louis Philippe'. His father, holding cheap the idea of any real dangers in France, told him to return at once to Pau, unless he could point out some other place which would cost less. William once again defied Anglesey, and was still in England in June 1841. At the general election in that month he got himself elected Member of Parliament for the borough of Andover, which once again put him beyond arrest, and necessitated his living in England. Not surprisingly he showed no signs of reforming whatever, and his debts continued to mount. A further strain was at this time placed upon Anglesey, for his son never missed an opportunity to abuse, misrepresent and malign his long-suffering parent publicly, in the most shameful manner. 'I love my father better than anything in the world'; he wrote to Beer, '*better* than my *children*, whom I worship, but I am driven half mad when he rows me, and when I allow my violent temper to get the better of me I would say, or do anything.'

*   *   *

The present point is perhaps a good one for following William's career to the end of his father's life, though in fact Anglesey was not to be seriously troubled by his son beyond the end of 1846, for at that time William went abroad, never to return. Into the intervening years, however, he managed to pack a series of infamies unparalleled by any in his earlier life. These were of such a nature that before long his father's attitude of distress and pity had hardened to one of unrelenting sternness. In the end impersonal justice was the sole good feeling that he was able to muster towards his son.

By the end of 1843, William's financial situation had become so bad that the whole of his allowance was under stoppages for debt, and he was forced to live exclusively upon his naval half-pay of £3 15s. od. a week.

His shady man of business described him at this time as 'lodging up 3 pairs of stairs, a chop or steak and pint of porter for his daily meal, and without the Marquis's countenance and not a shilling in his pocket'. These privations were made no easier to bear by his mounting suspicions of his wife's faithlessness. These culminated in a notorious case which he brought against Lord Cardigan, later to become famous as the leader of the charge of the Light Brigade. Suspecting Fanny of an intrigue with Cardigan, William employed a disreputable 'private detective', named Winter, to lie beneath a sofa in the Paget's temporary London residence, so as to witness what took place when Cardigan called upon Lady William. Winter's report was that they had twice in the space of one afternoon committed adultery upon a sofa near to the one under which he lay. When the case came to court, however, Winter was nowhere to be found. 'My Lord,' wrote William to Cardigan, 'I charge you with the *wicked and infamous crime* of having bought him, and sent him "out of the way". Having done so you may go forth to the world and declare your innocence ... but you are not in my opinion one jot the less of a scoundrel for having debauched my wife, nor of a liar and a coward for having acted the part you have done.' To Anglesey, William wrote pathetically begging, at this moment of humiliation, to be received back into his father's arms. 'I am an INJURED MAN & GOD IS MY WITNESS; as far as Lady Wm. is concerned, *a most innocent one....* I will give up ... all my old associates, every one of them. FORGIVE THIS ONCE!! and shame and disgrace befall me if I disappoint you. Only don't make me afraid of you, the only thing on earth I do fear!... *Try me!*' Anglesey's reply shows his agony of mind:

'Although I think your whole conduct is perfectly atrocious, and as regards myself and knowing as you do my nervous sufferings, absolutely inhuman, yet I do not abandon you. I feel that I ought to have discarded you long ago without a single shilling nevertheless I have continued your allowance after having repeatedly pd your debts and I have taken charge of your 3 sons. [He had made himself responsible for the younger sons soon after their parents' marital troubles had started.] All this I shall continue to do, but ... at present I am most unhappy to say that it is wholly out of my power to throw a shield over you; and I feel perfectly assured that your presence in my house would close my doors against every friend & relative which I have.'

Before the case came on, William's solicitor had tried to persuade Anglesey to appear as a witness, and also to obtain permission for William junior to testify as to the affection which had subsisted in the past between his parents. In reply Anglesey wrote:

'I really do not believe it would be possible for Lord William's counsel to extract from my testimony any fact that could be deemed favorable to his case, and I have no doubt that the counsel for the Defendant might upon cross-examination elicit facts that might materially damage Lord William's case.

'In regard to their son, William Paget, I think it would be highly indecorous ... that a *son* — a youth of 13 years, should be brought into court with a view of criminating his mother, and I must believe that such a step would produce feelings in the court that would be entirely sinister to Ld William's interests. Under these circumstances I must deprecate the idea of calling into court, William Paget or myself: and in addition I have to say that I am by no means in a state to undertake the journey.'

Though abortive in December 1843, through Winter's disappearance, the case of Paget versus Cardigan was resumed in the following February. This time Winter gave his evidence, but the jury, without so much as waiting for the judge's summing-up, and without retiring, returned a verdict for Cardigan. The Solicitor-General, who defended him, declared that the object of the action had been to 'extract money from a wealthy nobleman, unpopular with the public'.[38] The jury probably felt, as must posterity too, that there was some truth in this assertion.

*   *   *

The next three years of William's tragic career are characterized by a further deterioration in his financial and moral state. Often in the past he had given cheques knowing them to be worthless, but now, in desperation, he resorted to more criminal methods for the raising of cash. On more than one occasion he borrowed money in advance on security of his half-pay, and then drew the half-pay himself when it became due. In January 1846 he thus defrauded Lord Adolphus FitzClarence (the third son of William IV by Mrs Jordan). In this case, Anglesey was forced to intervene to save his son from an intolerable public scandal, from a possible sentence of transportation, and from ignominious dismissal from the Navy (from which, instead, he was allowed to retire in the normal way). William's next step was to enter the profitable business of offering to obtain, for a consideration, places in Government Offices, often using as bait the names of his father (by then Master-General of the Ordnance) and his brother Clarence (Secretary to the Master-General). In two years he had made by this method £1,100 to supplement his legitimate annual income. In the summer of 1846, having ceased to be a Member of Parliament, he avoided arrest on a charge connected with this illegal traffic only by fleeing the country.

How he spent the rest of his life (he died at the age of 70 in 1873) is not known, except that for some years he seems to have resided in Cadiz, leading a comparatively respectable existence, and that in 1848 his father increased his allowance by £200 a year. Thus for the last seven years of his life Anglesey was spared the appalling tension and excitement to which his second son had for so long subjected him.[39]

CHAPTER FOURTEEN

While immense conscript armies paced the Continent, Palmerston's bold words were backed by an ill-organized regular force of some 130,000 men, of whom less than half were in Europe, and a small fleet slowly changing over from sail to steam.

Keith Feiling: A History of England[1]

IT is now necessary to go back to 1845. In that year Sir Robert Peel, who had headed a Conservative government for four years, resigned the Premiership, having failed to carry the Cabinet with him in his plan for the complete repeal of the Corn Laws: a measure which Lord John Russell, leading the Whig opposition, was advocating simultaneously. The Queen therefore sent for Russell. On hearing this news from his old friend Blake, who as usual was in the centre of things at Woburn, Anglesey was far from happy. 'I do not think that *we* are *yet* ready for harness', he wrote. The difficulties which confronted Lord John appalled him. 'What *can* be done *will* be done by little John the great.... He must try to outstride the seven leagued boots in which the public is now moving. It must be neck-or-nothing work — nothing short of the compleatest *Free Trade and so forth*. Well — Success to him.' Within a fortnight Russell had given up the attempt to form a government, Lord Grey's son (who had succeeded his father earlier in the year) refusing to serve if Palmerston went to the Foreign Office. Russell wrote to Anglesey to say that had the matter proceeded he should have asked him whether he felt his health equal to the post of Master-General of the Ordnance. 'I am truly *very old* for Office', came the reply, 'and moreover, a great sufferer, nevertheless my health and strength do not seem to be impaired either bodily, or (as I really believe) mentally, and therefore altho' I do not in the least degree court office, yet if you had required my services I should have held it to be a duty to obey the call, and you would have had in me a zealous friend and admirer.'[2]

Russell supported Peel, who had resumed office, in the repeal of the Corn Laws, but opposed a new coercion bill for Ireland. On this Peel was

318

beaten, and in July, Lord John, having overcome Grey's opposition to Palmerston, became Prime Minister for the first time. He called Anglesey to the Ordnance in the most flattering manner, and the Queen, on the Prime Minister's recommendation, made a special addition to the total number of officers holding the highest rank in the army, 'in order', as Prince Albert put it, 'to satisfy Lord Anglesey with the dignity of Field Marshal'. Char, taking the waters in Bath, heard from her husband on July 2nd. 'The D. of Wellington', he wrote, 'remains as Commander in Chief, and I have consented to go to the Ordnance.... This will sadly interfere with my sailing propensities, but really I have had such pressing solicitations from many, many friends not to withhold my humble services, on *public* grounds, that I have given in.'[3]

*   *   *

In 1830, when Lord Grey was finding difficulty in filling the office, Anglesey's one year's experience at the Ordnance in 1827 had led him to describe it as 'this charming department'. Nineteen years later his view of it was still the same, though many changes had taken place in the meantime. In 1827, for instance, he had been the last holder of the office to be a member of the Cabinet. Since then, though the number and variety of the functions which fell to his department were greater in 1846 than in 1827, the general influence and importance of the Master-General had steadily declined. One year after Anglesey's death, the Office of Ordnance was finally broken up and its functions transferred elsewhere. By that time it had been in existence for nearly four hundred and fifty years. It is a sad commentary upon the demise of a great department of state that the very last entry in the minute-book of the Board of Ordnance should have read: 'Tenders accepted for emptying privies in Ireland, 31 December, 1856.'[4]

The charm which Anglesey detected in the department consisted in the enormous variety of its functions. The Master-General acted in two capacities: one military, the other civil. He was, by virtue of his office, commander-in-chief of the artillery and of the engineers, both bodies of scientific and highly trained men. No officer was commissioned in either corps except upon the submission of the Master-General, which meant that he had considerable patronage. In his civil capacity, he presided over the Board of Ordnance, which besides being responsible for the provision, inspection, holding and issue of all military arms, and much other equipment for both the Navy and the Army, supplied food and fuel for all troops at home. The Board stored and issued everything provided centrally for the army, and for other services as well, even such diverse ones as the convict stations, the Metropolitan Police and the Irish Revenue Department. In modern times the Ordnance had been run on model lines. A Committee set up in 1828, the year after Anglesey's first tenure of the office, recommended that its system might well be followed in other branches of the administration.

There were two further aspects of the post which appealed to Anglesey. It brought him into close contact with Wellington, once again Commander-in-Chief, and it provided him with a salary of £3,000 a year. Further, he managed to get his son Clarence appointed as the Master-General's official secretary, and his grandson Henry Paget as an aide-de-camp.[a] Another favourable point was that he was able to attend to his duties for more than half of the year from Beaudesert.

Since the formation of the Royal Military Academy in the eighteenth century, the Master-General had been Captain of the Gentlemen Cadets of the Royal Artillery. The very first problem which confronted Anglesey after assuming office was connected with applicants for entry to this institution. About seventy youths were entered annually, but he found that his predecessor, his brother-in-law Murray (who died a few days after relinquishing office), had left a waiting-list of nearly five hundred. To one of many fresh applicants, Anglesey was forced to write: 'This is quite overwhelming. Every one of these [500] has had hopes held out to him.... To guard against a breach of promise, I ought not to add another name for the next three years, and', he concluded, 'do you think that my tenure of office is worth a third of that time?' In passing, it should be noted that in the event it turned out to be worth twice that time![5]

Another applicant, Assheton Smith, his neighbour in North Wales, to whom Plas Newydd was at this time let, was told that if he could produce a scheme for solving the cadet problem, the Master-General would make him 'a present of Plas Newydd, or any other trifle you may fancy.' To add to the list of applicants would place him, he said, 'in the predicament of breaking a promise. This I would not do to get my leg back again.' To his old friend, Cloncurry, in a similar context, he wrote, 'With respect to your *modest* request for two Clerkships, you might as well expect to extract Gold from a dust hole. My persecutions upon this subject are fearful and my *ayes* in proportion to my *noes*, are about as 1 to 100! Alas! Alas! What a life I lead.'[6]

*   *   *

Left: 'Char', Marchioness of Anglesey, 'One-Leg's' second wife, in old age

Below: The Marquess of Anglesey when Master-General of the Ordnance, aged 83

to be inserted

Shall we have another
touch at 'im?

no, no, it won't
but it all right

same at Yesterday
June 18 1840
Duke of Wellington

For the best part of six years, Anglesey presided over his 'charming' department. The routine work alone was heavy, especially for a man of his advanced years. The stream of papers which never ceased to reach him wherever he might be — whether in his office in Pall Mall, at Cowes Castle, or at Beaudesert — taxed his eyes and brain to the full, yet neither failed under the strain and the numerous memoranda and extensive correspondence which flowed from his pen retained their habitual force and clarity of expression to the end. A casual glance at his letter-books shows at once the variety of matters with which he dealt from day to day; beside the endless applications for jobs and patronage, there were inventors and inventions, sane and crackpot, to be investigated and assessed; disorders in the Academy to be dealt with by firm disciplinary action; the building of barracks in Hong Kong and the provision of stores for New Zealand; 'an ingenious method of carrying the pouch belt and knapsack'; the supply of 'iron travelling hot furnaces'; the introduction of percussion shells, and the comparative merits of 'the Paget Carbine'[b] and another type of fire-arm for the Yeomanry. In reply to Lord Morpeth's request for some obsolete guns for decorative purposes, the Master-General wrote: 'My dear Old Jobber — In my private capacity (being a merchant of copper) I ought to promote the expenditure of the metal knowing that what you take away from Ordnance Store must be replaced from my

facing: SCENE AT UXBRIDGE HOUSE, BURLINGTON GARDENS,
on the 25th anniversary of the Battle of Waterloo, June 18th, 1840

L

mines or from others of the Trade, but as Master-General seriously
speaking I have no more right to give away those state guns than you have.
All Ordnance Guns no longer useful are always recast, but if you will
obtain the sanction of the Treasury you shall have them.'[7]

* * *

By far the most important subject with which Anglesey had to deal,
and which dominated his tenure of office, was the state of the national
defences. He was one of a small number of distinguished military men,
Wellington conspicuously at their head, who for some time had been
anxiously aware that Britain's defensive deficiencies were an open invitation to a successful invasion of Britain. Wellington had been literally
losing sleep over the problem for years past.

> 'It is matter of regret as well as astonishment,' he wrote to Anglesey,
> 'not only that I should not have made any of the three last Adminis-
> trations sufficiently sensible of its existence, with your assistance in
> respect to the present administration; but that, in fact, the Gentry of
> the Country, the great landed Proprietors, the Publick and Parlia-
> ment appear to entertain no suspicion of its existence.
>
> 'It consists in one simple fact! The appreciation of Steam Vessels
> at sea has exposed all parts of the coasts of this Empire ... to be
> attacked and devoured by an enemy, at all times, and in any state of
> weather!'[c]
>
> 'There is no protection against this danger excepting a superior
> Fleet at sea! We all know to what chances, risks, and mistakes the
> operation of such a force is exposed. We have no security however.
> We have works for the protection of our ... Naval Dockyards; but
> supposing them to be armed, we have not men in sufficient number
> even to occupy them for their defence against a serious attack.'

This was one of a large number of similar letters addressed by the Duke
to Anglesey: letters which Greville described as being 'very strong'.
Anglesey showed them to the Prime Minister, and they did something to
awaken the Government to the dangers.[8]
Anglesey himself was fully aware of the urgency of the matter.

> 'I am at a loss', he told the Duke, 'to find out the best means of
> making known to the Country the real danger in which it is, at the

very moment at which we are writing. No one dare stand up & state to the House of Commons the extent of our imminent peril. The Government (and indeed all Governments, Whig and Tory) are more afraid of that Body, than of an Enemy (for such France is) armed at all points, and in a perfect state of Preparation to pounce upon us at a moment's notice, and with a confidence that if their attacking forces escape our naval armaments (and some of the various detachments they would probably push out simultaneously *must* escape our Squadrons) they would meet with no resistance on land, for if we could be certain of the very point at which their great effort would be made, I fear you would hardly be able to scrape together 15,000 men of all arms to meet it!

'What is to be done?

'Do let us make some effort to save our Country.

'The Ministers must be called upon to act *vigorously* and *immediately*, and if they were to begin today, I doubt if we shall still be in time to avert the evil, but it behoves us to make the effort, and I will join with you in any course that you may point out to effect our object.'[9]

As early as September 1846 Anglesey had started his campaign for bringing up to date the fortifications of the British Isles. 'I do most anxiously hope', he wrote to the Duke, 'for your most valuable aid and opinion, & whenever you may from time to time be disposed to make *reconnoisances* [*sic*], I shall be ready to attend you at a day's notice.' The two veterans in fact made a number of visits to the defensive works on the south coast and on the Thames in the years that followed, both together and separately, on horseback and by steamer. On one occasion Anglesey, inspecting the defences of the Channel Islands in his yacht, made so bold as to look into Cherbourg, which he found 'amply protected. I did not see any shew of Force there.'[10]

He was remarkably successful, with others, in persuading Ministers to make money available for increased defence works. This achievement was carried through in the face of the general atmosphere of parsimony and scepticism prevailing at the time, which ensured that the increase in the Army, the strengthening of the militia, and the other measures which were necessary to the minimum defence of the country, were not in fact put in hand.[d] Though Palmerston, and to a lesser degree the Prime Minister, became increasingly aware of the needs which Wellington and

Anglesey never ceased to indicate to them, they were too weak to overcome either the financiers among the Whigs, who insisted that Parliament would never agree to an increased income tax, or the Radicals, led by Cobden who, like their heirs in the twentieth century, taught the fallacy that unilateral disarmament was the path to peace. It would be tedious, since no invasion was in fact attempted at that time (or indeed at any time since), to detail the immense efforts which were made by Anglesey and others in the late 'forties and early 'fifties to rally the Government and public opinion to a realization of their perilous position. Let it suffice to say that an enormous amount of his time and energy was taken up by them.

The country as a whole might never have become generally aware of these preoccupations of her leading military experts, had not a memorandum upon the subject by one of them been the cause of a famous calculated indiscretion. Without doubt the ablest man on the staff of the Ordnance was Sir John Burgoyne. He had crossed Anglesey's path on more than one occasion. It was he who, as an engineer officer in Spain in 1808, had blown up the bridge at Castrogonzalo at the last possible moment, during the early stages of the retreat to Corunna (see p. 85 above). In 1831 Anglesey had appointed him Chairman of the Board of Public Works in Ireland, a post which he had retained for fifteen years. In 1845 he had become Inspector-General of Fortifications under the Ordnance, and as such was the Master-General's right-hand man. Soon after Anglesey's arrival at the Ordnance, Burgoyne had drawn up for him a long and masterly exposition of the defenceless state of the country.[11] It was this closely argued paper, put before the Cabinet by Anglesey, with his own comments, which more than anything else brought Palmerston round to a full realization of the perilous position. A copy of it was sent to Wellington, who wrote a letter[12] to Burgoyne, dated January 9th, 1847, reiterating at length his views upon the case. A year later this letter appeared in the *Morning Chronicle*. It had not been marked 'confidential', nor was it even written in the Duke's own hand; indeed it was clearly intended by him to have at least as wide a distribution as Burgoyne's cabinet paper which had drawn it forth. 'I have no objection', Wellington told Anglesey on February 6th, 'to Lord Palmerston making any use he pleases of my letter to Sir John Burgoyne of the 9th January.' It is all the more surprising therefore that the Duke became, some time after the publication of the letter, so incensed with Frances, Lady Shelley, who had taken the lead in propagating the letter's contents outside official circles, that it took two years for his deep friendship with her to be restored. Anglesey told Burgoyne that he was certain that the Duke 'at first laughed at' the fact of publication, and was far from 'disagreeing with me when I said that I thought his opinion upon the matter would be most beneficial, by opening the eyes of our people to the dangerous position of the country'. The trouble was that the radical press made fun of the Duke's letter, and the public reception of it showed that it was considered by many to prove that he was in his dotage; this so offended his *amour-propre* that he felt bound to reverse his original views on the matter, and to punish Lady Shelley cruelly both by private letter and by public reproach. It needed the charming tact of her husband, Sir John Shelley, to heal the breach. 'Good evening, Duke,' said Shelley at a party in 1850. 'Do you know it has been said, by someone who must have been present, that the cackling of geese once saved Rome? I have been thinking that perhaps the cackling of my old goose may yet save England!' 'By God, Shelley,' replied the Duke, 'you are right: give me your honest hand.'[13]

*   *   *

There was one vital and awful matter which transcended all others in the minds of public men in the late 1840s. It affected Anglesey directly at two points; first, as a landlord. In October 1846 Thomas Beer, just back from a tour of the Anglesey estates in Ireland, wrote to their owner: 'The all absorbing subject now is the total failure of the Potatoe Crop, and how the poorer tenantry are to be relieved, and the labouring people to be fed, who had that for their only food.' The local agent considered the failure to be equal in value to more than one year's rent, and he did not expect to collect on the next rent day more than half the usual receipt. He recommended making a twenty per cent cut, although the following year he did not expect to collect anything like the remainder. Anglesey, on the other hand, thought it

'infinitely better to give every timely assistance that is possible and to regulate that assistance by the real and honest wants of the Parties, without regarding threats and the Clamour of non-payments of any rent at all. This will never be permitted, and the right principle to act upon is this: To exact repayment in labour for every advance of money or food to those who are distressed and really require aid. I would act liberally and kindly, but I would not enter into any Bargain in respect of future Rents, for the present can only be considered as a temporary visitation. Let there be no positive want, but let there be a very marked difference between the idle whose object may be to live upon Alms, and those who are really industrious and deserving.'

This excellent advice was probably more easily carried out on Anglesey's Irish estates than on many others, particularly in southern Ireland, for as Beer wrote, 'the tenantry (as is the case to the North of Ireland) on your Lordship's Estate, are on the whole an orderly and quiet people.'[14]

From a public point of view, the Master-General of the Ordnance had no direct part to play in the horrors of the Irish famine, but his other preoccupations suffered considerably from the seconding of Sir John Burgoyne to take charge of the relief organization in Dublin set up by the government. This urgent appointment was originally intended to last for only three months, but the Prime Minister extended it beyond that period, much to Anglesey's and Sir John's own inconvenience, though undoubtedly to Ireland's benefit. Burgoyne kept Anglesey informed of his work. 'Nothing can be more arduous or more *fearful* than my business here,' he wrote, ' ... where a false step may do great mischief, & the imputation of faults, which Your Lordship knows never spared in Ireland, leads to a course of rancourous censure.' And again as his task drew to a close: 'The breaking off from feeding three millions of people to their being left on their own resources all in the course of about six weeks, was rather an awful operation; but the period of gathering the autumnal crops, their abundance, the fall in prices, & the fine weather are favorable circumstances, & we are closing our issues to Union after Union, with less inconvenience than we had expected — but great distress will soon arise again, & many extra measures must be adopted yet, before Ireland can be in anything like a state to take care of its own poverty.'[15]

To Sir Edward Blakeney, the Commander-in-Chief in Ireland, Anglesey in October 1847 dared 'not open upon the wide field of Irish distress and Irish misconduct. Depend upon it,' he wrote, 'England will no longer feed that country whose soil if properly worked would yield produce for a triple population.' Relating the problems of Ireland to those of Britain's defences, he went on: 'The money that has been expended in that unhappy land would have enabled the Empire to have placed itself in perfect security from foreign aggression and insult and to have assumed an attitude of defiance to all her enemies. This, alas! is far, very far from

being the case; we want everything! But what we most want is *Men*. We
ought to have an increase of at least 200,000.'[16]

Anglesey's last letter to Lord John Russell, before he finally left office
at the age of eighty-three, shows that he was still pegging away at the
same vital subject:

'*23 Janry, 1852*.... Apropos of our conversation yesterday, I must
upon further reflection say that your 80,000 volunteers (alone)
won't do. An augmentation of 40, (or at least) 30,000 men of the
Regular Army *might* do, but for anything like *security* the Militia
should be enrolled also, for you may depend upon it, that if this
country is attacked, it will be upon an enormous scale, and we ought
instantly to prepare to meet it with corresponding energy, and such
as would prevent the re-embarkation of a single man. But to effect
this, our Levies really must be well drilled & exercised & not a
moment should be lost. I cannot but think that if these demands upon
the Country were manfully made, they would be nobly responded
to.'[17]

*   *   *

During the years of his last term of office Anglesey was never so
infirm as to have to relinquish his favourite pastimes. At Beaudesert,
while his sons and guests were 'slaving and slaying all day', he took
'matters more easily, and 3 or 4 times a week *after* completely finishing my
dispatches, which I never fail to do, I take my gun, and (wonderful to
say) generally bring home 6 or 8 or so brace of Black Game, &c., J.
[possibly the keeper or a favourite dog] growling at my bad shooting,
the spectators in admiration that I can shoot at all.... I read all evening,
as long as is not bad for the eyes, and then Patience comes in aid.' In
December 1852 he announced to his friends and relations his intention of
placing 'shooting concerns upon a new footing. All are to come as they
like. There will be 3 days a week for covert shooting, the prescribed
number of guns will be announced at the breakfast table, and gentlemen
will arrange amongst themselves who are to be so employed and who are
to devote themselves to the Ladies.' How this further evidence of Anglesey's radical outlook struck the sporting conservatives of the eighteen-
fifties, there is no way of telling. His liberal hospitality at Beaudesert was
matched by that at Uxbridge House, where those who wished to dine of

an evening merely inscribed their names upon a slate kept for the purpose in the hall, under the watchful eye of the porter. He had, none the less, a powerful dislike of the professional diners-out who abounded in nineteenth-century society. He was known to refer to the activities of these spongers as 'cruising for a cutlet'.[18]

Certainly up to the summer of 1852, Anglesey never missed spending at least a part of the season at Cowes. In July of the previous year he and his 'dear boys' had set off for the Isle of Wight in separate yachts, he in his beloved *Pearl*, they in another named *Serpent*. From Cowes that morning he wrote to Char:

> 'There has been and still is so very severe a gale that you will be glad to hear that *Pearl* took up her moorings here at 6 o'clock this morning, and without an accident or the straining of even a rope yarn, as the saying is, altho' it has blown terrifically, and, in the most critical part of the passage, with a deluge of rain. I am most anxious to hear of my dear *Boys*, altho' I feel assured that they had the good sense to bear up and run for shelter which somehow or other, I never with all my good intentions and resolutions, am able to effect.'

He had lost sight of *Serpent* off Beachy Head in a 'very heavy uncomfortable sea'. A little later the gale had increased to such force that, having earlier stowed the mainsail and set the trisail, he now had to take

> 'two Reefs in the foresail, put the bowsprit in the slings and set the storm jib, and at it we went with the faint hope of getting round the Owers before dark. This however we were unable to accomplish, for the sea was indeed tremendous, and it had become so thick with such furious squalls of wind and rain that we had to grope our way as best we might in almost utter darkness, notwithstanding a full moon. At length ... we *tumbled upon* the Nab Light (for we really could not see twice the length of the Cutter), and finally took up our moorings here.... It really has been blowing a hurricane and poor *Pearl* has been smothered.'

This alarming night, it seems, had no ill effect upon Anglesey at the age of eighty-three. His 'dear boys', it is comforting to learn, being less adventurous than their father, had done as he hoped, and they turned up next day unscathed.[19]

The previous year, his friend the Emperor Nicholas, finding that his yacht the *Queen Victoria*, which had been built at Cowes, had not proved herself successful at 'a trial of speed made at Cronstadt', sent her over to the builder for advice and alterations. The builder, however, was not very helpful. The captain of the Imperial yacht was therefore ordered to consult Anglesey. 'You are the best judge on the subject,' wrote the Russian Ambassador, ' ... and I shall not fail to tell the Emperor that I have put his yacht under your own patronage.'[20]

* * *

His family and friends at times found him a rather formidable figure, though always a lovable one. The new fashion of afternoon tea, introduced in the 'forties by the Duchess of Bedford, did not meet with his approval, and he forbade his womenfolk to indulge the habit. This, however, did not stop them: they merely hid the tray under the sofa when the patriarchal footsteps were heard in the passage. One of his grandsons, a cornet in the Blues, found himself placed under arrest for failing to salute his Colonel. The unfortunate young man received the message: 'You may cut your grandfather when you like, but by G-d you *shall* salute your Colonel.'[21]

To the Lieutenant-Colonel of the Blues he wrote on one occasion:

'I am informed that Lord Otho FitzGerald has again applied to be allowed to serve on the Staff of the newly appointed Lord Lieutenant of Ireland. This is the third Governor General to attend upon whom he has received this indulgence, and by which he has thrown the Regimental duty, which *he* should have been performing, upon *his brother officers*! It is clear that it is not for *filthy lucre* that he shirks Regimental service ... it is not to learn something of his profession ... it is purely to lead the most idle and unprofitable of lives, and therefore I desire you to inform him, that he may be assured I will *never* recommend him for promotion in the R.H. Guards until after he shall have done an ample share of Regimental Duty.'

A father, wishing to gain a commission for his son in the Blues, received a reply similar to many sent by colonels of the Household Cavalry, past and present. 'It appears that your son has not attained the standard of height required for the Regiment of *Giants*, and altho' *I* set little value upon the stature of a man (& by the bye, neither does the *world*, for *it* has it that there is a great preponderance of *little* over *big* heroes) yet I must say that with our enormous helmets, and heavy jacked boots and gauntlets upto the elbows, it really does require much bulk to contend with these obstructions, and to avoid the appearance of being smothered by such incumbrances and lost amongst our *Leviathans....* I would rather advise his taking another line of service.'[22]

To a middle-aged nephew, on the point of quitting the army, he wrote: 'I cannot condemn you for the decision...but I own I should have better liked to see you in the full current which would have floated you down to the Colonelcy of a Regiment. My ambition was that we should all be Sailors or Soldiers, but it is otherwise ordered. This will probably lead you to a wife, whom you will probably secure as a good Nurse when you are reduced to a pair of Gouty Cloth Shoes! If you happen to be discharged at this moment, get into the train and come down here tomorrow.'[23]

* * *

The great event of the summer of 1851 was the International Exhibition held in Hyde Park. As Master-General, Anglesey supplied a number of sappers to help in constructional work, and also examples of the latest types of artillery. Letters of thanks from Prince Albert and from Earl Granville, who was in charge of the detailed arrangements, testify to the interest which he took in the 'Great Exhibition'. At the opening ceremony he was to be seen arm in arm with the Duke of Wellington, whose entry, as Cobden angrily noted, caused all other objects of interest to sink to insignificance.[24]

ii

I am a dreadful sufferer, but I keep going.
Anglesey to Cloncurry.[25]

It might be expected that Anglesey's grounds for quitting office just before his eighty-fourth birthday were connected with old age or ill health, but this was not the case. His final retirement came about upon the resignation of the Government of which he was the oldest member.[e] Towards the end of 1851, Palmerston, without consulting any of his colleagues, had formally recognized the new French government formed by Napoleon III after the *coup d'état* of December 2nd. Russell at once demanded and received the Foreign Secretary's resignation; but Palmerston soon hit back. In February 1852 he moved an extension to the Militia Bill which Russell, on Wellington's and Anglesey's prodding, had introduced as a minimum measure of protection against invasion. The amendment was carried by eleven votes, and the Government at once resigned. Thus, in his eighty-fifth year, Anglesey closed his official career, but his interest in politics remained alive to the very end. When, on Russell's fall, Stanley, his old colleague and antagonist of Irish days, became Tory Prime Minister as Lord Derby, Anglesey was for giving him a chance, but when he hung on after being defeated in the general election of 1852, he was caustic in his comments.

'I cannot for the life of me', he told the Duke of Bedford, 'make out how the very awkward squad, in whose incompetent hands the safety and interests of the Country are now placed, can carry on the duties of its charge, even in a time of repose and considerable prosperity; but what would it, what could it do if difficulties either internal or external were to assail it! I tremble at the prospect! But I am told and I fear that our own camp is in a very unsettled and disorderly state. How deplorable, how pitiful it is, that, with a host of able, of honest, of liberal and of independant men — many of them practiced statesmen — there should be mixed up amongst them so many unworthy crotchets; such jealousy, hatred, malice and all uncharitableness; that, with a vast mass of talent in the market, out of which there might be formed an invincible Government, we are to allow those Blunderers to retain office and bring disgrace on the Country. Such things ought not to be: they might be averted: but who will undertake to bring together so many jarring interests!'[26]

When, after Derby's short-lived administration had collapsed, just such a government as Anglesey desired had been formed under Lord Aberdeen, he was delighted. He wrote to Lord Lansdowne, who had refused to undertake the task which had fallen to Aberdeen, 'there is enough of strength of intellect and of talent to supply men for *two* Cabinets.' As to the new Prime Minister (though he would have preferred Lansdowne), Anglesey's slight acquaintance with Aberdeen gave him a high opinion of his integrity; 'he has not however I fear a very winning manner.' As to what Anglesey may have thought of the foreign policy of the Government immediately before the declaration of war with Russia, there is no record, for that event took place only a month before his death, when his infirmities made it difficult for him either to write or to talk. There remains only the very old man of action's complaint, written four months before the end: 'It is terrible to be so old as to have no chance of having a finger in the pie.'[27]

*   *   *

The last years of Anglesey's life were darkened by two great sorrows. On September 14th, 1852, the Duke of Wellington died. For years past they had been the closest of old cronies, frequently dining in each other's houses, drawn together at social functions not only by the affinity in their ages and the fact that they were virtually the only survivors of their generation of military heroes, but also by the ever-increasing deafness which they shared. In the House of Lords, on occasion, distinguished peers in full forensic flood would be disconcerted to find attention wandering from their speeches to the entry of two very old gentlemen conducting a noisy dialogue which would continue long after they had taken their seats. Now all that was over, and Anglesey remained the solitary survivor of a great comradeship, and the only senior commander present at Waterloo to outlive his chief. Now, too, with the exception of members of the Royal Family, he had the distinction of being the only living Field Marshal in the British Army.

To Charles Wellesley, the second son of the Duke, Anglesey wrote on hearing the news of his father's death: 'Whatever may be the arrangements for the funeral of your illustrious father, I beg you to believe and I request you to make known to Douro [the 2nd Duke] ... that if there is any part I could take upon the occasion of this dreadful calamity, which might enable me to evince my unbounded veneration for, and affectionate attachment to that invaluable friend and unerring Chief I would avail myself of it with avidity and at a moment's notice.' In consequence, at the great state funeral in St Paul's on November 18th, the most spectacular ever accorded to a non-royal personage — the procession watched by a million and a half spectators, the cathedral crammed with 20,000 others — Anglesey was given the honour of bearing the dead Field Marshal's baton. Detained at the great west door for more than an hour because the complicated machinery for removing the coffin from the bier (which weighed twelve tons and was drawn by as many horses) failed at first to work, he frequently exclaimed that he had never been so cold in his life before. Nevertheless his friend Lord Seaton (Colborne of Corunna days) states that 'all the *old* boys bore the breeze well, and I have not heard that they suffered from it.'[28] As the coffin slowly sank through the floor, Anglesey, moved by an irresistible impulse, stepped forward and, with tears streaming down his cheeks, placed his hand upon it, in a moving gesture of farewell.

*　　*　　*

The second and perhaps more desolating bereavement which Anglesey suffered was the death of his beloved Char. She died at Uxbridge House on July 11th, 1853, three days before her seventy-second birthday. On New Year's Day three and a half years earlier, she had written her husband a touching letter, which showed that the circumstances of her elopement and second marriage had not been banished from her mind, and that her preoccupation with religion, for which she had been noted at the time of that marriage forty-one years earlier, was as strong as ever. It is such a typical product of the mid-Victorian mind that it is here reproduced almost in full.

'We have both been mercifully preserved through a length of years beyond the usual allotment to man, & I sincerely hope that you may still be spared for the sake of many to whom your existence is of so much importance! My own life is of little use to any Body — but time *must* be short for us both, & life fast dying away, & our latter days can *only be valuable* to ourselves as giving us a longer period for preparation to meet our Heavenly Father.... It is a solemn subject for *us* to reflect upon *by-gone days*, past to us as if they had never been, but not so with God; in his memory every sin is recorded, and to him we must ere long give an account of all our deeds as if he were in ignorance — This we are distinctly told in his holy word, but in that blessed Book we are as clearly promised *perfect forgiveness* if we approach him deeply humbled under a sense of our sins — I feel certain that you go with me now in these things, altho' we may differ upon more trifling points our hopes and dependance rest entirely in our Saviour; without his mediation & death, what would have become of *us?* —
'If it should please God to take me first I am sure that my dying moments will be soothed by the reflexions which your *present* state

of mind affords me, & I pray God that you may go on daily advancing in holiness, for there is need of improvement in all of us! We have all the same means given by which *alone* we can be carried forward, & in the end obtain what we ask for — the Kingdom of Heaven — *There* I trust my dearest that we shall be re-united, joined by all our dear Children *yours* & *mine* — I must beg of you to convey my kindest love & *best* wishes to those of *your* Children who may like to receive the last expressions of affection & gratitude from one who was deeply sensible of their invariable kindness, and altho' some may have shewn more *generosity of feeling* towards me than others I shall die in the same spirit of kindness towards them all — I had no right to expect it from any — and for yourself, my dearest, pray accept every assurance of my entire forgiveness, *as I ask for yours* upon any subject which may have occur'd between ourselves to cause unhappy feelings on either side — Let us look forward to the joyful expectation of meeting hereafter in that blessed Kingdom where all will be peace & harmony — Your bodily sufferings have been fearful! — only equal'd by the patient submission with which you have borne them, (I really believe) in dutiful submission to the will of God — If the humble prayers of an humble Individual can avail anything mine will surely have been heard, so constantly offer'd up for your support under your trials, and above all, for your spiritual welfare, & they will continue to my life's end — God bless you....

'I have directed that Adelaide may have my little personal property, composed of a few articles (not worth dividing) with a reserve of some Trinkets to the other Children, but of course you will make what alterations you please. I hope you will always keep my old gold repeating Watch and let Uxbridge have it at your death — He was always kind to me & to *my Children* which I have deeply felt.

'I beg of you to allow My Burial to be as quiet as possible but *take care that I am really dead* beforehand — The less expence the better pleased I should be, & therefore let me be peacefully & *quietly* deposited wherever I may happen to die.

'Once more God bless you!

'B[eau] Desert, Jany 1850.'[29]

The funeral took place quietly, as was her wish, and she was buried in the crypt of Lichfield Cathedral, in the presence of her husband and only eighteen other official mourners, all of them close male relations. With Lady Anglesey's passing, there had vanished from the London scene a familiar sight, for the old lady, suffering perhaps from slight *folie de grandeur*, never drove out in the metropolis without outriders preceding her carriage-and-four. This was in contrast to her husband's more economical mode of transport: to the very last weeks of his life, if he was not riding his horse, he was to be seen driving a two-horse curricle, a single groom perched up behind.

'I have nothing to say of myself', he told his daughter, Lady Sandwich, a week or so after the funeral, 'save that I am well, but that every hour seems to increase the gloom occasioned by our irreparable loss, and I do believe that it will still increase, nor have I the least disposition to throw it off. On the contrary I rather indulge in it.

'All this, however, need not, ought not, does not interfere with our worldly concerns, and experience shews that the most grievous afflictions are softened down by time, and yet I am perfectly certain that the impression of the amiable qualities of your excellent mother, will never be effaced, no, not even weakened, in those who loved her (and who did not love her who knew her!), and so we have only to indulge in our sorrows, and not attempt to shirk them.'[30]

Less than a month later his son George caused him further grief, for he took the inopportune moment to announce his desire to marry his first cousin, Agnes, daughter of Sir Arthur Paget. Anglesey objected not only to the close relationship, but also to the fact that she had no fortune. There were more pathetic reasons, too.

'I have much and earnestly tried to reconcile myself to a measure which has for some time appeared inevitable,' he informed his son, 'but the truth is (as is indeed the case in the loss of your excellent mother) the more I reflect upon it, the more I endeavour to extract from it future good from present evil, the less do I succeed and the more gloomy and distressing are the prospects. There may be selfishness in this. I cannot deny it. In your mother I lose an amiable, an agreeable, an attached companion of near 50 years. Upon you I had set my heart as upon a trusty *crutch*, on whom to lean, and with but little more than your professional duties to abstract you from me. Upon your success and advancement in your profession I had looked forward with the anxious hope that a brilliant career was opening to you which might bring honor upon the family. Such hopes vanish at once. At your age and that of Agnes [George was thirty-five and Agnes twenty-two] it would be absurd in me to attempt to put a veto upon your union, and with the view of turning you from it, to diminish the means on which you might have counted. I can do no such thing. You may be assured that I shall make no unfavourable alterations in my intentions towards you.... I shall lament in silence the step you are about to take, but I will not thwart your wishes, and in proof of the absence of all unkindly feeling, I will place in your hands, in aid of outfit, the same sum that your sisters had as a trousseau upon their marriage. You have my blessing and hearty prayers for your happiness.'[31]

*   *   *

The last two letters preserved in Anglesey's own hand — by now, for the first time, showing signs of shakiness — well illustrate the pathos of a lonely, failing, deaf old man. The first of these he wrote on November 2nd to his daughter, Lady Sydney:

'My dearest Emily,
'What are you about — Who is with you — Who do you expect? When I know all this *honestly*, I shall think of offering myself to you, but you know that I am no better than a mute. I go on Friday to see how the Pearl is getting on [alterations were being made to his beloved yacht]. I shall return in the evening.'

And later the same day, upon receiving an answer:

'When your company leave you, I will pay you a visit, but I do most seriously beg of you not to betray me to anyone of your party — It is unexceptionable, yet I should not feel comfortable amongst them.'[32]

*   *   *

On the morning of February 1st, 1854, as Anglesey was taking his customary morning's walk, a gentleman who knew him by sight noticed him leaning against a lamp-post. He approached, and discovered that 'his weakness', in the words of The Times, 'was the result of an attack of paralysis.' In other words he had suffered a stroke. He was helped back to Uxbridge House, where medical aid was at once called in.[33]

On March 28th, Britain and France declared war upon Russia. In early April, Anglesey wrote to his son Clarence, who had sailed with the naval expedition sent to the Baltic at the beginning of March: 'I with difficulty hold a pen. I am very bad, indeed a cripple. For three weeks I have not left my chair or bed, and can scarcely move a muscle over every part of my body. This must be my excuse for not writing *much*, for I have *much* to say.' In a postscript he added that Lord Raglan, who had been appointed to command the expedition to the Crimea, and the Duke of Cambridge, the Commander-in-Chief, had gone that day to Paris, so as to co-ordinate the Anglo-French army. 'I wonder what the Cronstadt Fleet will do? Stay at home I suspect. I fear they [the Russians] have no ships at Revel for you.... Alas! That I can have no chance of going out to see you, but I am prostrate. Pearl promises exceedingly well. She *might* I believe be out by June, but what chance have I? Alas none.... I hope you use Steam as little as possible. Reserve it for great occasions.'[34]

These, so far as can be established, are his last written words. At six o'clock in the evening of Friday, April 29th, eighteen days short of his eighty-sixth birthday, he died at Uxbridge House, surrounded by a large number of sons, daughters, daughters-in-law, sons-in-law, and grand-children. His last words are said to have been: 'What brigade is on duty?' When assured that it was not his own, he seemed much relieved that he was not neglecting his turn.

*   *   *

It had at first been the intention of the family that the interment should be private, but the Queen made it known that she wished there to be a state funeral. Accordingly, on Thursday, May 4th, the body lay in state in the mortuary room at Uxbridge House, and on the following morning, at half past ten, it was borne through the streets of London to King's Cross station. On top of the coffin the dead man's coronet and Field Marshal's baton lay upon a crimson velvet cushion. The hearse was drawn by six horses with black ostrich-feathers and escutcheons, and accompanied by an escort of the Blues, whose band played 'The Dead March' from *Saul*. The procession included four mourning coaches, each drawn by four horses, containing the chief mourners, followed by 'the late Marquis's carriage and horses; the Queen's carriage; Prince Albert's carriage; the Duchess of Gloucester's carriage; the Duchess of Kent's carriage. The French Ambassador's carriage followed next; and after that, sixty belonging to the nobility and gentry; the melancholy cavalcade', reported the *Illustrated London News*, 'proceeding *en route* to the terminus.' The special train arrived at Lichfield station at half past four. The body was then conveyed to the George Hotel, where two hundred men of the Staffordshire Militia formed a guard of honour around it. Several thousand people filed past the coffin that evening, as it lay in the assembly room of the hotel. It was covered all over with crimson Genoa velvet, studded with gold nails; over each of the massive gold handles was a Marquess's coronet, while the head panel was adorned by the badge of the Garter, and the panel at the foot by that of the Bath. The coffin plate bore the following inscription:

> The Most Honourable
> HENRY WILLIAM PAGET
> First Marquess of Anglesey,
> Earl of Uxbridge,
> Baron Paget of Beaudesert,
> Field Marshal,
> Colonel of the Royal Horse Guards,
> Lord-Lieutenant and Custos Rotulorum of the
>   Counties of Anglesey and Stafford,
> Constable of Carnarvon Castle,
> Ranger of Snowdon Forest,
> Vice-Admiral of the Coast of North Wales and
>   Carmarthenshire,
> Captain of Cowes Castle,
> Privy Councillor,
> K.G., G.C.B., K.St.P., G.C.H.,
> Knight of Maria Theresa of Austria,
> Knight of St George of Russia,
> Knight of William of Holland.[35]

The funeral next day was preceded by the tolling from an early hour in the morning of the great bell of the cathedral. Soon after eleven o'clock the procession left the hotel and made its way along streets lined by men of the various Staffordshire regiments. The hearse, with the Paget arms blazoned on the pall, was followed by carriages containing a veritable host of family mourners. 'It is questionable', commented *The Times*, 'whether on any previous occasion so many immediate relatives and connexions followed the head of a family to his last home.' When the service was over, the body was lowered into the family vault from a point outside the cathedral walls. Today a small brass plaque, not easy to discover, is the sole indication of the whereabouts of Anglesey's last resting-place.

*   *   *

The passing, thirty-nine years after Waterloo, of the 'Iron Duke's' second-in-command at that memorable battle was little noticed by the press or by the public at large. Attention, not unnaturally, was almost wholly focused upon the month-old war with Russia. The dispatch of troops to the East, and the news which daily poured in of the attitudes and intentions of Britain's allies, filled the newspapers to the virtual exclusion of less pressing matters. *The Times*, however, in a telling leading article about Anglesey's death crystallized, for those who read it, contemporary opinion upon what it called

'an event which, in the course of nature, might have been looked for long before it really occurred.' It went on: 'It can scarcely be denied that his civil abilities were such as distinguished him among several successive generations of patrician legislators. To the qualifications or position of a statesman we believe that he never throughout his long career made any pretension. The field of battle was a more appropriate scene for his exertions.... Since the soldier's drawn sword first glittered in the sunshine, never did a more fearless or more chivalrous officer support the honour of his country than the brave old man to whose memory we are now endeavouring to offer a tribute of respect....

'He was one of the few links left between the present and the past. It requires almost as violent a mental jerk for a man who is now in the prime of life to realize to himself the society of the PRINCE REGENT, as it would to form a just appreciation of that period of French history in which LOUIS XV gave himself up to the sway of Madame DE POMPADOUR. If we want to know anything of the period in which EDMUND BURKE perorated to empty benches, and wrote for immortality — when SHERIDAN burnished up witticisms, and forgot to pay his debts — we must painfully fag our way through histories and contemporary memoirs, and collections of letters, and gossip.

Even then, it is probable that a reader will only dress up the impressions of his own time in the outward costume of another, with regard to their essence and reality. That is all we could hope to do with the period when GEORGE, Prince of Wales, first broke away from his pedagogues, and burst upon the town. Lord ANGLESEY was a youth then — the contemporary of that very dissolute Prince whom we buried at Windsor a quarter of a century ago — a jaded voluptuary, exhausted with well-nigh seventy years of luxury and self-indulgence. Let those who are not in the habit of recurring to dates reflect that GEORGE III came to the throne in the year 1760 — rejoicing, as he said — poor man! — in the name of Briton; that GEORGE, Prince of Wales was born in 1762, and the Marquis of ANGLESEY in 1768. He was thus a year older than NAPOLEON BONAPARTE, and NAPOLEON died on the 5th of May, 1821 — that is to say, 33 years ago — at the age of 52.... To most of us the *Diaries* of Lord BYRON offer much agreeable information as to the condition of London society when he was a young man, just returned from the Levant. He tells us of the dandies and exquisites of that time, and to us they are historical figures. Now, these men were to Lord ANGLESEY mere boys. He had rounded Cape Forty before they devised their waistcoats, or established their impertinent canons of bad taste. He had been a dandy when they were learning to walk, or, more probable still, lay puling in the arms of their nurses. He had become a man and put away childish things. He had won reputation with the Duke of YORK in Flanders. He had married his first wife; children had been born to him; and his marriage had been dissolved. He had courted death at the cannon's mouth — at the lance's point — by the sabre's edge, in order to shake off an existence which he thought insupportable, and never, surely did man give greater proofs of sincerity. Upon this point of his history we will not enlarge, for certainly the moment is ill-chosen for reflecting upon failings and weaknesses which occurred half-a-century back, and were redeemed by half-a-century of devotion. For ourselves, we confess we take pleasure in the recollection of the old man's stately form as he was to be seen amongst us, the very model — as it is expressed by the hackneyed phrase — 'of an officer and a gentleman'. He was not only this. He belonged to a race of nobles who have passed away from among us; he was the last of the race, and we shall know them no more. Your modern English peer is a sharp land agent or conveyancer, or a jocular, hair-splitting law lord, or, if he be of a younger generation, he is a painful devourer of blue-books — a man ready to talk for three hours upon the condition of Central Asia, or the statistics of dandelions in the county of Salop; but a nobleman he is not in the sense in which Lord ANGLESEY was one. Society may possibly have gained by the change — we simply notify the fact that a genus is extinct of which Lord ANGLESEY was a brilliant example....

'We saw him continually and everywhere. In the parks, in the streets, in assemblies and parties, or stretching down Long Reach in the *Pearl*, with his great mainsail set, Lord ANGLESEY was ever about among his countrymen. More than this, he was always ready with a kind act for those whom he could oblige, and with a courteous denial for those who had asked from him that which it was not in his power to give. If he did not act the highest part in the world's history, all he did he did well, and that throughout well nigh fourscore years and ten.... Wherever the news of his death is told all will be sorry that "old Lord ANGLESEY is gone at last," and have a kind word and a kind thought for his memory. With him the old race of nobles is well-nigh burnt out.'[36]

NOTES

CHAPTER I (p. 19 to p. 23)

ᵃ THE BAYLY FAMILY. Unreliable evidence and family tradition suggest that the Baylys were descended from Renard de Bailleul, who came to England with William of Normandy,[1] and whose descendants included a line of Scottish kings and the founder of Balliol College, Oxford. Another was John Baillie, who is believed to have settled in the Island of Anglesey early in the sixteenth century, and to have been the forbear of LEWIS BAYLY, Bishop of Bangor. This distinguished divine, thought to have been born in Carmarthen, was the author of a book, *The Practice of Piety*, which enjoyed the widest fame among puritans in the seventeenth and eighteenth centuries, being translated into many languages. Bunyan ascribed to its influence the beginning of his spiritual experiences; it was republished in London as late as 1842. Bishop Bayly was chaplain to Henry, Prince of Wales, and on his death, to Charles I. His wife was the daughter of Sir Henry Bagenal (Bagnal) (1556?-98), who succeeded his father as Queen Elizabeth's marshal of the army in Ireland, and whose mother was the daughter of Sir Edward Griffith of Penrhyn, near Bangor in Caernarvonshire. Through Sir Henry's daughter came the Irish and Welsh estates of the Baylys and Pagets, including Plas Newydd, Anglesey. Bishop Bayly's son and heir, NICHOLAS BAYLY of Plas Newydd, was Governor of Galway and the Isles of Arran, and a Gentleman of the Bedchamber to Charles II. His son, EDWARD, created a baronet in 1730, was the father of SIR NICHOLAS BAYLY. (*See genealogical table I.*)

ᵇ THE CHAMPAGNÉ FAMILY. JANE CHAMPAGNÉ's father was the Very Reverend ARTHUR CHAMPAGNÉ, Dean of Clonmacnoise in Ireland, whose grandfather, Josias de Robillard, Chevalier Seigneur de Champagné, and his wife Maria (probably a granddaughter of Charles, Duc de la Rochefoucauld, and niece of the author of the famous *Réflexions ou Sentences et Maximes Morales*), had fled from France with their family after Louis XIV had revoked the Edict of Nantes in 1685. Maria has left an account of the manner in which her children were smuggled from France.

'On April 10th, 1687, my four daughters and my two youngest boys ... left La Rochelle. It was night. The head of a wine cask was knocked out, the wine was emptied into the sea, and they were put inside the cask. The vessel in which they sailed was only eighteen tons burthen. They paid twelve hundred francs for the passage.'

Maria with the rest of her family followed some months later.

'We were put down into the hold [she wrote] upon a quantity of salt, and for eight days we remained there well concealed, the ship being at anchor. The vessel was searched without our being discovered. We set sail, and arrived at Falmouth eight days after, not without trepidation and much risk.'[2]

Her husband escaped to Holland, came over to England from there as a captain in the army of William III, and died two months after his arrival. His youngest son fought at the battle of the Boyne, and married Lady Jane Forbes, a daughter of the second Earl of Granard. Their son was the father of Jane Champagné, whose mother was also of Huguenot stock.

Eight years before Jane's marriage to Henry Bayly, his sister had married Lord Forbes, later 5th Earl of Granard, whose great-aunt was Jane's grandmother. This double connection with the Granards points to a close friendship between the two families, and accounts for Jane's marriage taking place at Castle Forbes, the seat of the family. (*See genealogical table I.*)

° THE EARLY PAGETS. WILLIAM, 1ST BARON PAGET (1505-63): of his origins nothing is certain, though a lease among the family papers reveals the existence of a John Pachet, 'citizen and shereman', living in Coleman Street, London, not later than 1524,[3] and the records of the Court of Aldermen of London disclose that William Patchet, serjeant-at-mace, had a son living in 1527 who was vicar of St Stephen's, Coleman Street.[4] It is thought that this serjeant-at-mace, who was born near Wednesbury, Staffordshire, 'of mean Parentage', was the father of the first baron.[5] A Staffordshire historian, unsupported, states that the family were 'nailers, or rather nail factors, who gathered the nails from the forgers and placed them on the market as merchandise'.[6] Paget's low birth was the chief reason given when he was temporarily degraded from the Order of the Garter in 1552, it being said that 'he was no gentleman of bloud, neither of father's side nor mother's side'.[7] In the *Visitation of Staffordshire*, 1583, Paget's father is given as 'Pagitt, of London, mediocris fortunae vir'.[8] Pachets, Pacchets and Pacchettes occur between 1275 and 1452 in the *Gresley MSS* at Drakelowe. They are described as being of Nether Seal, Co. Leicester, not a great way from Burton-upon-Trent. In the catalogue of the *Gresley MSS* there are mentioned several agreements between the Gresley and Paget families concerning a fulling-mill at Burton. Those Paget family papers which are now at Burton contain grants of land at Spittelscheyle (Seal, Co. Leicester) made by Pouwerus Pachet in 1313, 1317 and 1322.[9] Collins' *Peerage* (1735) mentions a Lewis Paget, 'gentleman of Staffordshire', who in the 11th year of Henry VII signed a certificate relating to the office of Master of the Game of Cankerwood.

Paget, a protégé of Stephen Gardiner, served Henry VIII as a secretary of state, was one of his chief advisers, and an executor of his Will. From the 1540s onwards, many of the King's more delicate diplomatic negotiations were entrusted to him. The Emperor Charles V is said to have remarked that Paget deserved 'as well to be a King as to represent one', and in comparing the three English ambassadors who had been sent to him from time to time, that Wolsey had promised much and done nothing, Morrisson had promised and done much, while Paget had promised nothing and done all.[10] The *Spanish State Papers*[11] show him to have been an extraordinarily clever negotiator.

In the reign of Edward VI, one of whose governors he had been appointed by

Henry VIII, he was a supporter of 'Protector' Somerset. Two years after Edward's accession, Paget was arrested on a charge of conspiring against Warwick's life; this indictment having failed, his accounts as Chancellor of the Duchy of Lancaster were found to be corrupt. Thus the enemies of Somerset managed to deprive Paget of honours, lands and goods. On the death of Edward VI, having been partially restored to favour before that event, he joined Lady Jane Grey's council, possibly under constraint, for he was one of those who sanctioned the proclamation of Mary as Queen. With Mary and Philip he was for most of their reign in high favour, being made Lord Privy Seal in 1555 and employed once more upon foreign missions.

When Mary was thought to be pregnant, Philip applied to Parliament for an Act to make him Regent during the child's infancy, giving a promise that when the infant was of age to govern he would surrender the regency. In the Lords the Bill was on the point of being carried when Paget, it is said, asked 'Pray who shall sue the King's Bond?', meaning that Philip as Regent would virtually be King, and that as the King was paramount even above Parliament, no power in the country could keep him to his word. As a result of Paget's intervention the Bill was negatived.[12]

On the accession of Elizabeth I, Paget retired. Six years later he died, possessed of considerable fortune and large estates. Chief of these was that of Beaudesert, which had been granted him by Henry VIII. He obtained other church lands from time to time, including those of the dissolved Abbey of Burton, some of which still remain in the family. He also acquired estates at West Drayton and Uxbridge. [The deed of acquisition of the mitred Benedictine Abbey of Burton is dated 1546. The Abbey lands included properties in Derbyshire, Warwickshire, Leicestershire and Cheshire. The records of the Abbey, including Ethelred II's confirmation of an earlier charter, dated 1004, are remarkably complete and date from 956. The Letters Patent conveying the manor and lands of West Drayton (which had previously belonged to the Dean and Chapter of St Paul's, London) from the King to Sir William Paget (as he then was) are of the same date as the Burton Abbey deed, 1546.[13] These lands in Middlesex were sold by Henry Bayly in 1773 and 1778.]

Paget is credited with the following axioms: 'Fly the courte, Speke little, Care less, Desire nothing, Never earnest, In answer cold, Learne to spare, Spend in measure, Care for home, Pray often, Live better, And Dye well.'[14] It was said of him that 'his education was better than his birth; his knowledge higher than his education; his parts above his knowledge, and his experience above his parts.'[15] His portraits, depicting him in middle age, disclose a long face, wearing a sphinxlike expression upon it, with ginger hair, large nose and forked beard.[16]

His sons included HENRY, 2ND BARON, who died a few years after his father, and was of little consequence; THOMAS, 3RD BARON (1543/4-90), who partly rebuilt Beaudesert, and CHARLES (d. 1612). All three were Roman Catholic exiles and conspirators. The 3rd Baron was succeeded by his son WILLIAM, 4TH BARON (1572-1629), a staunch Protestant, who was with Essex at the taking of Cadiz in 1596. He was a Commissioner for Virginia, an original member of the Bermudas Company for the plantation of the Somers Islands, where a fort and a tribe were named after him, a member of the Council of the Amazon River Company, and had connections with the East India Company.[17] (See genealogical table I.)

ᵈ It is believed that he may, in the first place, have received a patent with limitation to heirs male; but no such patent is known to exist. By *fine I Mary*, he entailed his estates on his sons and their issue male, with eventual remainder to his own issue female, ignoring his heirs general, from which it may be deduced that he expected the barony to descend to the heirs male of his body.[18]

ᵉ THE LATER PAGETS. WILLIAM, 5TH BARON PAGET (1609-78) (son-in-law of Henry Rich, Earl of Holland, who was beheaded in 1649), voted, in 1640, against the King in the Lords, and was one of those who petitioned him to summon a parliament for the redress of grievances. It was only when he realized that the Parliament actually intended a resort to arms that he joined the King. His reasons were put in a letter which was read to the Commons. He raised a regiment for the King which did good service at Edgehill. His estates were sequestered by the Commonwealth, and he was fined £1,000. At the Restoration his petitions to make good his losses were not attended to. The compiler of a seventeenth-century list of the gentry of Staffordshire described his character thus, 'Noe parts that I know of except a good stomack.'[19]

His eldest son, WILLIAM, 6TH BARON (1637-1713), was a distinguished diplomatist, first in Vienna, and then, from 1693, as ambassador-extraordinary to Turkey, where his prudent negotiations resulted in the Treaty of Carlowitz, 1699. He was much liked by the Sultan of Turkey, who personally persuaded William III to keep him on at his Court, and who loaded him with presents when he eventually left for home in 1702. Of these he presented twelve superb Turkish horses to Queen Anne. He undertook a number of other special diplomatic missions before he died. He was the father of the 1st Earl of Uxbridge (of the first creation), and uncle of Brigadier-General Thomas Paget, the maternal grandfather of Henry Bayly. General Paget became a Groom of the Bedchamber to George I in 1727, and later Governor of Minorca. (*See genealogical table I.*)

ᶠ Peter Walter's grandfather (also called Peter) had amassed a considerable fortune in the course of a dubious career as steward to several noblemen of the day, chief among whom was the Duke of Newcastle. At his death his estate was computed at £300,000.[20] He was the original of Peter Pounce in Fielding's *Joseph Andrews*, and is frequently alluded to by Pope, who referred to him as 'a dexterous attorney'.[21]

There are three isolated pieces of evidence showing connections between the Walter family and the Pagets and Baylys, but they do no more than accentuate the mystery which surrounds the relationship:

1 Peter Walter (grandfather) was at one time steward to the 1st Earl of Uxbridge (of the first creation), who died in 1743.[22]

2 The father of the Peter Walter who made the Will was called *Paget* Walter.

3 Up to her death in 1828, an annuity of £300 was paid by the head of the Paget family to Mrs Bullock, the only child of the Peter Walter who made the Will.[23]

ᵍ Two years after his marriage, but eleven years before the Will came into effect, Henry Bayly wished to borrow money on the securities of the Dorset Estates. Counsel's opinion was sought, but it has not been possible to discover whether he in fact achieved his purpose.[24]

ʰ THE EARLS OF UXBRIDGE OF THE FIRST CREATION. The 7TH BARON
PAGET (d. 1743) was created Earl of Uxbridge in 1714, soon after his appointment as
envoy-extraordinary to the Elector of Hanover, who was to come to England later
that year as George I. He had been M.P. for Staffordshire from 1695 to 1711, was a
Lord of the Treasury, and Captain of the Yeomen of the Guard.

His son, THOMAS CATESBY PAGET (1689-1741/2), a Gentleman of the Bedchamber to
George II, was an amateur poet and writer, whose works 'were compos'd for the
Noble Author's own Amusement in the Country, during the intervals of bad Weather,
in Hunting-seasons'. They so closely imitated Pope's that Paget was thought for some
time to be the author of the anonymous 'Essay on Man'.[25] He was the father of the
8TH BARON, second and last Earl of Uxbridge of the first creation, who was reputed
to have an inordinate love of money. (*See genealogical table I.*)

ⁱ This he did by placing him under William Cramer and Jan Dussek. Later he
procured for him the post of organist at St Mary's Church in Stafford, and as late as
1810 he is to be found in a similar one at Rugely, near Beaudesert. In 1789, Lord
Uxbridge installed an organ in Uxbridge House in London and engaged the leading
performers of the day to play upon it. Among these was Charles Wesley, nephew of
the great evangelist and elder brother of the more famous musician Samuel Wesley.
Charles Wesley gave recitals at Uxbridge House every year up to 1811.[26]

ʲ The Westminster School lists (kindly made available by the joint editors of the
Record of Old Westminsters) show Paget to have been placed in III Form on his
admission (8 Sep. 1777); to have been in 28th place in IV Form in July 1779; in 6th
place in February and 9th in April 1780. In July that year he moved up to V Form
and in 1781 to 'Shell', in which he was placed 18th later in the year. At this point the
lists stop. This information shows him to have been a schoolboy of about average
scholastic achievement.

ᵏ Robert's boat-building yard was one of a number on the South Bank. It continued
in being, on the site of the present St Thomas's Hospital, till 1852.[27]

ˡ Captain William Paget, R.N., was a year and a half younger than his brother. He
died in 1794, as the result of the reopening of a wound inflicted some years before
by an assassin in Constantinople. In the previous year, at the early age of 24, he had
been promoted post captain, and given command of the *Romney*, 50 guns. On 17th
June, 1794, while escorting a convoy westwards from Smyrna, he captured a French
frigate (*La Sybille*, 48 guns) and three merchantmen, after a brilliant action which
lasted an hour and ten minutes. When the French commodore surrendered his sword,
Paget, in recognition of his bravery, gave him his own in exchange. *La Sybille* lost
55 killed and 103 wounded, *Romney* only 10 killed and 28 wounded. That Paget was
an outstandingly skilful officer the details of the action amply show;[28] that he was
deeply loved and respected by officers and men is clear from the high praise lavished
upon him at his death three months later. Captain Thomas Fremantle, later to become
a distinguished member of Nelson's 'band of brothers', writing from Gibraltar to his

brother William Fremantle, says, 'You will be sorry, tho' not acquainted with him to hear that my good and worthy friend Paget died on his passage from Smyrna. What we who loved him have so truly felt upon this melancholy subject you must judge.... I had almost said I wished you had known him but you are in happiness in not. I do not think in my life I ever saw a man of so amiable a disposition, a better officer, or one who was so universally beloved & respected.... I almost dread the funeral in the morning.'[29]

CHAPTER II (p. 24 to p. 40)

[a] No letter telling his father of his misfortune survives.

[b] On arrival at Calais Paget had reported to his father that M. St Germain was 'half dead' but would write as soon as he had recovered from his seasickness, which he said 'was worse than he ever experienced'. They had not been long at Lausanne before the tutor was 'very ill indeed; he looked wretchedly and speaks thoroughly like a sick man.'

[c] A traveller who met Paget soon afterwards, wrote home that the young man had been 'banished the republic for life'. He went on: 'the commandant of a French city would have laughed at such a circumstance, as childish, and beneath his attention; and I think the magistrates of Geneva should have been satisfied with reprimanding the offenders, if only in consideration of their being young men and foreigners; but impatient of opposition to their authority, and fearful that private disturbance might produce general insurrection, they judged with violence and punished with severity.'[1]

[d] The police report on this incident tells a rather different story. On July 25th there took place some horse races at Plan-les-Ouates, organized by a number of young Englishmen staying in Geneva and Lausanne. In the evening there was a dinner in the famous 'Les Balances' inn, where Paget had been staying for a week. At two in the morning of the 26th, *four* of the party of fifteen Englishmen (Charles Parkhurst, who was lodging in Geneva; Francis Sykes, aged 20, an officer in the dragoon guards; Henry Weston, son of a resident of Lausanne, and Paget), '*wanting to go for a run in the country*', woke up M. Cayla the Mayor, to obtain permission for the gates to be opened. When Cayla refused, they insulted him and became riotous, whereupon he sent for the guards, with whom they fought. They were imprisoned for six days until the Duke of Gloucester, who was staying at Coppet, intervened on July 31st, asking for their release. They were handed over to the Duke next day and he ordered them to leave the town.[2]

[e] The Tory, George Rose, wrote at about this time that Uxbridge had 'threatened to turn his eldest son, Lord Paget, out of Parliament if he voted with Mr Pitt in his late opposition to Mr Addington.'[3]

CHAPTER III (p. 41 to p. 54)

ᵃ Lieutenant (7th Royal Fusiliers), March 11th; captain (23rd Fusiliers), March 25th; major (65th Foot), May 20th, and lieutenant-colonel (16th Light Dragoons) June 15th, 1795.

ᵇ On 16th May, 1801, he was made full colonel of the regiment in place of Sir David Dundas.

For a full report upon the numerous regimental papers at Plas Newydd dealing with the 7th Light Dragoons (Hussars) during Paget's period of command, see 'The Life of a Light Cavalry Regiment' by T. H. McGuffie, which is appearing serially in *The Journal of the Society for Army Historical Research*. The first instalment appeared in vol. XXXVIII, no. 154, June 1960.

ᶜ His sister Louisa, writing in 1801 to her fiancé, said that 'as Paget left Lady Paget a fortnight after they were married, I shall be neither surprized or disconcerted at your going to your Regt and leaving me, a week after we are married.'[1]

CHAPTER IV (p. 55 to p. 62)

ᵃ Very similar tactics were used by Paget at Benavente in 1808 (see p. 85).

ᵇ The day's casualties were: 7th Light Dragoons, 2 killed, 9 wounded or missing; 11th Light Dragoons, 9 killed, 18 wounded.

ᶜ The 7th's strength on September 25th had been 669 all ranks. On October 24th it had sunk to 389.

ᵈ Edward Ball Hughes later fell desperately in love with Paget's daughter, Jane, who at the last moment, it is said, turned him down flat.

CHAPTER V (p. 63 to p. 88)

ᵃ A Spanish army had won a great victory against the French at Baylen in the south in July, but another had been beaten five days before at Medina de Rioseco in the north.

ᵇ Including Moore. The other two besides Paget were the Hon. John Hope, and Mackenzie Fraser. Moore, together with Hope, Paget and Fraser, on landing on August 25th, had tried to persuade Dalrymple to stand aside as they themselves had done, so as to allow Wellesley to retain command of his division; but Dalrymple would not.

ᶜ Joaquin Blake was of Irish blood. There were a number of such officers in the Spanish armies.

ᵈ Moore's request was made to Baird on December 2nd, but Paget, in Baird's absence it appears, opened the letter containing it, and was therefore better able to press Baird for permission to take three regiments instead of one, as well as most of the horse artillery.¹

ᵉ Up to December 14th Paget's command consisted of Edward Paget's infantry division (20th, 1/52nd, 28th, 91st, 1/95th); one brigade R.A.; 10th and 15th Hussars under Slade; horse artillery; Beresford's brigade (9th, 42nd, 2/52nd); 7th Hussars, and four companies of 2/95th.

On December 20th his command had been extended to embrace the whole of the advanced corps. This consisted of:

10th and 15th Hussars — at Melgar de Abajo, Melgar de Arriba, Galleguillos de Campos;

7th Hussars — at Santervás de Campos;

18th Hussars; 3rd Hussars, King's German Legion — at Villalón de Campos.

Also under his command came:

Edward Paget's reserve infantry division — at Villahamete [Villagomez la Nueva], Vega de Ruiponce, Oteruelo de Campos [nr Villalba de la Loma]. (See map p. 79.)

ᶠ Oman's description of Slade is most unflattering. He was only capable, he says, of going forward to carry out a definite order, it being necessary that he should simply be put like a tram on a line 'and shoved forward', or he would slacken pace and come to a stop 'from want of initiative and moving power'. Paget's contempt for him is well illustrated by Captain Gordon's account of an incident on the advance: 'Lord Paget rode along the flank of the column giving directions respecting the order of the march and precautions to be attended to, which he desired the General to repeat to the squadron officers of the Tenth; but no sooner had Slade left him than his lordship called one of his aides-de-camp, whom he ordered to "ride after that damned stupid fellow" and take care that he committed no blunder. This speech — which, to say the least of it, was very ill-timed — was made within hearing of a number of officers and soldiers and was calculated to deprive the Brigadier even of the slight degree of respect previously entertained for him by the troops.'²

ᵍ Realizing this, Paget disobeyed an order from the Horse Guards that Slade's brigade should consist of three regiments (the 7th, 10th and 15th Hussars) and that Stewart should have only two (the 18th Hussars and the 3rd Hussars of the King's German Legion), and transferred his own regiment, the 7th, from Slade's to Stewart's command.

[The 7th, 10th, 15th and 18th Light Dragoons were in the process of conversion from dragoons to hussars between 1803 and 1807, though the Warrant which officially sanctioned the change was not published until 1811. In most contemporary records reference is made both to light dragoons and hussars. In this chapter each regiment is referred to as hussars.]

h Charles Stewart had been most active during the whole of Moore's advance. On one occasion, with one squadron of the 18th Hussars he entered Valladolid and carried off £3,000 and a very valuable consignment of cotton found there.

All Paget's cavalry regiments were constantly in touch with enemy troops in the vital days preceding the junction, invariably driving them back and taking a number of prisoners. One of these, a French major, gave Moore extremely important and accurate information regarding the enormous size of Napoleon's army.

i Paget's orders to Slade ran as follows:

'The 10th Hussars with 4 guns will march from Monastero [probably Monasterio de Vega] so as to arrive at the Bridge at Sahagún precisely at half-past six tomorrow morning. The whole will march as light as possible, leaving the forage to be brought forward by the country carts with the baggage, which will march at daybreak under escort of such men and horses as are not fit for a forced march. The guns will move without ammunition wagons, the two remaining ones, with everything belonging to the artillery, will come on with the baggage. The object of the movement is to surprise Sahagún. The picquet at the Bridge will be driven in briskly. If serious opposition is made, a squadron or more may be dismounted, who, followed by a mounted squadron, will enter the town, make for the General's and principal officers' quarters to make them prisoners. It is only in case of absolute necessity that the guns must be used. The grand object is to drive the enemy through the town, on the other side of which Lt.-General Lord Paget will be posted with the 15th Hussars. The moment this object is in way of being accomplished, two squadrons of the Tenth must be detached to the left of El Burgo Ranco [?], where the enemy has a picquet of from 60 to 100 men. These must be briskly attacked and made prisoners. This done they will return to Sahagún.'

Morgel de Alaxo [sic]: *20th Dec., 1808, ½9 p.m.*

As will be seen (Note n, p. 352), Slade and the 10th did not in fact arrive on the field until the pursuit had commenced.[3]

j With him went his A.D.C., Captain Thornhill, and a personal escort of twelve men of the 7th Hussars.

k 'Lord Paget', wrote Captain Gordon in his Journal, 'immediately ordered us to form open column of divisions and trot, as the French, upon our coming in sight, made a flank movement, apparently with the intention of getting away; but the rapidity of our advance soon convinced them of the futility of such an attempt. They therefore halted, deployed from column of squadrons, and formed a close column of regiments, which, as it is their custom to tell off in three ranks made their formation six deep. During the time the two corps were moving in a parallel direction, the enemy's flankers, who came within twenty or thirty yards of our column, repeatedly challenged, "Qui vive?", but did not fire, although they received no answer.'

The distance separating the two lines was variously reported by eye-witnesses, the truth lying somewhere between 80 and 400 yards.[4]

[1] The adjutant of the 15th Hussars says that 'the French officers who were taken declared that they had never seen such determined charging, which they should not have stood in the manner they did, but that they thought us Spanish Cavalry, and their error owing to the mist of the morning was not discovered until we were upon them. They however fought well for a few minutes, and finding it was English Cavalry they became astonished and it was sauve qui peut.'[5]

[m] In reference to the successful charge made against the French at Emsdorf soon after the raising of the 15th in 1760.

[n] The tardy appearance of Slade with the 10th and his two guns at this moment contributed to the disorder, for in the half-light they were thought to be another body of the enemy. Slade's 'dilatory proceedings', as Captain Gordon scathingly puts it, which prevented the 10th's arrival on the field until after the action, were in part due to a lengthy speech which he made to his troops before starting. This he is said to have concluded with the words, 'Blood and slaughter — march!'

Paget, according to Gordon, 'allowed the body he pursued to escape by sending an officer, with a white handkerchief as a flag of truce.... The French took advantage of the delay this occasioned.'[6]

[o] 'One', wrote Paget to his father, 'is a strong, low grey horse, very easy and sure-footed in his walk and canter, and perfectly quiet. I destine him for your riding, and will send him by the first safe opportunity. Coming from your old regiment, and given in so handsome a manner, I know you will ride him with pleasure.'[7]

[p] No final decision can be arrived at as to the numbers engaged at Sahagún, but on a careful weighing of the evidence available on both sides (and there is a rare quantity of it), it is pretty safe to say that each had between four hundred and fifty and five hundred sabres in the field; writing to Arthur Paget however, Paget says, 'I judged them [the French] to be between 6 & 700 Men, but from the reports of Prisoners they must have amounted to 750,' while in the same letter, and in another to his father, he speaks of the 15th as having 'about 400' men.[8] The truth would seem to be that Paget was slightly outnumbered by Debelle.[9]

[q] Nearly forty years afterwards a special clasp was given for Sahagún to be worn with the Peninsular medals.

'Sahagún' is inscribed on the colours of the 15th Hussars. It is the only regiment (except the 34th Foot) which has to itself the glory of one combat throughout the Peninsular War.

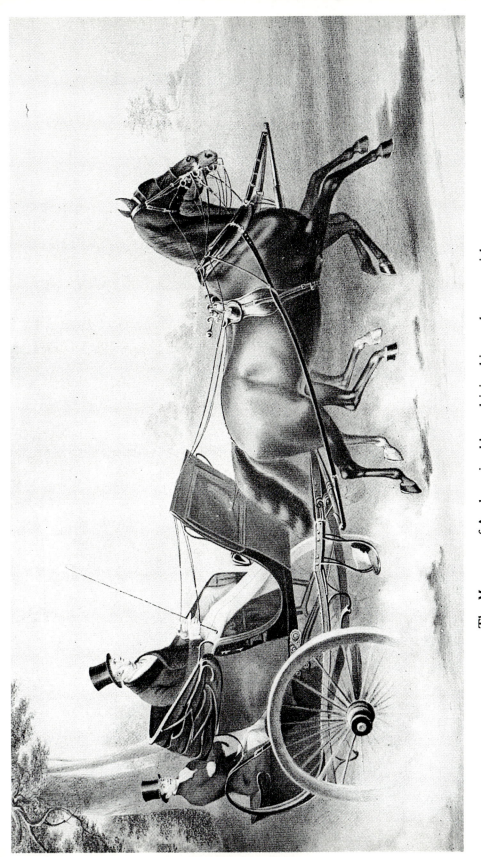

The Marquess of Anglesey in old age driving his two-horse curricle

As Colonel of the 7th Hussars.
Statuette by William Theed

ʳ Captain Gordon records that a lieutenant of the 15th, being too ill to be moved, had to be left behind in charge of a Spanish doctor. 'Lord Paget left a letter, addressed to the commanding officer of any French troops which might enter the town, requesting kind treatment, ... and offering, in the event of his recovery, to give any officer of the same rank taken prisoner on the 21st in exchange for him.' It is pleasant to relate that the officer recovered and returned to England.[10]

ˢ Paget had ordered Slade to lead this squadron, but the feeble brigadier was too slow for him; he 'moved off at a trot', says Captain Gordon, 'but had not advanced far when he halted to have some alteration made in the length of his stirrups. An aide-de-camp was sent to inquire the cause of the delay, and the squadron was again put in motion; but the General's stirrups were not yet adjusted to his mind, and he halted again before they had advanced a hundred yards. Lord Paget, whose patience was by this time quite exhausted, then ordered Colonel Leigh to take the lead.'[11]

ᵗ Captain Gordon claims only fifty.

ᵘ On the conversion of light dragoon regiments to hussars, the officers and other ranks were directed to wear mustachios on the upper lip.

ᵛ On December 31st Napoleon reached Astorga. Butler says that his escort was

'so slender that had Lord Paget, who was close at hand, been aware of it, one cannot doubt that Napoleon would have been in imminent peril of becoming his prisoner.' He adds that 'an encounter did, in fact, take place, of a singular kind, for the brigade of Rioult d'Aveney was watering its horses at a brook close to Astorga, when a large party of British hussars came down to the farther bank for the same purpose. Each side was in watering order without arms, and at a later period of the war would probably have finished its occupation in the most friendly manner. At this period French and English did not know each other so well, and in mutual alarm both parties mounted and galloped away.'[12]

ʷ Inflammation of the conjunctiva or mucous membrane which covers the front of the eyeball, and is reflected on to the inner surface of the eyelids.

CHAPTER VI (p. 89 to p. 112)

[For a list of the chief sources used in these notes, see note 1, p. 395.]
ᵃ According to Lady Harriet Cavendish, Henry Wellseley was 'quite a Héro de Romance in person and manner'.

ᵇ The result of this pregnancy was a son, Gerald Wellesley; but the date of his birth is a mystery. Upon his tombstone at Stratfieldsaye it appears as October 31st,

1809. Yet it would appear that this is false, for only just over four months later, on March 4th, 1810, Charlotte gave birth to a daughter, Emily Paget (see p. 109), though there can be no real certainty about this date either.

Gerald was admitted to Trinity College, Cambridge, in March 1826: the record of admissions states that he was then seventeen, which, if correct, puts October 31st 1809 out of the question. What evidence there is, therefore, points to the end of 1808. It is just possible that the '1809' on the tombstone is an honest mistake for '1808'.[1]

c Arthur Paget himself at this time was a central figure in a scandal which bears some resemblance to the one described in this chapter. In May 1808 he had eloped with the beautiful Lady Boringdon (née Augusta Fane, daughter of the 10th Earl of Westmoreland, and sister-in-law of Car Paget's brother, the 5th Earl of Jersey). Lord Boringdon divorced his wife by Act of Parliament dated February 14th, 1809; two days later she married Arthur Paget, and within six weeks of that ceremony gave birth to a daughter by him. The members of the Paget, Villiers and Fane families most closely concerned, seem to have been united in feeling that Arthur acted honourably in rescuing Augusta from an unhappy marriage to a man whom she (and they) despised. Lord Boringdon, who was a close friend of Canning's, was created Earl of Morley in 1815. He seems to have had many enemies, in spite of a large fortune and a country house boasting of at least a hundred bedrooms: Lady Caroline Lamb, on the other hand, spoke in September 1808, of 'poor Lady Bor[ingdon]'s fate connected with such a man as Sir A[rthur] P[aget]'.[2]

d i.e. without her becoming pregnant. She did in fact become so (see p. 109).

e Lady Caroline Lamb had written to Lady Bessborough in September 1808: 'Lady Paget's … I fear is not a happy prospect; she has always been well spoken of hitherto, I believe, but was certainly injudicious in her husband's absence, in going … with the D. of Argyll to Lady Borringdon.'[2]

f Baron Tuyll was a Dutchman of very good family who had emigrated from Holland at the end of the eighteenth century and entered the 7th Hussars. He soon became Paget's A.D.C. and close friend, serving with him in the Corunna campaign. He was a man of sedate character with highly polished manners and unfailing good nature, much liked in high society both in London and abroad. He was a devoted friend and admirer of Paget's, to whom he made himself useful in many capacities, especially in Ireland, first as A.D.C. in 1828, and later as private secretary.[3]

g At this time Edward Paget proposed a joint letter to Paget from himself, Arthur and Charles, stating that as they had all failed to prevail upon him to give up Lady Charlotte and return to his family, they still had 'one painful duty to perform, that of conscientiously stating to him what we knew from positive facts relating to her which proved her to be a most artful deceitful woman. We meant then to recount the several acts to prove the assertions — & to say that tho' we did not count upon this exposure having the effect of moving him, still we felt it a paramount duty to ourselves and to him to declare our sentiments towards her, which we were persuaded in a very short

time his own conviction would satisfy him upon.' This letter, however, on consideration, the brothers thought it better not to send as it would 'do no practical good'.

ʰ This correspondence was not made public until May 16th.

ⁱ Farington in his Diary entry for May 26th says that Paget's 'motive for returning
was on acct of his children, but he would visit Lady Charlotte Wellesley whenever
he pleased. — She is at Brompton. — She had been remarked', he adds, 'for great
levity of manner before she was married.'
Miss Berry saw Paget walking with four of his children in Kensington Gardens on
July 1st.

ʲ It seems possible that the arrangement whereby Henry Wellesley took Charlotte
under his protection until his divorce bill became law [see p. 109], had already taken
effect. If this were so, it would account for Paget's being able to accept the challenge
without fear that his death would leave Charlotte refugeless. On the other hand, it is
just conceivable that Henry Wellesley expressly undertook to protect his erring wife,
should Paget be killed in the duel, thereby freeing him to accept the challenge. There
is no evidence either way, but there must have been some new factor to induce Paget
to accept in May what he had felt bound to refuse in March [see p. 102].

ᵏ Emily Paget, who married Viscount Sydney in 1832 and died in 1893.

ˡ Indeed, it was said that Car left London ('to act her part in this bare-faced and
indecent farce') in the Duke's carriage! This was in fact untrue: Paget paid £157
for a landau to convey Car and two of her children from London to Scotland, her
own carriage being under repair.

ᵐ In 1816 the Prince Regent gave a grand dinner at Carlton House, at which
Paget (then Marquess of Anglesey) and Henry Wellesley were guests. A relation of
Wellesley's wrote that the Prince took him and Castlereagh aside before dinner

'and said he was much distressed at Lord Anglesey and Henry being in the room
together; that he had never recollected it till he saw them, etc., etc., and he desired
me to take an opportunity of explaining to Henry that the circumstances had
arisen from mere misadventure. I told him that I was sure Henry was quite easy
about the matter, and I informed his R.H. that in a conversation I had lately had
with Henry, he had observed that he now considered Lord Anglesey as the best
friend he had ever had in his life. Castlereagh observed coolly that the meeting
was a fortunate circumstance, for it would be impossible they should not very
often meet, and therefore the sooner the thing was over the better; upon which
P.R. observed that Castlereagh was the most impudent fellow existing, and so
broke up the conversation. Henry did not seem at all annoyed at the meeting.'

Paget and Argyll had met and shaken hands in the hall of Carlton House at a
levée in June 1811.⁴

ⁿ General Dyott, who was a close friend and Staffordshire neighbour of Lord Anglesey's, wrote in his diary nineteen years after the divorce:

'The strict moralist perhaps may not approve of taking my daughter to visit Lady Anglesey, but situated as I felt myself towards the noble Marquis and the obligation I owed the family, added to the circumstance of her ladyship having called here to introduce her daughter to Eleanor, I naturally concluded I must either take Eleanor or give up my acquaintance altogether. Lady Anglesey's conduct cannot be justified. She has suffered for her misdeeds; they should not be visited on her children. And as Mrs Littleton, Lady Sophia Gresley, etc., had been to stay at Beaudesert, I did no longer hesitate in accompanying my daughter.'

The wife of the Irish Under-Secretary would never call on Lady Anglesey when Anglesey was Lord Lieutenant in 1828.

Paget's sister, Caroline, announcing to old Lady Uxbridge, a week after Waterloo, that Char had come over to be at her wounded husband's side, says, 'My Lady arrived last night and I am going ... to *Swallow my Pill* at one o'clock.' On hearing that Paget (who had succeeded his father as Earl of Uxbridge in 1812) had been created Marquess of Anglesey, she wrote to her mother: 'I rejoice that Paget has this honor — But I am sorry to have dear old Uxbridge sunk into a Second Title — & again I rejoice that [Lady Anglesey] will no longer bear the same name with your pure, virtuous, precious Self.'[5]

º For instance, up to the time of his Waterloo wound, Caroline Capel had not spoken to her brother, nor he to her, but Caroline Paget (his eldest daughter, who was then nineteen) wrote on June 30th, 1815, to Char (who was her stepmother): 'I am most happy to hear you and the Capels are friends. I felt sure they never would resist — at such a moment. I was certain Lady Caroline *must* go to Him and I knew Him too well not to be certain he would not refuse seeing her.'[6]

CHAPTER VII (p. 113 to p. 118)

ᵃ The annual produce of the landed property in 1802, not including the copper-, lead- and coal-mines, was over £28,000. Over the seventeen-year period 1819-35, Anglesey's *total* income averaged £76,200; for the same period his average total expenditure was £77,800, an average overspending of £1,600 p.a.[1]

ᵇ This is a table centre-piece of silver gilt, made by Paul Storr, in the form of a sturdy triumphal column. At its base recline four lions; surmounting it are four prancing chargers held by two winged goddesses. The column itself is completely encrusted with trophies in shallow relief, while the base panels contain the Prince of Wales's arms, the Paget arms, and two relief representations of hussars in action. It is inscribed:

'This piece of plate is presented to
Lieutenant-General Lord Paget by the
Prince Regent, by H.R.H. The Duke of
Cumberland, and the inscribed officers
of the Hussar Brigade who served under his
Lordship's command in token of their
admiration of his high military acquirements and
of the Courage and Talent constantly displayed
by him in leading the Hussars to Victory against
the French cavalry during the Campaign on the
Peninsula in 1808.'

CHAPTER VIII (p. 119 to p. 154)

a There is a story that Wellington's recommendation of Combermere to succeed
Edward Paget as commander-in-chief in India in 1825 was questioned on the ground
that difficult operations were in prospect. The Duke is said to have replied: 'At any
rate he can take Bhurtpore.'[1]

b The Duke of York is supposed never to have much liked Wellington, thinking
him false and ungrateful. This has been much exaggerated by some modern writers,
though Greville quotes York as saying of the Duke 'that at Waterloo he got into a
scrape and allowed himself to be surprised', attributing 'in great measure the success
of that day to Lord Anglesea, who ... was hardly mentioned, and that in the coldest
terms, in the Duke's despatch.'[2]

c A small vessel was 'appropriated exclusively for the conveyance of the horses
belonging to His Lordship and Staff — in number forty.'
His first General Cavalry Order was dated 'Ninove, 3 May 1815,' and began as
follows:
'1. Lieutenant General The Earl of Uxbridge, in announcing that he has been
placed in the Command of the Cavalry of this Army, by Field Marshal His Grace the
Duke of Wellington; begs to express the high sense he entertains of the Honor that is
conferred upon him.
'2. He expects from this Cavalry everything that can be attain'd by Discipline,
Bravery, and a high sense of Honor.'[3]

d As late as June 15th, Lieutenant-Colonel Macdonald was appointed to command
the six troops of horse artillery actually attached to the cavalry.[4]

e This was an arrangement of administrative convenience, especially as regards
forage supply. It meant that small units were scattered over a large area and therefore
incapable of speedy concentration. It was Uxbridge's intention, given time, to have
formed his seven brigades into divisions. Lord Greenock says that 'In consequence of
the suddenness of the order to advance to meet the Enemy on the 16th of June, the
measure of forming the Cavalry into Divisions, which I know to have been Lord

Anglesey's intention, had not taken effect.' Sir Evelyn Wood goes so far as to say that this omission 'was the cause of the loss of many lives on the 18th June.'[5]

Two cavalry regiments were in Ghent, acting as bodyguard to Louis XVIII, and one cavalry brigade was in reserve between Ninove and Grammont.

The British and King's German Legion cavalry brigades were made up as follows:

1st (Household)	Major-General Lord E. Somerset	
	1st Life Guards	}
	2nd do.	About 1,200 sabres.
	Royal Horse Guards (Blues)	
2nd (Union)	Major-General Sir W. Ponsonby	
	Royal Dragoons (Royals)	About 1,200 sabres, though effective strength probably only 900.[6]
	2nd Dragoons (Royal Scots Greys)	
	Inniskilling Dragoons (Inniskillings)	
3rd	Major-General Sir W. Dörnberg	
	1st Light Dragoons, K.G.L.	About 1,260 sabres.
	2nd do.	
	23rd Light Dragoons	
4th	Major-General Sir J. Vandeleur	
	11th Light Dragoons	About 1,160 sabres.
	12th do.	
	16th do.	
5th	Major-General Sir C. Grant	
	7th Hussars	About 1,360 sabres.
	15th do.	
	2nd Hussars, K.G.L.	
6th	Major-General Sir Hussey Vivian	
	10th Hussars	About 1,280 sabres.
	18th Hussars	
	1st Hussars, K.G.L.	
7th	Colonel Sir F. O. Arentschild	
	13th Light Dragoons	About 1,000 sabres.
	3rd Hussars, K.G.L.	

Total: about 8,460 sabres.

Royal Horse Artillery	Major Bull's (Howitzer) Troop.
	Lieutenant-Colonel Webber-Smith's (Light) Troop.
	Lieutenant-Colonel Sir Robert Gardiner's (Light) Troop.
	Major Whinyates's (Light, plus Rockets) Troop.
	Captain Mercer's (9-pounder) Troop.
	Major Ramsay's (9-pounder) Troop.
Reserve	{ Lieutenant-Colonel Sir Hew Ross's (9-pounder) Troop.
	{ Major Bean's (Light) Troop.

Total: 36 guns.

The foreign cavalry brigades were made up as follows:

1st Hanoverian	Colonel Van Estorff	
	Prince Regent's Hussars	} About 1,680
	Bremen and Verden Hussars	sabres.
	Cumberland Hussars	
Brunswick Cavalry		
	Regiment of Hussars	} About 920
	Squadron of Uhlans	sabres.
1st (Netherlandish)	Major-General Trip	
	1st Dutch Carbineers	} About 1,230
	2nd Belgian do.	sabres.
	3rd Dutch do.	
2nd (Netherlandish)	Major-General de Ghiny	
	4th Dutch Light Dragoons	} About 1,080
	8th Belgian Hussars	sabres.
3rd (Netherlandish)	Major-General van Merlen	
	5th Belgian Light Dragoons	} About 1,080
	6th Dutch Hussars	sabres.

Total: about 5,990 sabres.

½ Gey van Pittius's   Dutch Horse Battery
½ Petter's   do.

Total: 8 guns.

Grand total: (including officers, etc.) about 14,500 men and 44 guns.

[f] A number of smaller reviews was held before and after this one. On May 24th Uxbridge inspected the heavy cavalry: on May 25th, the hussars. Gibney, medical officer of the 15th Hussars, describes a review of his regiment on June 9th. 'We were turned out at 3 a.m. [to be] inspected by General Grant.... As usual General Grant found fault; ... but Lord Uxbridge, who came on the ground about 10 o'clock, evidently thought otherwise, for he complimented the Regiment in the most handsome way, telling us we were, as he had always known us to be, both willing and able to undertake anything; and that ... the movements were well and accurately performed. This was consoling after General Grant's abuse.'

Thirty-five years later an old trooper of the 7th reminded Uxbridge of his only encounter with him: it took place at 5 a.m. on the day of this review, and well illustrates Uxbridge's informality. The trooper, bringing a letter to another officer, 'trotted sharp down the yard of your Quarters.... On my return', he wrote, 'you were stood at your door with nothing on but your shirt, not even a pair of slippers; you asked me if I had brought anything for you; I replied "No"; you said you wished I had, and bowing to my salute you turned in.'[7]

[g] Gibney says that Colquhoun Grant [who is not to be confused with his namesake who was Wellington's chief intelligence officer] was well known 'to be somewhat innocent of cavalry'; but he is almost alone in this opinion, though it is true that a considerable part of Grant's career had been spent with the infantry.[8]

ʰ To two officers of the 7th Hussars, Uxbridge said: 'You gentlemen who have engaged partners had better finish your dance and get to your quarters as soon as you can.'

At seven o'clock that morning Wellington finally decided that his true point of concentration should be Quatre-Bras. He only then gave orders for his whole army (with important exceptions) to move eastwards towards that village. He then rode over to see Blücher, who was awaiting Napoleon's attack in his position at Ligny. Not until the middle of the afternoon did he return to Quatre-Bras, where he found the battle in progress and Picton's infantry only just coming on to the field.

When, early in the morning of the 16th, the cavalry regiments had received their orders to move towards Enghien, Vandeleur's brigade was the nearest to Quatre-Bras, the 11th Hussars being some 45 miles from it. It is therefore not surprising that in spite of Uxbridge's efforts to hasten them on [see note j below], none of his cavalry arrived in time to take part in the battle of Quatre-Bras. The state of the roads, too, was very bad from much recent rain; added to which it was extremely hot and thundery — weather not conducive to extreme exertion. The 11th arrived at about 8 p.m. One squadron was immediately thrown out to form the advanced picket in front of Quatre-Bras farmhouse, but except for desultory skirmishing the battle was over, and the French had withdrawn whence they had come. The remainder of the brigade arrived at about 10 p.m., but the best part of the other brigades did not arrive till the early morning of the 17th, nor did the horse-batteries.⁹

ᶦ The original MS of these orders, in Uxbridge's hand, has been added to the Plas Newydd papers by the kindness of Miss I. F. Jacob, a descendant of Captain Wildman. They have not been published before. What is of special interest is the time at which they were written, namely a quarter of an hour before midnight.

'*June 15th, 1815* — ¾ *past* 11 P.M.

'GENERAL CAVALRY ORDERS.

1 The Cavalry will march immediately from the Left to Enghein.
2 Whatever Brigade arrives first within a mile of Enghein, will choose a convenient Spot near the road, to form in Column of half Squadrons at quarter distance.
3 The Brigades as they arrive in succession will form in rear of that first form'd.
4 The Baggage will march in the rear of each Brigade under a sufficient guard.
5 The Royal Horse Artillery of the Cavalry will also march by Troops independently to near Enghein. Lieut. Col. Webber Smith's Troop is attached to Maj. Genl. Sir C. Grant's Brigade. Lt. Col. Sir Robt. Gardiner's is attach'd M. Genl. Sir H. Vivian's Brigade.
6 An Officer of each Brigade, and an Officer per Troop from the Rl. H. Artillery will meet Lt. Genl. The Earl of Uxbridge at the Hotel Royal at Enghein.

'UXBRIDGE, Lt. Gl.

'Such Sick as are unable to march, will be sent to Brussels. Horses unable to march with the Brigades will be sent to Ninove.'

ʲ Uxbridge had gone straight on to Quatre-Bras. Many years later he wrote:

'The E. of Uxbridge pushed forward, and finding at each of these towns [Grammont, Enghien, and Nivelle], pressing orders for the advance of the Cavalry, he left directions to expedite its march. At 2 p.m. [probably later, in fact] he reached Quatre Bras having between that place and Nivelle met some wounded and many fugitives. The Corps of the Prince of Orange had been for some hours warmly engaged with a very superior force.... The Duke of Wellington had arrived and as the day advanced the post was reinforced by the arrival of several Brigades of Infantry. The only Cavalry at hand was that of the Duke of Brunswick. It behaved gallantly but was too inferior in numbers to that of the French, to make any material impression.[10]

k This was Napoleon's force from Marbais, not Ney's in front of Quatre-Bras.

l The equivalent of many volumes has been written on Ney's waste of the whole of the morning of the 17th without attacking; all that it is necessary to say here is that Wellington and Uxbridge were very lucky that Napoleon was not in Ney's place.

Ney had been joined by d'Erlon's corps which had spent the 16th marching and counter-marching between the two battlefields of Quatre-Bras and Ligny; he therefore found himself immensely stronger on the morning of the 17th than at any time on the 16th.

m In 1846, when Master-General of the Ordnance, Anglesey wrote to Wellington: 'I perfectly recollect being very much puzzled with our heavy 9-pounders in the retreat on the 17th of June, 1815, and longed for the 6's just for that particular purpose.'[11]

n In places the horses sank right up to their girths. 'Some of the hussars who were driven in upon us were so covered with mud that it was impossible to distinguish their features', wrote Lieutenant Hamilton of the Greys.[12]

o Vandeleur ought perhaps to have allowed Vivian to pass through his brigade instead of withdrawing as Vivian approached. 'The incident', says Fortescue, 'showed the danger of allowing brigades to manoeuvre on their own account without the control of a divisional commander.'[13] (See note e, p. 358.)

p Standish O'Grady (1792-1848) was the son of the first Viscount Guillamore. With both father and son Uxbridge had subsequent dealings. The father was Chief Baron of the Exchequer in Ireland during Lord Anglesey's first Irish administration in 1828, and was retired by him at the beginning of his second administration in 1831, the Irish peerage being created on the Lord Lieutenant's recommendation. The son, by then a lieutenant-colonel, was also in Ireland at the time. Anglesey found him 'a sharp, useful fellow'. He married the Lord Lieutenant's niece, Gertrude Jane, daughter of Berkeley Paget, in December 1828, during her uncle's first administration. Her son (the first Lord Guillamore's grandson) was, as a young man, at the Royal Military Academy during Anglesey's second term as Master-General of the Ordnance. In December 1851 his mother received the following letter:

'Dear Lady Guillamore,

'I have received your letter and can only express my deep regret that my sense of truth and fair dealing absolutely forbid me from giving to your son a Certificate of good conduct.

'Believe me, affectly. yours,

'ANGLESEY'[14]

[q] Muddled and inaccurate reports of what happened at Genappe circulated in London after the campaign. To counteract these, Uxbridge published a letter eleven days after the action, addressed to his 'dear brother officers' of the 7th, in which he said:

'It has been stated to me, that a report injurious to the reputation of our regiment has gone abroad; and I do not therefore lose an instant in addressing you on the subject. The report must take its origin from the affair ... near Genappe, when I ordered the 7th to cover the retreat. As I was with you, and saw the conduct of every individual, there is no one more capable of speaking to the fact than I am. As the Lancers pressed us hard, I ordered you (upon a principle I ever did, and shall act upon) not to wait to be attacked, but to fall upon them. The attack was most gallantly led by the officers; but it failed: it failed because the Lancers stood firm, had their flanks secured, and were backed by a large mass of cavalry. The regiment was repulsed but did not run away. No – it rallied immediately; I renewed the attack. It failed again from the same cause. It retired in perfect order, although it had sustained so severe a loss; but you had thrown the Lancers into disorder, who being in motion, I then made an attack upon with the Life Guards, who certainly made a very handsome charge, and completely succeeded. This is the plain honest truth. However lightly I think of Lancers under ordinary circumstances, I am of opinion that, posted as they were, they had a most decided advantage over the Hussars. The impetuosity, however, and weight of the Life Guards carried all before them. And while I exculpate my own regiment, I am delighted in being able to bear testimony to the gallant conduct of the former.

'Be not uneasy, my brother officers, you had ample opportunity, of which you most gallantly availed yourselves, of revenging yourselves on the 18th for the failure on the 17th; and after all what regiment, and which of us individually, is certain of success? Be assured that I am proud of being your colonel, and that you possess my utmost confidence.

'Your sincere friend,

'ANGLESEY, Lieut.-General'[15]

'In covering the retreat on the 17th' Uxbridge 'found the Lance had some advantage over the Sword.' It is likely that the 7th had never fought against lancers before, and it is known that the pennons, at a later date always removed before action, had been left on the lances, which probably alarmed the horses of the 7th.[16]

[r] In fairness to the 23rd, it should be said that they had just witnessed the squadron of the 7th defeated by the *lanciers*, after repeated charges, and that by the time the Life Guards had 'gone about' (for, at the moment when they were ordered to charge, they were heading northwards), the enemy horsemen were well clear of the houses

and half way up the incline. Of more importance still, the Life Guards were heavy cavalry, big men on big horses.[17]

ˢ Captain Kelly who led this charge, writing to Uxbridge later in the year, gives a fuller and slightly different account.

'When the Hussars and Light Dragoons were repulsed the Household Brigade had retired thro' Genappe in Column of Divisions left in Front. Some time afterwards the 1st Life Guards were halted on the *Chaussée*, countermarched Divisions and stood in column fronting the Enemy, at which time I commanded the rear half Squadron of the Column (viz. the left). As the enemy approached the head of our column, by some misunderstanding or other the Regiment put about & retired a little in confusion, upon which I quitted the rear Division and went towards the enemy, when I saw Your Lordship alone within a few paces of them, saying "They dare not come on, they only need to be properly attacked and they will retire." Our Column fronted again and were tilting a few seconds with the head of the Enemy's Column, the Enemy still rather advancing, and as *I did not see any Officer* of the 1st Life Guards or other Corps in *Front* of the front rank of the leading Division of that Corps on the Chaussee I placed myself there, having quitted Your Lordship's side for that purpose, when I heard Your Lordship make use of the words before recited, and calling out to the Men to follow me, I rode singly into the leading Division of the Lancers.... The Corporal Major of the Regiment was the next man after me, and then and *not till then*, the whole Column charged.'[18]

Five officers of the 7th were taken prisoner during the abortive attack on the *lanciers*, but when the Life Guards attacked, two of them 'caught a couple of spare French horses & made their escape'. Another, Captain Elphinstone, got away on the night of the 18th, having been brought before Napoleon that morning. The Emperor 'spoke to him for some time very civilly and on going away said to an officer "I desire you will treat these officers well in every respect as British officers deserve." ' When Napoleon asked Elphinstone: 'Who commands the cavalry?' he received the answer 'Lord Uxbridge.' Napoleon replied 'No. *Paget.*' The other two prisoners died of their wounds; they were Major Hodge and the adjutant, Captain Myers.[19]

ᵗ The southern slope (i.e. that towards the French) was also, in places, very steep. At one point the helmets of the French cavalry, halted 150 yards south of the crest, could only just be seen by the British infantry standing atop the ridge.[20]

ᵘ Fortescue states that 'of two thousand troopers and horses that had charged, over one thousand horses, and from seven to eight hundred men were killed, wounded, and missing.'[21]

ᵛ There is doubt as to whether the Duke was in fact a witness of the charge itself. It is possible that he came on the scene from the right of the line after it had been launched and only saw the aftermath. This might in part account for his failure to appreciate its true worth, both in his dispatch and later when discussing the battle.

ʷ [See p. 135.] Vandeleur says that subsequent to the discretionary order, 'an order came from the Duke or Lord Anglesey to close to the Infantry, which had left a vacancy by closing to its right.' No indication of the timing of this order is given. Wood says that Vandeleur was 'an officer who, however brave, was more accustomed to wait for orders than act on his own initiative. He had served for a long time under the Duke, and knew how heavily he could vent his wrath on officers who moved without orders.' Uxbridge told Siborne that 'the second line (excepting only a small part of Sir J. Vandeleur's Brigade — in fact, I believe, only two Squadrons of the 12th, under Sir F. Ponsonby) had not followed the movements of the Heavy Cavalry.'[22]

ˣ Contemporary critics made much of this supposed inferiority of the light cavalry. This probably arose from the misunderstanding about the repulse of the 7th Hussars at Genappe the day before [see p. 362], and from the fact that on that occasion the *lanciers* were in a small degree superior to the *sabreurs*. According to Colonel James Stanhope's journal, quoted by Fortescue, Uxbridge at one time 'rode up to the Guards of Maitland's brigade and said, "Well done, men. By God, we stand on you. If I could only get my fellows to do the same! But by God, they won't budge — but I'll try again." The writer', comments Fortescue, 'adds that the Light Cavalry in that part of the field [the right] were of little profit, partly because they were brought up for small isolated attacks instead of in a mass. This, however, is quite unconfirmed, rather indeed contradicted, by other authorities; and it is probable that Uxbridge was speaking of some of the foreign cavalry which, it is well known, refused to follow him.'[23] (See note aa, below.)

ʸ Grant left one squadron of the 15th watching the right. The rest of his brigade, since he had scented the trap at Hougoumont, was now available for Uxbridge's counter-attacks, which followed elsewhere.

ᶻ The 7th, 23rd, 1st and 3rd Hussars K.G.L., the remnants of the heavy brigades, two regiments of Brunswick cavalry, and (though they proved useless) three brigades of Dutch-Belgian cavalry in reserve. Of these last Uxbridge scathingly wrote: 'The Belgian and Brunswick Cavalry assisted occasionally in the pursuit.'
There is very little evidence as to how much and in exactly what manner Wellington interfered in the movements of the cavalry during the battle. Preserved at Apsley House, however, is an order respecting the cavalry, which was probably sent at about this period in the battle. It is written in pencil upon a strip of prepared skin, and reads: 'We ought to have more of the Cavalry between the two high Roads. That is to say, three Brigades at least, besides the Brigade in observation on the Right & besides the Belgian Cavalry & the D. of Cumberland's Hussars. One heavy & one light Brigade might remain on the left.'[24]

ᵃᵃ General Trip was the commander of the Dutch-Belgian brigade, which consisted of one Belgian and two Dutch regiments. He was specifically mentioned in Wellington's dispatch; not the only case of mistaken praise in that remarkable document. He was the brother of Uxbridge's erstwhile A.D.C., who at Waterloo was senior A.D.C.

to the Prince of Orange. Horace Seymour says that Uxbridge 'tried all in his power to lead Trip's brigade on and while *he* was advancing, I believe I called his attention to the fact of his not being followed.'

Seymour gave evidence at the subsequent court martial of the Cumberland Hussars' colonel, to the effect that Uxbridge,

'seeing that Regiment moving to the rear (about five o'clock), desired me immediately to halt it. On delivering the order to the Colonel, he told me that he had no confidence in his men, that they were Volunteers, and the horses their own property. All this time the Regiment continued moving to the rear, in spite of my repeating the order to halt, and asking the Second in command to save the character of the Regiment by taking the command and fronting them. I was unsuccessful, and in the exigence of the moment I laid hold of the bridle of the Colonel's horse, and remarked what I thought of his conduct; but all to no purpose. I then returned to Lord Anglesey, and reported what had passed. I was again ordered to deliver the message to the Commanding Officer of the Regiment, that if they would resume their position in the Line, that he was to form them across the high road *out* of fire. They did not even obey this order, but went, as was reported, altogether to the rear.'

Compare Farington's diary [July 14th, 1815] where Sir Thomas Lawrence repeats conversations he has had with Wellington, who was with Uxbridge at this time:

'His Lordship again repeated his order [to the commanding officer of the Cumberland Hussars] & the Duke added to it another unless the Hanoverian should [not] comply with the first. The aide de camp rode back and again gave the order as before, but without effect, & seeing that the Hanoverian would not advance, He then said, "As you do not attend to the order given I have another from the Duke of Wellington which is *that you fall back to the rear of the Army.*" This the Hanoverian readily complied with, saying it was very considerate of the Duke when engaged in so much action to think of his corps with so much care.'[25]

bb Horace Seymour, who had earlier been dispatched to Vivian by Uxbridge, was sent by the former with an officer and a patrol to make certain that the cavalry seen was in fact Prussian, 'which, on proving,' he later wrote, 'I made the best of my way to Lord Anglesey, whom I found with the Duke of Wellington, to whom I reported what I had seen. Sir Alexander Gordon questioned me as to my certainty of it being the Prussians with whom I had communicated, I assuring him that it was so. I was desired by the Duke of Wellington to tell General Bulow that the Duke wished him immediately to send him Prussian Infantry to fill up the loss that had taken place in his Lines.' Seymour does not state specifically that Uxbridge went himself to reconnoitre.[26]

cc (1788-1871), novelist and journalist. This poem first appeared in *The Morning Post.* It has often and erroneously been attributed to George Canning.[27]

dd The saw which is thought to have been used in the operation was presented in 1960 to the National Army Museum at Sandhurst by Rear-Admiral James Powell, a descendant of the surgeon of that name who is believed to have wielded the instrument. Thirteen years later, when viceroy of Ireland, Lord Anglesey gave a helping hand to Mr Callander, surgeon to the 7th Hussars, who, as he told Lord Hill, the Commander-in-Chief, 'was appointed by the Duke of Wellington's directions to attend me after my wound.'[28]

ee Lord Lauderdale told Baron Stockmar that it was he who brought to Char the intelligence of her husband's lost leg. 'Contrary to his wishes,' wrote the Baron in his diary, 'she had been informed of his arrival; and, before he could say a word, she, guessing that he brought her news of her husband, screamed out "He is dead!" and fell into hysterics. But when he said, "Not in the least; here is a letter from him", she was so wonderfully relieved that she bore the truth with great composure.'[29]

CHAPTER IX (p. 155 to p. 181)

a Nevertheless Anglesey was said to have sent a letter to the King acquainting him with the public feeling against what was going on, 'for which the King cut him at the Levée. Lord A. thought it might be accidental, but he was re-cut, and more decisively, at the next Levée.'[1]

b This incident has been attributed to the Duke of Wellington, on the sole authority, it seems, of G. W. E. Russell, writing in 1898. Russell, who states in the preface to his recollections that his memory is impaired, was claiming to quote his uncle, Lord John Russell. On the other hand the newspaper notices which appeared on Anglesey's death in 1854 give the story as applying to him and not to the Duke. These obituaries do not seem to have been questioned either at the time or later, nor, so far as can be discovered, is the story given in any of Wellington's obituaries of two years before.

Lord Penrhyn told Augustus Hare in 1881 that he was riding behind Anglesey in St James's Park on one of these occasions, when 'Lord Anglesey backed his horse between the trees, set his teeth and hissed back at the yelling people. Then he said, "If every man of you were a hundred men, and each of them had a hundred hands, and a bayonet in each hand, I should still do my *duty*!" Then the people cheered him.'

Mrs Pitt Byrne gives an amusing account of a similar incident:

'My father used to talk of having seen the Duke of Wellington and the Marquis of Anglesey riding side by side to and from the House, and as it was known they shared the same opinions, they were uniformly met by unsuppressed cries of execration.... One day when thus pursued by the marks of disapprobation of the populace, the Duke as usual was taking it quite coolly, merely smiling benignly when the yells were at their loudest, but the Marquis became irritated, and showed his indignation by frequently turning round with an angry expression. This increased the insolence of the crowd, so that when the two heroes passed as usual, through the Horse Guards into the Park, they were followed by a general rush of the rabble. Here they assumed a livelier pace, and the Duke rode away; but the Marquis lingered behind, and at length making a sudden stop, he veered round and demanded of his persecutors whom this movement seemed at once to have awed, "Why do you hiss me?" The answer came in the form of loud shouts, "The Queen! The Queen!" But the Marquis exclaimed, "If you want me to vote against my conscience, I must tell you I had rather you ran me through the body!" This brave answer produced loud cheers from the crowd, but the next moment the cry "The Queen!" was taken up, the gallant Marquis, finding there was nothing to be done with the pig-headed mob, spurred his horse to a gallop, and left them yelling behind.'[2]

c This caused quite a flutter among the physicians attending the Duke. Sir Joseph Laffan, Anglesey's chief medical attendant at this time, writing to him on November 29th, said that

'since it became known that yr Lordship forwarded the receipt for the broom medicine to the Duke of York and that I had suggested it to you, the medical folks are determined that no more medicines or suggestions from this quarter shall be listened to, and they affect to blame me for not communicating it directly to Sir Harry [Halford].'

And again on December 6th:

'The purest feelings of disinterested friendship led you to take an interest in the fate of H.R.H. the Duke of York, and induced you to recommend a medicine which is allowed on all hands to have done good. Who would not be happy to offer an advice which after all was referred to, and approved by the Duke's Physicians — & administered under their sanction & approbation!! and became therefore *their medicine* & not yours. Is it to be endured that a set of *selfish knaves* & *fee-catching* doctors shall censure ... the man who having suffered himself, knows how to feel for the sufferings of his friend, & recommends for his adoption the means of obtaining immediate relief!!! No! You have deserved well of yr country & yr Prince.'[3]

d Sir Hussey Vivian, now a Member of Parliament and, since 1825, Inspector-General of Cavalry, had informed Anglesey that he knew 'no one so well calculated' for the Ordnance, and 'no one to whom the Officers of the Corps have so long looked with anxiety to see filling the situation.'[4]

e The Colonelcy of the Royal Horse Guards (the Blues), then as now, was a position of especial honour, combining the position of Gold Stick-in-waiting. Anglesey did in fact become Colonel of the Blues in 1842 (see p. 311).

f On January 21st Anglesey wrote to the King accepting, should the Constableship of the Tower be offered to him conjointly with the Colonelcy of the Blues, but nothing came of the offer.[5]

ᵍ Mrs Arbuthnot was, of course, a highly prejudiced lady, the staunchest of champions of her great friend, Wellington, and something of a prude into the bargain, which did not endear Anglesey or his family to her.

ʰ   '*Private.*

'My dear Anglesey,

'I have a very sincere pleasure in offering you the situation of Master Genl of the Ordnance, & Mr Canning's letter will explain the value which I set upon your Services.

                              'Always Your Sincere Friend,

'*St James's Palace, April 13th, 1827.*'   'G.R.

It had been thought in some quarters that Anglesey would go to the Horse Guards. The Duke of Clarence, who had just been made Lord High Admiral, wrote on April 14th: 'I hear you are Commander-in-Chief, which God grant may be true', adding characteristically that he hoped he would make his son George [FitzClarence] 'one of your Aides-de-Camp'.ᶠ

ⁱ 'I would ask you', wrote Londonderry to Anglesey on April 17th, 'if you would be the man that would assist in depriving the King and the Army of a Duke of Wellington without every effort in your comprehensive mind to avert it — in which act, would you have the most pride? In accomplishing the restoration of England's glory and Europe's wonder? — or in mounting the tottering seat upon such a man's expulsion? To return good for evil is the highest instance of virtue. If the Duke was in your way to the Office he has been driven from, and if he did not wish you to obtain it, which I told you at the time I wished and thought he ought to have done, for God's sake don't let that remembrance bear on the present moment.'

To this lecture Anglesey replied:

'I have undertaken the Office I am to hold at the express command of the King and ... if the happy moment were to arrive when by a cordial reconciliation with the King, His Majesty could again avail himself of the Duke of W's valuable services, I should not hesitate but should joyfully and with the most good intentions, seize the earliest moment of resigning into the Duke's hands the situation he is in every respect so very much more capable of filling than I am.'ⁱ

ʲ Wellington had shown a number of friends his correspondence with Canning 'to account', as he wrote to Anglesey on April 21st, 'for recent transactions' and 'in consequence of the Misrepresentations & gross abuse of me in the Govt &c Papers.' To Torrens he had expressed a wish that Anglesey should see the letters before he formed his judgment. On April 23rd the Duke showed them to him at the Ordnance.ᵏ

ᵏ Kingston Lacy Hall (home of the Tory politician, Henry Bankes) is about 120 miles from London and 100 miles from Windsor. There and back in two days, at the age of fifty-nine, was a remarkable achievement. In the same year he journeyed from

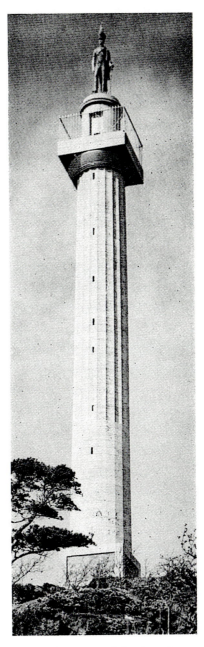

The Marquess of Anglesey's
column at Llanfairpwll

The Marquess of Anglesey, aged 83
Wax relief by Richard Cockle Lucas

London to Beaudesert, a distance of about 125 miles in something less than twelve hours, an average speed of over 10 m.p.h. In Ireland a year later he left Dublin in his carriage-and-four at 5 a.m. and arrived at Knocklofty before 4 p.m. the same day: a distance of 111 miles covered in less than 11 hours.[9]

When he was forty, he had 'contrived to ride seventy-four miles' in nine and a half hours 'upon tired bidets' over mountainous country in Spain, an average speed of $7\frac{3}{4}$ m.p.h. [see p. 72].

[1] Mrs Arbuthnot was exceedingly angry with the Duke for resuming the command of the Army. Compare her account of Anglesey's mission, written two years later, with that of Palmerston, who was, of course, a member of the Cabinet at the time.

'The Duke of Wellington came here today', wrote Mrs Arbuthnot on May 9th, 1829, 'to shew us a dispatch which had been intercepted of the Swedish's minister's. It gave an account of a conversation he had had with Lord Anglesey [who] complained of the Duke most bitterly, said he had conferred the greatest obligations!! ... that he had travelled all night to take him the offer of his resuming the Command-in-Chief, & that he had been the cause & the only cause of the King (who hated the Duke) sending for him to make him his Minister, & nothing but his influence wd have made the King do it. He certainly did go down into Dorsetshire to offer to the Duke to resume the command of the army, but the Duke owed him no thanks; it was a desperate effort to uphold an impotent Govt & nothing cd exceed his insolent manner of telling the Duke he must decide instantly & take it at once or not at all, for which the Duke turned him out of the room. But the most impudent lie of all is his pretending *he* caused the King to send for the Duke! He was the most violent of all against the Tories. When the Duke took the command of the Army, he said, "Thank God, the d——d Tories were done for," and he was foremost in urging Lord Holland and Brougham upon the King &, if he cd have seen the King at the time, wd have tried to make himself head of a new Government.'[10]

[m] To Lansdowne, Anglesey wrote on September 6th, 'when the King becomes familiarised with you, and discovers that Whigs do not *all* bite (for it must be admitted that there are a few who use their teeth) His Majesty will gradually get rid of his strong prejudices.'[11]

[n] A further embarrassment for a weak government was the news of the battle of Navarino, and the controversy which followed it. Anglesey's son, Clarence, was in action during the battle as a midshipman in the *Talbot*. So also was Horatio, aged fourteen, the third son of Sir Charles Paget, whose letter to his sister describes the action:

'We have had a fight with the Turks and we have sunk, burnt and destroyed all that there were and I am quite well.

'Best love to Papa and Mama, Brothers and Sisters, I am ever your affectionate Brother,

'HORATIO

'P.S. We have had in the Talbot seven killed and sixteen or seventeen wounded.'

Lord Grey, in whose government Anglesey was later to serve, also had a son in the *Talbot*. 'Our young Mids.,' wrote Anglesey, 'you will have heard, have been fighting side by side and very gratifying mention is made of both of them. The performance of the Talbot was very distinguished and they are truly fortunate in having commenced their career in so good a school.'[12]

o While the King was making up his mind as to who should head a new administration, a further storm had broken over poor Goderich's head. Without consulting Herries and at the instigation of Huskisson, the Prime Minister had nominated Lord Althorp to the chair of the Finance Committee. Herries, rightly indignant, insisted on resigning unless he as Chancellor of the Exchequer, was made chairman, while Huskisson was equally determined to resign unless Althorp was. Though, according to Goderich, the King considered 'this matter between Huskisson and Herries practically a dissolution of the Government', he told Goderich that he was 'very anxious not to have an *exclusive* Government'.[13]

p Herries's private secretary wrote to his principal on January 5th that Lyndhurst was with Goderich and Huskisson on the 4th, when he had declared his immediate determination 'to communicate with the King in order that the state of the Government might not come upon H.M. unawares; and it was then settled that Lord Anglesey should accompany the Chancellor to the King. In about an hour, however, he received a letter from Lord Anglesey, declining to go with him on the ground of his ill health.'[14]

q Charles Arbuthnot wrote to Peel that by that time

'Canning may have come to the determination of abolishing the Lord Lieutenancy. This has certainly been one of his recent projects. He flew into a passion upon hearing that Spring Rice, the Duke of Leinster, and others were scheming to have no more Ld Lieutenants; and he told Herries that he wd send for them and let them know that they shd follow his measures — not he theirs. The meeting took place. They were not convinced by Canning, but he was nearly so by them. For a day or two his notion was that the Lord Lieutenancy must be done away with.'

Surprisingly enough, O'Connell in 1831, when Hume wished to see the office abolished, sprang to its defence saying that all Irishmen were unanimous upon the expediency of maintaining it.[15] In fact there were to be Lords Lieutenant of Ireland for another ninety-four years.

r This part of the speech, distorted and magnified beyond recognition by the pro-Catholics, caused Anglesey much embarrassment in years to come. Four days after the debate, O'Connell lashed out at 'the noble deserter, the gallant Marquess who says the sooner we fight the better.... Your medals and your glory and your honours have floated to you on the young blood of Catholics, and now you spurn our petition.' In time O'Connell talked of Anglesey's threat 'to cut down the Catholics with his broad sword'; in fact, he at no time uttered words remotely related to these.[16]

[8] A. J. Balfour, nearly eighty years later, referred to the relationship between viceroy and chief secretary as 'that practical paradox', and compared it to that of a constitutional sovereign with his prime minister.[17]

CHAPTER X (p. 182 to p. 221)

[a]

'Lord Chancellor	Lord Lyndhurst
Lord President	Lord Bathurst
Privy Seal	Lord Ellenborough
Chancellor of the Duchy	Lord Aberdeen
President of the Board of Control	Lord Melville
Master-General	[Lord Beresford]
Secretary of State Foreign Dept.	Lord Dudley
Home	Mr Peel
Colonial	Mr Huskisson
Chancellor of the Exchequer	Mr Goulburn
Pres. of the Board of Trade	Mr Grant
Secy at War	Lord Palmerston
Master of the Mint	Mr Herries'

[b] The chief legal posts in the Irish government were filled as follows: Sir Anthony Hart, the Lord Chancellor, who was politically neutral, and master of his business; Plunket, Chief Justice of the Common Pleas, and Bushe, Chief Justice of the King's Bench, who were decidedly liberal and pro-Catholic. Doherty, the Solicitor-General, was a competent lawyer and mild politically, soon becoming an intimate of the Lord Lieutenant's, while Joy, the Attorney-General, was, like Gregory, a determined upholder of Protestant ascendancy.

[c] Melbourne told Queen Victoria in 1838 that Anglesey's personal luggage consisted of thirty-six trunks.[1]

[d] The mistake did in fact leak out. A London newspaper reported it, expressing doubt as to whether the King's declaration in council without Anglesey being present, was strictly legal.[2]

[e] In the summer he was on his horse each morning by seven o'clock.[3]

[f] In March he told Lamb that he was convinced that the system of bringing both parties boldly together in society would answer ultimately and lay the foundation of permanent good.

Between March 4th and April 19th he gave fourteen and attended three dinner-parties, held three levées and two 'drawing-rooms', and gave four Balls. He also attended the theatre four times, and went to one concert.[4]

g Croker, the Secretary to the Admiralty, who visited him at Phoenix Park at this time, wrote in his diary that Anglesey put the highest confidence in Lord Holland — 'so high, indeed, as to leave him the arbiter of whether he is to stay in office or not'.[5]

h The Association leaders even tried to persuade Anglesey's son, William, to stand. Anglesey told Holland that 'O'Gorman Mahon who had been sent to Ennis, & who suddenly came back crestfallen at the defection of Macnamara, actually called upon Wm. Paget, before he went to announce the event to the Association, to implore him to stand. William, of course, laughed in his face.'[6]

i P. V. Fitzpatrick states that Sir D. Roose, High Sheriff of Dublin, first conceived the idea of O'Connell's standing. He adds that Roose suggested the movement to Anglesey, who 'was greatly struck with it, and gave it his warmest approbation, enjoining, however, secrecy as to his having been spoken to on the subject.' This seems very unlikely, though it is possible that Anglesey did not actively discountenance the idea.[7]

j Tuyll reported that Sir Edward O'Brien, who had calculated on bringing six hundred of his tenants to the poll for Fitzgerald, 'had the mortification ... of seeing them *all* marched in by two Priests to vote for O'Connell'. On another occasion 'a posse of priests went out four miles to meet Sir A. Fitzgerald, who was bringing in about 70 or 80 of his tenants to vote for Mr F[itzgerald] and actually forced them away from him.'[8]

k When it got out that Tuyll had attended the meeting, Lamb had remonstrated with Anglesey, who replied: 'Tuyll was too bad. All foreigners have an unconquerable propensity to attend debating clubs, & he has the rage more than any other. He told me that he was to go some day & that he was to be *hid* I know not where. But enough of this, it is an unfortunate occurrence & I have felt it much, but there is no use in grumbling about it.'[9]

l 'There is at Ennis', Anglesey wrote to Peel, 'near 300 Constabulary. At Clare Castle (close at hand) 47 artillery, with 2 6-pounders; 120 cavalry; 415 infantry. Within 36 hours, 28 cavalry, 1367 infantry & 2 6-pounders.... At a further distance, one Regiment of cavalry & above 800 infantry. If this cannot keep one County quiet, we are in a bad way.'
Anglesey directed the sheriff and the magistrates to avoid calling upon the military as long as the public safety would permit. He ordered the commander of the troops 'to avoid collision to the last moment, but on no account to allow the use of *blank* cartridges'.[10]

m Palmerston, when he visited Dublin later in the year, understood that Doherty was 'the guiding adviser of Lord Anglesey'.[11]

n Though, as an old man, he wrote that he knew more of the Duke's intentions than he was able to reveal to Anglesey.[12]

^o Cloncurry was one of those who formed what he called the viceroy's 'extra-official council'. Other members were George Villiers (later Earl of Clarendon), Anthony Blake, Chief Remembrancer of Ireland (sometimes described as 'the back-stairs Viceroy'), and W. H. Curran. In his memoirs Cloncurry states that they 'met very frequently at dinner, as well as at other periods, when matters occurred respecting which Lord Anglesey wished for information and advice. And so often, and at such uncertain times, was this assistance called for, that it was my habit to have post-horses constantly ready at Lyons [Cloncurry's country seat], in order to enable me to obey His Excellency's summons.'[13]

^p To Sir Henry Parnell on September 21st Anglesey wrote,

'Lt. Colonel Gosset has just told me of a conversation which took place yesterday in which you stated that I had said to Lord Cloncurry that I had expectations of the Catholic question being granted if the Leaders could be prevailed upon to restrain the meetings.

'I find that he assured you I had not expressed that expectation & I now confirm what he said. In fact, I have no grounds for forming any opinion of the intentions of the King's Ministers upon that subject.

'I have invariably stated whenever I have given any opinion upon the subject that it was purely and simply my own opinion; and that I had no authority from Ministers to utter upon the question. The real truth is that I cannot even guess at their future proceedings in regard to it. If you should have quoted me in a contrary sense you will much oblige me by correcting the misapprehension.'[14]

^q Lord Forbes was present throughout the interview.

^r The Duke of Cumberland thought Anglesey should be impeached for seeing O'Connell.[15]

^s *The Times* sarcastically put it that she 'was not deemed by the Government of Lord Anglesea to have performed any meritorious services'.[16]

^t Sir John Byng, the Commander-in-Chief in Ireland, told Palmerston that 'being asked by Lord Anglesey where he would place two regiments which were coming over from England, he said at once that he would send them among the Protestants of the north, who were much more violent and likely to disturb the public peace than the Catholics of the South; and they went accordingly to Belfast.'[17]

^u To the King Peel wrote that 'all the disposable force in Great Britain has been stationed, as far as possible, within immediate reach of Ireland, and the Lord-Lieutenant has discretionary power to summon the whole of that force to his assistance, without waiting for orders from the Horse-Guards, should he deem it necessary.'[18]

^v Cloncurry succeeded only in postponing the resolution; it was carried at a later meeting of the Association.

A leading article in *The Times* upon 'the real cause' of Anglesey's later recall, suggested that the tactics of Downing Street would never admit the production of any correspondence 'between a meddling chief on this side of the water, and the no less proud but more dignified representative of his Majesty on the other, the subject of which is reported to have been an interdiction of all acquaintance between the gallant Marquis and the most popular member of the Irish peerage [i.e. Cloncurry], from whom the Lord Lieutenant had been in the habit of obtaining highly useful knowledge upon the state of the country.'[19]

w The King described Anglesey's letter as 'nothing but a proud and pompous farrago of the most *outré* bombast, of eulogium upon himself [Anglesey], his political principles, and his government of Ireland'.

The ultra-Tory Lord Bathurst thought the letter plausibly written, 'and well for the purpose'. 'Lord Anglesey', he wrote to Wellington, 'intends, and intended from the beginning, to take a popular course. It gratifies his vanity, of which he has an abundance; and his spleen against a government which he dislikes.'[20]

x In fact this was an invention of Sheil's, Anglesey not knowing of the existence of the Duke's letter until he received it from Curtis. 'Some friend of Mr Sheil', wrote Anglesey in the margin of Curtis's covering letter, 'probably suggested that I might wish to see it.' This calumnious mistake was taken up and made much of by the enemies of Anglesey's policy.[21]

y Anglesey's letter, it would appear, was published without the knowledge of Dr Curtis, though Anglesey was led to believe otherwise by Dr Murray, the Catholic Archbishop of Dublin, to whom Curtis had sent the viceroy's letter.

In a memorandum made by John Wilson Croker, the Secretary to the Admiralty, on January 9th, in which he recounts a conversation which he had with the Duke who entered fully into the whole affair with him, Wellington is quoted as saying that the letter which announced to the Lord Lieutenant that he was to be relieved was received on December 30th. This is correct, but the account continues:

'*The Duke.* — "Now you know his letter to Dr. Curtis is dated the 23rd, yet I cannot help suspecting that it is antedated, and that it was not really written till he had had my letter of recall." *Croker.* — "What, do you think he had the boldness to ante-date his letter a whole week?" *The Duke.* — "Why, there are circumstances that incline me to think so, though I admit there are difficulties as to *time*, which are in the way of that conclusion." '

This unworthy suspicion, besides being quite contrary to what one would expect from so patently honourable a man as Anglesey, is disproved by the fact that Curtis's reply to Anglesey's letter is dated *December 25th*. The original of that letter is among the Plas Newydd papers, and the clarity of Curtis's handwriting can leave no doubt as to the date-heading.

There was at the time, and there still persists, a belief that Anglesey's recall was the result of his letter to Dr Curtis. This was clearly not so, as a week divides the date of the cabinet meeting (December 24th) at which the recall was decided upon, and the date on which Anglesey's letter was published (January 1st). Though in the eyes of the public the letter made it easier to justify the action, to say, as his enemies did, that the making public of the letter, even had there been no other reasons, would have warranted the recall, is to overlook the fact that he only authorized its publication two days *after* he knew that he was to be relieved, and as a direct result of that knowledge.[22]

z This type of coat, which he continued to wear to the end of his days, irrespective of changes of fashion, came to be known as the 'Paget blue coat'. An old Jew once asked the father of Sir Algernon West, whether a certain gentleman walking down Pall Mall was Lord Anglesey. Having received an affirmative reply, he added: 'I would not give him half a crown for his coat.'

As the years went by, those who adopted Anglesey's unfashionable garb came to be known collectively as the 'old Anglesey school of dressers'.[23]

aa Concomitant with the Relief Bill, another was passed which had for object the disfranchisement of the 40s. freeholders. These little men, for the most part the tenants of Protestant landlords, had been given the vote for electioneering purposes in 1793. Anglesey's comment on their extinction was pungent. 'As long', he wrote, 'as they allowed themselves to be driven to the hustings like sheep to the shambles without a will of their own, all was well; not a murmur was heard. But the moment these poor people found out the value of their tenure, the moment they exercised their power constitutionally [as they had done at the Clare election], that instant they are swept out of political existence.'[24]

CHAPTER XI (p. 222 to p. 241)

a On May 17th Croker wrote: 'I have not heard the name of Goderich whispered, nor Palmerston, nor the Grants; but the latter trio of course are included under the word Huskisson. They would certainly make a very respectable government in point of talent and station. In the Lords, Grey, Lansdowne, Holland, Melbourne, and Anglesey. In the Commons, Brougham (if not Chancellor!), Huskisson, Palmerston, the Grants, Mackintosh, Althorp, Graham, Stanley.'[1] This was much the shape which the Grey Government actually took. Huskisson was removed from the scene by his tragic death at the opening of the Manchester and Liverpool railway in September.

b The Duke of Cumberland as early as July 1829 had heard, but told Anglesey that he disbelieved, rumours of a junction of the Whigs with the government. Anglesey thought it highly probable. 'The Duke of Wellington knows', he replied, 'that he cannot rally to him upon his own terms all his former friends, the Tories. He knows he cannot stand as he is. He is determined to hold on as long as he can, & he will be content to pick up all the stragglers he can enlist. He is in head a Tory, but if he can catch a wavering Canningite, (if such there be), he will not reject him.'[2]

e This was hardly an exaggeration. Economic distress was dire and rick-burning and other large-scale disturbances common. Even Wellington a few weeks later admitted that there existed 'a sort of feverish anxiety in every man's mind about public affairs. No man can satisfy himself of the safety either of this country or himself.'[3]

d In 1826 Anglesey had succeeded his brother Edward as Captain of Cowes Castle, a sinecure bringing in about £175 a year. This he held until his death, when the post was abolished. It had originally been a military appointment, the castle of West Cowes being one of a number of small defensive semicircular batteries erected by Henry VIII. Anglesey continued a series of improvements to the amenities of the building which had been started before his time, eventually making the apartments there into a pleasant small house in which he and his family lived for a part of each year.[4]

e The other ministers were:
Lord Brougham, Lord Chancellor;
Lord Althorp, Chancellor of the Exchequer;
Lord Durham, Lord Privy Seal;
Lord Palmerston, Foreign Secretary;
Lord Goderich, Colonial Secretary;
Sir James Graham, First Lord of the Admiralty;
Lord Auckland, President of the Board of Trade;
Charles Grant, Board of Control;
Lord John Russell, Paymaster of the Forces;
Duke of Richmond (Anglesey's son-in-law), Lord Carlisle and Mr Wynne, junior ministers.

CHAPTER XII (p. 242 to p. 278)

a It had obstructed, so far as it could, the introduction of Catholics to posts now open to them for the first time. One of Anglesey's aims, as soon as he returned to Dublin, was to assist worthy Catholics to obtain situations. For Richard Lalor Sheil, of whom he had a high opinion, he arranged a seat in Parliament by making his Dorsetshire 'rotten borough' of Milborne Port available to him; for Cloncurry he obtained an English peerage and for O'Connell, later on, a 'Patent of Precedency' at the Bar.

b The nearest Anglesey ever got to O'Connell's view was when in August 1831, despairing of the Government's ability to get things done for Ireland, he wrote to Lord Holland, 'the inconvenience, or I might say, the impossibility of legislating for Ireland in Downing St., is so obvious to me that if it were not that no Parliament in Dublin would be free to do its duty, as Ireland now is, I would be against the Union.'[1]

c Lord Talbot in a mischievous letter to Gregory suggested that one of the reasons for his dismissal was that Lady Anne Gregory (his wife) 'would never *call* upon Lady Anglesey' on account of the scandal of 1809.[2]

d (See p. 184). Tuyll now became Anglesey's private secretary.

e Nevertheless Anglesey might have protested against it had he thought it sufficiently important to do so, for a letter which he had received as early as November 20th clearly showed O'Connell's aversion to Doherty. In this letter O'Connell referred to 'the most wanton *assault*' which 'the gentleman who is understood to be your Solicitor General' made upon him in the Commons on the previous night, and declared that nothing he had said in 'our last conversation ... could be construed into any pledge' to give support to the Administration, 'or to accept any kind of favour, even from Your Lordship. I cannot conclude this last communication with which I shall ever trouble Your Lordship [!] without expressing my unfeigned regret that a nobleman so revered in Ireland as Lord Anglesey should be likely to place himself in a situation in which the popularity he so honourably earned may suffer diminution.' Yet a conciliatory reply from Anglesey produced another letter from O'Connell six days later in which he expressed his 'most anxious desire for the success of your administration in Ireland. I am quite convinced', he went on, 'you will dissipate the remnants of the old factions.... I am persuaded that you will do every thing for Ireland that can be done by a Lord Lieutenant and an English Parliament.... Be assured', he concluded in his oily manner, 'that if one so powerless as myself, and, naturally, so insignificant, can in any degree facilitate the spread of the benefits which you *intend* for Ireland, I will be most happy to co-operate — if that be not too strong a word — in my humble sphere — without offering that which you would scorn to accept — any sacrifice of principle.'[3]

f The difficulties experienced in the Irish law appointments as well as their immense importance in the eyes of Irishmen are shown by the numerous letters upon them in the Plas Newydd papers which passed between Anglesey and the Cabinet in late November and early December. The final arrangements were:
Lord Plunket, Lord Chancellor;
Doherty, Chief Justice of the Common Pleas;
Joy, Chief Baron of the Exchequer;
Blackburne, Attorney-General;
Crampton, Solicitor-General.

g How many times Anglesey saw O'Connell in London in November and December and exactly what transpired are not known, but what is certain is that he could get no assurances from him that he would change his tune on agitation for repeal. One of the objects of the interviews was at the behest of the Cabinet to see whether O'Connell would take any post under the new Government. 'Lord Anglesey', he wrote, 'sent for me and talked for two hours, to prevail on me to join the Government; he went so far as to discuss my private affairs in order to prevail on me to repair my fortunes!' But though Anglesey soon tired of this rather undignified attempt to persuade the poacher to turn gamekeeper and told Melbourne that he was convinced it was hopeless to entertain any further expectation of conciliating him, the Cabinet, egged on by Sir Henry Parnell and others, continued their efforts, offering him through secret negotiators, the Mastership of the Rolls, and other lucrative legal appointments. O'Connell, of course, turned them all down. 'He is flying at higher game than a Judgeship', Anglesey explained, 'and he is secure of a better income from the deluded people than *any Government* can venture to give to *any Person* whatever.'[4]

h The majority of his letters to Ministers and other semi-official correspondence during his two Irish administrations were entered by clerks into a number of letter-books; these and a mass of letters received by him, as well as numerous memoranda and miscellaneous papers, have been deposited by the present author with the Public Record Office, Northern Ireland.

Between November 1830 and September 1833, Anglesey wrote nearly 300 letters to Lord Grey; nearly as many again to Lord Holland, and considerable numbers to Melbourne and the Chief Secretary. All these, as well as many hundreds of less important communications, were written in his own hand.

i On the evening of March 1st, the day on which Lord John Russell introduced the plan in the Commons, Grey wrote to Anglesey:

'There is the greatest anxiety as to the proposed measure of Reform, the secret of which has been perfectly kept. Members were in the H. of Commons as early as half past six this morning to secure places.... The measure is a strong one. 60 Boroughs disfranchised [including Milborne Port of which Anglesey was patron]; 47 reduced to one member — additional members given to great towns, and to counties; reducing the Commons to 600. The County elections to remain as they are, as to the right of voting, with addition of £10 copy holders, and tenants holding leases, for 21 years, of £50 a year rent; and the counties which have additional members to be divided. The right of voting in towns and boroughs to be householders rated £10 a year — all other rights to be merged in this, when the present possessors die off.... The term of seven years not to be changed in the original Bill; but five may be consented to, if necessary. Ballot to be resisted.

'I was bound by a rule which was not allowed to have any exception, not to mention this before — and even now, pray don't communicate it, till you have seen it in the papers.

'Ireland and Scotland must have separate Bills.'[5]

j When, three years later, the Lords were obstructing the Irish Church Bill, Anglesey wrote 'for my part, the folly of *my brethren* will go far to reconcile me to a Republic. I would fight upon my stumps to put down Radicalism, but I would not budge an inch to restore an unjust preponderance to Aristocracy.'[6]

k Newspaper gossip at this time said that Anglesey had written to the King to say that in the event of a dissolution he could not answer for Ireland. Croker went further and wrote: 'I learn that Ministers consulted Anglesey as to a dissolution; he replied that it would throw Ireland into anarchy. This staggered them; and they begged him to withdraw that letter. He answered that he could not, for that every hour increased his original conviction.' In fact, long before his opinion had been asked Anglesey had told Stanley that though he dreaded a dissolution – 'it would play the devil here' – he saw that recourse would have to be had to it. His having written to the King was utterly false. 'If I *had* written', he protested, 'I should have said that if the *present* Government dissolved Parliament I *would* answer for Ireland, *even now* [April] in its disturbed state, but that if a new Anti-Reforming Government were formed & that *it* appealed to the people, then I would *not* answer for tranquillity. Indeed I would answer for it that there would be frightful agitation.'[7]

[l] Lady Mayo was a sister of Winthrop Mackworth Praed, the poet, who was a strong anti-Reformer.

[m] In those days peers could vote by proxy in all divisions except those which took place when the House was sitting in committee.

[n] Comparatively small numbers of peerages favourable to the government were in fact made both before and after the passing of the Bill. These included Cloncurry in September 1831, and Uxbridge, who was summoned to the House in January 1833 as Baron Paget. Anglesey, on hearing from Grey that this was to be done, wrote: 'You are very kind to Uxbridge. I am sorry that he has an anxiety to be made a Peer, as I fear I may thereby lose the County of Anglesey [which Uxbridge represented in the Commons]. It will, however, fall into the hands of a supporter, and I would not for the world, interfere with Uxbridge's wishes.'[8]

[o] The Irish Reform Act became law on August 7th. Naturally enough it did not restore the franchise to the 40s. freeholders, who had been deprived of it in 1829 (see p. 199 and note aa, p. 375). It gave to Ireland only five new seats, and did not extend the franchise to the same extent as the English Act. O'Connell and his 'tail' found in its provisions ample cause for complaint, but most of Anglesey's attempts to widen its scope received scant attention from the Cabinet. 'This measure was the least successful of the three [English, Scottish and Irish],' says Erskine May. 'Complaints were immediately made of the restricted franchise which it had created; and the number of electors registered proved much less than had been anticipated.'[9]

[p] Some glaring examples were:
Castletown, Cloyne: 3,279 Catholics, 17 Protestants; incumbent paid £414
Mansfield, Armagh: 1,063 Catholics, 4 Protestants; incumbent paid £216.
Clonmult, Cloyne: 1,195 Catholics, 1 Protestant; incumbent paid £176.

[q] Under this Act composition was voluntary only. The Lord Lieutenant if applied to by an incumbent or by a certain number of tithe-payers, could summon a special vestry for the purpose of agreeing upon a composition. This was based on the average price of corn for the last three years.

ʳ Althorp and Russell were both true church reformers but Stanley dominated the Cabinet to an amazing extent. Littleton, who became Irish Secretary in May 1833, wrote in his diary an account of the cabinet meeting he attended on July 21st that year. He concluded the entry: 'Lord John Russell expressed a good stout reforming opinion about the Irish Church Bill, which found no echo. I could clearly see that Stanley was the clog or dead-weight to the movement of the Government in the direction of real Church Reform.'

Grey had told Anglesey in June 1831 that it was absolutely indispensable that Stanley should become a member of the Cabinet. To this, with mild misgivings the Lord Lieutenant had agreed. At the same time he suggested that he too should be of the Cabinet. This Grey thought might be difficult as the Lord Lieutenant was neces-sarily absent at all times, and could not therefore perform the duties of a member of the Cabinet. Anglesey replied that it had been suggested to him that there might be awkwardness in appearing to place the Secretary over the Governor, 'as in the case of Sancho Panza in that of Barataria, and I therefore thought that my appointment, although, in fact, merely nominal might avoid the apparent anomaly, but I do assure you that I am perfectly satisfied with the decision.'

Anglesey told Cloncurry that he did not think Stanley very anxious to uphold him. 'I do believe he would prefer a more *submissive master*,' he wrote. 'You must see that I work at great disadvantage. He knows all *my* schemes, and I know few of his, until he finds himself in a difficulty. Thus all my projects, when laid before the Cabinet, if he does not go the *whole* length with me, (and half-measures are worse than useless), are probably thwarted by him. He tells his own story, and I have no one to support and back my views.'[10]

ˢ The plan included provisions, as did all the schemes, for the extinction of a further tax, known as Church Cess, the most obnoxious of all the imposts upon Roman Catholics. Its purpose was to maintain Protestant churches and to meet the expenses of Protestant religious services. It was under the exclusive management of Protestant vestries, and varied according to the purposes for which it was applied. 'It might', said Althorp, 'be increased by abuses of management, or it might be diminished by frugality; but in neither case had the Catholic the means of exercising any control over the money so levied upon his property.'[11]

ᵗ The Lord Lieutenant's salary in 1662 was £3,684 8s. 9d.; in 1763, £12,000; in 1784 £20,000, and from 1812 to 1831, £30,000.

Among numerous reductions in the official Household was that of the Master of the Riding House, whose salary was curtailed from £675 to £200. Of the sinecures, that of Clerk of the Council, which had been granted to Lord Clifden for life at £1,200 a year, was after his death 'to be regulated, and the duties executed in person'. Also to be abolished when the existing holders died, were the offices of Clerk of the State Papers, Keeper of the Records in Birmingham Tower, Constable of Dublin Castle, the House and Wardrobe Keeper and his assistant, nine different appointments connected with the defunct Irish House of Lords, and finally, sixteen customs officers. Among other financial reforms carried out by Anglesey on his own initiative and as a result of the report of the Select Committee on Civil List Charges, was the transference of the Lord Lieutenant's charitable fund (known as the Concordatum Fund) from the Civil List to Parliament. An example of how this fund had been employed, was the payment of a pension to the wife of a boatman at Carrick 'whose arm was broken by Lord Anglesey's carriage, when passing through that town in 1828'.

ᵘ The Establishment of State Musicians was:

Master & Composer	Seven Violins
Deputy Master & Director	Two Tenors
Attendant on Balls	Two Hautboys
Kettle Drummer	Two French Horns
Serjeant Trumpeter	Four Bass Violins
Five Trumpeters	Dulcimer

ᵛ Brougham says that in December 1832 he deemed a change absolutely necessary, and urged Grey to replace Anglesey by Melbourne or Goderich and to give Stanley the post thus made vacant. But Grey felt that he could not say to Anglesey, 'This is an arrangement which I require for the Government, and therefore you must submit to it whether you like it or not.' Referring to his offer of India, he told Brougham, 'I did, with respect to Lord Anglesey, endeavour to open the way for his retirement from the government of Ireland in the only way in which I could do so without being wanting to all the claims he has upon me — i.e., by making an arrangement which might be both honourable and agreeable to himself.' Since this had fallen through, he felt that there was nothing for it but to leave the general constitution of the Government as it was.[12]

CHAPTER XIII (p. 279 to p. 317)

ᵃ Wellington had advised the King that Peel should be Prime Minister. For the three weeks which elapsed before Peel arrived home, Wellington virtually carried on the government single-handed, so that Peel might have a free hand in the composition of his Cabinet. When Peel arrived, Wellington became Foreign Secretary. The administration lasted only four months, and was succeeded by Melbourne's.

ᵇ At some time previous to his going to Italy, Anglesey had consulted other homoeopathic doctors, including the celebrated Dr Quin of London and Drs Neckar, Schmid and Romani.

In detailing his past medical history to Dr Mauro, Anglesey admitted that he had at one time suffered from a venereal disease. 'Forty-six years earlier [in fact in 1786, see p. 24] he had had syphilis and had been cured within three weeks by the Emperor's surgeon-in-chief [probably Dr Tissot or Dr Lachans, see p. 25] ... since then he had had no further symptom of it. He believes that for some time he had had warts.' Hahnemann tells Mauro, in one letter, that he has seen a sympathetic cure which succeeded in curing warts: 'one takes a small piece of pork, rubs the warts lightly with it and gives it to a cur to eat or digs it into soft soil so that it putrefies.'

In insisting that constant exercise is the first essential, Hahnemann adds that in cold weather Anglesey is to cover his face with a gauze or crape veil.

Clarence Paget's ailments were said to be 'acute rheumatism', 'gonorrhoea with herpetic eruptions' and 'chancre'. The symptoms were a high fever in cold weather, swelling of the knees and feet (the knees were so sensitive that the slighest pressure 'even of his trousers' was painful), and inflammation of the right eye. 'There is a phimosis due to the scars of old chancre ulcers. The friction of coitus again causes gonorrhoea, and when this dies down, the knees start to swell again, etc.' Dunsford also asks advice about another anonymous young man, 'very moral, whom circumstances prevent from marrying' and who suffers from 'an excess of sexual desire the suppression of which drives him practically mad'. Platinum and other remedies have proved useless. Hahnemann tells Dunsford to give Clarence few or no medicines until he (Hahnemann) has had a chance to examine him, and meanwhile 'to regulate his way of life'. In the case of the moral young man, he remarks that if he is under twenty-seven, 'nocturnal pollutions occurring every eight to ten days are intended by nature to pacify the sexual urge. After that age nature demands marriage, reduces the pollutions and thereby torments the young man who is resisting the demands of nature.' He gives a remedy for producing nocturnal pollutions in a man under twenty-seven should they not occur naturally, and recommends avoidance of coffee and tea.

The drugs which seem to have been most successful in Anglesey's case were sulphur, arsenic, sabadilla and thuja. For the constipation, Hahnemann sent Anglesey a feather impregnated with nux vomica, from which he was to inhale.

At one point Hahnemann refused to send any more drugs, until his fee of thirty napoleons had been paid.

That Anglesey early grasped the principles of homoeopathy is shown by his remark to Arthur that for some time his sufferings had been produced by the remedies 'whose object is to bring on an artificial disease with the intention of beating out the natural one'. He rather pathetically added: 'That they have accomplished the first object I will vouch, let us hope that they will be equally successful in the second.'

Though no cure has yet been found for the tic douloureux (trigeminal neuralgia), Dr Wilfred Harris, who died in 1960, discovered in 1910 that the injection of alcohol into the nerve ganglion gave great relief to many sufferers.

James Hogg, 'the Ettrick Shepherd', gives a graphic description of the horrors of the disease:

'I never fan [felt] ony pain like the Tick Dollaroose. Ane's no accustomed to a pain in the face. For the toothach's in the inside o' the mouth, no in the face; and you've nae idea hoo sensitive's the face. Cheeks are a' fu' o' nerves — and the Tick attacks the hail bunch o' them screwing them up to sic a pitch o' tension that you canna help screeching out, like a thousan ools, and clappin' the pawms o' your haums to your distrackit chafts [jaws], and rowin' yoursell on the floor, on your groff ['on the groffe' = flat on the ground], wi' your hair on end, and your een [eyes] on fire, and a general muscular convulsion in a' your sinnies; sae piercin', and searchin', and scrutinisin', and diggin' and houkin', and tearing is the pangfu' pain that keeps eatin' awa and manglin' the nerves o' your human face divine. Draps o' sweat, as big as beads for the neck or arms o' a lassie are pourin' doun to the verra floor, soe that the folks that hears you roarin' thinks you're greetin' [weeping], and you are aye afterwards considered a bairnly chiel through the hail kintra. In ane o' the sudden fits I grappit sic haud o' a grape [fork] that I was helpin' our Shusey to muck the byre wi', that it withered in my fingers like a frush [brittle] saugh-wand [willow-stick] — and 'twould hae been the same had it been a bar o' iron. Only think o' the Tick Dollaroose in a man's face continuing to a' eternity!'[1]

[c] From Clarence's description of Hahnemann it seems that he had forgotten when he wrote his autobiography that the first time he had seen him was in Köthen in 1835, not in Paris in 1836.

[d] By 1840 Char was confined to a wheel chair, as a result, it seems, of acute rheumatism. Lord Dudley used to tell a story, which dates from about this period, of how one of her daughters, upon hearing her father give orders for the shooting of a mare, demanded to know the reason. When Anglesey explained to her that the animal was old and lame, she asked, 'Oh! Papa! When are you going to shoot Mama?'[2]

[e] Earl Granville was ambassador in Paris, and an uncle of Lord Francis Leveson-Gower who had been Irish Secretary in 1828. Lord Hatherton was E. J. Littleton, Irish Secretary in 1833, who had been raised to the peerage in 1835. Edward Ellice, known from his connexion with the fur trade as 'Bear' Ellice, was Secretary for War in Lord Grey's administration. 'Old Sugarloaf' was Count Scouvaloff, whose nickname had first been coined for his wife by the second Lady Morley, whose wit, incidentally, also led her to dub Prince Gorchakov, 'Prince Got-such-a-cough'.[3] This Lady Morley had married Lord Boringdon in 1809 after his first wife, née Lady Augusta Fane, had left him and eloped with Arthur Paget, whose wife she became (see note c, p. 354).

[f] Viscount Chelsea was the eldest son of Lady Cadogan and became the 4th Earl Cadogan. Miss Wellesley was the third daughter of the Hon. and Rev. Gerald Wellesley, whose wife was Lord Chelsea's aunt and Lady Anglesey's sister. The marriage was objected to because the parties were first cousins. It took place, notwithstanding, six months later.

The intermingling of Paget, Cadogan and Wellesley blood was carried a stage further in 1851, when the Angleseys' youngest daughter, Adelaide, married *her* first cousin, the Hon. Frederick William Cadogan, fourth son of Lady Anglesey's brother, the 3rd Earl Cadogan.

The 3rd Lord Graves was the eldest son of Anglesey's sister Mary, whose husband had committed suicide in 1830 (see p. 223 above). His first wife, the daughter of Marshal Berthier, Napoleon's chief-of-staff, had died in 1833.

[g] Bellini's *Norma* and Francesco Gnecco's *La Prova d'un Opera Seria* seem to have been given on the same night. *La Prova* provided the famous Neapolitan actor-singer Lablache with one of his favourite parts. It was in this year that he started giving singing lessons to Princess Victoria, who continued them for some time after

she became Queen. She later wrote of him that he was 'not only one of the finest bass singers, that we have seen, but a remarkably clever, gentleman-like man, full of anecdote and knowledge, and most kind and warm-hearted. He was very tall, and immensely large, but had a remarkably fine head and countenance. He used to be called "Le Gros de Naples". The Prince [Consort] and Queen had a sincere regard for him.'[4]

Giulia Grisi, niece of Grassini and sister of the famous ballet dancer, was at this time in her twenties. Bellini thought her the perfect Adalgisa in *Norma*.

John Liston was one of the great comic actors of the Haymarket and elsewhere during the early part of the nineteenth century.

[h] This formidable weapon consisted of twenty-five barrels, charged with a variety of missiles, and lighted simultaneously by a train of gunpowder. The King and his sons were unscathed, but more than forty people were killed or injured.

[i] By the following year, Clarence was completely recovered. He resumed his career in the Royal Navy by being appointed to command the *Pearl* corvette. This was a particular compliment to Anglesey, for it was he who had proposed to Sainty, the ship-designer, that a corvette should be built upon the lines of his yacht *Pearl*, which was the clipper of those days.

[j] The ship's boy, named William Heritage, on the *North Star*'s passage from Madeira to Barbados, had failed 'to lock the tank after going for water'. For this offence (a more serious one than it sounds, for fresh water aboard ship was a most precious commodity) he had been ordered to be flogged. Not long before he had received twelve strokes for another, unspecified offence. To avoid the second flogging he had committed suicide by throwing himself overboard. As a result of a letter from the boy's father to the Admiralty, William Paget had undergone two Courts of Enquiry in Halifax, Nova Scotia, both of which had honourably acquitted him. Upon his return home, Their Lordships, being dissatisfied, had ordered a third Court of Enquiry. To this William had quite rightly objected, insisting instead upon a full court martial. This was held aboard H.M.S. *St Vincent* in the first week of February 1831, under the presidency of the Commander-in-Chief, Portsmouth, Sir Thomas Foley, one of Nelson's famous 'Band of Brothers'. Its findings were conclusively in William Paget's favour.

[k] When Anglesey was a member of Lord John Russell's Government in 1846, he thought it right to inquire of Palmerston, the Foreign Secretary, whether as a Minister he should ask Louis Napoleon to shoot at Beaudesert. Palmerston replied that he did not himself see much objection 'to your giving young Napoleon a day's shooting at Feathered Bipeds as he has given up shooting at the Bourbons', but that he thought it best to consult the Prime Minister. Russell, however, thought it better to postpone the invitation for a year, as 'a man of such bad faith as Guizot might make it a pretext for creating disturbance in Ireland, or any other act of malice.'

When, in 1849, Napoleon had come to power, he asked Anglesey to stay at the Elysée. This, however, seems not to have come about. 'Allow me, Prince,' wrote

Anglesey in thanking him for the invitation, 'to take this opportunity of assuring you of the heartfelt satisfaction I have derived from observing your judicious and successful career, under circumstances the most trying and difficult, and where a combination of firmness, of forbearance, of discretion, and of decision, were absolutely necessary to the achievement of your patriotic efforts in the regeneration of your country, sincerely hoping that the termination of your glorious career may be as glorious as the commencement.'[5]

[1] Seven years later, in reply to a letter from Brougham complaining of the clocks supplied by the Ordnance department, Anglesey, who was then Master-General of the Ordnance, wrote in reference to Brougham's notoriously illegible handwriting: 'Our clocks are good, but we and other departments that have the pleasure of corresponding with you, require a decypherer, for by one of Mr Vulliamy's own make, I was full half an hour in guessing at your hieroglyphics, and upon my soul, they do not give me time for such employment.' The letter proceeds in this vein of friendly badinage, and shows that the personal friendship revived.[6]

m Lawrence's full-length, life-size portrait of Anglesey possessed by the Duke of Wellington, had been painted as the result of a request by the Duke that Anglesey should sit for it. It is a version of an earlier painting by Lawrence which now hangs at Plas Newydd. It was bought from the artist for £210 in 1818, when Wellington 'was making a collection of the pictures of the principal officers whom I had the honour of commanding during the War'. The picture was not delivered to Apsley House (where it now hangs) until 1830, soon after Lawrence's death. At the time of its painting (in 1818) Anglesey asked the Duke to sit to the same painter, so that there might be a portrait of the victor of Waterloo upon the walls of Beaudesert.

'There was some delay about the Duke's sitting,' wrote Anglesey to his brother Berkeley from Dublin in 1831, 'but finally he did sit and the head was quite finished, and so it remained. I then came to this country, and you will know under what peculiar circumstances I quitted it. It was not a time to press the completion of the portrait, although I never lost sight of it, but, for decency's sake, one could not be coquetting by proposing that the Duke should have it completed, when we were supposed *to be very angry with each other*, although, in point of fact, this was not the case, at least on my part. The portrait, then, was not completed, and I always expected to be informed that this head was placed to my account, and so forth. Not, however, having heard anything about it, I desired Sanderson (I think) to write to you to ascertain how the matter stood. It now appears ... that such head is not forthcoming, and someone has probably contrived to possess himself of it. For this there appears no remedy, and I regret it, for although we did not separate upon the best terms, yet I should have liked much to have left a portrait of the D. of W. on the walls of old Beaudesert.'

[This head of the Duke by Lawrence could conceivably be that referred to under No. 13, Appx. B, in Ld G. Wellesley (later 7th Duke of Wellington) & J. Steegman, *The Iconography of the First Duke of Wellington*, 1935, 62.][7]

N

[n] Five years later, when the Emperor visited England, Greville described him as very imposing but without 'the highest aristocratic stamp; his general appearance,' he added, 'is inferior to that of Lord Anglesey ... (twenty-five years older), and to others.'[8]

[o] Melbourne thought Alfred and his sisters 'such complete Cadogans', but considered George Paget better looking than Alfred.[9]

[p] The barrister appearing for the plaintiffs in his opening remarks recalled that Uxbridge had been made a peer in the lifetime of his father (see note n, p. 379), which might, he said, lead the jury to speculate whether the defendant had been so raised to the peerage 'in order that, as a legislator, he might benefit his country, or that he might enjoy the priviledge of freedom from arrest (which was, until recent times, the right of all peers).'[10]

[q] See p. 166 above.

On another occasion, at the end of May 1836, Lord Hill had called on Anglesey at Uxbridge House.

'He came from the King,' wrote Anglesey in a memorandum. 'I said: "I guess your commission — You are to tell me that His Majesty has appointed *you* to [be Colonel of] the Fuzilier Guards, & that he wishes to place me at the head of the Blues [Royal Horse Guards]." "No," said he, "you are mistaken — The King has expressed himself in the most kind & flattering terms about you & has ordered me to offer *You* the Fuzilier Guards." Of course I expressed my deep sense of H.My's obliging consideration of me & begged Ld Hill to assure the King of my gratitude & to say that I did not accept, because I had a scruple, as an Officer of Cavalry to run away with one of the best things of the Infantry — that I had a further scruple, as feeling that it ought to be given to a Scotsman, & further that having been 39 years in the Regiment I now have [the 7th Hussars], I felt a disinclination to quit it.'

The 3rd Fusilier Regiment of Foot Guards became the Scotch Fusilier Guards [Scots Guards] in 1831. The vacancy was caused by the death of the late Colonel, the 5th Duke of Gordon, who as Marquess of Huntly had raised the Gordon Highlanders, and fought beside Anglesey in the Helder and Walcheren campaigns.[11]

CHAPTER XIV (p. 318 to p. 341)

[a] Henry Paget later became 3rd Marquess of Anglesey. In October 1851 his grandfather wrote to him thus: 'My dear Henry, I have received three letters on three consecutive days from you upon the subject of your anxiety to obtain a permanent situation ... at the Horse Guards. You have always seemed to me to be impressed with the idea that importunity in the setting forth of a claim founded upon the Services of your relatives ... would certainly obtain success. I am far from thinking so.'[1]

b The Paget Light Cavalry Carbine and the Paget Light Dragoon Pistol, though not, as sometimes stated, actually invented by Anglesey, were almost certainly adopted by the light cavalry at his instance. It is possible that he collaborated with the gun-maker Henry Nock upon the production of these weapons at about the time of his assuming command of the 7th. Their introduction is an important landmark in the history of fire-arms. Their revolutionary feature was the fastening to the barrel, near the muzzle, of the iron ramrod, so that in use it was never detached from the weapon. This was a conspicuous boon to the soldier who had to load in the saddle. The Paget ramrod came to be used on all subsequent cavalry carbines and pistols down to the end of muzzle-loading in 1867, not only in Britain but also on the Continent and in America.[2]

c This, of course, was the new and frightening factor. Both Wellington and Anglesey were constantly aware of the changed conditions brought about by the invention of the steam-engine, both at sea and on land. Though he perforce accepted, Anglesey never relished them. In 1847 he told the Bishop of Bath and Wells that he would like to 'level every rail road throughout the Empire and to explode steam both by sea and by land, but I do not know how to set about effecting this most desirable object!' To Clarence in 1853, he wrote: 'I have the same regret at the substitution of steam for canvass that I feel that I should have had if I had lived in the days when the employment of gunpowder to kill your enemy at a distance was introduced, instead of the more animating practice of doing it à l'arme blanche, when the best man was sure to win.' (See, also, p. 337.)

There were other signs of progress with which he was not in sympathy. In the 1820s he had violently objected to the building of Telford's great suspension bridge over the Menai Straits, for reasons which are not clear. As to the effect upon navigation which would be produced by the Britannia tubular railways bridge, completed in 1850 near the suspension bridge, he felt that though it might not obstruct the channel, 'yet it must, I apprehend, cause very inconvenient eddy winds in passing under it.'[3]

d The nearest the Government ever got to taking effective action was when Russell proposed in the Commons in February 1848 to reorganize the militia (Wellington wanted it actually called out), and slightly to augment the regular forces (Wellington wanted an increase of at least 20,000 men), with an increase of income tax from sevenpence to one shilling. The change of Government in France which came about while the debate continued, and the lack of support in the House, induced the Government to drop these measures. In 1849 considerable reductions were made.

e Anglesey was succeeded at the Ordnance by Lord Hardinge, the very last holder of the office. There is a story that Hardinge, immediately upon Anglesey's retirement, wrote to Lord Londonderry advising him to apply for the post, but before he could do so, Hardinge himself was offered and had actually accepted it, without letting Londonderry know. Uxbridge, retailing the story to his father, wrote: 'Lord Londonderry I am told has not spoken to [Hardinge] since.'[4]

ABBREVIATIONS
USED IN THE SOURCE NOTES

Only those sources which occur more than once in the source notes
are included in this list.

I UNPUBLISHED SOURCES

APP	The papers of Sir Arthur Paget, other than those printed in *The Paget Papers* and *The Paget Brothers*. In the possession of The Lady Phyllis Benton
Grey (Durham)	The papers of Earl Grey, in the possession of Durham University
Harness MSS	The papers of William Harness, other than those printed in *The Letters Home of William Harness*. In the possession of Mrs C. M. Duncan-Jones
Hickleton Papers	The papers at Hickleton. In the possession of the Earl of Halifax
Ilchester MSS	The papers of Lord Holland. In the possession of the Earl of Ilchester
Jeayes	Jeayes, I. H., *Descriptive Catalogue of the … Muniments … at Plas Newydd*, 1934
Le Marchant MSS	The papers of Major-General J. G. Le Marchant. In the possession of his descendants
Londonderry MSS	The papers of Charles Stewart (Vane), 3rd Marquess of Londonderry. In the possession of the Marquess of Londonderry
PNP	The Plas Newydd Papers. In the possession of the present author. (The majority of the MSS referring to the two Irish administrations have been transferred to the Public Record Office, Northern Ireland.)
PRO/HO	The Public Record Office, Home Office papers
PRO/WO	The Public Record Office, War Office papers
RA	The Royal Archives, Windsor Castle. In the possession of Her Majesty the Queen
Spencer MSS	The papers at Althorp. In the possession of Earl Spencer
Wildman	Letter dated June 19th, 1815, from Captain Wildman, A.D.C. to the Earl of Uxbridge, to his mother, Mrs Wildman. In the possession of Lieut.-Colonel Cyril Paget. (The letter has been printed in *The Listener*, June 24th, 1954, pp. 1085-7, and broadcast on the Third Programme of the B.B.C., introduced by Sir Grimwood Mears, K.C.I.E.)

II PUBLISHED SOURCES

Arbuthnot	Aspinall, A., *The Correspondence of Charles Arbuthnot*, 1941
Aspinall	Aspinall, A. (ed.), *Three Early Nineteenth Century Diaries*, 1952

Bagot	Bagot, J. (ed.), *George Canning and his Friends*, 1909
Bessborough	Bessborough, Earl of, and Aspinall, A. (ed.), *Lady Bessborough and her Family Circle*, 1940
Booth	[Booth, J. (ed.)] *The Battle of Waterloo ... by a near observer*, 1815-17
Canning's Ministry	Aspinall, A., *The Formation of Canning's Ministry*, 1937
Capel Letters	Anglesey, Marquess of (ed.), *The Capel Letters*, *1814-1817*, 1955
Carnock	Carnock, Lord (ed.), 'The Diary of the Adjutant of the XVth Hussars', *The Journal of the Society for Army Historical Research*, special publication no. 4, 1936
Clarence Paget	Otway, Sir A., Bt (ed.), *The Autobiography and Journals of Lord Clarence Paget, G.C.B.*, 1896
Cloncurry	*Personal Recollections of the Life and Times of Valentine, Lord Cloncurry*, 1849
Cockayne	Cockayne, G. E., *The Complete Peerage*
Colborne	Moore Smith, G. C., *The Life of John Colborne, Field Marshal Lord Seaton*, 1903
Creevey	Maxwell, Sir H., Bt (ed.), *The Creevey Papers*, 1903
Croker	Jennings, L. J. (ed.), *The Correspondence and Diaries of John Wilson Croker*, 1885
DEP	*Dublin Evening Post*
DMR	*Dublin Morning Register*
Doyle	Fitzpatrick, W. J., *The Life, Times and Correspondence of Dr Doyle, Bishop of Kildare*, 1861
Duncan-Jones	Duncan-Jones, Caroline M. (ed.), *The Letters Home of William Harness, an Officer of George III*, 1957
Dyott	Jeffery, R. W. (ed.), *Dyott's Diary*, *1781-1845*, 1907
EHR	*The English Historical Review*
EP	Paget, Harriet M. and Eden (ed.), *Letters and Memorials of General Sir Edward Paget, G.C.B.* [privately printed, 1898]
Farington	Greig, J. (ed.), *The Farington Diary* [Joseph Farington, R.A.] 1924
Fortescue	Fortescue, Hon. (Sir) J. W., *A History of the British Army*, 1899-1930
Fortescue MSS	*HMC Report on the MSS of J. B. Fortescue*, 1927
Frazer	Sabine, E. (ed.), *Letters of Sir A. S. Frazer, K.C.B.*, 1859
Geo IV	Aspinall, A. (ed.), *The Letters of George IV*, *1812-1830*, 1938
Gibney	Gibney, Dr, *Eighty Years Ago*, 1896
Girlhood	Esher, Viscount (ed.), *The Girlhood of Queen Victoria*, 1912
Gleig	Gleig, G. R., *Personal Reminiscences of the Duke of Wellington*, 1904
Gordon	Wylly, H. C. (ed.), *A Cavalry Officer in the Corunna Campaign*, *1808-1809, the Journal of Captain Gordon of the XVth Hussars*, 1913
Gregory	Gregory, Lady (ed.), *Mr Gregory's Letter Box*, *1813-1830*, 1894
Greville	Strachey, L. and Fulford, R. (ed.), *The Greville Memoirs*, *1814-1860*, 1938

Greys	Almack, E., *The History of the 2nd Dragoons, 'Royal Scots Greys'*, 1912
Gronow	Greco, J. (ed.), *The Reminiscences and Recollections of Captain Gronow, 1810-1860*, 1890
Guest	Guest, Montague, and Boulton, W. B., *The Royal Yacht Squadron: Memorials ... from the Official Records*, 1903
Hansard (C)	*Hansard's Parliamentary Debates*, House of Commons
Hansard (L)	*Hansard's Parliamentary Debates*, House of Lords
HMC	The Historical Manuscripts Commission
Hope-Johnstone MSS	The papers of J. J. Hope-Johnstone of Annandale, Historical Manuscripts Commission, 1897
Ilchester	Ilchester, Earl of, *The Chronicles of Holland House, 1820-1900*, 1937
JAHR	*The Journal of the Society for Army Historical Research*
Kennedy	Kennedy, Sir J. Shaw, *Notes on the Battle of Waterloo*, 1865
Le Marchant	Le Marchant, D., *Memoirs of Major-General J. G. Le Marchant* [privately printed, 1841]
Leveson-Gower	Granville, C., Countess (ed.), *Lord Granville Leveson-Gower: Private Correspondence, 1781-1821*, 1916
McDowell	McDowell, R. B., *Public Opinion and Government Policy in Ireland, 1801-1846*, 1952
McGuffie	McGuffie, T. H., 'Kelly of Waterloo', *JAHR*, XXXIII, 1955
Mercer	Mercer, C. (Fortescue, Hon. (Sir) J. W. (ed.)), *Journal of the Waterloo Campaign*, 1927
Miss Berry	Lewis, Lady Theresa (ed.), *The Journal of Miss Berry, 1783-1852*, 1865
Mrs Arbuthnot	Bamford, F. and Wellington, 7th Duke of (ed.), *Journal of Mrs Arbuthnot, 1820-1832*, 1950
O'Connell	Fitzpatrick, W. J. (ed.), *The Correspondence of Daniel O'Connell*, 1888
Oman	Oman, (Sir) Charles W. C., *Wellington's Army, 1809-1814*, 1913
Palmerston	Ashley, Hon. E., *The Life and Correspondence of Henry John Temple, Viscount Palmerston*, 1879
P. Bros.	Hylton, Lord (ed.), *The Paget Brothers, 1790-1840*, 1918
Peel	Stanhope, Earl and Cardwell, Lord (ed.), *The Memoirs of Sir Robert Peel*, 1856
PP	Paget, Sir Augustus, G.C.B. (ed.), *The Paget Papers, diplomatic and other correspondence of the Right Hon. Sir Arthur Paget, G.C.B., 1794-1829*, 1896
Raikes	Raikes, Thos., *A Portion of the Journal kept by Thomas Raikes, 1831-47*, 1856-8
7th H	Barrett, C. R. B., *The 7th (Queen's Own) Hussars*, 1914
Shelley	Edgcumbe, R. (ed.), *The Diary of Frances, Lady Shelley, 1787-1817*, 1912
Siborne	Siborne, H. T. (ed.), *Waterloo Letters*, 1891
Stanhope	Stanhope, Earl, *Notes of Conversations with Wellington*, 1888

Stockmar	Müller, F. Max (ed.), *Memoirs of Baron Stockmar by his son Baron E. von Stockmar*, 1872
Victoria	Benson, A. C. and Esher, Viscount, *The Letters of Queen Victoria, 1837-1861*, 1907
Vivian	Vivian, Hon. C., *Richard Hussey Vivian, 1st Baron Vivian, a Memoir*, 1897
Walpole	Toynbee, Mss Paget (ed.), *The Letters of Horace Walpole*, 1905
Wellington (D)	Gurwood, Lt-Col. (ed.), *The Dispatches of Field Marshal the Duke of Wellington ... 1799-1818*, 1837-8
Wellington (SD)	Wellington, [2nd] Duke of (ed.), *The Supplementary Despatches, Correspondence and Memoranda of Arthur, Duke of Wellington*, 1858-72
Wellington (D:NS)	Wellington, [2nd] Duke of (ed.), *Despatches, Correspondence and Memoranda of Arthur, Duke of Wellington (New Series)*, 1867-80
West	West, Sir Algernon, *Recollections 1832-86*, 1899
Wood	Wood, Sir Evelyn, V.C., *Cavalry in the Waterloo Campaign*, 1895
XV H	Wylly, H. C., *XVth (the King's) Hussars, 1759-1913*, 1914

SOURCES
QUOTED IN THE TEXT

CHAPTER I (p. 19 to p. 23)

[1] Quoted in Locke (A. Audrey), *The Seymour Family*, 1911, 46

[2] Which took place at Castle Forbes in Ireland, the seat of the Earl of Granard. The marriage was confirmed in Dublin on 10 July 1767. Parish of St Anne's, *Dublin Parish Register Society*, 60

[3] [n.d. ?16 Dec. 1798], Ly Louisa Paget to Hon. Mrs Sneyd, PNP

[4] 19 Oct. 1839, *Girlhood*, II, 270

[5] Abstracts of wills of Peter Walter, sen. and jun., 6 Jan. 1769, PNP

[6] 27 Nov. 1845, Anglesey to Mrs Berkeley Paget, PNP

[7] 'Peter Pindar' [J. Wolcot or C. F. Lawler], *Tears of St Margaret's*, 1792

[8] Ly Stafford to Ld G. Leveson-Gower, *Leveson-Gower*, I, 85

[9] The author is indebted to Mr Sidney Crawford of Adelaide, Australia, for bringing this story to his attention

[10] 1 Nov. 1785, PNP

[11] Memorandum by Anglesey [n.d. ?1840], PNP

[12] Paget to Uxbridge, 1 Nov. 1785; 17 Oct. 1786, PNP

CHAPTER II (p. 24 to p. 40)

[1] Reynolds (F.), *The Life and Times of Frederic Reynolds, by himself*, 1826, I, 367

[2] Paget and St Germain to Uxbridge and Css of Uxbridge, Aug. 1786 to Oct. 1788, PNP

[3] St Germain to Uxbridge [n.d. ?Oct.-Nov. 1786] (translated from the French), PNP

[4] St Germain to Uxbridge, 20 Jan. 1787, PNP

[5] St Germain to Rev. G. Champagné, 22 Apr. 1787, PNP

[6] PNP

[7] Queen Charlotte to Css of Uxbridge, 25 Dec. 1800, PNP

[8] PNP

[9] Paget to Arthur Paget [n.d. ?1807], *P. Bros.*

[10] Feb. 1791, *Walpole*, XIV, 363

[11] Ld H. FitzGerald to A. Paget, 24 Dec. 1790; 3 Jan.; 9 Dec. 1791, *P. Bros.*, 3, 5, 7

[12] *Bon Ton Magazine*, I (1791), 365-6

[13] Apr. 1791, *Walpole*, XIV, 411; XV, 313. See also *Miss Berry*, I, 441

CHAPTER III (p. 41 to p. 54)

[1] *Leveson-Gower*, I, 86

[2] Memorandum by Anglesey [n.d. ?184?], PNP

[3] Duncan-Jones, 35, 39

[4] Duncan-Jones, 42

[5] Duncan-Jones, 38

[6] Harness to Mrs Harness, 23 May 1794, Harness MSS

[7] Duncan-Jones, 48

[8] Duncan-Jones, 48

[9] Duncan-Jones, 45

[10] A. Wesley to Sir C. Fortescue, 20 Dec. 1794, *Wellington (SD)*, XIII, 1

[11] Duncan-Jones, 66

[12] Atkinson (C. T.), 'Gleanings from the Cathcart MSS, Pt. IV, The Netherlands, 1794-5', *JAHR*, XXIX (1951), 153

[13] Stanhope, 182. For a fuller account of the campaign as seen through Paget's and Edward Paget's eyes, see Anglesey (Marquess of), *Two Brothers in the Netherlands, 1794-5*, an edition of their letters to Uxbridge and Css of Uxbridge, 3 May 1794 to 9 Dec. 1795 (PNP), *JAHR*, XXXII (1954), nos. 130-1

[14] 16 Jan. 1804, PNP

[15] 'Statement of facts by Lady Paget' in 'Decreet Divorce: Lady Paget v. Lord Paget, 1810', PNP

[16] Jersey to Georgiana, Css Spencer [8 June 1795], Spencer MSS

[17] *Le Marchant*, 58

[18] Le Marchant to Mrs Le Marchant, Aug. 1797, Le Marchant MSS

[19] 19 July 1798, Le Marchant MSS

CHAPTER IV (p. 55 to p. 62)

[1] PRO/WO orig. corres. 1/180, 145, 205, 215

[2] Cannon (R.) (ed.), *Historical Records of the British Army: 7th (Queen's Own) Hussars*, 1842, 66n.

[3] PRO/WO orig. corres. 1/180, 241, 345, 377

[4] PRO/WO orig. corres. 1/180, 391, et seq., muster-roll (25 Oct.-24 Nov.) 9 Dec. 1799

[5] Charles Paget to A. Paget, 1 June 1805, *P. Bros.*, 35

[6] 13 Feb. 1805, *Farington*, III, 60

[7] Ly L. Erskine to J. Erskine, 27 Jan. 1801, PNP

[8] Ly L. Erskine to A. Paget, 24 Nov. 1805, *P. Bros.*, 50

[9] Paget to A. Paget, 28 Sep. 1801, APP

[10] Ly L. Erskine to A. Paget, 25 Aug. 1805, *P. Bros.*, 39

[11] R. H. Vivian to his father, 14 Aug. 1803, *Vivian*, 56

[12] *Gronow*, II, 89; *Girlhood*, II, 66; *Colborne*, 219

CHAPTER V (p. 63 to p. 88)

[1] Londonderry MSS

[2] Paget to A. Paget, 17 Aug. 1808, *PP*, II, 383

[3] *Colborne*, 86

[4] 24 Aug. 1808, Londonderry MSS

[5] Paget to Uxbridge, 28 Aug. 1808, *EP*, 94

[6] Edward Paget to Css of Uxbridge, 10 Oct.; 11 Oct. 1808, *EP*, 102-3

[7] *EP*, 114

[8] E. Paget to Css of Uxbridge, 13 Nov. 1808, *EP*, 104

[9] Berkeley Paget to Uxbridge, 16 Nov. 1808, *EP*, 107

[10] R. H. Vivian's Diary, 19 Nov. 1808, *Vivian*, 74

[11] Paget to Uxbridge, 3 Dec. 1808, *EP*, 111

[12] Paget to A. Paget, 23 Nov. 1808, *PP*, II, 384

[13] Paget to A. Paget, 24 Nov. 1808, *PP*, II, 386-7

[14] Paget to Uxbridge, 3 Dec. 1808, *EP*, 113

[15] Paget to Uxbridge, 4 Dec. 1808, *EP*, 113-14

[16] *EP*, 116

[17] Paget to A. Paget, 22 Dec. 1808, *PP*, 388

[18] *Gordon*, 102

[19] Paget to A. Paget, 22 Dec. 1808, *PP*, 388-9

[20] Article [by Murray (Sir John)], *Quarterly Review*, LVI (1836), 447 and n.

[21] *Papers relative to Spain and Portugal, presented to Parliament in 1809*, 221

[22] Fortescue, VI, 352

[23] Paget to A. Paget, 28 Dec. 1808, *PP*, 389

[24] Paget to Moore, 29 Dec. 1808, PRO/WO 1/236, 261-4

[25] *Colborne*, 97, 386

[26] Sturgis (J.) (ed.), *A Boy in the Peninsular War; the Services ... of Robert Blakeney ... 28th Regiment*, 1899, 48

[27] *Gordon*, 175

[28] Anglesey to Grey, 30 July 1834, *PNP*

[29] *Gordon*, 194

CHAPTER VI (p. 89 to p. 112)

[1] It has not been thought necessary to give individual references for the detailed transactions of the elopement and divorce in this chapter; the chief sources for these are:

1   A. Paget to and from his brothers and others, APP

2   PNP

3   Somerset House and House of Lords records of the proceedings of the Consistory Court

4   'Evidence in Wellesley's Divorce Bill', 9 Feb. 1810, House of Lords

5   'An Act to dissolve the Marriage of ... Henry Wellesley with ... Lady Charlotte Wellesley ... and to enable him to marry again ...', 22 Feb. 1810', 2 Anno 50 Geo 3 (House of Lords)

6   Draft MS memorandum in hand of Sir A. Wellesley [n.d.], Duke of Wellington's MSS at Apsley House

7   Matthew Lewis to Css Grey [n.d. 1810], Hickleton Papers

8   Webster (Sir C.) (ed.), 'Some Letters of the Duke of Wellington to his brother, William Wellesley-Pole', RHS, *Camden Miscellany*, XVIII, 1948, nos. 22, 23

9   *Farington*, V, 174-5

10   Bickley (F.) (ed.), *The Diaries of Sylvester Douglas, Lord Glenbervie*, 1928, II, 73, 89, 104

11   *Miss Berry*, II, 383

12 *Leveson-Gower*, II, 365, 428
13 *Bessborough*, 172
14 Leveson-Gower (Sir G.) and Palmer (Iris), *Hary-O: The Letters of Lady Harriet Cavendish, 1796-1809*, 1940, 307-11
15 *P. Bros.*
16 *Capel Letters*
17 Fortescue, VII
18 Paterson (James), *A Compendium of English and Scottish Law*, 1860, 290
19 Newspapers and journals, daily and weekly
² Fremantle (A. F.), *England in the Nineteenth Century, 1801-1810*, 1930, II, 416
³ Paget to Css of Uxbridge, 27 Nov. 1787, PNP
⁴ Foster (Vere) (ed.), *The Two Duchesses*, 1898, 330-1
⁵ Queen Charlotte to Css of Uxbridge, 2 July 1809, PNP
⁶ Paget to Coote, 1 Aug. 1809, PRO/WO, 30/8 vol. 366
⁷ Fortescue, VII, 79
⁸ *Fortescue MSS*, X, 83; [n.d. 1811], *P. Bros.*, 227
⁹ Frances, Css of Jersey to A. Paget, [n.d. 1810]; C. Paget to A. Paget, 13 May 1811, *P. Bros.*, 152, 172

CHAPTER VII (p. 113 to p. 118)

¹ 19 Mar. 1812, *Fortescue MSS*, X, 227
² Galloway to A. Paget, 6 Mar. 1810, *P. Bros.*, 132
³ Charles Paget to A. Paget, [n.d.], and 30 June 1811, APP
⁴ Css of Uxbridge to A. Paget, 17 Apr. 1805; Paget to A. Paget, 28 July; Charles Paget to A. Paget, [n.d. Nov.]; Paget to A. Paget, [n.d. 1811]; [n.d. Dec. 1810]; *P. Bros.*, 31, 202, 224-5, 226-7, 150-1
⁵ Charles Paget to A. Paget, 18 June 1811, *P. Bros.*, 192
⁶ Anglesey to Gregory, 1 July 1828, PNP; PRO/HO, 42-143

CHAPTER VIII (p. 119 to p. 154)

¹ *XV H*, 230
² Paget to A. Paget, 12 Aug. 1811, *P. Bros.*, 210
³ Wellington to Torrens, 2 Dec. 1812, *Wellington (SD)*, VII, 485; Paget to Le Marchant, 1811, *Le Marchant*, 157-8; *Gronow*, II, 3
⁴ *Wellington (D)*, XII, 11; PNP
⁵ *Wellington (SD)*, X, 19; *Wellington (D)*, XII, 292; *Wellington (SD)*, X, 42, 169 (28 Apr. 1815), 84
⁶ Oman, 103
⁷ Darling to Uxbridge, 15 May 1815, PRO/WO, 3/537 DAG; *Frazer*, 520
⁸ Ly C. Capel to Dowager Css of Uxbridge, 13 June 1815, *Capel Letters*, 109
⁹ Siborne, 3-4
¹⁰ *Frazer*, 521-4
¹¹ These figures are taken from James (W. H.), *The Campaign of 1815*, 1908, 322-4, who based them chiefly on Siborne and the works of van Loben-Sels and de Bas
¹² Gibney, 173

[13] *Wellington (D)*, XII, 433; *Wellington (SD)*, X, 436-7, 463; Dörnberg to Uxbridge, 13 June 1815, PNP (discovered in 1958 in a state of dilapidation in the office of Lowe & Co., the family's solicitors for many years); Wildman; *Capel Letters*, 237n.

[14] *Wellington (D)*, XII, 472

[15] Wildman

[16] Memorandum by Uxbridge [n.d.], PNP

[17] *EHR*, 1888, 550; Wildman; *XV H*, 242; Siborne, 154; see also a rather muddled account of Uxbridge's personal actions at this time in Mercer, 145-50

[18] Siborne, 4; Fortescue, X, 334

[19] *Greys*, 61; *EHR*, 1888, 550; *XV H*, 242

[20] Siborne, 156

[21] Wood, 103-4; for O'Grady's account see Siborne, 132-3

[22] Siborne, 96; McGuffie, 103

[23] Anglesey to Croker, 15 Mar. 1852, PNP; Siborne, 7; see also the works of Houssaye (149), Pontécoulant (185) and Gourgaud (79), as well as other French writers who try to make out that the retreat was chaotic. All reliable modern accounts, backed by contemporary evidence, some not available when the Frenchmen were writing, support Uxbridge's view given here

[24] Fraser (Sir W. A.), *Words on Wellington*, 1889, 1, 4; compare *Shelley*, I, 103

[25] Mercer, 157

[26] Eaton (Charlotte A.), *The Days of Battle*, 1853, 125; *Greys*, 62; Wood, 119, Siborne, 35-6

[27] Wood, 125

[28] Memorandum by Uxbridge [n.d.], PNP

[29] Siborne, 16, 105; Wood, 130-1, 146-8

[30] *Frazer*, 556; Siborne, 188

[31] Siborne, 8, 238

[32] Wood, 140-1; Atkinson (C. T.), *The History of the Royal Dragoons, 1661-1934*, 1934, 307-8

[33] Siborne, 9-10

[34] Siborne, 74; see also 70, 83 and 87 for different accounts all confirming that the Greys were in support, not in the first line, 41 ('the Blues supporting', in Somerset's own account); Arthur (Sir George), *The Story of the Household Cavalry*, 1909, II, 609; Siborne, 72

[35] PNP; *Colborne*, 222

[36] Kennedy, 115

[37] PNP; see also Siborne, 11

[38] Kennedy, 117; Wood, 166

[39] Fortescue, X, 375

[40] Siborne, 12

[41] Captain Dance in conversation with Farington, 25 Aug. 1815, *Farington*, VIII, 33; Captain Dance to his father, Pflug-Harttung (J. von), *Belle Alliance*, Berlin, 1915, 289; Wildman

[42] Wildman; PNP; see Booth, I, 136-7, for an extract from a letter of a Captain Paget who had been 'some hours in Buonaparte's company', which confirms that this view of Uxbridge was expressed by Napoleon at St Helena

[43] Siborne, 17, 20
[44] PNP
[45] Vivian's reply to Gawler in *The United Services Journal*, July 1833, 312
[46] From the journal of General Allan, Wellington's private secretary, 15 July 1815, *The Times*, 18 June 1934
[47] Wildman
[48] Wildman; Anglesey to Croker, 1 Mar. 1852, PNP; Webster (Sir C.) (ed.), *Some Letters of the Duke of Wellington to his brother William Wellesley-Pole*, Camden Miscellany, XVIII, 1948, letter 31; Stanhope, 183; see also Greenock's account in Siborne, 15, and *Shelley*, 103
[49] Report by Major-General E. Vincke upon 5th Hanoverian Brigade at Waterloo, which, as colonel, he commanded. The men were of the Landwehr battalion Gifhorn, *Staatsarchiv Hannover*, Han. Des. 41 E XXI k, 3; *Greys*, 66; E. Senior to Anglesey, 26 May 1851, PNP
[50] Wildman; Curling (H.), *Recollections of the Mess-table*, 1855, 98
[51] Paris to Uxbridge, 10 July 1815, PNP; Adeane (Jane) and Grenfell (Maud), *Before and After Waterloo: Letters from Edward Stanley*, 1907, 261-2; Stanhope, 183
[52] *Capel Letters*, 118, 120; Wildman; *Clarence Paget*, 2
[53] Graves to Dowager Css of Uxbridge [n.d.], PNP; the patent was dated 4 July 1815, but the announcement was made earlier
[54] 29 June 1815
[55] *Farington*, VIII, 21; *The Times*, 11 July, 27 July 1815
[56] *Lichfield Mercury*, 11 Aug. 1815
[57] P. Bros., 289

CHAPTER IX (p. 155 to p. 181)

[1] *Stockmar*, I, 53; PNP
[2] Uxbridge to Prince Regent [n.d. 1814], RA
[3] 28 Feb. 1804, *P. Bros.*, 17; see also Dr Dodeswell to Paget, 6 Mar. 1804, PNP; Malmesbury (Earl of), *Diaries and Correspondence*, 1844, IV, 292
[4] Anglesey to Prince Regent, 3 Aug., RA; Liverpool to Prince Regent, 6 Sep.; Cumberland to Lauderdale, 10 Nov.; Anglesey to Lauderdale, 22 Nov. 1815, *Geo IV*, II, 106, 126, 132
[5] Archduke John to Metternich, 11 Mar. 1816, Corti (Count), *Leopold I of Belgium*, 1923, 37; 3 Jan. 1840, *Girlhood*, II, 290; see also Holland (Lord), *Further Memoirs of the Whig Party, 1807-1821* (ed. Lord Stavordale), 1905, 246
[6] Uxbridge to A. Paget, 12 Jan. 1815, *P. Bros.*, 268; Prince Regent to Northumberland, 23 Jan. 1818; Anglesey to Prince Regent, 24 Nov.; Prince Regent to Anglesey, 10 Dec.; Liverpool to Bloomfield, 2 Dec.; Anglesey to Prince Regent, 14 Dec., 17 Dec. 1817, *Geo IV*, II, 215, 216, 218, 219, 226, 241
[7] Anglesey to Cloncurry, 9 Sep. 1830, *Cloncurry*, 407
[8] Bagot, II, 102
[9] Deputy Garter's printed instructions for Lord High Steward [n.d. 1821], PNP; Lockhart (J. G.), *The Life of Sir W. Scott*, Edinburgh, 1902-3, VI, 322 (letter from Scott, under pseudonym 'An Eye-witness' to James Ballantyne, ed. *The Edinburgh*

Weekly Journal, in which it appeared); *Military Calendar,* (?); Hon. Mary Hope-Johnstone to Sir W. Johnstone Hope, 22 July 1821, *Hope-Johnstone MSS*

[10] *Geo IV,* III, 192

[11] Anglesey to C. Paget, 21 Jan. 1827, PNP

[12] *Mrs Arbuthnot,* II, 78

[13] Vivian to Anglesey, 7 Feb. 1827, PNP

[14] *Canning's Ministry,* 128, 189

[15] Canning to Anglesey, 13 Apr. 1827, PNP

[16] Anglesey to Londonderry, 2 Apr., PNP; Vivian to Knighton, 15 Apr. 1827, *Geo IV,* III, 221

[17] Londonderry to Wellington, 17 Apr.; Londonderry to Mrs Arbuthnot, 18 Apr., *Canning's Ministry,* 101, 115; 2 May 1827, *Hansard (L),* XVII, 497

[18] Wellington to Anglesey, 15 Apr.; Anglesey to Wellington, 16 Apr. 1827, *Wellington (D:NS),* III, 643–4

[19] Canning to Anglesey, 13 Apr. 1827, PNP

[20] Holland to George Tierney, 23 Apr., *Canning's Ministry,* 160; *The Times,* 28 Apr.; Stapleton to Bagot, 27 Apr. 1827, Stapleton (E. J.), *Some Official Correspondence of George Canning,* 1887, II, 309

[21] *Shelley,* II, 156

[22] George IV to Wellington, 21 May, *Wellington (D:NS),* IV, 35; *Mrs Arbuthnot,* II, 122; see also Seaford to Granville, 29 May, *Canning's Ministry,* 233; Anglesey to Wellington, 1 June 1827, PNP

[23] PNP

[24] *Mrs Arbuthnot,* II, 135; Beaconsfield (Earl of), *Endymion,* Hughenden edition, 1881, 13; George IV to Goderich, 12 Aug. 1827, *Geo IV,* III, 284

[25] For the King's and Goderich's letters to Wellington which Anglesey took with him to Dorsetshire, and for Wellington's answers to both, as well as the King's letter to the Duke of 17 Aug., see *Wellington (D:NS),* IV, 95–7; Goderich to Anglesey, 15 Aug. 1827, PNP; *Palmerston,* I, 120

[26] PNP

[27] Anglesey to Goderich, 26 Aug., 6 Sep.; Lansdowne to Anglesey, 3 Sep. 1827, PNP

[28] Goderich to George IV, 11 Dec., *Geo IV,* III, 344; Lansdowne to Anglesey, 17 Dec., PNP; George IV to Knighton, 16 Dec., *Geo IV,* III, 350; Anglesey to Lansdowne, 18 Dec. 1827, PNP

[29] Lyndhurst's recollection 1826–1832, Moneypenny (W. F.), *The Life of Benjamin Disraeli,* 1910, Appendix B, I, 387–9

[30] 10 Jan. 1828, *Mrs Arbuthnot,* II, 157; for further light on Anglesey's part in the dissolution of the government, see letters to and from Goderich, Huskisson and Lyndhurst, Dec. 1827 and Jan. 1828, PNP; 24 Feb. 1828, *Dyott,* II, 17

[31] PNP; *O'Connell,* I, 148

[32] *Mrs Arbuthnot,* II, 155

[33] Anglesey to A. Paget, 27 Aug. 1827, PNP

[34] Cumberland to George IV, 28 June; Lyndhurst to Knighton, [?20 Dec.] 1827, *Geo IV,* III, 264, 353; Bagot to Binning, 16 Apr. 1827, Bagot, II, 385; Paget to A. Paget [n.d. 1807], *P. Bros.,* 62; *Hansard (L),* 51: 57 Geo III, 16 May 1817; 52: 59 Geo. III, 17 May 1819; 54: 2 Geo IV, 16 Apr. 1821; 53: 3 Geo. IV, 21 June 1822

[35] From MS copy in PNP, which varies unsubstantially from the report in *Hansard* (*L*)

[36] Holland to Anglesey, 18 Mar.; Anglesey to Holland, 24 Mar. 1827, PNP

[37] Anglesey to Lamb, 17 Sep. 1827, PNP

CHAPTER X (p. 182 to p. 221)

[1] Wyse (Sir Thomas), *Historical Sketch of the late Catholic Association*, 1829, I, 381

[2] Wellington to Anglesey, 21 Jan., *Wellington* (*D:NS*), IV, 207; Peel to Anglesey, 25 Jan., Anglesey to Peel, 27 Jan.; Lamb to Anglesey, 23 Jan., PNP; Eldon to Ly F. Banks, 25 Jan. 1828, Twiss (H.), *The Life of Lord Eldon*, 1844, III, 27

[3] *Greville*, I, 235

[4] *London Gazette*, 19 Feb. 1828

[5] *DEP*, 26 Feb. 1828

[6] *DMR*, 19 Feb. 1828

[7] Forbes to Anglesey, 6 Aug. 1827-5 Feb. 1828; Anglesey to Lamb, 17 Sep. 1827, PNP

[8] *Dublin Weekly Register*, 1 Mar. 1828

[9] McDowell, 17

[10] *Greville*, I, 235

[11] Anglesey to Lamb, 17 Sep. 1827, PNP

[12] Davis (H. W. C.), 'Catholic Emancipation', *Cambridge Modern History*, X, 1907, 637-8

[13] Anglesey to Lamb, 29 Mar., 27 Apr. 1828, PNP

[14] Anglesey to Peel, 14 May; Peel to Anglesey, 26 July; Holland to Anglesey, 21 May 1828, PNP

[15] *DEP*, 21 Feb. 1828

[16] Lamb to Anglesey, 24 Feb.; Anglesey to Lamb, 25 Feb. 1828, PNP

[17] *DEP*, 1 Mar.; *DMR*, 1 Mar.; *Weekly Freeman's Journal* (Dublin), 8 Mar. 1828; *DMR* (Article by Ly Morgan), 6 Feb. 1829; Anglesey to Lamb, 2 Mar. 1828, *PNP*

[18] *DEP*, 18 Mar.; *DMR*, 18 Mar. 1828

[19] *Addresses ... presented to ... the Marquis of Anglesey ... 1828-1829, including ... Answers*, Dublin, 1831, 5-6; *DMR*, 10 Mar.; 19 Apr. 1828

[20] Moore (T.), 'Thoughts on the Present Government of Ireland, 1828', *Poetical Works of Thomas Moore, collected by himself*, 1841, VIII, 272

[21] Anglesey to Peel, 12 Apr.; Lamb to Anglesey, 24 Mar. 1828, PNP

[22] Anglesey to Lamb, 26 Apr.; 14 May 1828, PNP

[23] Holland to Anglesey, 13 June 1828, PNP

[24] 2 June 1828, *PP*, 390

[25] Lamb to Anglesey, 26 May, 3 June, PNP; Gleig, III, 268; Anglesey to Holland, 1 June; Anglesey to Lamb, 24 May; Holland to Anglesey, 4 June; Anglesey to Wellington, 13 June; 16 June; Anglesey to F. L. Gower, 21 June 1828, PNP

[26] *Peel*, I, 123

[27] Anglesey to Peel, 21 June; 23 June 1828, PNP

[28] Tuyll to Anglesey, 29 June-4 July 1828, PNP

[29] Fitzgerald to Anglesey, 29 June; Anglesey to Lamb, 29 Apr.; Anglesey to Peel, 30 June 1828, PNP

[30] Anglesey to Lamb, 28 June; Anglesey to Holland, 1 July; Tuyll to Anglesey, 5 July 1828, PNP

[31] Anglesey to F. L. Gower, 2-3 July; F. L. Gower to Anglesey, 7 July; 27 July 1828, PNP

[32] Anglesey to A. Paget, 27 July; Anglesey to C. Paget, 17 Aug. 1828, *PP*, 397-9

[33] 28 Sep. 1828, *Wellington (D:NS)*, V, 93

[34] *Peel*, 184

[35] 14 Aug. 1828, *Peel*, 203-4

[36] Anglesey to F. L. Gower, 27 July; F. L. Gower to Anglesey, 31 July 1828, PNP

[37] Wellington to George IV, 1 Aug.; George IV to Wellington, 3 Aug.; Wellington to Peel, 6 Aug. 1828, *Wellington (D:NS)*, IV, 570, 573, 575

[38] Wellington to Peel, 26 Aug. 1828, *Wellington (D:NS)*, IV, 666

[39] Anglesey to Holland, 4 Aug. 1828, PNP

[40] *Palmerston*, I, 183

[41] Anglesey to Peel, 26 July; Peel to Anglesey, 30 Aug., PNP; Anglesey to A. Paget, 2 Aug., *PP*, II, 398; *Palmerston*, I, 184; Ilchester (Earl of) (ed.), *The Journal of Henry Edward Fox, 4th Baron Holland, 1818-1830*, 1923, 133; *Greville*, I, 312; Anglesey to Wellington, 11 Aug.; F. L. Gower to Anglesey, 21 Aug. 1828, PNP

[42] Peel to Wellington, 24 Aug., *Wellington (D:NS)*, IV, 662; Anglesey to Peel, 26 Aug.; see also Peel to Anglesey, 30 Aug. 1828, *PNP*

[43] Anglesey to Peel, ?10 Sep., *Peel*, I, 207; Anglesey to Holland, 2 Oct. 1828, PNP

[44] Peel to Anglesey, 27 Sep., *Peel*, I, 230; Anglesey to Wellington, 6 Oct.; Wellington to Anglesey, 10 Oct. 1828, *Wellington (D:NS)*, V, 112, 121

[45] 5 Nov. 1828, *Wellington (D:NS)*, V, 214; *The Times*, 14 Jan. 1829

[46] Anglesey to Peel, 2 Oct., *Peel*, I, 233; Wellington to Peel, 30 Sep. 1828, *Wellington (D:NS)*, V, 100; Anglesey to Melbourne, 13 July 1832, PNP

[47] *Palmerston*, 182

[48] Wellington to Peel, 14 Oct. 1828, *Wellington (D:NS)*, V, 138

[49] Anglesey to Wellington, 24 Sep. 1828, PNP

[50] *Creevey*, II, 195; 24 Nov. 1828, *Wellington (D:NS)*, V, 280

[51] Holland to Anglesey, 21 Oct., PNP; A. Paget to Anglesey, 27 Oct. 1828, *PP*, II, 405

[52] Wellington to Phillpotts, 6 Nov., *Wellington (D:NS)*, V, 221; *Palmerston*, I, 184; Anglesey to Wellington, 14 Nov. 1828, PNP

[53] Anglesey to Wellington, 23 Nov., PNP; Wellington to George IV, 26 Nov. 1828, *Wellington (D:NS)*, V, 288

[54] Wellington to Anglesey, 28 Dec. 1828, *Wellington (D:NS)*, V, 366; Ly Anglesey to John Sanderson, 31 Dec. 1828, PNP

[55] 24 Dec. 1828-5 Jan. 1829, Robinson (L. G.) (ed.), *Letters of Princess Lieven*, 1902, 170

[56] *Palmerston*, 185n.

[57] Curtis to Wellington, 4 Dec.; 22 Dec.; Wellington to Curtis, 11 Dec. 1828, *Wellington (D:NS)*, V, 308, 326, 352

[58] Ilchester, 103; copy of Anglesey to Curtis in PNP

[59] Peel to Anglesey, 10 Jan. 1829, PNP; *Greville*, I, 238

[60] Anglesey to A. Paget (incorrectly dated 'Phenix [*sic*] Park, Jan. 27th'; Anglesey left Ireland before that date), *PP*, II, 409

[61] *DMR*, 20 Jan. 1829; Villiers (G.), *A Vanished Victorian ... the Life of the 4th Earl of Clarendon*, 1938, 64; Ly Anglesey to Anglesey, 19 Jan. 1829, PNP

[62] Ilchester, 103

[63] Anglesey to Cloncurry, 12 Mar. 1829, *Cloncurry*, 335

[64] See Anglesey to Blake, 6 Feb. 1829, PNP

[65] *Hansard* (*L*), 20, 507; see also *Hansard* (*L*), 20, 545

[66] Anglesey to George IV, 30 Jan. 1829, PNP; *Mrs Arbuthnot*, II, 234

[67] Anglesey to Holland, 13 Jan., 4 May, PNP; 7 May 1829, *Cloncurry*, 399

[68] Anglesey to Clarence Paget, 4 Oct. 1849, PNP

[69] Anglesey to Cloncurry, 23 Sep. 1851, PNP

CHAPTER XI (p. 222 to p. 241)

[1] *Cloncurry*, 399.

[2] 1 June 1829, *Mrs Arbuthnot*, II, 279; Ilchester (Earl of), *Lady Holland to Her Son, 1821-1845*, 1946, 104

[3] 'Copy Case with Opinion of the ... Attorney-General; Report of evidence ... to sustain the action ... against ... Gerard [*sic*] Callaghan ... at suit of Lady Agnes Byng' [n.d.], PNP; *Leinster Journal*, 25 Mar.; *Dublin Evening Packet*, 26 Mar.; *Star of Brunswick*, 28 Mar.; *The Times*, 27 Apr.; 4 May; 1 Sep.; *DMR*, 11 May 1829; Dss of Bedford to Ly G. Grey, 21 Jan. [1843 or 1844], Hickleton Papers

[4] *Gentleman's Magazine*, Mar.; *The Times*, 9-11 Feb.; 22 Jan., *Greville*, I, 363; 9 Jan.; 17 May, *Mrs Arbuthnot*, II, 325, 358; Cumberland to Eldon, 14-19 Feb. 1830, *Geo IV* (Appendix), III, 505

[5] Croker to V. Fitzgerald, 3 May 1830, *Croker*, II, 58

[6] Croker to V. Fitzgerald, 11 May 1830, *Croker*, II, 59

[7] Memorandum, June 1830, PNP

[8] 4 June 1830, *Mrs Arbuthnot*, II, 362

[9] J. Sanderson to Forbes, 23 Mar.; J. Sanderson to Ly Anglesey, 20 Feb.; 17 Apr.; Anglesey to Uxbridge, June 1830, PNP

[10] 20 Mar.-4 Dec. 1829, Ld William Paget's papers, PNP

[11] J. Sanderson to Col. Edwards, 28 June; J. Sanderson to Rev. Rowlands, 8 July 1830, PNP (transferred to the Library of the University College of North Wales, Bangor)

[12] 24 July 1829, *Greville*, I, 305

[13] Anglesey to Holland, 30 Apr. 1833; memorandum, 1 Nov. 1830, PNP

[14] Anglesey to Holland, 18 Aug. 1830, Ilchester MSS

[15] Grey to Anglesey, 16-18 Nov. 1830, PNP

CHAPTER XII (p. 242 to p. 278)

[1] ?Nov. 1830, PNP

[2] Forbes to Anglesey, 9 June, PNP; O'Connell to C. Sugrue, 20 May, *O'Connell*, I, 189; Anglesey to P. Mahony, 25 Apr.; 14 Nov. 1829, PNP

[3] *DMR*, 13 Nov.; see also Anglesey to Cloncurry, 7 Nov. 1830, *Cloncurry*, 407

[4] 16 Jan. 1831, *Shelley*, II, 206

[5] Confidential memorandum by Anglesey, 20 Sep. 1833; Anglesey to Melbourne, 4 Dec., PNP; Anglesey to Holland, 11 Dec. 1830, Ilchester MSS

[6] P. Mahony to Gossett, 25 Nov. 1830, PNP; Anglesey to Cloncurry, 15 Dec. 1830, *Cloncurry*, 411-12

[7] O'Connell to E. Dwyer, 29 Nov.; 1 Dec., *O'Connell*, I, 235-6; Anglesey to Cloncurry, 19 Dec., *Cloncurry*, 413; Anglesey to Melbourne, 21 Dec. 1830, PNP

[8] Anglesey to Melbourne, 24-6 Dec.; Anglesey to Grey, 29 Dec., PNP; 30 Dec. 1830, *Greville*, II, 98

[9] Grey to Anglesey, 29 Dec. 1830, PNP; Anglesey to Ly Anglesey [n.d.], quoted in *Greville* (22 Jan. 1831), II, 109

[10] *Doyle*, II, 263; Anglesey to Holland, 23 Jan. 1831, PNP

[11] O'Connell's public letter was dated 5 Apr.: it is quoted in *Doyle*, II, 274; Anglesey to Grey, 23 May 1831, PNP

[12] *O'Connell*, 1831-3

[13] *O'Connell*, II, 321-2

[14] 15 Jan. 1831, PNP

[15] O'Connell to E. Dwyer, 29 Nov. 1830; O'Connell to P. V. Fitzpatrick, 17 Sep. 1833, *O'Connell*, I, 235, 388; Anglesey to Holland, 29 Jan.; 20 Dec. 1831; memorandum by Anglesey [n.d. early 1831], PNP

[16] PNP

[17] Anglesey to Cloncurry, 9 Sep. 1830, *Cloncurry*, 405; Grey to Anglesey, 1 Mar.; Anglesey to Grey, 4 Mar. 1831, PNP

[18] Grey to Anglesey, 24 Mar.; 21 Apr.; Holland to Anglesey, 20 Apr.; Melbourne to Anglesey [n.d. 21 Apr.]; see also Stanley to Anglesey, 21 Apr. 1831, PNP

[19] 23 May 1831, PNP

[20] Anglesey to Grey, 23 May; Holland to Anglesey, 29 Apr.; Anglesey to Holland, 2 May 1831, PNP

[21] Grey to Anglesey, 3 Sep.; 8 Oct.; Anglesey to Grey, 5 Sep.; 22 Nov. 1831, PNP

[22] Grey to Anglesey, 9 Jan. 1832, PNP

[23] Grey to Anglesey, 17 Feb.; Anglesey to Grey, 19 Feb. 1832, PNP

[24] See Grey (H., Earl) (ed.), *The Reform Act, 1832; correspondence of Earl Grey with William IV and with Sir H. Taylor, 1830-2*, 1867, II, 96-116

[25] Anglesey to Grey, 23 Apr. 1832, Grey (Durham)

[26] Anglesey to Holland, 9 and 12 May; Anglesey to Stanley, 14 May 1832, PNP

[27] Anglesey to Stanley, 17 May; Anglesey to Grey, 11 and 12 May, PNP; Wellington to Lyndhurst, 10 May, *Wellington* (*D:NS*), VIII, 304; Grey to Anglesey, 20 May 1832, PNP

[28] Holland to Anglesey [n.d. 18 or 19 May 1832], PNP

[29] Anglesey to Stanley, 17 May 1832, PNP

[30] PNP

[31] Anglesey to Stanley, 19 June; Stanley to Anglesey, 21 June; 4 Aug. 1831, PNP

[32] Quoted in Lampson (G. Locker), *A Consideration of the State of Ireland in the Nineteenth Century*, 1907, 150n.

[33] Wakefield (Edward), *An Account of Ireland, statistical and political*, 1812, II, 486

[34] Anglesey to Grey, 15 Apr. 1831, PNP

[35] Anglesey to Grey, 16 Mar. 1832, PNP

[36] Anglesey to Ld John Russell, 12 Dec. 1843, PNP

[37] Anglesey to Holland, 20 Apr.; 9 July, PNP; Melbourne to Anglesey, 25 Oct.; Anglesey to Melbourne, 28 Oct. 1831, PNP

[38] Melbourne to Anglesey, 25 Oct.; Anglesey to Melbourne, 28 Oct. 1831, PNP

[39] Cabinet Paper by Anglesey, 18 Jan. 1832; Anglesey to Ld J. Russell, 12 Dec. 1843, PNP

[40] Grey to Anglesey, 5 Feb.; Anglesey to Holland, 12 Feb.; 21 Oct. 1832, PNP

[41] *Palmerston*, I, 285; Anglesey to Holland, 9 Mar.; 30 Apr. 1833, PNP

[42] Anglesey to Holland, 23 June 1833, PNP

[43] Anglesey to William IV, 14 July 1833, PNP

[44] See E. J. Littleton's Diary, 20 July, Aspinall, 349; William IV to Anglesey, 17 July; Holland to Anglesey, 22 July 1833, PNP

[45] *Cloncurry*, 391

[46] *Report from Select Committee on Civil Government Charges*, 'Reports from Committees', IV, 14 Oct.; Anglesey to Stanley, 1 Sep. 1831, PNP

[47] *Cloncurry*, 389-90

[48] Anglesey to Holland, 2 Dec. 1831; Anglesey to Melbourne, 16 Mar. 1833, PNP; McDowell, 198-9

[49] Anglesey to Grey, 23 July 1831, PNP

[50] Anglesey to Grey, 28 Mar., Grey (Durham); *Pilot* (Dublin), 2 Dec. 1831; Inglis (Brian), *The Freedom of the Press in Ireland, 1784-1841*, 1954, 206-7

[51] Anglesey to Grey, 15 Apr. 1831, PNP

[52] PNP

[53] Anglesey to Holland, 19 July 1833; Grey to Anglesey, 3 Nov.; Anglesey to Grey, 6 Nov. 1832, PNP

[54] 3 Nov. 1833, *Creevey*, II, 265

[55] Grey to Anglesey, 13 Jan.; Anglesey to Grey, 15 Jan.; Holland to Anglesey [n.d. ?20 Jan.], 1833, PNP

[56] Anglesey to Holland, 21 Jan. 1833, PNP

[57] See Reid (Stuart J.), *The Life and Letters of 1st Earl of Durham, 1792-1840*, 1906, I, 215

[58] Grey to Anglesey, 27 Mar.; Anglesey to Grey, 27 Mar.; Littleton to Anglesey, 24 and 29 June; Anglesey to Littleton, 30 June 1833, PNP

[59] Anglesey to Grey, 6 Sep.; Holland to Anglesey, 26 July; Anglesey to Holland, 9 Aug. 1833, PNP

[60] Anglesey to A. Paget, 23 Jan. 1835, *P. Bros.*, 335

CHAPTER XIII (p. 279 to p. 317)

[1] 11 July 1841, PNP

[2] Holland to Anglesey, 2 Sep. 1833; Dr Dodeswell to Anglesey, 28 Oct. 1827, PNP; Anglesey to 'the Brotherhood', 19 Feb. 1834, *P. Bros.*, 332

[3] Sir J. Murray to J. Sanderson, 11 Dec. 1833, PNP; Anglesey to 'the Brotherhood', 19 Feb. 1834, *P. Bros.*, 331

[4] PNP. (The extracts given here have been freely translated from the broken French of the original.)

⁵ Anglesey to A. Paget, 15 Apr., *P. Bros.*, 333; Anglesey to Cloncurry, 27 Apr. 1834, *Cloncurry*, 368

⁶ Anglesey to A. Paget, 27 Nov. 1834, APP

⁷ Ponsonby to Anglesey, 3 Apr. 1830; Burdett to Anglesey [n.d. 1835/6?], PNP; Weiss (Dr Karl Erhard), 'Die Krankheit des Marquis d'Anglesea und ihre Heilung durch Hahnemann, aus Hahnemanns literarischem nachlass bearbeitet', *Allgemeine Homoeopathische Zeitung*, CLXIX (1921); Dunsford (Dr Harris), 'Observations pratiques, offertes à la Société homoeopathique gallicane, communiquées le 17 Septembre 1835', *Bibliothèque Homoeopathique, publiée à Genève par une société de médecins*, VI (1836), 263-5

⁸ Ly Cowper to Pss Lieven, 25 Sep. 1835, Sudley (Lord) (ed.), *Lieven-Palmerston Correspondence, 1828-1856*, 1943, 104; Melbourne to Anglesey, 26 Sep. 1835, PNP

⁹ *Clarence Paget*, 22-3

¹⁰ Anglesey to Ly Anglesey, 8 Jan.-7 Mar. 1836, PNP

¹¹ *Raikes*, III, 133

¹² 11 Feb. 1831-11 Oct. 1837, Ld William Paget's papers, PNP

¹³ Anglesey to Clarence Paget, 17 Jan. 1837; Anglesey to Col. Clavering, 4 Sep. 1846; Anglesey to Rev. Erskine Neale, 11 Aug. 1848, PNP. See also d'Orsay to Lichfield, 19 Oct. 1841, Connely (W.), *Count D'Orsay*, 379

¹⁴ Draft of speech in Anglesey's hand, PNP

¹⁵ *Annual Register*, 1837, 64

¹⁶ Lever (Tresham) (ed.), *The Letters of Lady Palmerston*, 1957, 216, 259; Deerhurst to Anglesey, 18 Nov. 1829, PNP

¹⁷ Cardigan and Lancastre (Css of), *My Recollections*, 1909, 58-9; 17 Jan. 1838, *Greville*, IV, 14

¹⁸ Anglesey to Brougham, 21 Jan. 1838, PNP

¹⁹ Brougham to Anglesey, ?Mar. 1839; Anglesey to Brougham [n.d. Mar.] 1839, PNP

²⁰ 5 June 1838, *Girlhood*, I, 344; Wellesley to Anglesey, 28 May; Anglesey to Wellesley, 28 May 1841, PNP

²¹ 24 June 1838, *Greville*, IV, 67; draft of speech in Anglesey's hand, PNP

²² Anglesey to Wellington, 27 Nov.; Wellington to Anglesey, 8 Dec.; Wellington to J. Lucas, 20 Dec. 1840, PNP

²³ 21 Aug. 1839, PNP

²⁴ Anglesey to Palmerston, 21 Nov.; Palmerston to Anglesey, 22 Nov. 1838, PNP

²⁵ Lieven to Anglesey, 5 Apr.; 19 Apr. 1830, PNP

²⁶ *Clarence Paget*, 30-48

²⁷ Anglesey to Ly Anglesey, June-Aug. 1839, PNP. For a more complete edition of this correspondence, see Anglesey (Marquess of), 'A Visit to Russia, 1839', *History Today*, II (1952), 710

²⁸ Guest, 45-6

²⁹ 14 Jan. 1840, *Greville*, IV, 225; 18 Nov. 1838, *Girlhood*, II, 71; see Lindsay (W. A.), *The Royal Household*, 1898

³⁰ 13 June 1838, *Girlhood*, II, 349

³¹ Jerrold (Clare), *The Early Court of Queen Victoria*, 1912, 235

³² *Annual Register*, 1842, 338

[33] Thomas Beer to Anglesey [n.d. 1842], PNP; 21 Mar. 1842, *Victoria*, I, 487

[34] 9 July 1838; 24 Apr. 1839, *Girlhood*, I, 365, II, 155

[35] Colonel Brotherton to Anglesey, 26 May 1840; Clarence Paget to Captain D. Pack, 5 Jan. 1850, PNP

[36] Wellington to Anglesey, 12 Dec.; Anglesey to Wellington, 14 Dec.; George Byng to Anglesey, 16 Dec. 1842, PNP

[37] Whyte to Anglesey, 23 Dec.; Anglesey to Whyte, 25 Dec. 1842, PNP

[38] *Annual Register*, 1844, 23

[39] May 1838-48, Ld William Paget's papers, PNP

CHAPTER XIV (p. 318 to p. 341)

[1] Feiling (Keith Grahame), *A History of England from the Coming of the English to 1918*, 1950, 860

[2] Anglesey to A. R. Blake, 12 Dec.; Russell to Anglesey, 20 Dec.; Anglesey to Russell, 21 Dec. 1845, PNP

[3] Memorandum by Prince Albert, 6 July 1846, *Victoria*, II, 102; Anglesey to Ly Anglesey, 2 July 1846, PNP

[4] Anglesey to Grey, 28 Nov. 1830, PNP; Board of Ordnance books, PRO

[5] Anglesey to Ld FitzHardinge, 27 July 1846, PNP

[6] Anglesey to J. Assheton Smith, 27 July; Anglesey to Cloncurry, 10 Nov. 1846, PNP

[7] Anglesey to Morpeth, 2 Dec. 1847, PNP

[8] Wellington to Anglesey, 3 Apr., PNP; 18 Apr. 1847, *Greville*, V, 439

[9] Anglesey to Wellington, 31 Mar. 1847, PNP

[10] Anglesey to Wellington, 10 Sep. 1846; Anglesey to Auckland (First Lord of the Admiralty), 8 Aug. 1847, PNP

[11] For full text see Wrottesley (G.) (ed.), *Military Operations of Sir John Burgoyne*, 1859, 1

[12] For full text see Wrottesley (G.), *The Life of Sir John Burgoyne*, 1873, I, 444

[13] Wellington to Anglesey, 6 Feb. 1847; Anglesey to Burgoyne, 11 Feb. 1848, PNP; *Shelley*, II, 411

[14] T. Beer to Anglesey, 5 Oct.; Anglesey to T. Beer, 8 Oct. 1846, PNP

[15] Burgoyne to Anglesey, 24 Apr.; 13 Sep. 1847, PNP

[16] Anglesey to Blakeney, 25 Oct. 1847, PNP

[17] PNP

[18] Anglesey to Ly Anglesey, 7 Sep. 1849; Anglesey to Css of Sandwich, 1 Dec. 1852, PNP; West, I, 77-8; Guest, 45-6

[19] Anglesey to Ly Anglesey, 14 July 1851, PNP

[20] Brunnow to Anglesey, 21 Aug. 1850, PNP

[21] Young (G. M.), *Early Victorian England, 1830-65*, 1934, I, 97; *P. Bros.*, xiii

[22] Anglesey to Bouverie, 29 Mar. 1852; Anglesey to H. Seymour, 11 Dec. 1851, PNP

[23] Anglesey to Frederick Paget, 19 Dec. 1853 (letter in possession of Mrs Fowler of Enborne, Newbury)

[24] Prince Albert to Anglesey, Oct. 1851; Granville to Anglesey [n.d. 1851], PNP; Chancellor (F. B.), *Prince Consort*, 1931, 159

[25] Anglesey to Cloncurry, 23 Sep. 1851, PNP
[26] Anglesey to Bedford, 3 Sep. 1852, PNP
[27] Anglesey to Lansdowne, 7 Jan.; Anglesey to Clarence Paget, 28 Dec. 1853, PNP
[28] Anglesey to Charles Wellesley, 16 Sep., PNP; Seaton to his son, 8 Dec. 1852, Colborne, 346
[29] PNP
[30] Anglesey to Css of Sandwich, 26 July 1853, PNP
[31] Anglesey to George Paget, 26 Aug. 1853, PNP
[32] Anglesey to Ly Sydney, 2 Nov. 1853, PNP
[33] The Times, 3 Feb. 1854
[34] Anglesey to Clarence Paget, 10 Apr. 1854, PNP
[35] The Morning Advertiser, 1 May; The Illustrated London News, 13 May 1854
[36] The Times, 1 May 1854

SOURCES
QUOTED IN THE NOTES

NOTES TO CHAPTER I (p. 343 to p. 348)

[1] Delisle (Léopold), *Liste des Compagnons de Guillaume le Conquérant à la Conquête de l'Angleterre en 1066*, Caen, 1862

[2] 10 Jan. 1690. Translation from MS at one time in the possession of Sir Erasmus Burrowes, Bt, Agnew (Rev. D. C. A.), *Protestant Exiles from France*, 1871, II, 125

[3] Copy lease, Ford-Pachet [n.d. ?1517-24], [(Jeayes, no. 897), transferred to Middlesex CRO (446/Ed. 319)], PNP

[4] 14 May 1527, Rep. 7 fos., 196, 198b

[5] Dugdale (Sir William), *Baronage of England*, 1675-6, II, 390

[6] Hackwood (F. W.), *Glimpses of Bygone Staffordshire*, Lichfield, 1925, 58

[7] Nichols (J. G.) (ed.), *Literary Remains of King Edward VI*, Roxburghe Club, 1857, II, 410

[8] Harleian MSS, 1077, f.7

[9] [(Jeayes, nos. 1047-51), transferred to Burton-upon-Trent Borough Archives], PNP

[10] Anon., *Scrinia Reclusa, or Brief Remarks upon the Reigns of several … English Princes, with the Characters of their Favourites*, 1709, 237

[11] See, particularly, Gayangos (Pascual de) and Tyler (Royall) (ed.), *Calendar of … State Papers relating to the negotiations between England and Spain*, VII, 1889: XII, 1949

[12] Lodge (Edmund), *Portraits of Illustrious Personages of Great Britain*, 1835, II, 6-7

[13] Jeayes, PNP

[14] From a Commonplace book possessed in 1818 by Ld Boston, *Gentleman's Magazine*, LXXXVIII, pt. I, 119

[15] Lloyd (D.), *State Worthies*, 1766, I, 99

[16] The chief portraits of the first Baron Paget are:
Anon., Anglo-German school, TQL, c. 1545 (Plas Newydd)
Anon., H & S, c. 1560 (Plas Newydd)
Anon., HL (National Portrait Gallery, 961)

[17] Cockayne, X, 283

[18] Cockayne, X, 278

[19] [n.d.], Staffordshire CRO, 100-1

[20] Article by Waters (E. C.) in Nichols (J. G.) (ed.), *The Herald and Genealogist*, 1874, VIII, 1-5

[21] Cobbett (W.) and Wright (J.) (ed.), *Parliamentary History of England …* , IX (1811), 482n.

[22] Cockayne, X, 288n.

²³ A/c books, PNP; Lipscomb (George), *History … of the County of Buckingham*, 1847, II, 596

²⁴ 6 Jan. 1769, PNP

²⁵ [Anon. (Paget (T. C.)], *Miscellanies in Prose and Verse*, 1741, 1; Orford (Earl of), *Catalogue of Royal and Noble Authors*, 1806, IV, 177

²⁶ C. Wesley to Css of Uxbridge, 20 Aug. 1811, PNP; Blom (Eric) (ed.), *Dictionary of Music and Musicians*, 1954, I, 359; V, 700

²⁷ Markham (Maj.), *Recollections of a Town Boy at Westminster*, 1903, 107-8

²⁸ Hon. W. Paget to Uxbridge, 1 July; copy in APP; *London Gazette*, 16 Aug. 1794

²⁹ T. Fremantle to W. Fremantle, 1 Oct. 1794 (copy of extracts), PNP

NOTES TO CHAPTER II (p. 348)

¹ 14 Sept. 1787, Watkins (Thomas), *Travels through Switzerland … 1787, 1788 and 1789*, 1794, I, 169-70

² For this information the author is indebted to Mr Ronald Armstrong (as for much else), Sir Gavin de Beer, F.R.S., and to M. Gustave Vaucher, State Archivist, Republic and Canton of Geneva, Switzerland

³ Harcourt (Rev. L. Vernon) (ed.), *The Diaries and Correspondence of the Rt Hon. George Rose, 1744-1818*, 1860, II, 142

NOTES TO CHAPTER III (p. 349)

¹ Ly Louisa Paget to James Erskine, [n.d. ?20 ?Feb. 1801], PNP

NOTES TO CHAPTER V (p. 349 to p. 353)

¹ Ward (S. G. P.), 'Some Fresh Light on the Corunna Campaign', *JAHR*, XXVIII (1950), no. 115, 118n.

² Oman, 151; *Gordon*, 66

³ *XV H*, 149

⁴ *Gordon*, 101-2; Carnock, 17

⁵ Carnock, 19

⁶ *Gordon*, 99, 107

⁷ Paget to Uxbridge, 23 Dec. 1808, *EP*, 115

⁸ Paget to A. Paget, 22 Dec. 1808, *PP*, 388; Paget to Uxbridge, 23 Dec. 1808, *EP*, 115

⁹ Compare the two extremes in Oman and Fortescue, neither of whom can have seen Carnock or *Gordon*, for these had not appeared when they were writing.

¹⁰ *Gordon*, 133

¹¹ *Gordon*, 134

¹² Butler (L.), *Wellington's Operations in the Peninsula*, 1904, I, 113-4

NOTES TO CHAPTER VI (p. 353 to p. 356)

[For a list of the chief sources used in this chapter and in the notes to it, see p. 395.]

¹ *Admissions to Trinity College, Cambridge*, IV

² Ly C. Lamb to Ly Bessborough, 17 Sep. 1808, *Bessborough*, 172

³ See *Raikes*, 242-4

⁴ Wellesley-Pole to Bagot, 5 July 1816, Bagot, II, 29-30; Argyll to A. Paget, 22 June 1811, *P. Bros.*, 195

⁵ *Dyott*, II, 65-6; *Gregory*, 321; *Capel Letters*, 117-8

⁶ PNP

NOTES TO CHAPTER VII (p. 356 to p. 357)

¹ PNP

NOTES TO CHAPTER VIII (p. 357 to p. 366)

¹ Fortescue, XI, 366-7

² *Greville*, I, 120

³ PRO/WO 1/660, 549; PNP

⁴ *Frazer*, 537, but see also 556

⁵ Siborne, 14; Wood, 49

⁶ Wood, 120

⁷ Gibney, 172-3; J. Hatherly to Anglesey, 30 July 1850, PNP

⁸ Gibney, 172

⁹ *Account of Service in 7th Hussars by Sir William Verner* (unpublished), 1853, II, 5. See Tomkinson (Lt-Col.), *The Diary of a Cavalry Officer ... 1809-1815*, 1895, 279, for the disappointment felt by the 16th Hussars at not being in time to take part in the battle

¹⁰ PNP

¹¹ 1 Oct. 1846, PNP

¹² *Greys*, 62

¹³ Fortescue, X, 335

¹⁴ Anglesey to Grey, 2 Dec. 1830; Anglesey to Ly Guillamore, 12 Dec. 1851, PNP

¹⁵ *7th H*, I, 384; see also Siborne, 6; *Farington*, VIII, 19

¹⁶ Siborne, 11; McGuffie, 103

¹⁷ See particularly Wood, 105-6

¹⁸ Kelly to Anglesey, 9 Sep. 1815, PNP

¹⁹ Wildman; Booth, I, 118

²⁰ Wood, 123

²¹ Fortescue, X, 366

²² Siborne, 8-9, 105; Wood, 146; Müffling (Baron von), *Passages from My Life* (ed. P. Yorke), 1853, 245

²³ Fortescue, X, 415

²⁴ PNP; Wellington Museum (Victoria and Albert Museum), Apsley House

²⁵ Siborne, 18-19; *Farington*, VIII, 19

²⁶ Siborne, 20

²⁷ *Morning Post*, ?Oct. 1815; Gaspey (Thomas), *Many-Coloured Life*, 1842, 1; *Notes and Queries*, 3rd series, II (Oct. 1862), 339

²⁸ Anglesey to Hill, 22 July 1828, PNP

²⁹ *Stockmar*, I, 53

NOTES TO CHAPTER IX (p. 366 to p. 371)

¹ Lyttleton to Bagot, 8 Aug. 1820, Bagot, II, 100

² Russell (G. W. E.), *Collections and Recollections*, 1898, 22; *Morning Chronicle*, 1 May; *Reynold's Newspaper*, 7 May 1854; Hare (Augustus J. C.), *The Story of My Life*, 1900, V, 335; [Byrne (Mrs W. Pitt)], *Gossip of the Century*, 1892, I, 25-6

³ Laffan to Anglesey, 25 Nov.; 6 Dec. 1826, PNP

⁴ Vivian to Anglesey, 27 Dec. 1826, PNP

⁵ Anglesey to George IV, 21 Jan. 1827, PNP

⁶ George IV to Anglesey, 13 Apr.; Clarence to Anglesey, 14 Apr. 1827, PNP

⁷ Londonderry to Anglesey, 17 Apr.; Anglesey to Londonderry, 19 Apr. 1827, PNP

⁸ Wellington to Anglesey, 21 Apr.; 22 Apr. 1827, PNP

⁹ *Dyott*, II, 9; *DMR*, 13 Aug. 1828

¹⁰ *Mrs Arbuthnot*, II, 271-2; see also *Geo IV*, III, 284

¹¹ Lansdowne to Anglesey, 3 Sep. 1827, PNP

¹² C. Paget to Anglesey, 19 Dec., PNP; Anglesey to Grey, 9 Dec., Grey (Durham); see also Anglesey to Lansdowne, 18 Dec. 1827, PNP

¹³ Goderich to Anglesey, 9 Jan. 1828, PNP

¹⁴ Herries (E.), *Memoir of J. C. Herries*, 1880, II, 52-3

¹⁵ Arbuthnot to Peel, 6 July 1827; *Canning's Ministry*, 254; 31 Aug. 1831, *Hansard* (C), 3rd Series, VI, 932

¹⁶ Report of meeting of British Catholic Association on 21 May, *The Times*, 23 May 1825

¹⁷ Balfour to Dudley, 15 Aug. 1905, Petrie (C.), *Walter Long and His Times*, 1936, 95

NOTES TO CHAPTER X (p. 371 to p. 375)

¹ 17 Aug. [1838], *Girlhood*, I, 384

² *Morning Herald*, 1 Mar. 1828

³ Anglesey to Holland, 7 June 1828, PNP

⁴ Lamb to Anglesey, 18 Mar., PNP; *DMR*, 4 Mar.-19 Apr., 1828

⁵ *Croker*, II, 422

⁶ Anglesey to Holland, 1 July 1828, PNP

⁷ *O'Connell*, I, 160

⁸ Tuyll to Anglesey, 1 July 1828, PNP

⁹ Anglesey to Lamb, 26 Apr.; see also Anglesey to Peel, 28 June; Gosset to Tuyll, 21 June 1828, PNP

¹⁰ Anglesey to Peel, 30 June; Anglesey to Gregory, 27 June 1828, PNP

¹¹ *Palmerston*, 184

¹² Strafford (Alice, Css of) (ed.), *Personal Reminiscences of the Duke of Wellington by Francis, 1st Earl of Ellesmere*, 1904, 70

¹³ *O'Connell*, I, 286; *Cloncurry*, 332

¹⁴ PNP

¹⁵ Holland to Anglesey [n.d.], PNP

¹⁶ *The Times*, 14 Jan. 1829

¹⁷ *Palmerston*, 184

¹⁸ Peel to George IV, 27 Sep. 1828, *Wellington (D:NS)*, V, 87

¹⁹ *The Times*, 14 Jan. 1829

¹⁰ George IV to Wellington, 20 Nov.; Bathurst to Wellington, 25 Nov. 1828; *Wellington* (*D:NS*), V, 275, 287

¹¹ Curtis to Anglesey, 22 Dec. 1828, PNP; see also W. Holmes to Mrs Arbuthnot, 17 Jan. 1829, *Arbuthnot*, 114

¹² See Curtis to Anglesey, 25 Dec. 1828, PNP; Curtis to Wellington, 2 Jan. 1829, *Wellington* (*D:NS*), V, 413; compare *Greville*, I, 232; *Croker*, II, 4; see also *Arbuthnot*, 112n.

¹³ West, I, 15; Bryant (Sir Arthur), *English Saga*, 1940, 45

¹⁴ Quoted in Walpole (Sir Spencer), *History of England*, 1878-86, II, 519

NOTES TO CHAPTER XI (p. 375 to p. 376)

¹ Croker to V. Fitzgerald, 17 May 1830, *Croker*, II, 62

² Anglesey to Cumberland, 2 July 1829, PNP

³ Buckingham (Duke of), *Memoirs of ... the Court and Cabinets of William IV and Victoria*, 1861, I, 188

⁴ *List of Officers....* [Army List], WO, 1826; 1827; 1853; 1855; PRO/WO 55/1548; Barber, *Picturesque Illustrations of the Isle of Wight....* [n.d., c. 1832-50], 34; [Worsley (R.)], *The History of the Isle of Wight*, 1781, cix (Appx. XL)

NOTES TO CHAPTER XII (p. 376 to p. 381)

¹ Anglesey to Holland, 12 Aug. 1831, PNP

² 11 Jan. 1831, *Gregory*, 321

³ O'Connell to Anglesey, 20 and 26 Nov. 1830, PNP

⁴ O'Connell to W. N. Bennett, 31 Dec., *O'Connell*, I, 237; Anglesey to Melbourne, 21 Dec., et seq., 1830, PNP

⁵ Grey to Anglesey, 1 Mar. 1831, PNP

⁶ Anglesey to Holland, 7 June 1833, PNP

⁷ Croker to Hertford, 22 Mar., *Croker*, II, 112-3; Anglesey to Stanley, 22 Feb., 21 Apr. 1831, PNP

⁸ Anglesey to Grey, 27 Oct. 1832, PNP

⁹ May (T. E.), *The Constitutional History of England ... 1760-1860*, 1861-3, I, 358; see also II, 402-3

¹⁰ E. J. Littleton's Diary, 21 July 1833, Aspinall, 350; Grey to Anglesey, 13 June; Anglesey to Grey, 15 June 1831, PNP; Anglesey to Cloncurry, 1 Feb. 1832, *Cloncurry*, 438

¹¹ 12 Feb. 1833, *Hansard* (*C*), 3rd series, XV, 561-577

¹² Brougham (Henry, Lord), *Life and Times of Brougham by himself*, 1871, III, 235-8

NOTES TO CHAPTER XIII (p. 381 to p. 386)

¹ Weiss (Dr K. E.), 'Die Krankheit des Marquis d'Anglesea....' *Allgem. Homoeo. Zeit*, CLXIX (1921); Anglesey to A. Paget, 23 Jan. 1835, *P. Bros.*, 337; *The Times* (obituary notice of Dr W. Harris), 29 Feb. 1960; Hogg (James), 'Noctes Ambrosianae' no. XXXV, *Blackwood's Edinburgh Review*, Jan. 1828.

² [Julian Field], *More Uncensored Recollections*, 1926, 100

³ Leveson-Gower (Hon. F.) (ed.), *Letters of Harriet, Countess Granville, 1810-1845*, 1894, II, 199

⁴ Note by Queen Victoria in Grey (Lt-Gen. Hon. C.), *Biography of the Prince Consort*, (privately printed) 1866, 336

⁵ Palmerston to Anglesey, 11 Oct.; Ld J. Russell to Palmerston, 11 Oct. 1846; Anglesey to Louis Napoleon [n.d. 1849], PNP

⁶ Anglesey to Brougham, 29 Sep. 1846, PNP

⁷ Anglesey to Berkeley Paget, 29 Nov. 1831; Berkeley Paget to Wellington, 11 Dec. 1832, Wellington (Evelyn, Duchess of), *Catalogue of ... Pictures ... at Apsley House*, 1901

⁸ *Greville*, V, 178

⁹ Jerrold (Clare), *The Early Court of Queen Victoria*, 1912, 235; 8 Nov. 1838, *Girlhood*, II, 66

¹⁰ *Annual Register*, 1842, 338

¹¹ PNP; PRO/WO 3/82, 227; Maurice (Sir F.), *The History of the Scots Guards....*, 1934, II, 43, 246-7

NOTES TO CHAPTER XIV (p. 386 to p. 387)

¹ Anglesey to Major Henry Paget, 24 Oct. 1851, PNP

² The information upon which this note is based was kindly provided by Mr Robert Scurfield in amplification of his 'British Military Smoothbore Firearms', *JAHR*, XXXIII (1955), 149. See also Aerts (W.) and Brown (Maj. R.), 'British Firearms at the time of Waterloo', *JAHR*, XXV (1947), 67-69

³ Anglesey to Bishop of Bath and Wells, 18 Oct. 1847; Anglesey to Clarence Paget, 13 Aug. 1853; Anglesey to Burgoyne, 11 Oct. 1851, PNP

⁴ Uxbridge to Anglesey, 2 Oct 1852, PNP

INDEX

INDEX

Page numbers in italic refer to references in the Notes; numbers in bold refer to principal references.

O   417

Henry Bayly 9th Baron Paget of Beaudesert ; 1st Earl of

1
Lady Caroline (i) = HENRY WILLIAM = (ii) Lady Charlotte
Villiers   1st MARQUESS OF   Wellesley (née
(1774 – 1835)   1795 ANGLESEY   1810 Cadogan)
                        (1768 – 1854)   (1781 – 1853)

2   **3**
Sir Arthur = Lady Augusta
(1771–1840)   Boringdon (née
        1809 Fane) (b.1786)
William
(1769–1795)
                Lady Caroline = Hon J.T. Capel
                (1773–1847) 1792 (1769 – 1819)

4   **5**
Jane   = George 8th Earl
(1774–1842) 1797 Galloway (1768–
                            S
                            (

1
Lady Caroline = Charles, 5th Duke
(1796–1874)   of Richmond
[5s., 5 dau.] 1817 (1791–1860)

2 **3**
Lady Jane = Francis 2nd
(1798–1876)   Marquess of
[2s., 4 dau.] 1824 Conyngham
                    (1797–1876)

4 **5**
Lady Augusta = Arthur 1st Baron
(1802–1872)   Templemore
[6s., 2 dau.] 1820 (1797–1837)

6 **7**
Lady Agnes = George
(1804–1845)   Earl
[3s., 3 dau.] 1829 Stra
                    (1806

Henry (Earl of = (i) Eleanora Campbell (1799–1828)
Uxbridge)   1820
2 Marquess of   1833
Anglesey   = (ii) Henrietta Bagot (1815–1844)
(1797–1869)   1860
            = (iii) Ellen Burnand (d.1874)
             [no issue]

Lady Georgiana = Edward 2nd
(1800–1875)   Baron Crofton
[4s., 1 dau.] 1833 (1806–1869)

Lord William = Fanny
(1803–1873)   Rottenb
[3s.]   1827 (d.1875

Henry 3rd
Marquess of
Anglesey
(1821–1880)
[and 2 dau.]
[no issue]

Henry 4th = (ii) Blanche
Marquess of   Curwen
Anglesey   1874 (d.1877)
(1835–1898)

Henry 5th
Marquess of
Anglesey
(1875–1905)
[no issue]

Lord Alexander = Hon. Hester
(1839–1896)   Stapleton-
        1880   Cotton
                (d. 1930)

Charles 6th Marquess of Anglesey = Lady Marjorie Manners
(1885–1947) [and 1 other s. and 2 dau.] 1912 (1883–1946)

Henry 7th Marquess of Anglesey
(1922–) [and 5 dau] [the present author]